ENTERTAINING UNCERTAINTY
IN THE
EARLY MODERN THEATER

Stage Spectacle and Audience Response

Lauren Robertson's original study shows that the theater of Shakespeare and his contemporaries responded to the crises of knowledge that roiled through early modern England by rendering them spectacular. Revealing the radical, exciting instability of the early modern theater's representational practices, Robertson uncovers the uncertainty that went to the heart of the playgoing experience in this period. Doubt was not merely the purview of Hamlet and other onstage characters, but was in fact constitutive of spectators' imaginative participation in performance. Within a culture in the midst of extreme epistemological upheaval, the commercial theater licensed spectators' suspension among opposed possibilities, transforming dubiety itself into exuberantly enjoyable, spectacular show. Robertson shows that the playhouse was a site for the entertainment of uncertainty in a double sense: its pleasures made the very trial of unknowing possible.

LAUREN ROBERTSON is Assistant Professor of English and Comparative Literature at Columbia University.

ENTERTAINING UNCERTAINTY IN THE EARLY MODERN THEATER

Stage Spectacle and Audience Response

LAUREN ROBERTSON

Columbia University, New York

CAMBRIDGE
UNIVERSITY PRESS

CAMBRIDGE
UNIVERSITY PRESS

University Printing House, Cambridge CB2 8BS, United Kingdom

One Liberty Plaza, 20th Floor, New York, NY 10006, USA

477 Williamstown Road, Port Melbourne, VIC 3207, Australia

314–321, 3rd Floor, Plot 3, Splendor Forum, Jasola District Centre, New Delhi – 110025, India

103 Penang Road, #05–06/07, Visioncrest Commercial, Singapore 238467

Cambridge University Press is part of the University of Cambridge.

It furthers the University's mission by disseminating knowledge in the pursuit of education, learning, and research at the highest international levels of excellence.

www.cambridge.org
Information on this title: www.cambridge.org/9781009225151
DOI: 10.1017/9781009225137

First published 2023

A catalogue record for this publication is available from the British Library.

Library of Congress Cataloging-in-Publication Data
NAMES: Robertson, Lauren (College teacher), author.
TITLE: Entertaining uncertainty in the early modern theater : stage spectacle and audience response / Lauren Robertson.
DESCRIPTION: Cambridge, United Kingdom ; New York : Cambridge University Press, 2022. | Includes bibliographical references and index.
IDENTIFIERS: LCCN 2022025446 | ISBN 9781009225151 (hardback) | ISBN 9781009225137 (ebook)
SUBJECTS: LCSH: English drama – Early modern and Elizabethan, 1500–1600 – History and criticism. | Theater audiences – England – History – 16th century. | English drama – 17th century – History and criticism. | Spectacular, The, in literature. | Theater audiences – England – History – 17th century. | Theater – England – History.
CLASSIFICATION: LCC PR658.A88 R6295 2022 | DDC 822/.309–dc23/eng/20220822
LC record available at https://lccn.loc.gov/2022025446

ISBN 978-1-009-22515-1 Hardback

For Chester

Contents

Figures

All illustrations are used by permission of the Folger Shakespeare Library.

Acknowledgments

I owe thanks to the many people who provoked me into uncertainty and restored me to resolution in the process of writing this book.

The idea for *Entertaining Uncertainty in the Early Modern Theater* was sparked in a graduate seminar taught by Joe Loewenstein at Washington University in St. Louis. I am grateful for his mentorship, a bolstering balance of rigor, enthusiasm, and patience, which modeled the precision of thought and expression to which I still aspire.

In Columbia's Department of English and Comparative Literature, I am incredibly lucky to be surrounded by colleagues both brilliant and generous. Sarah Cole, Denise Cruz, Jenny Davidson, Austin Graham, Matt Hart, Edward Mendelson, Dustin Stewart, and Dennis Tenen have all shared invaluable advice and encouragement. Jim Adams's invitation to give a talk on *King Lear* to a lively group of Columbia alumni helped me clarify the reading of the play that appears in Chapter 1. The responses I received to a department works-in-progress presentation helped shape Chapter 5; Erik Gray subsequently offered galvanizing feedback on the whole project, carrying me through a revision of the introduction just as New York went into lockdown in March 2020. Julie Crawford, Eleanor Johnson, Molly Murray, Jim Shapiro, and Alan Stewart each read multiple chapters with precision and care; I am deeply appreciative, and still a bit overwhelmed, when I register their collective contribution to the pages that follow. There simply aren't thanks enough in the world for the incomparable Jean Howard, whose clear-eyed wisdom helped me both see what the book could be and chart the path to its completion.

Material support from Columbia University was essential to the book's completion. Leave provided by the Junior Faculty Development Program and the Chamberlain Fellowship gave me the time to finish it, and funding from the Hettleman Junior Faculty Summer Research Grants Program allowed me to undertake necessary research at the British Library.

The book benefited from people and support beyond Columbia, as well. Brad Gregory's inspiring direction of an interdisciplinary seminar at the

Folger Shakespeare Library helped me frame the project for a broad audience. Members of the Rutgers Medieval-Renaissance Colloquium, who read Chapter 1, and the Yale Renaissance Colloquium, who listened to material from Chapter 3, asked excellent questions. The students in Rhodri Lewis's graduate seminar on tragedy at Princeton engaged incisively with the introduction and Chapter 1; Rhodri's further questions and conversation proved essential as I finalized the manuscript for publication. Anita Gilman Sherman generously invited me to lead a seminar on theatrical skepticism with her at the 2019 Shakespeare Association of America conference; the participants' fantastic papers and invigorating discussion left me with whole new sets of ideas. I am particularly grateful to Anita for her ongoing support since.

At Cambridge University Press, Emily Hockley expertly guided me through the publication process, and the book was made better by the press's two anonymous readers, who offered serious, substantive feedback. George Laver's, Natasha Burton's, and Thirumangai Thamizhmani's assistance as I prepared the manuscript was instrumental.

Material from Chapter 3 originally appeared as "False Evidence and Deceptive Eyewitnesses: The Theatricality of Uncertainty in *The Picture* and *Cymbeline*" in *Renaissance Drama*, where it benefitted enormously from Will West's incisive comments; material from Chapter 5 originally appeared as "'Bootless are your thoughts': Audience Expectation and Surprise in the Caroline Commercial Theater" in *Publicity and the Early Modern Stage*, expertly edited by Allison Deutermann, Musa Gurnis, and Matthew Hunter. I thank the University of Chicago Press and Palgrave Macmillan for permission to include this material in revised and expanded form.

I am endlessly grateful to the friends who, in serving as writing partners, improved the book with their insight and made the solitary process of writing one less so: Joe Albernaz, Caralyn Bialo, Adhaar Desai, Allison Deutermann, Aubrey Gabel, David Hershinow, Jayne Hildebrand, Matthew Hunter, Laura Kolb, Debapriya Sarkar, Steven Swarbrick, Hannah Weaver, and Michael West. Meg Dobbins's, Kelly Oman's, and Merrill Turner's life-saving commiseration has stretched across multiple years and states. Musa Gurnis has read multiple drafts, listened to talks and practice talks, asked the best questions, and shared the best theater tickets for over a decade. Maggie Heim is a friend for all time.

The love and encouragement of my family, especially my parents, Tom and Kim, and my sister Marta, is foundational. My husband Chester has listened to all the ideas that made it into this book and many more that did not; he's also reliably made me laugh every single day as I've worked on it and dinner almost as often. It is dedicated to him.

Introduction
Convention

Cultivating Uncertainty in the Early Modern Theater

> What are thou that usurp'st this time of night
> Together with that fair and warlike form
> In which the majesty of buried Denmark
> Did sometimes march? (1.1.45–48)[1]

Hamlet's Ghost, "stalk[ing]" onstage in its heavy armor (1.1.49), raises more questions than it answers. Its sudden appearance, just as Barnardo begins to relate having seen the "guilty thing" or "apparition" or "dreaded sight" or "questionable shape" the night before (1.1.147, 27, 24; 1.4.43), would seem to affirm the very power of theatrical representation itself: on the stage, a ghost can invade its own story.[2] Yet from the perspective of the play's original spectators, it is not clear that *Hamlet*'s Ghost would have looked much like one at all. The commercial theater had not settled on a conventional representation for its ghosts by 1600, nor would it in the subsequent decades of its operation. Ghosts continued to appear onstage in an array of attire into the seventeenth century: wearing a *"leather cassock and breeches, boots [and] a cowl"* (5.4.127sd), *"crown'd, with Scepters in their hands"* (505), clad *"all in white, stuck with jewels, and a great crucifix"* (4.4.42sd).[3] They do not seem to have regularly, or even frequently, appeared in armor.[4] Encased in a bulky metal shell, the spectacle of *Hamlet*'s supposedly immaterial spirit marching onto the Globe stage in the middle of the afternoon likely did not announce itself as a ghost so much as exactly what it was: an actor, entirely alive and material to the point of excess.[5] As the appearance for theatrical ghosts settled into a conventional emphasis on "their immateriality, their invisibility" by the nineteenth century, the materials of the Ghost's representation to which the play draws repeated attention – its "fair and warlike form" resembles "the very armour" worn by King Hamlet (1.1.59) – became an "increasing

I

embarrassment" for audiences and readers of Shakespeare's play.[6] Yet this evolution toward embarrassment sheds light on a possible audience response to the spectacle at the moment of its original staging. If *Hamlet*'s Ghost "embarrassed" its Elizabethan spectators, it did so in the senses that the word conveyed when it was introduced to the English language during Shakespeare's lifetime: to block, to impede, to confuse, to perplex.[7] The excessive materiality of *Hamlet*'s Ghost was an interpretive roadblock – "a mote," as Horatio describes it, "to trouble the mind's eye" (I.I.III). At a moment when the theater had not yet decided on a standard representation for its ghosts, the sudden appearance of one in *Hamlet* likely invited spectators to share in the very uncertainty that the play's characters variously exhibit about it.[8] A supposedly spectral visitor who is materialized by a living actor and allegedly resembles a dead king could just as easily be a demon. Who's there? No one, onstage or in the playhouse, knows.[9]

It goes without saying that *Hamlet*, which includes perhaps the most famous uncertain rumination in the whole of English literature, is a play about doubt. Horatio doubts whether the figure he has just seen is really the ghost of Hamlet's father; Hamlet wavers back and forth about the Ghost, too, and in the process manages to doubt nearly everything else, from the nature of death's undiscovered country to the sincerity of his uncle's prayer. But what the Ghost's visual ambiguity reveals is that *Hamlet* is more than just a dramatic representation of various responses to uncertainty – detached skepticism in Horatio's case, crushing mental torment in Hamlet's. The play just as deliberately entangles its spectators in uncertainty from its very opening scene, which renders the Ghost semiotically illegible by underscoring the means by which the spectacle is brought into being. *Hamlet* makes a paradigmatic drama of uncertainty not simply by representing it on the stage, but by producing it in the playhouse.

This book is about the phenomenology of the early modern English commercial theater, and it takes as its premise that this theater and the culture in which it arose were epistemologically akin; they shared, that is, the same basic form.[10] It is commonplace to describe early modernity in England as Janus-faced, a period of epistemological flux: modes of thought that were actively unsettled through the sixteenth and seventeenth centuries did not simply disappear, but lingered in aggravated relation to the burgeoning methodologies and disciplines that would eventually replace them. Yet the form of theatrical representation that emerged within this mosaic of cultural change was itself oppositional – and more than that, acutely attuned to its own opposition. All theater is, at heart, paradoxical, "a presentation of an *imagined* act."[11] But the insistently metatheatrical, highly experimental early modern theater regularly invited its spectators to dwell in that paradox by drawing attention to its fictional representations *as* theatrical presentations, its imagined acts *as* stagecraft.[12] London's commercial theater industry prospered at the close of the sixteenth century because it transformed the very shape of its culture into entertainment; it rendered the essential contrariety of early modernity, quite simply, spectacular.

The theater enacted that transformation, I will suggest, by actively and repeatedly entangling its spectators in uncertainty. The cultivation of playgoers' unknowing was less the result of a singular agenda than the London theater's emergence as an innovative commercial enterprise, one that responded to the demand for "Play[s] *Spick and span new*" by offering its spectators fresh stories and spectacles nearly every day of the week.[13] Working quickly, practitioners borrowed material freely from one another, invented new representational practices and dramatic genres, and exploited the very conventions they codified. The last decade of the sixteenth century alone saw the transformation of the medieval Vice into the early modern villain, the development of the dramatic sequel, the invention of the history play, the cultivation of the soliloquy, and the flourishing of the complex semiotics of disguise plots. These and other dramatic experiments regularly put plays in contested relation to the formal resources of the theater itself, and the result was often spectacular incoherence: representations that were brazenly, even deliberately, at odds with the mechanics of their own production. As in the case of *Hamlet*'s Ghost, this troubling of what spectators saw in the theater, whether by accident or design, impeded what they could know about the fictional worlds unfolding before them onstage.

Yet that uncertainty served a theatrical purpose, for it enabled spectators' imaginative participation in stage performance.[14] In a theater with no scenic backdrops and relatively little stage furniture, much of the labor required to realize its fictional representations fell to spectators themselves. ("Think, when we talk of horses, that you see them" [Prologue.26], the speaker of *Henry V*'s prologue implores.)[15] Theatrical apprehension, simultaneously imaginative and interpretive, is a spatiotemporal process that depends on the smooth transmission of meaning from stage to audience. Such transmission requires the security of interpretive discernment and expectation: A revenger who announces, toward the end of a tragedy, that he is about to stage his own play will likely kill at least one of the dramatic participants; the actor playing his victim will likely remain prone on the stage floor until he is carried off. But interspersed with these reliably conventional moments were those that deliberately frustrated spectators' abilities to apprehend the action unfolding before them: An actor playing a seemingly dead character hops up from the stage floor without warning; a revenger gleefully introduces his play only to get straight to the business of murdering without staging it at all.[16] What I term "uncertainty" in the chapters that follow does not name a particular feeling or response, then, so much as a concrete theatrical effect: the disturbance of the phenomenological tie that linked early modern spectators to performance. It is certainly true that the effectiveness of *all* art, in all times and places, depends on the careful interplay of familiarity and surprise. But the clash of the two was particularly volatile in the early modern theater, where spectators were required to make sense of a highly experimental art form while also making sense of playgoing as a new kind of social activity and "playgoer" as a new kind of social identity. And yet it was precisely because the theater encouraged its spectators' close imaginative and interpretive involvement with stage show that the very disruption of that participation worked counteractively to spur the dynamic process of performance itself.[17] Early modern performance ran on its audiences' uncertain responses to stage spectacle.

In focusing on the ways that the theater unsettled spectators' interpretive connection to performance, I depart from work that has so far been done in historical phenomenology, a methodology that seeks to identify the cultural practices and assumptions that shaped spectators' responses to what they saw in the playhouse.[18] Like these scholars, I take as a new formalist premise that the theater was not a closed semiotic system, and that audiences' responses to its spectacles were therefore necessarily conditioned by the discourses that spectators would have both consciously and unconsciously absorbed outside the playhouse and brought with them into the theater. Yet it is equally true that experiential familiarity with performance was itself a key form of tacit knowledge on which spectators relied to make sense of new plays. To be sure, we lack concrete evidence of how exactly playgoers responded to the spectacles of the commercial stage, and this book is not an attempt to reconstruct the panoply of early modern audience responses lost to us. It instead reads the plays in concert with the array of material evidence we do possess about the historical conditions of theatrical representation in order to make informed claims about the semiotic effects of various stage moments. The surviving playtexts of this period are material traces of the ephemeral event of performance, and the same lines that have been read for decades in service of the search for thematic meaning contain troves of untapped evidence about what the plays *did* on the stage.[19] This book extricates those phenomenological effects.

Conventions of Uncertainty

A familiar explanation for the early modern commercial theater's success is that, over the seven decades of its operation, it increasingly rewarded theatergoers' experiential knowledge of its practices. Trends across the industry shaped the representational strategies of individual companies, and blockbuster plays sparked imitations for years into the future; there would arguably be no *Titus Andronicus* (1592), *Hamlet* (1600), *Antonio's Revenge* (1600), *The Revenger's Tragedy* (1606), or *The White Devil* (1612) without *The Spanish Tragedy* (1587).[20] At the same time, companies defined themselves by regularly staging plays that reused popular theatrical devices, while the repertory system ensured that spectators could reliably see old favorites alongside new plays.[21] Actors were typecast.[22] Genre announced itself as a determining framework from the opening lines of nearly every play spectators saw.[23] Above all, spectators' interpretive security depended on their recognition of conventions – those repeated devices, as Jeremy Lopez defines them, that were deployed onstage "in similar circumstances and accompanied with informational and ideational baggage similar to those other moments of its kind."[24] Theatrical conventions were dynamic collaborations with spectators through which meaning emerged in the moment-by-moment unfolding of a single performance. The repetition of common devices cultivated the theatrical literacies of early modern playgoers. As William N. West and others have shown, the semiotics of early modern dramatic representation were established intertheatrically; the significance of any single theatrical moment, especially for experienced playgoers, was always informed by its conventional overlap with the similar deployment of like devices in other plays.[25] Audiences increasingly made sense out of what they saw in response to the systems of meaning that the "reverberant constellation" of early modern drama produced.[26] In this account, the theater scene witnessed, from the Elizabethan to Caroline era, a gradual evolution of spectators into playgoers, playgoers into increasingly sophisticated critics.[27] If the commercial theater began as a site of eclectic, even haphazard experimentation with dramatic form, the various devices and practices it employed eventually hardened into conventions that reliably conveyed information and meaning, in the process cultivating "an audience of active taste, critical, discriminating and alert."[28]

But this is only part of the story. For even as spectators grew more experientially attuned to what they saw onstage, the theater did not consistently deliver to them the recognizable and familiar alone. Throughout the period, theater practitioners actively worked to remain an interpretive step ahead of their spectators who made sense of new plays with increasingly deep recourse to those they had already seen. Upsetting spectators' intertheatrical expectations thus meant upsetting the conventions that had generated them in the first place. As thinkers across the disciplines of the theater and artistic representation more broadly have long understood, the actions, language, gestures, and images that eventually coalesce into identifiable conventions often first emerge into view as surprising departures from the established conveyance of meaning on the canvas, the page, or the stage.[29] As Bert O. States puts it, the "efficient and invisible chips in the informational circuitry" of performance make their way into that conventional circuit as precisely their opposite: "anticonventions, or anti-signs" that interrupt the established transmission of meaning.[30] As I will show in Chapter 1, for example, disruptions to the conventions governing the removal of dead characters' bodies from the stage quite literally gave rise to the unexpected (and incredibly popular) reanimations of seventeenth-century tragicomedy. The emergence of the hybrid genre is itself evidence of the innovations spurred by conventional rupture. Yet rather than focusing solely on the theatrical consequences of these conventional disruptions – that is, on the coalescence of those disruptions into newly meaningful conventions – I isolate their immediate phenomenological effects because it was precisely by upending spectators' expectations that the theater exposed the limits of their theatrical acuity.[31] The volatile conventions of the early modern theater brimmed with potential to be revised, upended, and bent into new relations to one other; in producing these disruptive jolts to the otherwise smooth transfer of meaning from stage to audience, the theater imbricated surprise and familiarity to particularly potent effect.[32] "Performances in the Elizabethan playhouses," West writes, "were provocations toward meaning rather than representations of a meaning."[33] *Entertaining Uncertainty* argues that spectators of this theater were so provoked under constantly shifting semiotic circumstances; their interpretive judgment was honed not through an unwavering knowingness with regard to stage spectacle, but through moments when individual plays pushed beyond the ever-broadening horizons of their dramatic expectations.[34]

Forms of Uncertainty

Early modern theater practitioners could unsettle spectators' interpretive complacency because they understood what the Prague formalists would articulate four hundred years later: To gaze on stage spectacle is to see with doubled vision.[35] In the playhouse, spectators are required to apprehend the mechanics of stagecraft as the fictional elements for which they must substitute. A chair, dagger, and cushion on the stage can all signify royal accoutrement in the fiction, as Falstaff recognizes in *1 Henry IV* (1597), but these materials inextricably retain their status as technologies of representation, as Hal points out:

FALSTAFF. This chair shall be my state, this dagger my scepter and this cushion my crown.
PRINCE. Thy state is taken for a joint-stool, thy golden scepter for a leaden dagger and thy precious rich crown for a pitiful bald crown. (2.4.368–72)[36]

On the stage, the materials of representation are manifest paradoxes, both the fictional thing itself and the tool used to create it at once. Early modern spectators acknowledged this contradiction even in the process of registering their commitment to stage fiction. When Henry Jackson praised a performance of *Othello* at Oxford in 1610, for instance, he alluded to the boy player's material role in bringing the fictional Desdemona into being while conflating the two of them: "Desdemona, murdered by her husband in our presence, although she consistently delivered her speech well, moved us even more having been killed, when, lying on the bed, she implored the pity of those watching with her face alone."[37] Practitioners of the early modern theater regularly fragmented the fragile coherence of contradictory spectacles like the one Jackson describes; they exacerbated the inherent instability of theatrical form by drawing attention to both the material technologies and the conventional tools of their fictional representations.[38] Readers of Shakespeare's plays have long been attuned to moments when, as Luke Wilson puts it, "the actor speaks out from inside his character."[39] But this particular playwright was not uniquely capable of "being in uncertainties,"[40] nor was emphasizing the contradictory hybridity of the actor the only way that practitioners foregrounded the materials of theatrical representation.[41] In Philip Massinger's *The Picture* (1626), spectators were required to search, in the uneven lighting of Blackfriars, for the impossible change of colors in a magical miniature purportedly able to detect a wife's adultery; in Thomas Kyd's *The Spanish Tragedy*, playgoers' expectations about the harmlessness of performance were overturned during Hieronimo's deadly inset play. Along with Horatio, spectators saw the bulkily spectral figure that he claimed "harrow[ed] [him] with fear and wonder" (1.1.43); along with Olivia, they gazed on the sight of the strangely doubled Cesario that gave her such joy: "Most wonderful!" (5.1.221).[42] The theater's near-constant attention to the tropes and tools underlying its representations allowed it to inculcate in spectators the very uncertainty that its characters experience, for to draw spectators' attention to plays *as* plays is to point to the margins of theatrical form itself: where the technologies of theatrical representation began to break down, to reach their limits as tools of representation, to cease to contribute dependably to the creation of fictional worlds. The early modern theater regularly transformed the doubled vision it required of spectators into epistemological dilemmas with which they were interpretively forced to reckon.

Four hundred years later, the consequence of spectators' compelled attention to the mechanics of stagecraft would be described by Bertolt Brecht as the "alienation effect" (*Verfremdungseffekt*).[43] A Brechtian model, predicated upon the integrity of an enclosed mimetic representation against which moments of spectatorial estrangement are sharply registered, has been most influentially integrated into studies of the early modern theater through Robert Weimann's categories of the *locus*, the defined place of symbolic representation, and the *platea*, the unlocalized site of presentation. The former isolates the "picture of the performed," while the latter discloses "the process of the performer performing."[44] While Weimann is attentive to what he terms the "interplay" between both performance modes on the early modern stage, his model nevertheless construes the *locus* – the self-contained site of representational authority, where "matter of 'worthiness', the discourse of epic and romance, historical and novelistic narrative, could be presented" – as the foundational mode of early modern performance.[45] If the *locus* belongs to kings, to the *platea* is relegated the sidelined clown, who, in his indecorous commitment to playing himself rather than a fictional role, functions as a challenge to the mimetic representation which both precedes and outlasts him.[46] Weimann's methodology is, in part, New Historicist; in his earliest elucidations of the *locus* and *platea* binary, the "unsanctioned social energy" of the commercial stage is figured as a threat to the mimetic authority of Renaissance poetics.[47] And while the great contribution of New Historicist scholarship has undeniably been its demonstration of the ways that commercial playing on London's margins subverted authoritative modes of representation in the period, it is also true that this historical upheaval cannot be neatly mapped onto the process of performance as it unfolded, moment-by-moment, in the playhouse, which did not privilege representation over presentation but dynamically integrated them. The Ghost's armor places him in the *platea*; his status as a king lends him the authority of the *locus*. An awareness of both simultaneously unsettles spectators' interpretive capabilities and aligns them with the unknowing characters onstage; their alienation from the fictional world invigorates their imaginative involvement in it. Rooted in a claim about the imbrication of Renaissance modes of mimesis and popular forms of playing, Weimann's phenomenology constructs an anachronistic binary, better suited to the darkened theaters and proscenium stages of the twentieth century, that necessarily subordinates estrangement to absorption. In the early modern theater, by contrast, the self-consciousness of the *platea* did not disrupt absorption in the *locus*; rather, the *locus* required the *platea* to come into being in the first place.

This book supplies a new model by which to understand the interplay of representational and presentational performance modes in the early modern English theater. Rather than taking absorption in a mimetic representation as spectators' foundational relation to performance, it outlines the dynamic contingency of their imaginative participation in the realization of stage fiction. On the early modern stage, representations did not so much exist as continuously come into being, emerging through spectators' constant negotiation of their interpretive tether to the stage. This theater exacerbated, that is, what phenomenologists have identified as the fundamental condition of all sensory and embodied experience: the uncertain grounding in a world that is never fully perceptible. That world, Edmund Husserl writes, presents itself as "a *horizon of indeterminate actuality, a horizon of which I am dimly conscious.*"[48] In and beyond that horizon, the world is "on hand," if not fully there – an opacity which requires Husserl to "exercise the 'phenomenological' ἐποχή [suspension of judgment] that *utterly closes off for me every judgment about spatiotemporal existence.*"[49] The world emerges as a dynamic process of phenomenological apprehension and interpretive suspension, coming into being only at an interpretive distance from the observer. What tethers the observer to that world *is*, at heart, her uncertainty about it. And yet the very act of doubting, Maurice Merleau-Ponty suggests, allows one to grasp oneself

> as a particular thought, as a thought engaged with certain objects, as a thought in act; and it is in this sense that I am certain of myself. [...] I am a thought which recaptures itself as already posessing an ideal of truth (which it cannot at each moment wholly account for) and which is the horizon of its operations. This thought ... searches after clarity rather than possesses it.[50]

Uncertainty ignites the wish for interpretive lucidity by holding clarity at bay. Early modern theatricality heightened the effect of what Merleau-Ponty elsewhere describes as a primordial immersion in "the impression of an emerging order, an object in the act of appearing, organizing itself before our eyes."[51] By regularly inviting spectators to reflect on the tools of stagecraft, by upending their judgments about a play's unfolding action, and by exposing the limits of their visual acuity, performance in this theater required spectators, nearly continually, to negotiate and renegotiate their connection to the onstage world. That dynamic process of performance propelled their interpretive investment in the stage fiction.

Cultures of Uncertainty

Yet this account of theatrical uncertainty – one that does not *"negate"* the world or *"doubt its existence,"* but merely refrains from making judgments about it – could just as aptly describe the unsettled feeling of life at the end of the sixteenth century, for the early modern English commercial theater arose, thrived, and was eventually shuttered within a culture that experienced multifaceted and overlapping provocations to doubt.[52] This period's intellectual culture has been described as "possessing "a widespread concern – one might even say obsession – with the simultaneous experience of contrary states," its political culture as hovering "between attachment to the *status quo* [and] alienation from it," its religious culture as "ideologically restless."[53] London, home to the theaters that registered and reimagined these radical changes, was itself "a city in flux."[54] That this period saw the destruction of old modes of thought in an array of disciplines and, eventually, the gradual emergence of new ones is, by now, a familiar account of English early modernity. But what is harder to remember at a historical distance is that the people who lived through these epistemological shifts inhabited, for the most part, the interim; they existed in the midst of the very uncertainty that demarcated waning methods for finding truth and certainty from their nascent replacements.[55] Perhaps most familiar to scholarship on the theater of this period are the effects of the spiritual whiplash caused by the Protestant Reformation, which sparked a crisis of uncertainty across Europe by destroying the previously singular – and therefore, unshakably certain – criterion of religious knowledge.[56] In England, the effects of this destabilization were particularly keenly felt, as the country's official confessional alignment changed with each new monarch and sectarian splintering proliferated within religious communities.[57] "Great is the variety of Religion in this our age, and great is the contention about the truth thereof," Jesuit Leonardus Lessius admitted in 1618.[58] But this period's broader culture of uncertainty did not arise from confessional conflict alone. "Ambiguities, doubtes, and diuisions" emerged in response to provocations as public as the fraught question of Elizabeth I's successor and as private as the "double – sensed, incertain, and doubtful" origins of one's dreams.[59] These various and overlapping inducements of uncertainty called into question not only the fundamental criteria of knowledge, but the epistemological methods, both intellectual and vernacular, for arriving at them.

John Donne – who, as a Catholic convert to the Church of England around 1600, acutely embodied the contradictions of his country's confessional clashes – famously registered another facet of this multivalent circulation of uncertainty when he complained, in 1611, that the "new philosophy calls all in doubt."[60] Yet he refers in this case not to religious upheaval but the cosmological disorder produced by the Copernican upending of the geocentric universe.[61] Donne's depiction of fundamental doubt about the very order of the cosmos was part of a broader scientific shift that, by the opening of the seventeenth century, had begun to overturn centuries of reliance on classical scholastic thought as the means to come to certain knowledge about the natural world. The various empirical methods that emerged during these decades would eventually prompt the founding of the Royal Society and its commitments to the "Physico-Mathematicall Experimentall Learning."[62] Yet the gradual codification of these new epistemological methodologies fundamentally severed intuitive reliance on the workings of the world apparent to sensory experience.[63] "Suspension of judgement," would, in Francis Bacon's defense of utilitarian knowledge about the natural world, become a necessary waystation on the way to truth about the world as it appeared, if not as it actually existed.[64] The rise of probability in both scientific and legal fields made space for the lingering presence of doubt amid, finally, satisfactory certainty.[65] But at the turn of the century, a more uncomfortable reliance on increasingly suspect systems of knowledge and belief prevailed alongside the emergence of these new methods for finding truth.[66]

Bacon's directive to suspend judgment on the path to knowledge about the natural world originated in the precepts of classical skepticism, which slowly made their way into the libraries and writing of English authors in the second half of the sixteenth century – the same moment that the word "skeptic" was introduced to the English language.[67] While most playgoers were unlikely to have come in contact with the writing of Sextus Empiricus and were thus not directly acquainted with the principles of *epoché* (the withholding of assent, or the suspension of judgment) or the tranquilizing benefits of *ataraxia* (the removed calm produced by *epoché*), there is substantial evidence to suggest that these ancient writings on uncertainty did make an impression on several playwrights and writers in London.[68] Shakespeare and John Marston both incorporated Michel de Montaigne's skeptical ruminations into their plays; Christopher Marlowe quoted Sextus's *Against the Mathematicians* in *Doctor Faustus*; Thomas Nashe deployed skeptical logic in *The Terrors of the Night, or a Discourse of Apparitions*, his tract on dreams.[69] This renewed interest in ancient writing on uncertainty provided a philosophical counterpart to emergent empirical theories about vision, which gave increasing attention to its limitations and unreliability.[70] By the opening of the seventeenth century, Sextus's general observation that sensory experience varies from observer to observer had narrowed, in George Hakewill's 1608 tract *Vanitie of the Eie*, to a denigration of eyesight itself: Eyes, he maintains, are "false reporters in naturall, & artificiall things."[71] Whether or not Hakewill's or Nashe's readers were familiar with the tenets of classical skepticism or empirical theories about vision, these writers' approaches would have rung familiar to those who had been required to cultivate skeptical habits of mind in grammar school, where students learned to argue both sides of the question using *in utramque partem* reasoning.[72]

Politically, too, England was held in the grip of uncertainty through both the theater's emergence and its eventual closure. By the 1590s, the urgent question of Elizabeth I's succession had become a crisis. Catholic proponents of James VI of Scotland weaponized skeptical reasoning, using the same logic to undermine unwelcome arguments in favor of Elizabeth's successor that Protestant reformers used to discredit the succession of popes.[73] The theater industry, ordered closed in response to fears of civil disorder on the eve of the queen's death, felt the brunt of this anxiety about England's future.[74] The succession crisis would eventually find an uncertain bookend in the civil wars that would close the theaters in 1642 – a series of conflicts that, in the Revisionist account, was not an inevitable clash between the opposed Crown and Parliament, but the product of "a mosaic of contingencies, uncertain affinities, and local allegiances."[75]

Above all, London itself was a fitting site for the circulation of these intellectual, political, and religious uncertainties. Its population having nearly quadrupled through the second half of the sixteenth century, the city saw a massive influx of immigrants from both smaller English cities and the Continent. In London, to an extent unimaginable anywhere else in England, it was possible to be anonymous, as well as to come into regular contact with strangers. The city's newly acquired cosmopolitan status necessitated the widespread urban negotiation of a world whose parameters were constantly shifting and expanding. To live in London was to be confronted by the limits of one's own knowledge – about people, about the social world – within the very fabric of urban life.[76] Yet the theaters that staged the plays by Shakespeare and his contemporaries required London's teeming masses of people – life-long residents and newly arrived migrants among them, all of various social classes – to support their continual operation. The material conditions that gave rise to a commercial theater industry in this period at once enabled the distinctly metropolitan confrontation with uncertainty itself.[77]

The Entertainment of Uncertainty

This account of early modern England's culture of uncertainty is necessarily incomplete, and it is highly unlikely that any two people would have experienced these and other provocations to doubt in the same way. But it is reasonable to assume that, no matter how, or how often, they were so provoked, at some point the anxiety of irresolution and the fear of interpretive error would have been urgently felt by most people.[78] Contraries that meet in one, we might say, vex in many different ways and to many different degrees. What I mean to emphasize in tracing this cultural circulation of uncertainty, then, is that as a period of extraordinarily varied epistemological flux, the *form* that early modernity took in England – its "essential shaping principle" – was conceptual clash.[79] In the long history of skeptical thought, the ambiguity that produces uncertainty resides in the midst of this clash – on the ambivalent border, that is, separating mutually exclusive possibilities or choices. For Sextus Empiricus, the suspension of judgment followed from "the opposition of things. […] For example, we oppose what appears to what appears when we say: 'The same tower appears round from a distance and square from nearby'."[80] In the early modern English imagination, the grammatical link of those oppositions was "or." Hamlet articulates his own vacillation between countervailing choices with stark simplicity: "To be, or not to be – that is the question" (3.1.55). In *Paradise Lost*, Satan approaches our universe and appears to find his footing "On the bare outside of this world, that seemed / Firm land embosomed without firmament," only to hover between possibilities himself: "Uncertain which, in ocean or in air" (III.72–76).[81] Does water surround the land mass on which Satan alights, or is it air? The "omnipresence of 'or' " in Milton's epic does not so much encapsulate uncertainty as unfurl it, dispensing alternatives in a chain of contradiction.[82]

This reliance on "or" as the conjunction of doubt suggests that epistemological clash evades verbal attempts to render it with precision; irresolution merely exists in the spaces between possibilities that remain unembraced.

It is a central contention of this book, however, that early modern English theatrical form captured that ambiguity in a way that language alone could not. As a result, the theater rendered, more precisely than any other representational mode of the period, the very form of its culture into visible, exciting show. The duplicity of the theater's representations – at once the thing itself and the mechanisms by which it was realized – synthesized oppositions into the prismatic singularity of ambiguous stage spectacle. Far from resolving this contradiction, these spectacles exaggerated it, and as a result, made it enticing: *Hamlet*'s "questionable shape" "captiuated" because it was a ghost *and* an actor; Hermione's statue in *The Winter's Tale* "inthralled" because it was inert *and* alive.[83] Outside the playhouse, uncertainty unmoored, requiring constant hovering and wandering among countervailing possibilities. But uncertainty met its protean match in the theater, where skeptical intrigue and doubtful regard became the phenomenological and epistemological modes by which playgoers were invited to apprehend the very ambivalence of stage spectacle. This theater encouraged suspension in the contraries that constituted staged representation, cultivating a playhouse version of *epoché* that was a pleasurable end in itself.

The theater transformed uncertainty from a state to be traversed or merely endured – more often than not, the frustrating, even frightening, placeholder between choices or possibilities – into the very satisfaction of spectators' expectations. Playhouse uncertainty was entertaining. And it was so because, while uncertainty often served as a narrative waystation on the road to comic resolutions and tragic endings, it was a key reward of theatrical experience. The "cheerful excess of contradiction" prompted by the multiple disguises in *Look About You* (1599), the confusion surrounding the surprise ending of *The Spanish Tragedy*, the spectral mysteries of *Hamlet*, and Falstaff's ambiguous rise in *I Henry IV* were among the most popular spectacles of the commercial theater.[84] Treatises defending the moral efficacy of drama and poetry in response to antitheatricalist vitriol gradually gave way to encomia that not only acknowledged, but celebrated the theater's ability to create experiences of pleasurable unknowing.[85] William Cartwright's dedication in Beaumont and Fletcher's 1647 folio comments directly on such enjoyment:

> None can prevent the Fancy, and see through
> At the first opening; all stand wondring how
> The thing will be untill it is; which thence
> With fresh delight still cheats, still takes the sence.[86]

The opacity of the play's conclusion holds spectators in a state of unknowing until the conclusion reveals their ignorance – a "fresh delight" to match the pleasure of uncertainty that has been kept alive through the rest of the play's action. Toward the close of Ben Jonson's *The Magnetic Lady* (1632), a boy actor promises that the playwright has more tricks up his sleeve: "Stay and see his last act, his *catastrophe*, how he will perplex that, or spring some fresh cheat, to entertain the spectators with a convenient delight" (Chorus 4.21–23).[87] In Jonson's description of the twists and turns of dramatic plotting, perplexity is as delightful as the denouement it precedes.

Yet what is most striking about these Caroline and Interregnum characterizations of the theater's uncertain pleasures is how much they diverge from staged representations of doubt as "painful surgical probing": Hamlet's anguish, or Leontes's rage, or even the skeptic Lampatho's disgruntled sense, in Marston's *What You Will* (1601), that his university education was a waste ("The more I learnt the more I learnt to doubt," he complains [2.2.154]).[88] If not knowing outside the theater was akin to what John Calvin called the "endlesse maze [of error] wherof there is no way out again," inside it, the "*craftie* Mazes" of drama were sources of distinct pleasure.[89] "Let them enjoy their doubt; Be it either; Be it both," Donne exhorted in a 1628 sermon.[90] In transforming the frustration of uncertainty into the pleasures of entertainment, the commercial theater was the cultural institution of the period fitted to precisely this purpose. Theatrical uncertainty was entertaining, then, in a doubled sense: in the very process of constructing unknowing as a satisfying experience, the theater at once licensed playgoers' suspension among countervailing possibilities. The early modern playhouse was a site for the countenance of uncertainty within a broader culture defined by the opposition of epistemological clash. Contradictory spectacles lowered the stakes of unknowing; upended conventions freed interpretive error of material consequence. The theater made the entertainment of uncertainty possible.

Nor was theatrical uncertainty, as the many accounts of the wrenching (and occasionally satisfying) effects of doubt in the literary-philosophical history of skepticism would suggest, a solitary affair. Augustine's anguished self-interrogations, Montaigne's remove to his library, and Descartes's excision of the entire world apart from his mind imply that the struggle with uncertainty is assumed alone – a feature of doubting that its dramatic representation through the soliloquy would seem to confirm.[91] But in the playhouse, William Cartwright noted, "*all* stand wondering how /

The thing will be untill it is." The conditions of early modern spectator-ship promoted the formation of a theatrical community bound together by playgoers' collective interest in drawing and redrawing the horizons of their dramatic expectations. The emergence of that community was in part made possible by preexisting affiliations among frequent playgoers.[92] But it was also prompted by performance itself, as playgoers were col-lectively invited to register their recognition of the strange and surpris-ing set in relief to the familiar. And spectators' pleasurable confrontations with the limits of their theatrical knowledge extended beyond the occa-sion of performance: playgoers returned to familiar plays again and again, invited actors to re-perform beloved dramatic bits in alehouses after the show, and discussed their reactions to plays with one other.[93] One such account of postperformance conversation is particularly illustrative. In a satire directed at a female theatergoer, Richard Brathwaite accuses specta-tors of retiring to their coaches after a performance, "where you relaters bee / Of what your Eare did heare, or Eye could see."[94] Brathwaite almost certainly did not intend this castigation to bear any affinity with the plays themselves, and yet its evocation of varied perspectives brought together in an enthusiastic mishmash resonates with one dramatic example in particu-lar, in which individual uncertainties intermingle in the hope, left unre-solved, of collective consensus: the lovers of *A Midsummer Night's Dream*, who, unsure whether they have awakened or continue to dream, see "with parted eye, / When everything seems double" (4.1.188–89).[95] Their promise to recount their dreams to one another is an apt analogy for what the col-lectivity of theatrical experience made possible: not just the entertainment of uncertainty, but the communal withstanding of unknowing beyond the playhouse entirely.

From Dramatic Convention to Theatrical Community

The individual chapters of this book explicate the early modern theater's phenomenology of uncertainty by each privileging a single aspect of perfor-mance: bodies, time, props, space, and audience. The doubled semiosis of the actor's body is perhaps the unruliest of the theater's representational contra-dictions, for the liveliness of the actor can never be entirely subsumed by the stage fiction he inhabits.[96] In Chapter 1, I show that the early modern theater exacerbated this semiotic volatility by regularly requiring its actors not only to express death, but to feign it. From the late 1580s through the opening of the seventeenth century, plays that staged apparent deaths increasingly invited their spectators to apprehend the ambiguity of the lively stage corpse, entwining them in uncertainty by offering them less and less interpretive guidance about the actor's inevitable signs of life. Audiences gradually came to expect that they could not know the fictional status of apparent corpses. The conventions that eventually coalesced around stage corpses, I contend, enabled the rise of English tragicomedy, the hybrid genre that allowed for seemingly dead bodies to resurrect themselves without warning.

The set of practices that the theater eventually adopted regarding seemingly dead bodies invited spectators to embrace the sense that a dramatic narrative, poised at an interpretive crossroads, could turn in any one of many directions. By attending to moments of temporal suspension in the history play – the attempt, within the unrelenting forward succession of performance, to grind dramatic time to a halt – Chapter 2 outlines the theater's techniques for producing narrative suspense out of phenomenological uncertainty. Such suspense was especially hard to come by in the new genre, which dramatized well-known chronicles of English kings. But playgoers flocked to theaters to see these stories of succession through the 1590s, a moment when England's dynastic future remained crucially opaque. The theatrical invitation to *unknow* England's past trained spectators in speculative thinking oriented toward their own politically uncertain future. History plays transformed the anxious wait for Elizabeth's successor, that is, into the pleasure of theatrical possibility.

These attempts to set theatrical representation at odds with the formal conditions of its presentation were given new valence for the King's Men when they began to perform the same plays in different kinds of playhouses after 1608. Chapter 3 investigates the affordances and limitations of staging tiny props in both the small indoor Blackfriars and the large outdoor Globe. In Shakespeare's *Cymbeline* (1610) and *Antony and Cleopatra* (1606), as well as Massinger's *The Picture* (1629), small objects are deployed as metonymic evidence purporting to offer indubitable, privileged knowledge about a woman's inscrutable body. The objects' epistemological limitations became, in the Globe and Blackfriars, a phenomenological impasse, for the very conditions of the props' theatrical display would have variously exacerbated their narrative failures, undermining spectators' attempts to see the objects clearly. At an historical moment when empiricist methodologies and probabilistic thought promised to mitigate uncertainty, if not eradicate it entirely, the theater involved spectators in the failures of forensic investigation and evidential knowledge only to posit itself as a site for the capacious fulsomeness of spectacular display. The very ephemerality of theatrical spectacle becomes, in these plays, the alternative to the permanence of partial knowledge.

While the architectonics of the early modern playhouse contributed to spectators' uncertainty about stage spectacle, these structures also invited playgoers to confront the limits of their knowledge about one another. There is ample evidence to suggest that by the Caroline era, the broader theatergoing public contained within it the smaller subset of a theatrical community – those playgoers collectively invested in the cultivation of their dramatic knowledge and interpretive acuity. Chapter 4 offers a phenomenological prehistory of this community, locating its activation in the moment of performance. I trace the formation of this theatrical community alongside the dramatic trope of impersonation, which constructed the unknown depths and vicissitudes of individual identity as a function of the bifurcated structure of the playhouse. That formation of spatially relational identities extended from the stage to the amphitheater: constituted as a series of mirror images only partially revealed, London's theatrical community was produced by spectators' mutual recognition of their opacity to one another.

By the commercial theater's closure in 1642, frequent playgoers commanded a vast trove of knowledge about the devices, tropes, character types, and genres of the commercial theater. But those conventions were as exploitable as they were familiar, and in Chapter 5 I show how theater practitioners managed to surprise those spectators with especially long horizons of dramatic expectation. By looking back on the striking durability of revenge tragedy through the Caroline era, I show that knowing playgoers were most vulnerable to uncertainty in response to dramatic moments that recalled the commercial theater's beginnings – those moments, in other words, that unexpectedly made the eminently familiar newly strange.

The commercial theater's phenomenology of uncertainty arose from the material conditions of performance in the late sixteenth and early seventeenth centuries – conditions that crucially changed after the eighteen-year interruption of playing during the Interregnum. *Entertaining Uncertainty*'s coda traces the emergence of a new theatrical phenomenology in the Restoration theater, as London's playhouses were outfitted with the perspective scenery and proscenium frames that defined Continental and court performance. Plays that aimed to control and dominate spectators' imaginations replaced the more ambivalent spectacles of the earlier theatrical era, with a crucial consequence: though uncertainty itself did not disappear from English culture in the late seventeenth century, the playhouse no longer served as a site for its entertainment.

To claim that the commercial theater rendered the essential ambiguity of early modern culture spectacular is also to make the somewhat incredible suggestion that this theater succeeded because it simply monetized the experiences of uncertainty with which its spectators were already deeply familiar. Why were playgoers willing to pay, again and again, for *more* of the doubt that circulated so freely outside the playhouse? Yet this statement is less contradictory when we consider, as the chapters that follow will, what the essential unreality of theatrical experience accomplished. The very name of the Globe, early modern London's most famous playhouse, makes plain what the metatheatricality of the commercial theater's representational practices imply: the playhouse was not a refuge from the world itself, but a laboratory for navigating it. In the ostentatious artificiality of the theater's spectacles, uncertainty and possibility met. By promising unknowing for the price of admission, the commercial theater bolstered its playgoers' ability to weave among paradox and contradiction – pleasurably to withstand, that is, the doubt endemic to a culture in the midst of thoroughgoing epistemological change. This book aims to make a show of that doubled entertainment in the playhouse.

Notes

1 Act, scene, and line numbers follow William Shakespeare, *Hamlet*, ed. Ann Thompson and Neil Taylor (London: Arden, 2006).
2 See Stephen Booth, "On the Value of *Hamlet*," in *Reinterpretations of Elizabethan Drama: Selected Papers from the English Institute*, ed. Norman Rabkin (New York: Columbia University Press, 1969), 137–76.
3 Act, scene, and line numbers follow John Webster, *The White Devil*, ed. Benedict S. Robinson (London: The Arden Shakespeare, 2019); Richard Brome, *The Queen's Exchange*, in *The Dramatic Works of Richard Brome*, vol. 3 (New York: AMS Press, Inc., 1966); and Thomas Middleton, *The Second Maiden's Tragedy*, ed. Anne Lancashire (Manchester: Manchester University Press, 1978).
4 A late Jacobean exception is the anonymous *The Two Noble Ladies and the Converted Conjurer* (1622), which features a spirit "*Like a souldier in armour on his breast a sable shield*" (3.3.30sd). See *The Two Noble Ladies*, ed. Rebecca G. Rhoads (Oxford: Printed for the Malone Society by J. Johnson at the Oxford University Press, 1930). For more on the variety of ways that ghosts were represented in the early modern theater, see Ann Rosalind Jones and Peter Stallybrass, *Renaissance Clothing and the Materials of Memory* (Cambridge: Cambridge University Press, 2000), 245–68; and Alan C. Dessen and Leslie Thomson, *A Dictionary of Stage Directions in English Drama, 1580–1642* (Cambridge: Cambridge University Press, 1999), 100. It is worth noting, however, that when dramatic ghosts are talked about, as well as when characters pretend to be ghosts on the stage, the method of representation is fairly consistent. *A Warning for Fair Women* imagines "a filthie whining ghost / Lapt in some fowle sheete" (Induction.54–55); in *The Winter's Tale*, Antigonus similarly describes the possible ghost of Hermione

as dressed in "pure white robes" (3.3.21). In *The Night Walker*, two thieves entertain and subsequently reject the possibility of disguising themselves as ghosts with a "winding sheete" (2.1.47); in *The Atheist's Tragedy*, Languebeau *"pulls out a sheet, a hair, and a beard"* to disguise himself as the ghost of Montferrers (4.3.57sd). Act, scene, and line numbers follow *A Warning for Fair Women*, ed. Charles Dale Cannon (The Hague: Mouton, 1975); William Shakespeare, *The Winter's Tale*, ed. John Pitcher (London: Arden Shakespeare, 2010); John Fletcher, *The Night Walker*, ed. Cyrus Hoy, in *The Dramatic Works in the Beaumont and Fletcher Canon*, vol. 7 (Cambridge: Cambridge University Press, 1989); and Cyril Tourneur, *The Atheist's Tragedy*, in *Four Revenge Tragedies*, ed. Katharine Eisaman Maus (Oxford: Oxford University Press, 1995).

5   For more on materiality in *Hamlet*, see Margaret W. Ferguson, "*Hamlet*: Letters and Spirits," in *Shakespeare and the Question of Theory*, ed. Patricia Parker and Geoffrey Hartman (London: Methuen, 1985), 291-307; Janet Adelman, *Suffocating Mothers: Fantasies of Maternal Origin in Shakespeare's Plays, "Hamlet" to "The Tempest"* (New York: Routledge, 1992), 11–37; and David Scott Kastan, "What's the matter?" in *Formal Matters: Reading the Materials of English Renaissance Literature*, ed. Allison Deutermann and András Kiséry (Manchester: Manchester University Press, 2013), 249–53.

6   Jones and Stallybrass, *Renaissance Clothing*, 248, 243.

7   "embarrass, v. 1 and 2." OED Online. November 2019. Oxford University Press. www.oed.com/view/Entry/60793 (accessed November 3, 2019).

8   The play is more broadly interested in exploiting differing responses to theatrical spectacle: *Hamlet*'s play-within notoriously depends upon an array of conflicting reactions to Claudius's departure. See William N. West, *Theatres and Encyclopedias in Early Modern Europe* (Cambridge: Cambridge University Press, 2002). Stephen Booth similarly describes *Hamlet* as "the tragedy of an audience that cannot make up its mind." See "On the Value of *Hamlet*," 152.

9   It was the instability of the conventions surrounding ghosts that T. S. Eliot cited in his famous complaint about the semiotic volatility of the Elizabethan theater; as he put it, "what is fundamentally objectionable is that in the Elizabethan drama there has been no firm principle of what is to be postulated as a convention and what is not. The fault is not with the ghost but with the presentation of a ghost on a plane on which he is inappropriate, and with the confusion between one kind of ghost and another." My contention in this book is that such confusions do formative theatrical work. See Eliot, "Four Elizabethan Dramatists," in *Selected Essays, 1917–1932* (New York: Harcourt, Brace, and Company, 1932), 97.

10 Form is operative across different kinds of domains and discourses, Henry S. Turner writes, because it "permits the identification of reiterated patterns of arrangement in ideas, words, and other signifying units that occur in a relatively predictable way and that can be traced through the evidence of texts of all kinds." See Turner, *The English Renaissance Stage: Geometry, Poetics, and the Practical Spatial Arts 1580–1630* (Oxford: Oxford University Press, 2006), 20. This conception of form anticipates

the recent movement to describe form as patterned abstraction. See, for example, Anna Kornbluh, *The Order of Forms: Realism, Formalism, and Social Space* (Chicago: University of Chicago Press, 2019); and Daniel Shore, *Cyberformalism: Histories of Linguistic Forms in the Digital Archive* (Baltimore: Johns Hopkins University Press, 2018).

11 Bernard Beckerman, *Dynamics of Drama: Theory and Method of Analysis* (New York: Drama Book Specialists, 1979), 18.

12 That self-consciousness, as W. B. Worthen notes, has been matched in contemporary performances of Shakespeare's plays, which often foreground what he terms "the *technicity* of theatre." See Worthen, *Shakespeare, Technicity, Theatre* (Cambridge: Cambridge University Press, 2020), 27.

13 James Howell, *Epistolae Ho-Elianae* (London: Humphrey Mosley, 1645), Aaa2v.

14 Gina Bloom has compellingly described the early modern theater as "commodified interactivity." Taking her argument as a premise, mine pinpoints moments when such interactivity was both encouraged and thwarted. See Bloom, *Gaming the Stage: Playable Media and the Rise of English Commercial Theater* (Ann Arbor: University of Michigan Press, 2018), 13.

15 Line numbers follow William Shakespeare, *King Henry V*, ed. T. W. Craik (London: Arden Shakespeare, 1995).

16 In the case of the second example, I am thinking of Lodovico in Webster's *The White Devil*; I will treat the dramatic expectations created by the conventions of revenge tragedy in Chapter 5.

17 The question of whether the early modern theater was interested in the transmission of meaning at all is a matter of debate. Richard Preiss contests Jennifer Low and Nova Myhill's assertion that the early modern theater construed its audience "as a partner in the production of meaning." "Why do we assume early modern theatre understood itself," he asks, "to be about producing meanings?" Preiss's argument – that the rowdy behavior of audiences was itself a mode of competitive authorship in the playhouse – attends to different elements of theatrical experience than my own, but I share his sense that the theater of this period was not uniformly interested in ensuring interpretive significance or clarity. My contention, however, is that while this theater *did* enlist its audiences as producers of meanings, it also, often simultaneously, thwarted their ability to perform that very task. See Preiss, *Clowning and Authorship in Early Modern Theatre* (Cambridge: Cambridge University Press, 2014), 26; and Jennifer A. Low and Nova Myhill, Introduction, *Imagining the Audience in Early Modern Drama, 1558–1642* (New York: Palgrave Macmillan, 2011), 10. On spectators as producers of meanings, see also William N. West, who elucidates a sense of understanding in the theater that is at once cognitive and corporeal, encompassing the multifarious bodily pleasures of theatrical experience along with direct intellectual engagement with the play itself. West, *Common Understandings, Poetic Confusion: Playhouses and Playgoers in Elizabethan England* (Chicago: University of Chicago Press, 2021), 80–110.

18 Bruce R. Smith's work has established the foundations of the field; see Smith, *Phenomenal Shakespeare* (Malden, MA: Wiley-Blackwell, 2010). On theater-going as a historically and culturally specific corporeal experience, see especially Gail Kern Paster, *The Body Embarrassed: Drama and the Disciplines of Shame in Early Modern England* (Ithaca, NY: Cornell University Press, 1993); and Allison P. Hobgood, *Passionate Playgoing in Early Modern England* (Cambridge: Cambridge University Press, 2014). See also the special issue of *Criticism* 54.3 (2012), which builds on this foundational work by exploring phenomenology's "affinity with the theater's attempt to stage for its audiences minds and bodies and artifacts in dynamic relation." See Kevin Curran and James Kearney, *Criticism* 54.3 (2012): 353–64, esp. 358.

19 This methodology is aligned with what Paul Yachnin and Myrna Wyatt Selkirk identify as a move from "thematic to functionalist criticism – from an interest in what the plays mean to a focus on what they do." See Yachnin and Selkirk, "Metatheater and the Performance of Character," in *Shakespeare and Character: Theory, History, Performance, and Theatrical Persons*, ed. Paul Yachnin and Jessica Slights (New York: Palgrave Macmillan, 2009), 139–57, esp. 141.

20 Unless otherwise noted, I follow Martin Wiggins' dating of the plays' first performances. See Wiggins, *British Drama 1533–1642: A Catalogue*, 9 vols. (Oxford: Oxford University Press, 2012). For accounts of collaborative influence across companies, see Roslyn Lander Knutson, *Playing Companies and Commerce in Shakespeare's Time* (Cambridge: Cambridge University Press, 2001); and Tom Rutter, *Shakespeare and the Admiral's Men: Reading Across Repertories on the London Stage, 1594–1600* (Cambridge: Cambridge University Press, 2017).

21 For accounts of company styles, see, in particular, Sally-Beth MacLean and Scott McMillin, *The Queen's Men and Their Plays* (Cambridge: Cambridge University Press, 1998); Lucy Munro, *Children of the Queen's Revels: A Jacobean Theatre Repertory* (Cambridge: Cambridge University Press, 2005); Lawrence Manley and Sally-Beth MacLean, *Lord Strange's Men And Their Plays* (New Haven: Yale University Press, 2014); Andrew Gurr, *Shakespeare's Opposites: The Admiral's Company 1594–1625* (Cambridge: Cambridge University Press, 2009); Mary Bly, *Queer Virgins and Virgin Queans on the Early Modern Stage* (Oxford: Oxford University Press, 2000); and Bart van Es, *Shakespeare in Company* (Oxford: Oxford University Press, 2013). On the repertory system, see Roslyn Lander Knutson, *The Repertory of Shakespeare's Company, 1594–1613* (Fayetteville, AR: University of Arkansas Press, 1991).

22 See John Astington, *Actors and Acting in Shakespeare's Time: The Art of Stage Playing* (Cambridge: Cambridge University Press, 2010).

23 On genre as a governing interpretive framework across the commercial theater, see, for example, Jeremy Lopez, *Theatrical Convention and Audience Response in Early Modern Drama* (Cambridge: Cambridge University Press, 2003); and Jean E. Howard, "Shakespeare, Geography, and the Work of Genre on the Early Modern Stage," *Modern Language Quarterly* 64.3 (2003): 299–322.

24 Lopez, *Theatrical Convention*, 98.

25 See William N. West, "Intertheatricality," in *Early Modern Theatricality*, ed. Henry S. Turner (Oxford: Oxford University Press, 2013), 151–72; and Gina Bloom, Anston Bosman, and William N. West, "Ophelia's Intertheatricality, or, How Performance Is History," *Theatre Journal* 65.2 (2013): 165–82, esp. 179. Jonathan Gil Harris coins the term in *Untimely Matter in the Time of Shakespeare* (Philadelphia: University of Pennsylvania Press, 2009), 68–73. As a theoretical concept that seeks to explain how distinct plays create allusive constellations of significance beyond direct verbal reference, intertheatricality is indebted to Louise Clubb's explication of the "theatergram," which she defines as those "interchangeable structural units ... (characters, situations, actions, speeches, thematic patterns) which could be combined in dialogue and visual encounters to act out the fiction with verisimilitude." See Clubb, "Italian Stories on the Stage," in *The Cambridge Companion to Shakespearean Comedy*, ed. Alexander Leggatt (Cambridge: Cambridge University Press, 2002), 32–46, esp. 35. See also Clubb, *Italian Drama in Shakespeare's Time* (New Haven: Yale University Press, 1989).

26 West, "Intertheatricality," 152.

27 On "playgoer" as an emergent category in the period, see Michael West, "Were There Playgoers During the 1580s?" *Shakespeare Studies* 45 (2017): 68–76. On increasing appeals to the critical judgments and aesthetic discernment of Jacobean spectators, see Leo Salingar, "Jacobean Playwrights and 'Judicious' Spectators," *Renaissance Drama* 22 (1991): 209–34. On Caroline theatrical connoisseurship, see Adam Zucker and Alan B. Farmer, "Introduction," in *Localizing Caroline Drama: Politics and Economics of the Early Modern English Stage, 1625–1642*, ed. Adam Zucker and Alan B. Farmer (New York: Palgrave Macmillan, 2006), 1–16.

28 Martin Butler, *Theatre and Crisis 1632–1642* (Cambridge: Cambridge University Press, 1984), 108.

29 As Keir Elam puts it, these "transactional conventions are sufficiently powerful to ensure that there is no genuine ambiguity concerning the frame (i.e. everyone in the theatre knows more or less what is going on)." Deliberate ruptures to those transactions produce precisely the ambiguity that unsettled early modern spectators' interpretive relation to unfolding stage action. See Elam, *The Semiotics of Theatre and Drama* (New York: Routledge, 1980), 80.

30 Bert O. States, *Great Reckonings in Little Rooms: On the Phenomenology of Theater* (Berkeley: University of California Press, 1985), 12.

31 Others have recognized and productively attended to the disruption of convention in the early modern theater. As Jeremy Lopez rightly puts it, this theater regularly worked "to make an audience comfortable, even smug in its mastery of dramatic signals and information, and then casually [went] to the most extreme lengths to shock it out of its complacency." But where Lopez largely focuses on those conventions that interpretively situated audiences, my aim, building from the foundation of his wide-ranging and important work, is to emphasize moments of conventional anomaly and disruption. See *Theatrical Convention*, 133.

32 This emphasis on the pleasure of imbricated recognition and surprise intersects with work in adaptation studies; as Linda Hutcheon puts it, the "repetition with variation" of adaptation provides "the comfort of ritual combined with the piquancy of surprise." Yet while the competencies inculcated by conventions share traits with those produced by adaptation, the two are not entirely analogous: conventions provide interpretive frameworks rather than informational origins. See Hutcheon, *A Theory of Adaptation* (New York: Routledge, 2006), 4.

33 West, *Common Understandings, Poetic Confusion*, 110.

34 I borrow the term "horizon of expectations" from Hans Robert Jauss, who argues that the "interpretive reception of a text" is determined by its simultaneous reproduction and alteration within the broader scope of genre. In my own application of Jauss's concept, I widen dramatic genre to theatrical form, though the basic idea, that the interplay of norm and variation shapes audience response, holds. See Jauss, *Toward an Aesthetic of Reception*, trans. Timothy Bahti (Minneapolis: University of Minnesota Press, 1982), 23.

35 Jiří Veltruský's "Dramatic Text as a Component of Theater," in *Semiotics of Art: Prague School Contributions*, ed. Ladislav Matejka and Irwin R. Titunik (Cambridge: The MIT Press, 1976), 94–117, established the parameters of the semiotic approach to theater; František Deák traces the emergence and codification of that approach in "Structuralism in Theatre: The Prague School Contribution," *The Drama Review* 20.4 (1976): 83–94. For a semiotic approach that privileges performance as a live event over its realization of a dramatic text, see, in addition to Elam, *The Semiotics of Theatre and Drama*, Erika Fischer-Lichte, *The Semiotics of Theater*, trans. Jeremy Gaines and Doris L. Jones (Bloomington: Indiana University Press), 1992.

36 Act, scene, and line numbers follow William Shakespeare, *King Henry IV, Part 1*, ed. David Scott Kastan (London: Arden, 2002).

37 Original text: "At verò Desdemona illa apud nos a marito occisa, quanquam optimè semper causam egit, interfecta tamen magis movebat; cum in lecto decumbens spectantium misericordiam ipso vultu imploraret." Jackson recorded his impression of the performance in a letter written in September 1610. A transcription of the Latin text appears in *Records of Early English Drama: Oxford*, ed. John R. Elliott, Jr et al., vol. 1 (Toronto: University of Toronto Press, 2004), 387. The translation is my own. As Anthony B. Dawson interprets this eyewitness account, Jackson "ignor[es] ... the actual sex of the actor while at the same time praising him for the physical details of his impersonation." See "Performance and Participation" in Dawson and Paul Yachnin, *The Culture of Playgoing in Shakespeare's England: A Collaborative Debate* (Cambridge: Cambridge University Press, 2001), 11–38, esp. 19.

38 On the semiotic systems of interpretation that plays set up and subsequently upended for spectators, see Erika T. Lin, "'Lord of thy presence': Bodies, Performance, and Audience Interpretation in Shakespeare's *King John*," in *Imagining the Audience in Early Modern Drama, 1558–1642*, ed. Jennifer A. Low and Nova Myhill (New York: Palgrave Macmillan, 2011), 113–33.

39 Luke Wilson, *Theaters of Intention: Drama and the Law in Early Modern England* (Stanford: Stanford University Press, 2000), 177.

40 John Keats, *Selected Letters of John Keats*, ed. Grant F. Scott (Cambridge, MA: Harvard University Press, 2002), 60. Even as recent work on the early modern theater has productively broadened the period's dramatic canon by moving to consider Shakespeare in relation to his contemporaries, the perception that he was a uniquely ambivalent playwright – who alone managed to produce drama "in which no single argumentative position, no point of view, however passionately presented, is allowed to go unquestioned or unqualified" – remains. See Michael Neill, Introduction, *Antony and Cleopatra* (Oxford: Oxford University Press, 1994), 101. This book's focus on a wide range of playwrights suggests the opposite: that the production of uncertainty in the playhouse was less an epistemological technique at which Shakespeare was particularly adept than it was both a condition of the literary form in which he wrote and a preoccupation of the commercial industry in which he made his career. The wellspring of much of this attention to Shakespeare as a particularly skeptical playwright is Stanley Cavell's *Disowning Knowledge in Seven Plays of Shakespeare* (Cambridge: Cambridge University Press, 2003). Though Cavell's work is avowedly ahistorical, much of the work that it has inspired follows an intellectual historical framework, reading the drama in light of the skeptical crises that swept through Europe and England in the sixteenth centuries. See, for example, Graham Bradshaw, *Shakespeare's Scepticism* (Ithaca, NY: Cornell University Press, 1987); Ellen Spolsky, *Satisfying Skepticism: Embodied Knowledge in the Early Modern World* (Burlington, VT: Ashgate, 2001); David Hillman, *Shakespeare's Entrails: Belief, Scepticism, and the Interior of the Body* (New York: Palgrave MacMillan, 2007); Millicent Bell, *Shakespeare's Tragic Scepticism* (New Haven: Yale University Press, 2002); and James Kuzner, *Shakespeare as a Way of Life: Skeptical Practice and the Politics of Weakness* (New York: Fordham University Press, 2016).

41 For more on the doubled signification of the actor's body, see States, *Great Reckonings*; and Stanton B. Garner, *Bodied Spaces: Phenomenology and Performance in Contemporary Drama* (Ithaca, NY: Cornell University Press, 1994). In an early modern English context, see William N. West, "What's the Matter with Shakespeare? Physics, Identity, Playing," *South Central Review* 26.1 and 2 (2009): 103–26. I treat the doubled signification of the actor's body as theatrically engaged by the device of the false death in Chapter 1 and impersonation plots in Chapter 4.

42 Act, scene, and line numbers follow William Shakespeare, *Twelfth Night*, ed. Keir Elam (London: Arden Shakespeare, 2008).

43 What Brecht describes as a particular effect was the normative condition of theatrical experience in sixteenth- and seventeenth-century England: "The Chinese artist never acts as if there were a fourth wall besides the three surrounding him. He expresses his awareness of being watched. This immediately removes one of the European stage's characteristic illusions. The audience can no longer have the illusion of being the unseen spectator at an event which is

really taking place." Bertolt Brecht, "Alienation Effects in Chinese Acting," in *Brecht on Theatre: The Development of an Aesthetic*, ed. and trans. John Willett (New York: Hill and Wang, 1964), 91–99, esp. 92.

44 Robert Weimann, *Author's Pen and Actor's Voice: Playing and Writing in Shakespeare's Theatre* (Cambridge: Cambridge University Press, 2000), 184.

45 Weimann, *Author's Pen and Actor's Voice*, 184.

46 Preiss similarly suggests that in Weimann's model, "the authority of the stage is taken for granted"; see *Clowning and Authorship*, 63.

47 Weimann, "Bifold Authority in Shakespeare's Theatre," *Shakespeare Quarterly* 39.4 (1988): 401–17, esp. 407.

48 Edmund Husserl, *Ideas for a Pure Phenomenology and Phenomenological Philosophy: First Book: General Introduction to Pure Phenomenology*, trans. Daniel O. Dahlstrom (Indianapolis, IN: Hackett, 2014), 49.

49 Husserl, *Ideas*, 56.

50 Maurice Merleau-Ponty, "The Primacy of Perception and Its Philosophical Consequences," in *The Merleau-Ponty Reader*, ed. Ted Toadvine and Leonard Lawlor (Evanston, IL: Northwestern University Press, 2007), 89–118, esp. 98.

51 Merleau-Ponty, "Cezanne's Doubt," in *The Merleau-Ponty Reader*, 69–84, esp. 74.

52 Husserl, *Ideas*, 55. The phenomenological assumption that the world remains even in the face of doubt about what is contained within it is closer to a classical formulation of skepticism than a Cartesian one. For the intellectual prehistory of Cartesian doubt, see Richard Popkin, *The History of Scepticism from Savonarola to Bayle* (Oxford: Oxford University Press, 2003).

53 Bryan Crockett, *The Play of Paradox: Stage and Sermon in Renaissance England* (Philadelphia: University of Pennsylvania Press, 1995), 19; Butler, *Theatre and Crisis*, 24; Musa Gurnis, *Mixed Faith and Shared Feeling: Theater in Post-Reformation London* (Philadelphia: University of Pennsylvania Press, 2018), 160.

54 Jean E. Howard, *Theater of a City: The Places of London Comedy, 1598–1642* (Philadelphia: University of Pennsylvania Press, 2007), 4.

55 As Katherine Eggert describes it, this era created methods for "managing unpalatable knowledge" alongside the development of new modes of thought. See Eggert, *Disknowledge: Literature, Alchemy, and the End of Humanism in Renaissance England* (Philadelphia: University of Pennsylvania Press, 2015), 3.

56 Popkin terms this unsettling of the criterion of true religious knowledge *la crise pyrrhonienne*; see *The History of Scepticism, passim*. For work that marshals Popkin's framework in service of the study of religious doubt on the early modern stage, see, for example, William Hamlin, *Tragedy and Scepticism in Shakespeare's England* (New York: Palgrave Macmillan, 2005); Anita Gilman Sherman, *Skepticism and Memory in Shakespeare and Donne* (New York: Palgrave Macmillan), 2007; and John D. Cox, *Seeming Knowledge: Shakespeare and Skeptical Faith* (Waco, TX: Baylor University Press), 2007.

57 For work on the drama that treats the psychological and cultural effects of such confessional shifts, as represented by characters onstage, see, for example, Steven Mullaney, *The Reformation of Emotions in the Age of Shakespeare* (Chicago: University of Chicago Press, 2015); Stephen Greenblatt, *Hamlet in Purgatory* (Princeton: Princeton University Press, 2001); and Jonathan Dollimore, *Radical Tragedy: Religion, Ideology and Power in the Drama of Shakespeare and His Contemporaries*, 3rd ed. (Durham Duke University Press, 2004).

58 The effect was, as he put it, to cause the spiritually irresolute "continually [to] wauer" in the search for "tranquility of mind." See Leonardus Lessius, *A Consultation What Faith and Religion is Best to Be Imbraced*, trans. William Wright (Saint-Omer, 1618), 1. For more on these texts of spiritual irresolution, see Molly Murray, *The Poetics of Conversion in Early Modern English Literature: Verse and Change from Donne to Dryden* (Cambridge: Cambridge University Press, 2009), 86–92.

59 John Leslie, *A Treatise Concerning the Defence of the Honour of the Right High, Mightie and Noble Princesse, Marie Queene of Scotland, and Douager of France with a Declaration, as Wel of Her Right, Title, and Interest, to the Succession of the Croune of England* (Leodii [and Louvain]: Gualterum Morberium [and J. Fowler], 1571), 56; Richard Saunders, *Physiognomie* (London: Nathaniel Brooke, 1653), 235.

60 John Donne, "The First Anniversary: An Anatomy of the World," in *The Complete Poems of John Donne*, ed. Robin Robbins (New York: Routledge, 2013), 811–60.

61 Robin Robbins notes Donne's merely superficial knowledge of Keplerian theories about planetary movement, yet that lack of acquaintance with new scientific methodology, I would argue, is partly the point: Donne's fundamental doubt arises from the bizarre contention that the sun does not actually move, though it appears to. See *The Complete Poems*, 835.

62 As Peter Dear points out, this was an expression that John Wilkins could coin in 1660 without explanation "because so many of his peers now grasped [its] connotations." Peter Dear, *Discipline and Experience: The Mathematical Way in the Scientific Revolution* (Chicago: University of Chicago Press, 1995), 247.

63 As Mary Thomas Crane explains, the experimental proofs that would eventually provide explanations for the more speculative theories about the natural world only emerged retroactively. At the opening the seventeenth century, the new science, rather, "seemed to be separating the tangible surfaces of the world from their invisible material underpinnings." See Crane, *Losing Touch with Nature: Literature and the New Science in Sixteenth – Century England* (Baltimore, MD: Johns Hopkins University Press, 2014), 158. See also what Peter Dear has called the "precarious intelligibility" of a world that existed on the cusp of Aristotelian, inductive reasoning – which sought to explain universal knowledge supported by general experience – and knowledge constructed through the particularized experience of the experiment. Dear, *Discipline and Experience*, 11. For more on the severing of scientific truth from sensory experience in this period, see Barbara Shapiro, *Probability and Certainty in*

Seventeenth-Century England: A Study of the Relationships between Natural Science, Religion, History, Law, and Literature (Princeton: Princeton University Press, 1983). For an account of the seventeenth-century experimental method as "collectivized individual sensory experience," see Steven Shapin and Simon Schaffer, *Leviathan and the Air-Pump: Hobbes, Boyle, and the Experimental Life* (Princeton, NJ: Princeton University Press, 1985), 152.

64 Francis Bacon, *The New Organon*, ed. Lisa Jardine and Michael Silverthorne (Cambridge: Cambridge University Press, 2000), 23.

65 See Lorna Hutson, *The Invention of Suspicion: Law and Mimesis in Shakespeare and Renaissance Drama* (Oxford: Oxford University Press, 2007).

66 In addition to Eggert's *Disknowledge*, on the persistence of outmoded forms of thought alongside the emergence of new ones, see Thomas Kuhn's classic study of epistemological "crisis as an appropriate prelude to the emergence of new theories," in *The Structure of Scientific Revolutions*, 4th ed. (Chicago: University of Chicago Press, 2012), 156; and Steven Shapin, *The Scientific Revolution* (Chicago: University of Chicago Press, 1996), 4.

67 On the transmission (and reimagining) of ancient skepticism in late-sixteenth-century England, see William Hamlin, *Tragedy and Scepticism*; Luciano Floridi, *Sextus Empiricus: The Transmission and Recovery of Pyrrhonism* (Oxford: Oxford University Press, 2002); Charles Schmitt, "Philosophy and Science in Sixteenth-Century Universities: Some Preliminary Comments," in *The Cultural Context of Medieval Learning*, ed. J. Murdoch and E. Sylla (Dordrecht: Reidel, 1975), 485–537; and Michelle Zerba, *Doubt and Skepticism in Antiquity and the Renaissance* (Cambridge: Cambridge University Press, 2012).

68 On the governing principles of ancient skepticism, see Julia Annas and Jonathan Barnes, *The Modes of Scepticism: Ancient Texts and Modern Interpretations* (Cambridge: Cambridge University Press, 1985).

69 See Thomas Nashe, *The Terrors of the Night, or a Discourse of Apparitions* (London: William Jones, 1594). Nashe elsewhere alludes to a (now-lost) edition of Sextus's writings "latelie translated into English, for the benefit of vnlearned writers." See Thomas Nashe, "Somewhat to reade for them that list," in *Astrophel and Stella*, by Phillip Sidney (London: Thomas Newman, 1591), A4r. For the argument that Nashe refers to "The Sceptick," an essay that is essentially a loose translation of Book I, Chapter 14 of Sextus' *Outlines of Pyrrhonism*, see William Hamlin, "A Lost Translation Found? An Edition of 'The Sceptick' (c. 1590) Based on Extant Manuscripts [with text]," *English Literary Renaissance* 31.1 (2001): 34–51.

70 See Stuart Clark, *Vanities of Eye: Vision in Early Modern European Culture* (Oxford: Oxford University Press, 2007).

71 George Hakewill, *The Vanitie of the Eie* (Oxford: Joseph Barnes, 1608), 49.

72 As Joel Altman suggests, "Arguing both sides of the question was frequently employed as a method of political inquiry and (not infrequently) of politic hedging; it appears as a mode of theological speculation and even of scientific investigation. But it is also turned to use simply as a creative pastime, in which one need not proceed beyond disputation to secure

conviction; here, its value lay rather in exercising the inventive faculty to produce effective proofs." See Altman, *The Tudor Play of Mind: Rhetorical Inquiry and the Development of Elizabethan Drama* (Berkeley: University of California Press, 1978), 32. For more on *in utramque partem* reasoning as part of Elizabethan education from grammar school to university, see Lynn Enterline, *Shakespeare's Schoolroom: Rhetoric, Discipline, Emotion* (Philadelphia: University of Pennsylvania Press, 2012).

73 In 1595, for example, the authors of *A Conference about the Next Succession to the Crowne of Ingland*, who aimed to place Isabella of Spain on the throne, wrote regarding Elizabeth's successor that "albeit the neernes of each mans succession in blood, were euidently knowne, yet were it very vncertayne (as things now stand in Ingland and in the rest of Christendome rownd about) who should preuaile." A decade later, the Protestant polemicist (and former Roman Catholic priest) Thomas Bell would warn that "the Succession of Romish Byshops is not so certaine, as the Papists would beare the world in hand it is." See *A Conference about the Next Succession to the Crowne of Ingland* (Antwerp: A. Conincx, 1595), B4r; and Bell, *The Woefull Crie of Rome Containing a Defiance to Popery* (London: William Welby, 1605), 51. For more on the use of skeptical reasoning to "[destroy] the opponent," see Popkin, *The History of Scepticism*, 76.

74 See Leeds Barroll, *Politics, Plague, and Shakespeare's Theater: The Stuart Years* (Ithaca: Cornell University Press, 1991), 101.

75 Steven N. Zwicker, "'On First Looking into Revisionism': The Literature of Civil War, Revolution, and Restoration," *Huntington Library Quarterly* 78.4 (2015): 789–807, esp. 789.

76 This is not to suggest that people did not *try* to know all they could about their neighbors: in London and beyond, a culture of surveillance stridently pushed back against newly emergent forms of privacy in this period. See, in particular, Laura Gowing, *Domestic Dangers: Women, Words, and Sex in Early Modern London* (Oxford: Clarendon Press, 1996); and Lena Cowen Orlin, *Locating Privacy in Tudor London* (Oxford: Oxford University Press, 2008).

77 For more on the changing conditions of urbanization that made the growth of London's theater industry possible in the second half of the sixteenth century, see Howard, *Theater of a City*, 14–19; and Ian W. Archer, *The Pursuit of Stability: Social Relations in Elizabethan London* (Cambridge: Cambridge University Press, 1991).

78 To take a representative example: the Calvinist doctrine of predestination that rendered essentially unknowable whether one was saved or reprobate would have been widely familiar in post-Reformation England. Peter Marshall claims that "there appears to have been a broad cultural presumption in later Reformation England that salvation was widely accessible," though he also details examples of people driven to pathological fear over the status of their souls. There is a wide range of experience between these two extremes, and it is not hard to imagine moving to different places along that spectrum of anxiety at some or even many points in the course of one's life.

See Marshall, *Beliefs and the Dead in Reformation England* (Oxford: Oxford University Press, 2002), 201. George Puttenham hints at this preoccupation with the unknowable when he comments on the tendency to speculate about the fate of one's dead friends: "Our vncertaintie and suspition of their estates and welfare in the places of their new abode, seemeth to carry a reasonable pretext of iust sorrow." See Puttenham, *The Arte of English Poesie* (London: Richard Field, 1589), 38.

79 Raymond Williams, *Keywords* (Oxford: Oxford University Press, 1983), 138.

80 Sextus Empiricus, *Outlines of Scepticism*, trans. Julia Annas and Jonathan Barnes (Cambridge: Cambridge University Press, 2000), 11.

81 Book and line numbers follow John Milton, *Paradise Lost*, ed. Stephen Orgel and Jonathan Goldberg (Oxford: Oxford University Press, 2004).

82 Peter C. Herman, *Destabilizing Milton: "Paradise Lost" and the Poetics of Incertitude* (New York: Palgrave Macmillan, 2005), 43–59, esp. 43. Herman notes that "or" is the eighth most common word in *Paradise Lost*. Montaigne similarly recognized that doubtful alternatives had the potential for endless articulation: "To answere one doubt," he says of those who employ Socratic-style debates to seek after truth, "they give me three: It is *Hidraes* head." Michel de Montaigne, "Of Experience," in *The Essayes of Morall, Politike and Militarie Discourses of Lo: Michaell de Montaigne*, trans. John Florio (London: Edward Blount, 1603), 636.

83 William Prynne, *Histriomastix* (London: Michael Sparke, 1633), 81, 577.

84 Lopez, *Theatrical Convention*, 123.

85 On the quieting of these debates into the Jacobean era, see Amy J. Rodgers, *A Monster with a Thousand Hands: The Discursive Spectator in Early Modern England* (Philadelphia: University of Pennsylvania Press, 2018), 49.

86 William Cartwright, "Upon the Report of the Printing of the Dramaticall Poems of Master John Fletcher," in *Comedies and Tragedies Written by Francis Beaumont and John Fletcher* (London: Humphrey Robinson and Humphrey Mosley, 1647), d2r.

87 Act, scene, and line numbers follow Ben Jonson, *The Magnetic Lady, or Humours Reconciled*, ed. Helen Ostovitch, *The Cambridge Edition of the Works of Ben Jonson*, ed. David Bevington, Martin Butler, and Ian Donaldson, vol. 6, *1626–1636* (Cambridge: Cambridge University Press, 2012), 391–540.

88 Hamlin, *Tragedy and Scepticism*, 129. Act, scene, and line numbers follow John Marston, *What You Will*, in *The Works of John Marston*, vol. 2, ed. A.H. Bullen (London: J. C. Nimmo, 1887).

89 John Calvin, *The Sermons of M. Iohn Caluin vpon the Fifth Booke of Moses Called Deuteronomie*, trans. Arthur Golding (London: George Bishop, 1583), 505; Thomas Jordan, "To his friend the Author," in *The Plays and Poems of Philip Massinger*, vol. 2, ed. Philip Edwards and Colin Gibson (Oxford: At the Clarendon Press, 1976), 296. The maze as a spatial representation of uncertainty has strong poetic associations in the period. In his guide to poetry, for example, Joshua Poole glosses "maze" as "Perplexing, ambiguous, winding, uncertain, turning-blind, darksome, crooked, subtle, snakie, distractful, giddy, dizzy." See Poole, *The English Parnassus* (London: Thomas Johnson, 1657), 133.

90 John Donne, *Fifty Sermons* (London: M. F., J. Marriot, and R. Royston, 1649), 392.
91 On Shakespearean drama's depiction of skeptical solitude as tragic solipsism, see Cavell, *Disowning Knowledge.*
92 See Butler, *Theatre and Crisis*, 100–40.
93 Edmund Gayton reports that playgoers often "so courted the Players to re-act the same matters in the Tavernes, that they came home, as able Actors as themselves," and Thomas Fuller commends the complexity of Jonson's comedies by suggesting that they "took not so well at the *first stroke* as at the *rebound*, when beheld the second time." See Gayton, *Pleasant Notes upon Don Quixot* (London: William Hunt, 1654), 140; and Fuller, *The History of the Worthies of England* (London: Thomas Williams, 1662), 243.
94 Richard Brathwaite, *Anniversaries upon His Panarete Continued* (London: Robert Bostock, 1635), A7v.
95 Act, scene, and line numbers follow William Shakespeare, *A Midsummer Night's Dream*, ed. Sukanta Chaudhuri (London: Arden Shakespeare, 2017).
96 As Stanton B. Garner puts it, "the body represents a rootedness in the bio-logical present that always, to some extent, escapes transformation into the virtual realm." See Garner, *Bodied Spaces: Phenomenology and Performance in Contemporary Drama* (Ithaca: Cornell University Press, 1994), 44.

PART I

Dramatic Action

CHAPTER I

Bodies

Lively Corpses and the Rise of Tragicomedy

In the 1623 Folio edition of *King Lear*, the eponymous monarch's final words are a command: "Look on her," he says of Cordelia, "look, her lips, / Look there, look there!" (5.3.309–10).[1] The spectators who responded to it would not have all seen the same thing. Those standing or sitting farthest from the stage may have perceived nothing but the motionless woman, the spectacle confirming both her death and the return of Lear's delusion after his brief, bright moment of clarity upon reuniting with his youngest daughter. Playgoers who knew Raphael Holinshed's chronicle of the historical Leir's reign may have been confused, however, at the counterfactual sight of the dead Cordelia, who lives on in the history for several years after her father's death.[2] Still others unfamiliar with the historical narrative could have recently picked up the Elizabethan *Leir* play, newly printed in 1605, in which Cordelia remains alive to the play's conclusion; they may have searched, perhaps doubtfully, for signs of her resurrection.[3] Those spectators who had jostled their way through the Yard and pressed themselves to the very edge of the stage likely would have found them.[4] The boy actor, his lips fluttering as he exhaled, his chest rising and falling as he drew breath, would have evoked tantalizing signs of life even as he did his very best to play his part: the body of a dead woman. For these spectators, Lear's command may have brought a moment of false hope.[5]

I will return to *King Lear* at the close of this chapter, which is about the spectatorial expectations, thwarted and fulfilled, that were brought about by the practice of live actors expressing and feigning death in the early modern English commercial theater.[6] The inherent resistance of the actor's body to stable dramatic signification – it maintains, as Stanton B. Garner puts it, "a rootedness in the biological present that always, to some extent, escapes transformation into the virtual realm" – is a potent issue for the staging of death, for that semiotic instability renders ambiguous whether the signs of life the actor exhibits belong to the world of the playhouse or the play.[7] That liveliness also means that the revival of the fictional dead is always, at all times and in all places, a theatrical possibility.[8] But that potency took on special significance in early modern England, where the line between life and death was considerably blurrier than it is now. The possibility of revivification was as real outside the playhouse as it was within it. Resurrection, as the official language of the Church of England explained, was "the very locke and key of all our Christian religion and fayth."[9] At the most basic level, it is hard to imagine a playgoer in this period who was *not* deeply familiar with Lazarus's and Jesus's resurrections in the Gospels, as well as the depictions of the attempts to confirm Jesus's liveliness: "Euen doubting *Thomas*, who / reports would not beleeue," as a 1613 hymn succinctly put it, "By touch did feele and know, / that sure he was aliue."[10] Beyond this scriptural knowledge, the Protestant promise of bodily resurrection at the Last Judgment would have shaped the habits, anxieties, and hopes of many playgoers on a daily basis. But if *resurrection* was something that had happened in the distant past and would, at an undetermined future moment, happen again, *reanimation* was happening in the present – and frequently. Stories of apparently dead bodies reviving themselves were commonplace, and while medical treatises puzzled over the issue of how to discern liveliness in the moribund body, the possibility of reanimation remained so potent that the bereaved were advised to wait several days before burying their dead. Hamlet's description of death as "The undiscovered country from whose bourn / No traveller returns" was not simply false within a fictional world visited by just such a traveler (3.1.78–79); it also failed to describe the return of the dead to the world beyond the playhouse.[11]

Reanimations and resurrections did eventually make their way into the early modern playhouse, finding their greatest thematic richness in tragicomedy – the hybrid genre that, as John Fletcher famously claimed, "wants deaths."[12] The wonder that is so often said to describe the atmosphere of Shakespearean romance, in particular, often accompanies the unexpected – and sometimes unexplained – returns of characters thought to be dead: Thaisa, the Cymbeline brothers, Hermione.[13] Yet it took the commercial theater years of operation before the staging of these unexpected reversals became commonplace.[14] Even in a culture in which the possibility of resurrection was deeply felt, its depiction in the theater first required practitioners to subsume contemporary religious and medical debates about lively corpses into conventional stage practices.[15] Theater practitioners relied on various stage practices to shape playgoers' interpretive attention to dead and seemingly dead bodies, and in this chapter I track those practices that both disrupted old conventions and coalesced into new ones from the late 1580s through the opening decades of the seventeenth century. In the Elizabethan theater, I will argue, practitioners attempted to mitigate the semiotic instability of the actor's body by diverting spectators' attention from its ambiguous signification entirely. But as practitioners continued to experiment with the display of actual and apparent death in the theater, plays began to demand more frequently that spectators apprehend the liveliness of the stage corpse; as a result, they were increasingly asked to revise the conventional supposition that when a character died on the stage, his or her corpse would reliably stay dead.

The inculcation of spectatorial competencies regarding stage corpses, then, was at once training in the openness to the theatrical possibility that epitomizes tragicomedy. If, as Jane Hwang Degenhardt and Cyrus Mulready explain, tragicomedy "achieves a complex unity and tension by coming close to tragedy and then averting it," that swerve requires spectators in the playhouse to look closely for death itself, as expressed by the body of the actor.[16] This theatrical solicitation has complex phenomenological effects. Registering the body of the corpse necessarily enfolds the actor's recalcitrant liveliness into the world of the fiction, creating the interpretive space for the possibility of revival. Lear's demand to "look there," we might say, produces for the audience a wish to determine what that "there," if anything, is. Attention to the lively corpse suspends spectators at a point of narrative divergence, both inviting and frustrating their interpretive discernment of the plot's next turn. In the very process of cultivating playgoers' interpretive acuity and theatrical competencies, the broadening of possibility in the early modern playhouse forged the interpretive link between spectators and performance as uncertainty itself.

Apparent Death in the Elizabethan Theater

Late-1580s and early-1590s' drama frequently stages apparent deaths, though it overwhelmingly tends to solve the potential interpretive impasse of the trope – is the *character* feigning death, or merely the actor? – by warning spectators in advance of a character's counterfeited death. The sleeping potion serves as a theatrically expedient form of alert. The device allows characters to buy time, as in *Romeo and Juliet* (1595), to enact a moral shift in those fooled by the seeming death, as in *Much Ado about Nothing* (1598), to evade capture, as in *The Jew of Malta* (1589), and to defy the orders of corrupt rulers, as in *Cymbeline* (1610) and *Match Me in London* (1621).[17] But the sleeping potion is more than just a plot device: as a semiotic device, it frees spectators from their suspect reliance on the ambiguous, barely discernable signs of life or death suggested by the actor's body alone. In *Romeo and Juliet*, Friar Laurence's explanation of the sleeping draught's physiological effects at once serves as an interpretive guide to the apparently dead body that spectators will soon see on the stage:

> Through all thy veins shall run
> A cold and drowsy humour, for no pulse
> Shall keep his native progress, but surcease.
> No warmth, no breath, shall testify thou livest.
> The roses in thy lips and cheeks shall fade
> To wanny ashes, thy eyes' windows fall
> Like death, when he shuts up the day of life.
> Each part, deprived of supple government,
> Shall stiff and stark and cold appear like death,
> And in this borrowed likeness of shrunk death
> Thou shalt continue two-and-forty hours,
> And then awake as from a pleasant sleep.   (4.1.95–106)[18]

Supple vitality is rigid death; rose is ash; breath is not breath. The Friar's *enargeia*, which conjures Juliet's liveliness in the very process of describing its imminent withdrawal, evacuates the signifying force of the actor's body from the world of the play, so that the signs of life inevitably exhibited by the boy actor do not impinge on the dramatic representation. The sleeping potion device allows spectators simultaneously to *see* Juliet as dead within the world of the play and *know* that she is not.

Such interpretive sanction was crucial in the early modern theater, for playgoers were culturally primed to make the connection between sleep and death.[19] In the Protestant tradition, the characterization of the soul's restful period before the Last Judgment as sleep was so thoroughgoing that, as Carol Zaleski writes, it "reduce[d] the repertoire of images for the interim period to the single image of sleep."[20] "There is nothing more like to the graue, then our beds: to the winding sheet, then the sheetes of our beds," Francis Rodes wrote in 1622.[21] From "the long night of sleepe ... there is no awaking," Robert Horne preached in 1613, "till the last great trumpe call vs vp to iudgement."[22] The association was so common that Thomas Sparke could note in 1593 that "we finde it an vsuall thing in the Scriptures, immediately when men die, to say they fell a sleepe."[23] These comparisons were indeed supported by many biblical passages that described the afterlife with the Lord, as in a representative example from the Psalms, as sleep: "I will both lay me down in peace, and sleep : for thou, LORD, only makest me dwell in safety" (Ps. 4:8).[24] In the Protestant imagination, death, quite simply, *was* sleep.

Plays that chose not to disambiguate the actor's lively body with the sleeping potion device transformed this comforting conflation, then, into an epistemological quandary.[25] *The Famous Victories of Henry V* (1587), which stages Henry IV's apparent and actual death in juxtaposition, both foregrounds and offers a solution to precisely this spectacular problem. Scene 8 depicts Henry IV in bed, anxious about managing the details of his son's impending ascension to the throne: "But, good my lords," he directs, "remember my last will and testament concerning my son; for truly, my lords, I do not think but he will prove as valiant and victorious a king as ever reigned in England" (8.3–5).[26] If succession nears, so must the king's death, a supposition that Henry's order to "draw the curtains" of his bed would have visually reinforced (8.8–9).[27] But if the order offers seeming confirmation about the king's imminent demise in the form of literal closure, the prince instead treats the bed as a site of revelation: "Here is his body, indeed," he declares upon entering his father's chamber, "but his soul is whereas it needs no body" (8.14–15).[28] The deictic suggests that the prince has reopened the curtains, an action that trains spectators' attention on the king's body. Yet the display results in indeterminacy, for the seemingly dead king awakens, his crown having been prematurely seized by his son, moments later.[29]

King Henry's actual death follows upon the heels of his apparent one, a theatrical event that creates a new problem: how best to demonstrate that, *this* time, the actor's prone body represents death rather than sleep? The king tries again to retire: "Well, my lords," he admits, "I know not whether it be for sleep, or drawing near of drowsy summer of death, but I am very much given to sleepe. Therefore, good my lords, and my son, draw the curtains; depart my chamber; and cause some music to rock me asleep" (8.66–69). This time, the curtains stay closed. Though the next scene opens with repeated assurances that the king has indeed died – "my Lord Chief Justice heard that the old King was dead" (9.2–3), one character announces, just before another rushes onstage, crying, "Gog's wounds! The King is dead." (9.6) – his death itself is a spectacular lacuna, appearing in the playtext only as a stage direction. Placing repeated emphasis on an unstaged event seemingly coheres with *The Famous Victories's* habit, as Sally-Beth MacLean and Scott McMillin put it, of "referring to an incident instead of dramatizing it."[30] Taken together, though, these

episodes exhibit a theatrical savviness: when the play means to call King
Henry's death into question, his body is put on display; when his death
unequivocally occurs, it is decorously hidden from view. Narrative resolution requires closing the curtain on the problem of the ambiguously lively
body entirely.

Despite the commercial theater's exuberance for the display of death
and dying, these instances of apparent death highlight a nagging awareness: on the stage, death cannot unmistakably *show*. But death's opacity
was not a problem limited to the playhouse. As early modern medical treatises repeatedly insisted, death could be identified only by the
absence of signs of life. And life, as God's creation in Genesis had it,
was synonymous with breath.[31] In his thirteenth-century Latin treatise
De Proprietatibus Rerum, newly printed in English in 1582, Bartholomeus
Anglicus explained that when animal spirits are not allowed the reach the
brain, "breath is stopped, and the lyfe ended."[32] In 1638, Jesuit Robert
Bellarmine outlined "the usuall received opinion, that to live and *breath*
are one, and the same: for every thing that *breathes*, *liveth*, and that which
leaves to *breath*, ceaseth also to *live*."[33] This equation of life with breath
explains the prevalence with which characters in the drama wrongly claim
to see the dead breathing – inviting, of course, exactly the phenomenological confusion the Friar's speech in *Romeo and Juliet* seeks to avoid. In
Antonio's Revenge (1600), Pandulfo, mourning over the body of his dead
son Felice, suddenly – if doubtfully – claims to discern signs of life in
him:

> Methinks I hear a humming murmur creep
> From out his gelid wounds. Look on those lips,
> Those now lawn pillows, on whose tender softness
> Chaste modest speech, stealing from out his breast,
> Had wont to rest itself, as loath to post
> From out so fair an inn. Look, look, they seem to stir
> And breathe defiance to black obloquy.   (2.1.73–79)[34]

The formal hallmark of Marston's verse in *Antonio's Revenge* and elsewhere,
as Joseph Loewenstein has noted, is a sonic difficulty so extreme as to be
nearly unspeakable; this speech traces that very inability of utterance in its
depiction of a body and soul tenuously suspended in the balance of life
and death.[35] Pandulfo claims initially to hear a "humming murmur" exud-
ing from Felice's wounds, as if his entire body cries out for revenge. But
the subsequent image – speech that just barely escapes the mouth only to
collapse on the "tender softness" of Felice's lips – is a portrait of vivacity on
the brink of deathly enervation. By the end of the soliloquy, breath itself,

rather than speech, registers "black obloquy"; the life of which breath is a sign has been so wasted that it is nearly nonexistent. As with Lear's direction to look, the object of Pandulfo's pointing remains merely on the brink of coming into view.

Both within the playhouse and outside it, then, the discernment of breath remained a vexed endeavor. Even so, empirical tests for detecting breath frequently appeared in medical texts. In his anatomical treatise *Mikrokosmographia* (1615), the physician Helkiah Crooke details two of the most common: "A downy feather applyed vnto their mouth" and "a cleare looking glasse close vpon their mouths, for then if they liue the glasse will haue a little dew vpon it."[36] Both tests were notoriously unreliable, which caused many practitioners to favor one method over another."[37] Crooke himself prefers the mirror over the downy feather, for "sometimes," he cautions, "you shall not perceiue it [the feather] to shake."[38] Apoplectic bodies, in particular, were known to evade such empirical tests. Holinshed highlights one such famous example of apoplexy in his relation of Henry IV's apparent death: the king's "pangs so sore troubled him, that he laie as though all his vitall spirits had beene from him departed"; his advisors, "thinking verelie that he had béene departed, couered his face with a linnen cloth."[39] As *The Famous Victories* faithfully dramatized the event, Henry IV "suddenlie reuiued out of that trance," but his deceptive appearance reinforced the need for postmortem caution.[40] The only way to be sure of death, Crooke warned, was to hold off burying the body "til 2. or 3 dayes bee ouer, for some haue beene knowne so long after their supposed deaths to reuiue."[41] Even with the aid of tests that purported to make a show of life itself, the possibility that a dead body might suddenly revive remained disturbingly vivid.

Unable reliably to detect signs of life outside the theater, inside it the diagnostic test is prone to false positives. That Shakespeare makes use of the feather test in more than one play, then, suggests that he aimed to produce the ambiguity the device brings about, for in its very irrelevance onstage, the test insists that spectators register the semiotic instability of the actor's body. In Shakespeare's version of the Henry IV succession story, Hal's apparent confirmation of his father's death with a feather test heightens the uncertainty that *The Famous Victories* generates:

> By his gates of breath
> There lies a downy feather which stirs not;
> Did he suspire, that light and weightless down
> Perforce must move. My gracious lord? My father?
> This sleep is sound indeed. This is a sleep

That from this golden rigol hath divorced
So many English kings.   (4.3.162–68)[42]

The feather placed in front of the lips of the living actor, Hal asserts with confidence, does not move, a paradox that would have been exacerbated by the play's staging in an outdoor amphitheater. Playgoers closest to the stage might have detected a flutter of down and wondered whether it was the result of wind or the actor's breath. Those farther away, or in a place in the theater with poor sightlines, would have had to rely on other audience members to make a judgment about Hal's test, either by turning to their neighbors to commiserate or simply observing the reactions of other playgoers in the amphitheater's shared lighting. Inside the playhouse, the test's manifold faultiness becomes a meticulous technology for the inducement of spectators' uncertainty, encouraging doubt to spread through the theater space itself.

If Shakespeare seems to be working especially hard to render uncertain whether the king is dead or not at this moment – to create, that is, a narrative poised to turn, equally plausibly, in two opposed directions – that is likely because many playgoers had walked into the playhouse that afternoon with no doubts about his liveliness, for by 1597, Shakespeare's new play chronicled an eminently familiar story.[43] Frequent theatergoers may well have seen *The Famous Victories*; indeed, so potent was the memory of the anonymous Queen's Men's play that Shakespeare could allude directly to a moment from its performance in *Henry V* (1597).[44] Those spectators who had not seen the earlier play could have read about the confusion surrounding the king's death in the revised edition of Holinshed's *Chronicles* published in 1587. After 1598, theatergoers could have read *The Famous Victories* in quarto. For avid theatergoers, lovers of history, or readers of plays, the issue of Henry IV's liveliness was settled. The exaggerated uncertainty in Shakespeare's version of the scene thus theatrically counterbalances a narrative weighed down by inevitability.[45] As spectators scrutinized the actor playing King Henry's possibly dead body, the feather test transformed the determined account of what *happened* historically into an open investigation of what was *happening* on the stage.[46]

As theatrical devices, the sleeping draught and bed curtains permitted – even obliged – Elizabethan spectators to discount the semiotic force of the actor's body while he expressed or feigned death. *2 Henry IV*'s feather test marks a clear shift away from these earlier attempts to cordon the actor's liveliness from the onstage world. The first part of Shakespeare's Henriad occupies a more ambivalent middle ground, offering a glimpse of the theater's conventional treatment of stage corpses strained to the point of exhaustion and, finally, rupture. *1 Henry IV's* depiction of the Battle of Shrewsbury fills the stage with a frenzy of activity: after the injured king leaves the stage, Hal fights with Hotspur while Douglas engages with Falstaff. The fat knight's metatheatrical commentary as he cheers on his friend – "To it, Hal! Nay, you shall find no boy's play here, I can tell you" (5.4.74–75) – invites spectators to attend closely to the physical skill of the Chamberlain's Men, who deftly wield their weapons in an intricate choreography that conveys the chaos and risk of warfare.[47] But the scene keys up that attention only to overwhelm it with indeterminacy. In nearly the same moment, the battle produces one corpse and one "corpse": just before "*the Prince killeth Hotspur*," another stage direction indicates that Falstaff "*falls down as if he were dead*" (5.4.75sd).[48] The need to perceive the two bodies differently – to allow the signs of life exhibited by the actor playing Falstaff, and *only* the actor playing Falstaff, to infiltrate the world of *1 Henry IV* – puts more pressure on spectators' sensory and interpretive capacities than they can bear.

In the modern imagination, Falstaff's comic resurrection several lines later has been so thoroughly intertwined with our sense of his carnivalesque individuality – he "bulges out of the realistic frame of fiction," these readings go, embodying nothing less than life itself – that we risk missing the moment's potential for thoroughgoing uncertainty in performance.[49] Falstaff's rise sends contradictory signals: either the beloved knight is alive, or the actor playing him is merely preparing to exit. As Mariko Ichikawa argues, it was a convention, even a rule, in the early modern theater that corpses did not walk themselves offstage; to do so, she maintains, would have been "in every sense a step too far. It would have represented too radical a disruption of the illusion on which the play world depended."[50] But if the indeterminacy generated by Falstaff's rise takes just such a step, the action leading up to it strains the theater's convention for the removal of stage corpses to the point of exhaustion. After spotting Falstaff on the ground, Prince Hal bids his apparently dead friend farewell:

> What, old acquaintance! Could not all this flesh
> Keep in a little life? Poor Jack, farewell.
> I could have better spared a better man.
> O, I should have a heavy miss of thee
> If I were much in love with vanity.
> Death hath not struck so fat a deer today,
> Though many dearer in this bloody fray.

Embowelled I will see thee by and by;
Till then, in blood by noble Percy lie.   (5.4.101–09)

Hal's many allusions to Falstaff's size – "all this flesh," "heavy miss," "so fat a deer" – render his elegy comic, and it is commonplace to construe that tonal inappropriateness as evidence that Hal knows Falstaff is feigning death.[51] That reading suggests that everyone is – and indeed, has always been – in on Falstaff's joke: the prince himself, and through his awareness the play's audience, share the very perspective that generations of familiarity with *1 Henry IV* have produced.

Envisioning the scene as it would have been experienced in 1597, however, requires attention to an element of the speech that all readings of it have so far missed: that it is a series of stage directions enacting repeated false exits.[52] As they listened to Hal deliver these lines, spectators in the Theater would have also watched him try more than once to carry Falstaff offstage – to attempt, that is, to adhere to the very convention that Falstaff's standing seems so flagrantly to flout.[53] The sense of closure provided by the parallel structure of "better spared" and "better man" following Hal's "farewell" in the previous line is the first opportunity for the scene's apparent conclusion; the subsequent sets of rhyming couplets (ending on "vanity" and "fray") are the second and third.[54] Elizabethan spectators would have witnessed several extended bouts of effortful gesture on the part of the actor playing the prince, as he repeatedly attempts and fails to lift Falstaff before leaving in defeat. "In blood by noble Percy lie," he finally concedes, the picture of a prince who has once again failed, as it were, to carry out his duty. Such toggling back and forth between language and silence, discursive rhyme and indeterminate gesture, generates a sequence of actions that unfold in the ambiguous overlap between the play's single frame and its place within a broader conventional landscape: in the moments of silence, did spectators in the Theater perceive Hal saying goodbye to Falstaff or one actor attempting to adhere to a necessary bit of playhouse convention? Each time the actor playing Hal resumed his speech, he would have seemed to clear up the confusion, only to bring it about again in his next attempt to lift Falstaff from the stage. Death, Carol Chillington Rutter writes, "comes in at the end; it collects up final meanings."[55] The scene's refusal to end is thus also a refusal to settle into meaning, as the convention governing Falstaff's removal strains under his weight.

To suggest that the scene is not simply a winking acknowledgment of Falstaff's vivacity, however, is not to discount that it could well have been played for laughs. The spectacle of Hal's failure to lift Falstaff was undoubtedly one of the "humorous conceits" promised by the title page of the 1598 quarto, and a Restoration-era recollection of the Prince Charles's Men at the Fortune Theater indicates how it may have been initially received.[56] In John Tatham's *Knavery in All Trades, or, The Coffee-House* (1664), a group of gentlemen discusses the actor Richard Fowler, who, after exiting following a stage battle, "ne're minding to bring off his dead men; which they perceiving, crauled into the Tyreing house, at which, *Fowler* grew angry, and told 'em, Dogs you should have laine there till you had been fetcht off; and so they crauled out again, which gave the people such an occasion of Laughter, they cry'd that again, that again, that again."[57] This nostalgic recollection of the Caroline theater offers a portrait of spectators with different competencies and expectations than those watching Hal and Falstaff in 1597.[58] But it nevertheless suggests the pleasures of abrupt mimetic disruption: Hal's repetitive gestures are constructed as if to prompt just such laughter and cries of "that again, that again, that again."

The scene's comic potential simultaneously reveals its intimate tenderness. The actor playing Hal would have been required to wrap the actor playing Falstaff in an embrace in order to lift him, arranging the pair as a parodic *Pietà*; the image, perhaps inspiring simultaneous laughter and tears, may well have invited spectators to entertain the tragic possibility of Falstaff's death through its comic disruption of a familiar convention.[59] Layered on top of the spectators' jockeyed expectations produced by the repeated false closing couplets, then, is the potential for "affective disorientation," to use Sianne Ngai's phrase, produced by the simultaneous engendering of two contradictory feelings.[60] Ngai herself carefully distinguishes between affective bewilderment – that is, self-conscious confusion about what one is feeling – and epistemological indeterminacy. But at this moment of *1 Henry IV*, the two are crucially intertwined: the affective disorientation prompted by heightened metatheatrical attention would have primed Elizabethan spectators for the indeterminacy of Falstaff's rise from the stage floor moments later. The disruption of the phenomenological tether that links spectators to the performance becomes the occasion for multifaceted affective and interpretive engagement with the fiction itself.

While the question of how theatergoers collectively or individually reacted to Falstaff's false death is necessarily speculative, what is indisputable is that by inviting spectators to focus at hyperbolic length on a body that refuses to be removed from the stage, Shakespeare disrupts the smooth operation of a theatrical convention, and in so doing, provokes their uncertainty about what they see onstage. *1 Henry IV*, then, is crucially different from the other Elizabethan plays that include apparent deaths so far examined: Shakespeare frustrates theatergoers' sense of what turns this particular narrative will take by consciously upending their interpretive reliance on a theatrical convention that governs the unfolding of *all* plays. In its very inscrutability, Falstaff's rise offers a glimpse of the theatrical practices that would reshape performance into the seventeenth century – a future that Falstaff himself imagines. Acknowledging Hotspur, lying dead nearby, he registers a worry: "I am afraid of this gunpowder Percy, though he be dead. How if he should counterfeit too and rise?" (5.4.120–22). The question foregrounds the actor's vivacity in order to make the dead character glimmer with life. Such attention fully subsumes the inherent liveliness of the stage corpse into the dramatic fiction: *all* corpses, Falstaff suggests, may hop up from the stage at any moment.

He forecloses this theatrical possibility, however, almost as soon as he suggests it. Fearful that Hotspur might live, he stabs him, an action that decisively nullifies the semiotic significance of the actor's body. He then, as if dutifully following the conventional dictate for the removal of stage corpses, "*takes up Hotspur on his back*" (5.4.128sd). Yet just as he does so, Hal and Lancaster enter, and the scene continues for nearly forty more lines before the group exits. The staging in this interim, in which Falstaff both confirms and takes credit for Hotspur's death, is something of a mystery: what does Falstaff do with Hotspur's body? It is possible that he continues to carry Hotspur, though to do so would be, as David Scott Kastan notes, "an exhausting feat."[61] Although records of sixteenth- and seventeenth-century stagings of this moment do not exist, Kastan follows evidence from later productions in suggesting that Falstaff dumps the body on the ground at the moment he presents Hotspur to Lancaster and Hal – "There is Percy" (5.4.140), he announces – before picking him back up again at the end of the scene.[62] Tossing Hotspur's body around the stage in this way is an expedient solution to the scene's incredible physical demands, but it also enacts a mode of theatrical seeing distinct from the one encouraged by Falstaff's own rise. That prior mode recognizes the stage corpse's inherent liveliness, and with it registers the theatrical possibilities that exist beyond the bounds of a familiar stage convention. The other consciously reaffirms exactly those bounds, treating the actor's body, nearly to the point of hyperbole, as a lifeless, inanimate object.[63] So while *1 Henry IV* is certainly not the earliest example of a play that withholds from spectators the necessary tools by which to interpret the ambiguous spectacle of a lively stage corpse, it does consciously register the widespread theatrical possibility of reanimation that is opened up by breaking with the convention governing their removal.[64] In 1597, the ambiguity of Falstaff's rise and his nervous regard of Hotspur as a lively corpse together looked forward to a theatrical reality in which onstage corpses universally reverberated with the possibility of their own reanimation.

A little over a decade later, Thomas Middleton's *The Second Maiden's Tragedy* (1612) realized, with all the fiendish exuberance characteristic of Jacobean drama, just such a fantasy. That the play makes use of the semiotic instability of the actor's body is something of an understatement: it contains three apparent deaths – one of which was incorporated into the playtext during the rehearsal process – about which the audience is not warned in advance.[65] Sent to woo his daughter (the unnamed Lady) on the Tyrant's behalf, Helvetius falls at the sound of a gunshot when he is discovered by the Lady's lover Govianus; he lays on the ground, apparently dead, until Govianus commands him to rise: "Up, ancient sinner; thou'rt but mocked with death. / I missed thee purposely" (2.1.113–14).[66] Later, Govianus himself swoons as he attempts to murder the Lady, at her request; she aims to evade the Tyrant's command that she be given to him. Believing Govianus dead, the Lady takes matters into her own hands, stabbing herself; Govianus awakens after she has already died. A surprise resurrection is revealed at the conclusion of the play's subplot, which involves a husband who drives his wife to adultery by secretly testing her chastity: the dead Anselmus revives after another character reveals that his wife has indeed been unfaithful to him. Hearing the truth, he claims, has brought him back to life:

> O thunder that awakes me e'en from death
> And makes me curse my confidence with cold lips!
> I feel his words in flames about by soul;
> 'Has more than killed me.   (5.1.167–70)

On its own, this speech seems like more of the play's insistent exploitation of the blurry boundary between life and death. But its provenance makes the lines deserving of a closer look.

Anselmus's final speech is a late-stage revision to *The Second Maiden's Tragedy*, likely requested of Middleton by the King's Men before their first performance of the play at Blackfriars. The play survives only in the form of a playhouse manuscript, used as the company's promptbook, and it offers a tantalizing glimpse into the company's rehearsal process; in addition to instances of censorship by Master of the Revels George Buc, it contains revisions made during rehearsal and five speeches to be added to the script. While critical attention to these additions has focused almost entirely on the question of their authorship, from a theatrical standpoint, the revision enabling Anselmus's reanimation reveals an early Jacobean playing company exceedingly comfortable with requiring an audience, for a third time over the course of single play, to revise their judgment about a character's death.[67] Having Anselmus awake from death is certainly the simplest means to allow him an Aristotelian *peripeteia* (and with it, an opportunity for the actor playing him to deliver a final, impressive speech); it would have required more of the actors, already familiar with the original script by the time they gathered to rehearse, to adjust to a more extensive reworking of Anselmus's death scene.[68] That his resurrection shifts the burden of interpretive judgment onto audience members appears not to be a concern.

The apparent deaths in *The Second Maiden's Tragedy* require spectators to reassess their judgments about stage deaths for a variety of reasons: characters arise from seeming death, revealing that they were never actually dead at all, and claim to have been resurrected. It may be that the Tyrant, as Susan Zimmerman puts it, "moves to resuscitate the corpse with his own libidinal – or, as his fantasy would have it, creative – energy."[69] But the revisions to the playhouse manuscript at once reveal the creative energies responsible for the play's collective production. The play itself is a rejoinder to the Tyrant's failures, for if nothing else, *The Second Maiden's Tragedy* demonstrates that the theater gets the resurrections it wants. The play stages an outrageous fantasy of resurrection, as if funneling all of its culture's medical and biblical and cultural discourses about the lively corpse into the frenetic whiplash of its multiple surprising reanimations.

Yet the play also exemplifies the complete overturn of the conventions governing the removal of stage corpses that had defined the Elizabethan theater. With its many sudden revivals, *The Second Maiden's Tragedy* realizes a theatrical world in which corpses can hop up and away from death on a whim, without warning. Conspicuously absent from *The Second Maiden's Tragedy* are the overt explanations to explain apparent deaths to the audience, as in *Romeo and Juliet* or *Much Ado about Nothing*, or even ambiguous warnings that death will not be realized, as in *The Jew of Malta*. If, a decade earlier, the conventional way to treat an onstage corpse was to divert attention from it, by 1612 the theater had embraced all of the narrative possibility that the onstage corpse's semiotic volatility allowed:

apparent deaths, false deaths, returns to life from death. The revision granting Anselmus a brief resurrection, moreover, foregrounds the wide-ranging ramifications of the decisive break with one of the Elizabethan theater's foundational conventions, for a theater that privileges the surprising return of the corpse to life has necessarily less regard for the alleviation of its spectators' interpretive burdens. *The Second Maiden's Tragedy* evinces two key discoveries that would shape theater practitioners' experimentation through the Jacobean and Caroline eras: theatrical possibility requires audience uncertainty, and that uncertainty is born from the unannounced disruption of the conventions that inculcated playgoers' interpretive competencies in the first place.

Apparent Death in Tragicomedy

While *The Second Maiden's Tragedy* looks extreme next to Elizabethan treatments of apparent death, is not an outlier in a Jacobean context, for by the second decade of the seventeenth century, characters seemingly dead began hopping up from stage floors and rising from their coffins with some regularity. These surprising resurrections were a defining feature of tragicomedy, and in what follows I will argue that the emergence of the hybrid genre must be understood as, in part, the theatrical effect of the shift in stage practices regarding lively stage corpses. John Fletcher's *The Night Walker* (c. 1611) is a case study of the ways that these innovative breaks with convention would have been experienced by spectators. Though the play was billed as a comedy when it was first printed in 1640, it contains recognizable elements of Fletcherian tragicomedy, including a death not revealed as false until Maria, whom the audience has seen collapse in response to her husband's accusation of infidelity, rises from her coffin and speaks. The play lingers over the phenomenological ambiguity of Maria's surprise resurrection, deferring death's approach as Maria herself attempts to make sense of her own awakening. At the moment of her reanimation, Maria spectacularly embodies a narrative poised at the departure of multiple possible trajectories. The play construes the phenomenological experience of theatrical possibility, in other words, as uncertainty.

As its title suggests, much of *The Night Walker* takes place in the dark. Stage directions and dialogue indicate the presence of lights, candles, and torches onstage, and characters repeatedly stumble through the darkness.[70] The frequency of represented darkness in plays of this period suggests audiences must have enjoyed it, though the trope necessarily raises questions about how it would have been staged and experienced across outdoor amphitheaters and artificially lit indoor halls.[71] Such a question is frustratingly elusive when applied to *The Night Walker*, for the play's performance history is a blank until 1633, when it was performed at court (having been lightly revised by James Shirley) by the Queen's Men.[72] The title page of the 1640 quarto indicates that the company performed the play at the Cockpit, as well. Eventually, then, *The Night Walker* found a home in an indoor venue. But there is ample evidence about repertory styles and company resources, as well as textual evidence within the play itself, to suggest that *The Night Walker* was originally performed indoors.[73] Proceeding from the premise that Fletcher wrote *The Night Walker* for the Children of the Queen's Revels around 1611 – who by that year were playing at Whitefriars, the small indoor theater where the company moved following the loss of their lease of Blackfriars – I will suggest that *The Night Walker* exploits the performance conditions of the indoor playhouse in order not only to represent but to produce for spectators the failed attempt to see clearly in the dark.[74]

The cramped, artificially lit Whitefriars would have offered *The Night Walker* a glimmering, incandescent setting as the candlelight shone, through the haze of smoke, on the richly sumptuous fabrics worn by both actors and spectators onstage.[75] From its opening scene, *The Night Walker* makes the most of the indoor theater's atmospheric effects. "How rich she is in Jewels!" Maria's lover Frank Hartlove exclaims when she enters the stage for the first time (1.1.149), as she prepares to wed the elderly Justice Algripe. The playhouse's candlelight would have bounced off her jewelry, gleaming and glittering through the small space. At the same time, the comment works to train spectators' eyes on Maria – to observe, note, and examine her appearance.[76] Hartlove continues to register his observations about the jewels and his lover herself:

> Me thinkes they show like frozen Isicles,
> Cold winter had hung on her, how the Roses
> That kept continuall spring within her cheekes
> Are withered with the old mans dull imbraces?   (1.1.150–53)

Maria's marital obligation to Justice Algripe, as Hartlove sees it, has caused the life to go out of her. The color having gone from her cheeks, leaving her a ghastly shadow of the lively woman she once was, suits her to the smoky Whitefriars. Unlike Friar Laurence's speech, which preemptively deflects attention from the inherent liveliness of the actor playing Juliet,

Hartlove's language shapes the way spectators see Maria by incorporating into the fictional representation the atmospheric impressions made possible by the material conditions of the play's staging. Even before Maria rises from her coffin, spectators are encouraged to see her, in all her spectacular glittering and gleaming, as dead.

This focus on Maria as a spectral presence is an early primer in the faulty parallels *The Night Walker* will soon establish between seeing and understanding, blindness and ignorance. Searching for Maria after their wedding, Algripe calls out, "Give me a Torch" (1.7.2), and a few lines later, "Bring some lights, some lights" (1.7.25). He discovers her in a bedroom with Hartlove, where Maria has just rejected her lover's advances in order to preserve her chastity. But Algripe interprets the scene differently: "Mine eyes, mine eyes, / Oh how my head akes" (1.8.13–14), he laments, his seeming confirmation of her adultery equated with physically painful sight. Following Maria's apparent death, Wildbraine wanders Algripe's house at night with a candle, conjuring an image of disorder in the darkness: "Harke still, / In every roome confusion, they are all mad, / Most certaine all starke mad within the house" (2.3.9–11). The comically foolish Tobie embodies the chaos, fumbling blindly in the dark:

> I can finde no bed, no body, nor no chamber
> Sure they are all ith' cellar, and I cannot finde that neither
> I am led up, and downe like a tame asse, my light's out
> And I grope up and downe like a blind-man buffe
> And break my face, and breake my pate.   (2.3.55–59)

Set against these characters who find themselves lost in the darkness are the play's thieves, Lurcher and Snap, who navigate it, so they believe, with skillful ease. Seeing Maria and Algripe's wedding as an opportunity for their own gain, they prepare to steal a chest full of gifts from Algripe's house. Lurcher asks, "Are sure thou knowst the Chest?" "Though it were ith' darke sir, / I can goe to't," Snap responds (2.1.93–94). *The Night Walker*'s early scenes align the thieves' superior perspective with the narrative vantage of the play's spectators; unlike Algripe, the audience knows that Maria has not been unfaithful to her husband, and this crucial piece of information allows them figuratively to find their way in the dark – to see what Algripe cannot.

But the thieves soon learn that they are not as skilled at navigating the darkness as they believed. Having absconded from Algripe's house with what they assume is the wedding chest, they open it up to find they have instead taken Maria's coffin – with her body inside. "Our hast and want of light made us mistake," Snap sheepishly admits (2.4.43). Lurcher, Snap, and Mistresse Newlove now unexpectedly find themselves watching over a dead body. In part to mitigate against the reported possibility of prematurely burying those who were only apparently dead, warned against by Helkiah Crooke, the custom of watching over the corpse for two to three days and nights before the funeral remained a common practice into at least the early eighteenth century.[77] Though prayer for the dead and the use of candles for devotional purposes had been forbidden during the Reformation, these practices continued to be observed for decades after the new injunctions, though not without conflict. Around 1590, a group of Lancashire ministers asserted that "manifiolde popish superstition [had been] used in the buriall of the dead," going on to detail that the body had been "'all garnished with crosses, and sett rounde abowte with tapers and candelles burninge night and day."[78] Yet the custom of watching continued to be practiced, to varying degrees, by people of all social classes, though it gradually became associated with vulgar and rowdy behavior. Toward the end of the seventeenth century, John Aubrey explained that "at the Funeralls in Yorkshire, to this day, they continue the custome of watching and sitting-up all night till the body is interred," going on to describe the activities that accompanied such observance: "In the interim some kneel downe and pray (by the corps), some play at cards, some drink and take Tobacco : they have also Mimicall playes and sports."[79] *The Night Walker*'s staging conflates the playing and watching that, in this account, are described as concurrent activities: as they looked on the stage aglow with candlelight, spectators would have been invited to regard Maria's body as a corpse nearing its interment. "Theatrical watching," to borrow Stanton Garner's term, thus intermingles with the religious custom, one that carries with it the felt possibility of the corpse's sudden revival.[80] Both forms of watching are lookouts for life.

At this moment of heightened surveillance, real-world possibility merges with theatrical possibility: after the thieves' associate Mistress Newlove confirms that Maria is "cold, dead cold," (2.4.55) and Lurcher reassures Snap that "thou seest shee's dead, and cannot injure thee" (2.4.65), the seemingly dead woman rises from her coffin, causing the thieves to flee the stage in terror. The ambiguity about Maria's status – is she alive, dead, or a ghost? – continues even after Maria begins speaking, for she, too, is uncertain about whether she lives. In her attempt to confirm her vivacity, alone onstage, Maria attends to her own corporeality: "I am wondrous hungry," she comments, and "dead bodies eate not" (2.5.83). Her rumination, a comic allusion to Jesus's resurrection in the Gospel of Luke, would seem to confirm her own reanimation.[81] So, too, does her memory that she "was betrai'd, and swounded; my heart akes" (2.5.82); hers is a body in pain, one that would seem to be very much alive. But her speech as a whole is bookended with observations that seem to confirm her death – "I am very cold, dead cold" (2.5.79) and "Death, like a cake of Ice dwells round about me" (2.5.85) – her language both recalling Mistress Newlove's earlier assurance and Maria's own initial appearance onstage as a macabre, corpse-like spectacle in her wedding jewels. At the close of her speech she rushes offstage, her uncertainty about her own liveliness still unresolved.

As they watched this scene, Jacobean spectators might have noted that, encoffined but unburied at the time of her awakening, Maria has not received her customary burial rite, which bid departed souls farewell with one of the most notoriously controversial passages in reformed liturgy: "in sure and certein hope of resurrection to eternall lyfe."[82] The seeming confirmation of the individual's resurrection at the Last Judgment called into question the Calvinist doctrine of election.[83] What could it possibly mean to encapsulate both certainty and hope, except to tip the balance of unknowing toward surety rather than doubt? But *The Night Walker* theatrically preserves this contradiction by making Maria embody it, and in so doing, allowed spectators who had undoubtedly pondered the possibility of their own final resurrections to see the very paradox of that "sure and certein hope" play out onstage.[84] Maria's recognition of her own corporeality necessarily obliges spectators to confront the body of the actor playing her; in this regard, the moment is familiar, inviting spectators to engage in the fraught attempt to cordon off the signs of liveliness that belong to the world of the playhouse from those that signify unambiguously within the world of the play. But what differentiates this moment from earlier plays that encourage attention to the lively corpse is that Maria herself engages in exactly the same process of theatrical discernment that the play's spectators do. Maria's voiced uncertainty enfolds the "recalcitrant physiology" of the actor's body back into the represented ambiguity on the stage.[85] The physical body – cold, hungry, in pain – becomes the object of the character's attention, as if the uncertain Maria, in order to assure herself of her existence, reaches out from the imagined representation to probe the body of the actor playing her onstage. "The touching," Maurice Merleau-Ponty writes, "is never exactly the touched."[86] By doubtfully regarding herself as a lively corpse, Maria makes herself into a reverberant spectacle of that "never exactly," a comic version of the risen Jesus and doubting Thomas at once. The prismatic conflation of character and actor embodies the resurrectional paradox of certain uncertainty.

Maria's doubtful rumination following her rise from the coffin, then, phenomenologically encapsulates a narrative poised on the cusp of possibility; as she dwells in her own ambiguous ontological status, spectators themselves are suspended among the countervailing paths the plot might take. Will Maria live, or haunt the world of the play as a ghost, or simply be revealed as dead? At the moment she voices her doubt about her liveliness, they wait, unsure. The hovering ambiguity of the scene is only made possible by the material changes to the commercial theater's conventional practices over several decades of its operation. The gradual drive to scrutinize the actor's lively body, rather than to occlude it from spectators' interpretive attention or literal view, culminates in an explosion of theatrical possibility that inheres within a single spectacle. Spectators experience the sum total of the theater's innovation regarding the expression and feigning of death on the stage, in real time, as uncertainty itself: along with Maria, they watch, and wait, as the play pauses before taking its next turn. As a feature of *The Night Walker*'s moment-by-moment unfolding, narrative suspense is experienced as phenomenological suspension.

If the first half of *The Night Walker* invites spectators to dwell in the uncertain status of Maria's liveliness along with her, the second half of the play delights in the unexpected narrative reversals that are produced by unknowing. The play's characters become models of unsuspecting spectators, duped (often by means of the multifarious disguises for which the Children of the Queen's Revels were known) because they are unable to see through theatrical artifice: Maria dons a Welsh accent, Justice Algripe is made to endure a mock exorcism, and later, mock Furies descend upon him. The play's only instance of deception through disguise before Maria's reanimation foregrounds exactly this response to not knowing in the theater. In preparation for their intended theft of the wedding jewels, Lurcher and Snap don costumes "to fright those reverend watches" attending to Maria's supposedly dead body (2.1.38). Lurcher first suggests they wear a "devills face"; Snap rejects the idea, protesting that "weele have no shape so terrible" (2.1.43–44). Lurcher next proposes a "winding sheete," and Snap again protests its ghostly implications: "Thats too cold a shift, / I would not weare the reward of my wickednesse" (2.1.47–48). In both instances, Snap perceives a connection between the protean transformations of the actor through costume and its effects in the afterlife.[87] And when Tobie does see the outsized spectacle of the two thieves – Snap, wearing a turban and beard, sitting on Lurcher's shoulders – he makes exactly the assumption Snap had hoped to avoid: "Mercy upon me, the Ghost of one oth' Guard sure, / Tis the Devill by his clawes, he smells of Brimstone, / Sure he farts fire" (2.1.80–83). Tobie's material conflation of theatrical artifice with inner substance sets him apart as the play's fool, but his mistaken reaction to a staged ghost prefigures spectators' own frustrated attempt to interpret Maria's spectacular ambiguity after they have been led to believe that she is dead. Immediately before producing such an experience for spectators themselves, *The Night Walker* demonstrates that theatrical watching is comically and inevitably error-prone. The experience of uncertainty produced by the actor's body is just one instance of the theater's broader capacity not only to interpretively involve its spectators in performance, then, but to entertain them.

Nor is Maria's reanimation the only way *The Night Walker* orchestrates surprise spectators, for the action of the play culminates in Snap's revelation that *she* is actually Alathe, Justice Algripe's wife and Lurcher's sister in disguise.[88] In the final scene, Algripe agrees to grant Lurcher the land he has been withholding from him if both the contract entitling him to it and Alathe herself can be produced; at this demand, the stage directions explain that "*the* Boy *goes to* Maria *and gives her a paper: she wonders, and smiles upon* Hartlove, *he amaz'd approaches her: afterward she shewes it her mother, and then gives it to* Hartlove" (5.2.136sd). The unusually extended stage direction gives over to dumb show as Maria and Hartlove are left to convey their amazement through gesture and expression alone; spectators are invited to in share that feeling by filling in its verbal gaps with their own interpretive responses to the revelation. This spectacular, silent dramatic reversal is an occasion for deeply felt joy, a feeling that approaches the wonder associated with romance. In William Cartwright's description of this effect of Fletcher's drama, spectators "all stand wondring how / The thing will be untill it is."[89] In a play that is centrally concerned with the ambiguity produced by the vitality of the actor's body, this final surprise is *The Night Walker*'s last reminder that the materials of tragicomic possibility phenomenologically produce not only uncertainty itself, but the thrill of its experience.

Apparent Death in Repertory

By the time of *The Night Walker*'s probable first performance, the commercial theater no longer strictly adhered to the conventions that had once governed the treatment of stage corpses. Plays featuring surprise reanimations, including *The Second Maiden's Tragedy* and Tourneur's *The Atheist's Tragedy*, had already been staged by 1611; more, including Middleton's *The Witch* (1616), Fletcher and Massinger's *The Custom of the Country*

(1619), and Webster's *The Devil's Law Case* (1619), were to come as the second decade of the seventeenth century drew to a close. The record of court performances by the King's Men in the 1612–1613 season offers an illustrative look at how surprising reanimations in new plays might have been experienced by theatergoers in relation to those of repertorial standbys. That season, the company presented a spate of Shakespeare's plays at court that, taken together, feature a false death, a shuttling back and forth across the border dividing life from death, a (perhaps) miraculous return to life, and the well-worn sleeping potion device: *1 Henry IV* (listed as "The Hotspurr" in the court record), *Othello*, *The Winter's Tale*, and *Much Ado About Nothing*.[90] But while all of these plays contain reanimations that would have both demanded and frustrated audience interpretation at the time of their original performances, by 1612–13 they would have been entirely familiar to experienced theatergoers. Such familiarity and its effect on audience expectation makes the appearance of new plays containing surprise reanimations even more striking: Webster's *The White Devil*, Heywood's *The Iron Age* Part 2, Middleton's *A Chaste Maid in Cheapside*, and *The Honest Man's Fortune* premiered with various companies in 1613. If the lively stage corpse embodies the generic hybridity of tragicomedy, the theater's new commitment to coming close to death and averting it can also be seen as an attempt to make space for the unexpected within a theatrical landscape saturated with repertory performances of old plays. Exploiting the ambiguity of the actor's inherent liveliness extended the horizons of spectators' increasingly sophisticated theatrical expectations by continually thwarting them.

Francis Beaumont and John Fletcher's prologue to *The Captain* is a particularly illustrative explanation of the openness to uncertainty that the emergence of tragicomedy invited its spectators to inhabit. The earliest record of *The Captain*'s performance comes from the same 1612–13 court performance list for the King's Men, meaning that it would have been a new play among old Shakespearean favorites. Beaumont and Fletcher transform the prologue from its traditional function as an anticipatory response to critique into a commentary on the limits of interpretive judgment in the theater:

> To please you with this Play, we feare will be
> (So does the Author too) a mystery
> Somewhat above our Art; For all mens eyes,
> Ears, faiths, and judgements, are not of one size.
> For to say truth, and not to flatter ye,
> This is nor *Comody*, nor *Tragedy*,

Nor *History*, nor any thing that may
(Yet in a weeke) be made a perfect Play.   (Prologue.1–8)[91]

Beaumont and Fletcher foreground the variety of spectators' sensory
capacities and beliefs seemingly to highlight their inability to please
all audience members, but with a rhetorical flourish that acts as a dramatic twist in miniature – "not to flatter ye, / This is nor *Comody*,
nor *Tragedy*" – they turn instead to the generic ambiguity of the play
itself. The issue at hand is not whether the play is *good*, the playwrights
maintain, but what kind of a play it is at all. Such ambiguities, they
go on to acknowledge, will create interpretive roadblocks: those who
"love to laugh" and expect to see a comedy based on the love plot with
which the play opens, "may stumble on a foolish toy, or two" (12). In
Beaumont and Fletcher's estimation, the pleasurable uncertainty that
emerges from narrative misdirection is no less a constitutive element of
tragicomedy than the interpretive ability to "unweav[e] the complexi-
ties" of its plots.[92]

Beaumont and Fletcher's defense of the willingness to stumble interpretively is indicative of changes to the theatrical landscape by the early
decades of the seventeenth century more broadly. While it is true, as
Gordon McMullan suggests, that "tragicomedy assumes a sense on the part
of its target audience of theatrical history, an ability to recognise and appreciate the conscious redeployment of earlier modes," the hybrid genre just
as deliberately worked to upset that knowingness in the moment of performance.[93] Audiences seemed to enjoy such unsettling. Praise of Beaumont
and Fletcher, in particular, foregrounds the pleasure that inheres, as Claire
M. L. Bourne has detailed, in the paradox of "anticipat[ing] surprise."[94] The
"*craftie* Mazes *of the cunning plot*," trap spectators in a state of pleasurable
disorientation with regard to the play's unfolding action.[95] As John Dryden
would admiringly put it toward the close of the seventeenth century, the
"turn'd Design" of English drama "keeps the Audience in Expectation of
the Catastrophe."[96] That expectation is a prolonged state of unknowing, a
readiness to remain suspended in uncertainty that will ultimately culminate
in the frustration or reversal of one's dramatic expectations.[97] At the same
time, these characterizations of tragicomic plotting show that familiarity
with dramatic convention brings with it a simultaneous anticipation of the
uncertainty produced by unexpected breaks in the conventional circuit.
Apparent deaths found an especially comfortable home in a dramatic genre
that "wanted" them, but the increasing density with which they appeared
in plays of all genres speaks to the theater's eventual eagerness to exploit,
rather than explain away, the inherent semiotic the instability of the actor's

body, and in so doing, to transfer the interpretive responsibility of the resulting spectacular indeterminacy to playgoers themselves.[98]

With the theatrical opportunities of that indeterminacy in mind, I want to return to *King Lear*, to make a final suggestion about what spectators are simultaneously offered and denied by the spectacular ambiguity of the dead Cordelia. By the time Shakespeare held out hope of Cordelia's return to life only to crush it, unexpected reversals of seeming death had just begun to make their appearance in commercial theaters with some frequency: *The Trial of Chivalry* (1599) and *The Malcontent* (1603) had both featured reanimations, Marston's play staging false deaths both expected and surprising to the audience. In *Antonio's Revenge*, Pandulfo had wrongly claimed to see signs of life emanating from the lips of his dead son. Shakespeare himself had engineered Falstaff's rise from the stage floor, Prince Hal's doubt that his sleeping father lived, Hero's swoon that prompts Beatrice to pronounce her "Dead, I think" (4.1.113), and Desdemona's cries from beyond the grave.[99] Observant theatergoers might have noted his penchant for lively corpses and apparent deaths. As they watched Lear hold a stone and feather in front of the seemingly dead Cordelia's lips, some spectators may well have expected her ultimately to live precisely because of what they knew, not just of the Lear story itself, but of Shakespeare's other plays.

What I want to register, in short, is that despite the play's bleakness and horror – the extreme lengths it takes, in other words, to fulfill its designation as a tragedy – in 1606 *King Lear*'s very presence within the commercial theater's varied landscape corroborated what, for audience members, was certain: that Cordelia lives. Outside the playhouse, Holinshed's *Chronicles* confirmed the historical fact, ratified dramatically by the Elizabethan *Leir*. Inside it, the presence of the boy actor's breath, confirmed by the mirror and feather tests Lear administers, suggests the narrative reversal multifariously demanded by other sources. Within a broader theatrical milieu, Shakespeare's tendency to exploit the inherent liveliness of the corpse bends the arc of narrative expectation toward the reversal of Cordelia's reanimation. And still, she is dead. Critics have long noted the ways that this play, proto-tragicomically, raises comic expectations only to strike them down.[100] I mean to add one more to the list. Both Shakespeare's plots and the commercial theater as whole had begun to glimmer with the surprising revivals that turned tragedy into comedy – stories that wanted deaths instead of delivering them. The cruelty that readers and watchers of this play have registered for centuries is intensified by this nascent dramatic expectation. With the final scene in *King Lear*, Shakespeare suspends his spectators in the uncertainty of theatrical possibility only to deny them the very course of action that the commercial theater, through its innovative breaks with earlier conventions, had just begun to entertain. I would revise Ellen MacKay's observation, then, that at this moment the actor playing Cordelia "fail[s] to live up to the demands of his part."[101] The actor, rather, necessarily *exceeds* those demands; he fails to die down to them. Lying motionless onstage in Lear's arms, the boy actor registers a phenomenological possibility that simultaneously constitutes the counterfactual tragedy of Shakespeare's play and points forward to the surprising returns to life that would soon be widely embraced by the commercial theater. His breathing body tragically marks out the barely discernable horizon of this theater's future – a suggestion, denied, of what could be.

Notes

1 Act, scene, and line numbers follow William Shakespeare, *King Lear*, ed. R. A. Foakes (London: Arden Shakespeare, 1997).
2 In Holinshed's telling, Cordelia ascends the throne after Leir's death, ruling for five years until she is overthrown by her nephews. See *The Firste [Laste] Volume of the Chronicles of England, Scotlande, and Irelande* (London: John Hunne, 1577), 20.
3 See *The True Chronicle History of King Leir, and His Three Daughters, Gonorill, Ragan, and Cordella* (London: John Wright, 1605).
4 There is archaeological evidence for such crowding; as Holger Syme notes, "judging from the erosion around the stage area in the excavated Rose, audiences ... press[ed] as close to the action as possible." See Syme, "The Theater of Shakespeare's Time," in *The Norton Shakespeare: Third Edition*, ed. Stephen Greenblatt et al. (New York: W.W. Norton & Company, 2016), 93–118, esp. 94.
5 Stephen Greenblatt flattens the complexity of the moment when he argues that "to believe Cordelia dead, the audience, insofar as it can actually see what is occurring onstage, must work against the evidence of its own senses. After all, the actor's breath would have misted the stone, and the feather held to Cordelia's mouth must have stirred." Sensory evidence, a spectator's position within the theater, and previous knowledge of the Lear story variously combine in the phenomenological encounter with the boy actor's body. See Greenblatt, *Shakespearean Negotiations: The Circulation of Social Energy in Renaissance England* (Berkeley: University of California Press, 1988), 124.
6 The expression or feigning of death was not, of course, the only way this theater demanded spectators attend to the body of the actor. Crossdressing and disguise plots delighted in the intrusion of the boy actor's body upon the fiction; moments that required actorly skill, such as dancing, sword fighting, and clowning, offered similarly key occasions for the cleaving of actor from character. While my argument here is informed by these theatrical practices, my aim in this chapter is to track how the phenomenological effects of the lively corpse contributed to

experimentation with theatrical convention. For key work on gendered atten-
tion to the body of the actor, see Laura Levine, *Men in Women's Clothing: Anti-
theatricality and Effeminization, 1579–1642* (Cambridge: Cambridge University
Press, 1994); Stephen Orgel, *Impersonations: The Performance of Gender in
Shakespeare's England* (Cambridge: Cambridge University Press, 1996); Ann
Rosalind Jones and Peter Stallybrass, *Renaissance Clothing and the Materials of
Memory* (Cambridge: Cambridge University Press, 2000), 207–19; and Will
Fisher, *Materializing Gender in Early Modern English Literature and Culture*
(Cambridge: Cambridge University Press, 2006). On instances of actorly skill
in the playhouse, see Evelyn Tribble, *Early Modern Actors and Shakespeare's
Theatre: Thinking with the Body* (London: The Arden Shakespeare, 2017);
Erika T. Lin, "Recreating the Eye of the Beholder: Dancing and Spectacular
Display in Early Modern English Theatre," *Dance Research Journal* 43.1 (2011):
10–19; and Richard Preiss, *Clowning and Authorship in Early Modern Theatre*
(Cambridge: Cambridge University Press, 2014).

7 Stanton B. Garner, *Bodied Spaces: Phenomenology and Performance in
Contemporary Drama* (Ithaca, NY: Cornell University Press, 1994), 44.

8 As Carol Chillington Rutter writes of *King Lear*, "We know the actor who
plays Cordelia 'lives'. Cordelia could come back to life. Any body on stage,
potentially, might." See Rutter, *Enter the Body: Women and Representation on
Shakespeare's Stage* (New York: Routledge, 2001), 2.

9 "An Homilee of the Resurrection of our Sauiour Iesus Christe," in *The Second
Tome of Homilees* (London: Richarde Jugge, and John Cawood, 1571), 383.

10 William Barlow, *Psalmes and Hymnes of Praier and Thanksgiuing* (London:
John Beale, 1613), C4r.

11 Act, scene, and line numbers follow William Shakespeare, *Hamlet*, ed. Ann
Thompson and Neil Taylor (London: Arden, 2006).

12 John Fletcher, "To the Reader," *The Faithful Shepherdess*, ed. Cyrus Hoy, in
The Dramatic Works in the Beaumont and Fletcher Canon, vol. 3 (Cambridge:
Cambridge University Press, 1976), 497. There exists a robust body of work
on the spectacle of death in early modern drama: on the Renaissance fascina-
tion with death, see Michael Neill, *Issues of Death: Mortality and Identity in
English Renaissance Tragedy* (Oxford: Oxford University Press, 1997); Hillary
M. Nunn, *Staging Anatomies: Dissection and Spectacle in Early Stuart Tragedy*
(Burlington, VT: Ashgate, 2005); and Susan Zimmerman, *The Early Modern
Corpse and Shakespeare's Theatre* (Edinburgh: Edinburgh University Press,
2005). On the effect of the Protestant Reformation on dramatic represen-
tations of death, see Stephen Greenblatt, *Hamlet in Purgatory* (Princeton:
Princeton University Press, 2001); Huston Diehl, *Staging Reform, Reforming
the Stage: Protestantism and Popular Theater in Early Modern England* (Ithaca,
NY: Cornell University Press, 1997); and Steven Mullaney, *The Reformation
of Emotions in the Age of Shakespeare* (Chicago: University of Chicago Press,
2015). On the theatrical representation of lively corpses, see Tanya Pollard,
Drugs and Theater in Early Modern England (Oxford: Oxford University Press,
2005); and Farah Karim-Cooper, *Cosmetics in Shakespearean and Renaissance*

Drama (Edinburgh: Edinburgh University Press, 2006). While my work in this chapter is indebted to this scholarship, my focus is more strictly theatrical than thematic. By the distinction, I mean that through close attention to play-texts and the theatrical spaces in which they were produced, I give extended attention to the phenomenology of ambiguous and seeming death in the early modern theater, specifically the ways that the actor's vivacity frustrates active interpretation on the part of the spectator.

13 See, for example, T. G. Bishop, *Shakespeare and the Theatre of Wonder* (Cambridge: Cambridge University Press, 1996). On Fletcherian surprise and its "more [profound]" counterpart in Shakespearean romance, see Verna A. Foster, *The Name and Nature of Tragicomedy* (Burlington, VT: Ashgate, 2004), 20.

14 This is not to suggest that the early modern commercial theater invented staged resurrection, which was frequently dramatized in the mystery cycles that had been suppressed only a few years before the first permanent play-houses were built in London. But if the resurrections of Lazarus and Jesus, as well as the rising up of the dead on the day of the Last Judgment, were a narrative necessity in medieval cycle drama, the revivals and reanimations of the early modern theater became conventional by taking advantage of the actor's body as a formal resource.

15 The emergence of tragicomedy in the English theater is most often explained through the influence of Continental, particularly Italian, drama and dramatic theory on English playwrights. For more on the classical and Continental origins of English tragicomedy, see G. K. Hunter, "Italian Tragicomedy on the English Stage," *Renaissance Drama* 6 (1973): 123–48; and Tanya Pollard, "Tragicomedy," in *The Oxford History of Classical Reception in English Literature*, ed. Patrick Cheney and Philip Hardie, vol. 2, *1558–1660* (Oxford: Oxford University Press, 2015), 419–32. Lucy Munro's scholarship is an important exception to work that traces the emergence of tragicomedy in England from the Continent; in her account, the Queen's Men's company practices were central to the emergence of tragicomedy in the early seventeenth century. Her focus, however, is on the source texts the company used to produce their tragicomedies, rather than the conventional practices governing theater of the period more broadly. See Munro, *Children of the Queen's Revels: A Jacobean Theatre Repertory* (Cambridge: Cambridge University Press, 2005), 96–133.

16 Jane Hwang Degenhardt and Cyrus Mulready, "Romance and Tragicomedy," in *A New Companion to Renaissance Drama*, ed. Arthur F. Kinney and Thomas Warren Hopper (Hoboken, NJ: John Wiley and Sons Ltd, 2017), 417–40, esp. 419.

17 *The Jew of Malta* features a slightly more ambiguous use of the sleeping draught device: the play initially only implies that Barabas's "death" in Act 5 is feigned, though his later clarification – "I drank of poppy and cold mandrake juice, / And, being asleep, belike they thought me dead" – finally makes the use of the device explicit (5.1.80–81). Act, scene, and line numbers follow Christopher Marlowe, *The Jew of Malta*, in *The Complete Plays*, ed. Frank Romany and Robert Lindsey (London: Penguin Books, 2003).

18 Act, scene, and line numbers follow William Shakespeare, *Romeo and Juliet*, ed. René Weis (London: Bloomsbury Arden Shakespeare, 2012).

19 For more on the ways that Protestant discourse linked sleep and death, see Peter Marshall, *Beliefs and the Dead in Reformation England* (Oxford: Oxford University Press, 2002), 220–31.

20 Carol Zaleski, *The Life of the World to Come: Near-Death Experience and Christian Hope* (Oxford: Oxford University Press, 1996), 65.

21 Francis Rodes, *Life after Death* (London: Thomas Dewe, 1622), 21.

22 Robert Horne, *Life and Death Foure Sermons* (London: Francis Burton, 1613), 16.

23 Thomas Sparke, *A Sermon Preached at Whaddon* (Oxford: Joseph Barnes, 1593), F1r.

24 This and all other biblical citations follow *The Bible: Authorized King James Version with Apocrypha* (Oxford: Oxford University Press, 1997).

25 As Bartholomew Robertson described the pleasantness of death, for example, "*Lord Iesus Christ* ... hath changed the bitternes of death, and made it a sweet sleepe." See Robertson, *The Crovvne of Life* (London: John Marriot, 1618), A1r.

26 Scene and line numbers follow *The Famous Victories of Henry V*, in *The Oldcastle Controversy*, ed. Peter Corbin and Douglas Sedge (Manchester: Manchester University Press, 1991).

27 For the argument that stage beds were thrust onto the stage from the discovery space, see Sasha Roberts, "'Let me the curtains draw': The Dramatic and Symbolic Properties of the Bed in Shakespearean Tragedy," in *Staged Properties in Early Modern English Drama*, ed. Jonathan Gil Harris and Natasha Korda (Cambridge: Cambridge University Press, 2002), 153–74, esp. 157. For the argument that the drawing of bed curtains was conventionally associated in the early modern theater with death, see Frederick Kiefer, "Curtains on the Shakespearean Stage," *Medieval and Renaissance Drama in England* 20 (2007): 151–86, esp. 153.

28 Roberts suggests that beds were frequently treated as "a stage-within-a-stage, an intense and compelling visual and symbolic arena." See "The Dramatic and Symbolic Properties of the Bed," 153.

29 Readers of the play are given extra assurance from the stage direction that follows the king's command – "*He sleepeth*" (8.10sd) – that spectators, of course, do not receive. For more on stage directions that disambiguate uncertain moments in performance, see William N. West, "'But this will be a mere confusion': Real and Represented Confusions on the Elizabethan Stage," *Theatre Journal*, 60.2 (2008): 217–33.

30 Sally-Beth MacLean and Scott McMillin, *The Queen's Men and Their Plays* (Cambridge: Cambridge University Press, 1998), 134.

31 As Gen. 2:7 is rendered in the King James translation, "The LORD God formed man *of* the dust of the ground, and breathed into his nostrils the breath of life; and man became a living soul."

32 Bartholomeus Anglicus, *Batman vppon Bartholome his Booke: De Proprietatibus Rerum* (London: Thomas East, 1582), 28.

33 Robert Bellarmine, *Iacob's Ladder Consisting of Fifteene Degrees or Ascents to the Knowledge of God* (London: Henry Selle, 1638), 108–09.

34 Act, scene, and line numbers follow John Marston, *Antonio's Revenge*, in *"The Malcontent" and Other Plays*, ed. Keith Sturgess (Oxford: Oxford University Press, 1997).

35 Joseph Loewenstein, "Marston's Gorge and the Question of Formalism," in *Renaissance Literature and Its Formal Engagements*, ed. Mark David Rasmussen (New York: Palgrave, 2002), 89–114.

36 Helkiah Crooke, *Mikrokosmographia* (London: William Jaggard, 1615), 253.

37 See Kaara L. Peterson, *Popular Medicine, Hysterical Disease, and Social Controversy in Shakespeare's England* (London: Routledge, 2010), 85.

38 Crooke, *Mikrokosmographia*, 253.

39 Raphael Holinshed, *The Third Volume of Chronicles* (London: John Harison, George Bishop, Rafe Newberie, Henrie Denham, and Thomas Woodcocke, 1586), 541.

40 Holinshed, *Chronicles*, 541.

41 Crooke, *Mikrokosmographia*, 253.

42 Act, scene, and line numbers follow William Shakespeare, *King Henry IV, Part 2*, ed. James C. Bulman (London: Bloomsbury Arden Shakespeare, 2016).

43 Dating follows *Martin Wiggins, British Drama 1533–1642: A Catologue*, vol. 3, *1590–1597* (Oxford: Oxford University Press, 2013). The play's epilogue suggests it may have been presented at court during the 1597–98 revels season, which would indicate the play entered the Lord Chamberlain's repertory earlier in 1597.

44 See William N. West, "Intertheatricality," in *Early Modern Theatricality*, ed. Henry S. Turner (Oxford: Oxford University Press, 2013), 151–72.

45 As Phyllis Rackin points out, "dramatic irony is … endemic to the history play." That general irony was likely all the more heightened for *2 Henry IV*'s spectators given the recent wealth of opportunities to familiarize themselves with accounts of King Henry IV's death. See Rackin, "Temporality, Anachronism, and Presence in Shakespeare's English Histories," *Renaissance Drama* 17 (1986): 101–23, esp. 108.

46 Brian Walsh has shown that early modern history plays involved spectators in the temporal construction of historical narratives; to his compelling account of the genre's function, I would add that such involvement is often induced by inviting spectators' uncertainty about the direction of an unfolding narrative. I treat the inculcation of uncertainty in the history play in more detail in Chapter 2. See Walsh, *Shakespeare, the Queen's Men, and the Elizabethan Performance of History* (Cambridge: Cambridge University Press, 2009).

47 On early modern spectators' special appreciation of staged swordplay, see Tribble, *Early Modern Actors and Shakespeare's Theatre*, 67–100.

48 Act, scene, and line numbers follow William Shakespeare, *Henry IV, Part 1*, ed. David Scott Kastan (London: Arden, 2002).

49 James Calderwood, *Metadrama in Shakespeare's Henriad: "Richard II" to "Henry V"* (Berkeley: University of California Press, 1979), 71. For more readings of Falstaff in this vein, see C. L. Barber, *Shakespeare's Festive Comedy:*

A Study of Dramatic Form and Its Relation to Social Custom (Cleveland: Meridian Books, 1959), 67–73 and Hugh Grady, *Shakespeare, Machiavelli, and Montaigne: Power and Subjectivity from "Richard II" to "Hamlet"* (Oxford: Oxford University Press, 2002), 126–79.

50 Mariko Ichikawa, *The Shakespearean Stage Space* (Cambridge: Cambridge University Press, 2013), 135.

51 Calderwood claims, for instance, that Hal addresses Falstaff "precisely as if he knew he were faking death." See *Metadrama*, 83.

52 This reading of these lines is just that – a reading. There is no historical evidence to confirm that Elizabethan spectators watched Hal try to carry Falstaff offstage, and I know of no modern productions that have staged the scene this way. At the 2019 Blackfriars Conference, however, I had the good fortune to try out this staging with two actors with the American Shakespeare Center. It worked brilliantly.

53 Stage directions from various plays suggest both concerted attention to and creative solutions for ensuring the smooth removal of corpses from the stage throughout the period. As Alan C. Dessen and Leslie Thomson note, "bear" denotes care to removing stage corpses quickly, while "carry" often indicates the transfer of a body offstage in a chair. See Dessen and Thomson, *A Dictionary of Stage Directions in English Drama, 1580–1642* (Cambridge: Cambridge University Press, 1999), 22, 43.

54 For more on the sense of closure invited by rhyming couplets, see Katherine Bootle Attie, "Passion Turned to Prettiness: Rhyme or Reason in *Hamlet*," *Shakespeare Quarterly* 63.3 (2012): 393–423, esp. 407; and Warren D. Smith, *Shakespeare's Playhouse Practice: A Handbook* (Hanover, NH: University Press of New England, 1975), 102. For more on the manipulation of spectators' expectations through the deployment of false exits, see Steven Urkowitz, "Interrupted Exits in *King Lear*," *Educational Theatre Journal* 30.2 (1978): 203–210.

55 Rutter, *Enter the Body*, 2.

56 William Shakespeare, *The History of Henrie the Fourth; with the Battell at Shrewsburie, betweene the King and Lord Henry Percy, Surnamed Henrie Hotspur of the North. With the Humorous Conceits of Sir Iohn Falstalffe* (London: Andrew Wise, 1598).

57 John Tatham, *Knavery in All Trades, or, The Coffee-House a Comedy* (London: W. Gilbertson, and H. Marsh, 1664), E1r. See also Lopez's discussion of this story; I share his sense that although its "status is … somewhat doubtful," it is "vividly suggestive in terms of … questions of convention." *Theatrical Convention*, 1.

58 I will treat the responses of Caroline audiences to conventional disruption in detail in Chapter 5.

59 The clearest evidence of the early modern stage's ability to provoke tears comes from Thomas Nashe's defense of playgoing, in which he imagines the historical Talbot's response to his portrayal onstage: "How would it haue ioyed braue Talbot (the terror of the French) to thinke that after he had lyne two hundred

yeares in his Tombe, hee should triumphe againe on the Stage, and haue his bones newe embalmed with the teares of ten thousand spectators at least, (at seuerall times) who in the Tragedian that represents his person, imagine they behold him fresh bleeding." See Nashe, *Pierce Penilesse his Supplication to the Diuell* (London: John Busby, 1592), F3r.

60 Sianne Ngai, *Ugly Feelings* (Cambridge, MA: Harvard University Press, 2005), 14.

61 Kastan, *Henry IV, Part 1*, 334 n139.

62 A 1787 American reviewer, for example, noted the expediency of having "a stump of a tree on which *Falstaff* may rest the body of Hotspur, during his conversation with the *Prince*." See Arthur Colby Sprague, *Shakespeare and the Actors: The Stage Business in His Plays (1660–1905)*, (Cambridge, MA: Harvard University Press, 1944), 91.

63 The cumulative effect of these modes of looking, I want to suggest, goes beyond what Andrew Sofer characterizes as the mobile signifying force of the actor's body; in his estimation, "actor and prop are dynamic sign-vehicles that move up and down the subject-object continuum as they acquire and shed action force in the course of a given performance." The explanation of such a signifying continuum along which the actor's body can move is curiously devoid of the spectator's role in precisely that movement; as such, it does not allow for the possibility that the apparent corpse might, in crucially ambiguous moments, be seen by spectators as both subject and object at once. That excess of signification is predicated upon the active enlistment of the spectator as interpreter. See Andrew Sofer, "'Take up the Bodies': Shakespeare's Body Parts, Babies, and Corpses," *Theatre Symposium* 18 (2010): 135–48, esp. 136.

64 The anonymous *Locrine* (1595), which features the clownish Strumbo playing dead in order to avoid being killed in battle, likely served as Shakespeare's inspiration for Falstaff's fake death. For more on the relationship between the two plays and characters, see Michael Bristol, *Carnival and Theater: Plebeian Culture and the Structure of Authority in Renaissance England* (New York: Routledge, 1985).

65 Readings of *The Second Maiden's Tragedy* understandably tend to focus on the historicist and feminist implications of the Tyrant's idolatrous, necrophiliac devotion to the Lady's corpse, which he wrongly believes he can reanimate. For more on the spectacle of death in *The Second Maiden's Tragedy*, see Susan Zimmerman, *The Early Modern Corpse and Shakespeare's Theatre* (Edinburgh: Edinburgh University Press, 2005); Pollard, *Drugs and Theater*, 101–22; Karim-Cooper, *Cosmetics in Shakespearean and Renaissance Drama*, 67–88; Sara Eaton, "'Content with art?': Seeing the Emblematic Woman in *The Second Maiden's Tragedy* and *The Winter's Tale*," in *Shakespearean Power and Punishment: A Volume of Essays*, ed. Gillian Murray Kendall (Cranbury: Associated University Presses, 1998), 59–86; and Christine M. Gottlieb, "Middleton's Traffic in Dead Women: Chaste Corpses as Property in *The Revenger's Tragedy* and *The Lady's Tragedy*," *English Literary Renaissance* 45.2 (2015): 255–274.

66 Act, scene, and line numbers follow Thomas Middleton, *The Second Maiden's Tragedy*, ed. Anne Lancashire (Manchester: Manchester University Press, 1978).

67 For an overview of the attribution debate as well as the nature of the additions to the playtext, see James Purkis, *Shakespeare and Manuscript Drama: Canon, Collaboration, and Text* (Cambridge: Cambridge University Press, 2016), 101–40. While Eric Rasmussen has made the case that Shakespeare, as the official playwright of the King's Men, authored the additions, the consensus is now that Middleton was responsible for them. See Rasmussen, "Shakespeare's Hand in *The Second Maiden's Tragedy*," *Shakespeare Quarterly* 40.1 (1989): 1–26. Purkis ultimately argues for a collaborative understanding of the additions made in the playhouse, which, he suggests, bear "partial traces of the labour of different textual agents with overlapping and conflicting concerns." See Purkis, 137.

68 For a discussion of the scene as an Aristotelian reversal, see Julia Briggs, "*The Lady's Tragedy*: Parallel Texts," in *Thomas Middleton: The Collected Works*, ed. Gary Taylor and John Lavagnino (Oxford: Oxford University Press, 2007), 833–38, esp. 834. As Tiffany Stern details, the preparation for a play's staging was largely devoted to the solitary study of individual parts, rather than group rehearsal. See Tiffany Stern, *Rehearsal from Shakespeare to Sheridan* (Oxford: Oxford University Press, 2000), 52–70.

69 Zimmerman, *The Early Modern Corpse*, 102.

70 For more on lighting in the indoor theaters, see R. B. Graves, *Lighting the Shakespearean Stage, 1567–1642* (Carbondale, IL: Southern Illinois University Press, 1999); and Martin White, "'When torchlight made an artificial noon': Light and Darkness in the Indoor Jacobean Theatre," in *Moving Shakespeare Indoors: Performance and Repertoire in the Jacobean Playhouse*, ed. Andrew Gurr and Farah Karim-Cooper (Cambridge: Cambridge University Press, 2014), 115–36.

71 For more on the prevalence of staged darkness, see Lopez, *Theatrical Convention*, 102.

72 In his textual introduction to the play, Cyrus Hoy surmises that the bulk of Shirley's revisions are stylistic, taking the form of his characteristic clipped dialogue; substantively, Hoy concludes, "the text that we have seems to represent in the main the play that Fletcher wrote c. 1611." See Cyrus Hoy, "Textual Introduction," *The Night Walker*, in *The Dramatic Works in the Beaumont and Fletcher Canon*, vol. 7 (Cambridge: Cambridge University Press, 1989), 525.

73 *The Night Walker*'s 1611 date is relatively uncontroversial, having been mostly agreed upon since Baldwin Maxwell pinpointed a reference in the play to the bell installed in Lincoln Cathedral in late 1610. But Martin Wiggins has recently dated the play to 1615 based on other internal evidence. In the second half of the play, Maria disguises herself as a Welsh countrywoman; though she largely speaks in stage Welsh, she does use the phrase "du cat a whee" – the same one that Thomas Middleton gives to the Welsh gentlewoman in *A Chaste Maid in Cheapside*. According to Wiggins, because there is no immediate

reason for Maria to assume a Welsh disguise, Middleton's play must take priority. But Fletcher's plays have long been characterized as privileging scenic unity over dramatic coherence; the fact that a clear reason is not given for the particular features of Maria's disguise is in keeping with that dramatic style. Peter Hyland, too, has argued that accents were a common feature of stage disguises in this period. Based on the available evidence and Fletcher's dramatic style, it is entirely plausible that Middleton had *The Night Walker* in mind when he created a more fully realized Welsh character in *A Chaste Maid*. In sum, the priority of either play is simply not as clear as Wiggins maintains. See Maxwell, *Studies in Beaumont, Fletcher, and Massinger* (Chapel Hill: The University of North Carolina Press, 1939), 46–53; Wiggins, in association with Catherine Richardson, *British Drama 1533–1642: A Catalogue*, vol. 6 (Oxford: Oxford University Press, 2015), 455; and Hyland, *Disguise on the Early Modern English Stage* (Burlington, VT: Ashgate, 2011), 39. For more on Fletcher's (lack of) dramatic coherence, see Charles Squier, *John Fletcher* (Boston: Twayne Publishers, 1986), 15.

Questions about *The Night Walker*'s date raise questions about the play's company. While Fletcher was still writing for both the King's Men and the Children of the Queen's Revels in 1611, internal evidence suggests that *The Night Walker* was crafted for a boys' company. The play's casting list fits what Jean MacIntyre has identified as the resources of the Queen's Revels based on their repertory from 1609 to 1612; the parts include three gallants, one old man, one fool, five women, and one boy (a woman in disguise). In keeping with other Queen's Revels' plays, *The Night Walker* features multiple disguises in order to create the appearance of a larger cast size, including, in addition to Maria's Welsh Gentlewoman, a bookseller, a constable, a ghost, an angel, and two Furies. Beyond that, the play emphasizes its oldest character's lack of virility, delights in fart jokes, and makes homoerotic innuendo the centerpiece of interactions between Lurcher, an adult character, and Snap, a girl disguised as a boy – all common features of boys' plays. One interaction between Lurcher and Snap provides further evidence of both company and date. The moment takes place when the thief Lurcher prepares to trick Justice Algripe. Snap, his boy accomplice, supplies him, according to the stage direction, with a "*Gowne, Beard, and Constables staffe*" (4.1.106sd). When Lurcher asks Snap how he came by these items, the boy replies: "The staffe I stole last night from a sleeping Constable; / The rest I borrowed by my acquaintance with / The Players boyes" (4.1.108–10). The presence of these lines further weakens Wiggins' suggestion of a c. 1615 date; by that year, the Children of the Queen's Revels – the last of the boys' companies – had been shuttered for two years. The joke only works as a moment of self-referentiality for which the Queen's Revels were known. On the resources of the Children of the Queen's Revels at Whitefriars, see Jean MacIntyre, "Production Resources at the Whitefriars Playhouse, 1609–1612," *Early Modern Literary Studies* 2.3 (1996): 2.1–35. For more on the common characteristics of boys' company plays, see Mary Bly, "The Boy Companies 1599–1613," in *The Oxford Handbook of Early Modern*

Theatre, ed. Richard Dutton (Oxford: Oxford University Press, 2009), 136–50. For more on the self-referentiality of Queen's Revels plays in particular, see Lucy Munro, *Children of the Queen's Revels*, 37–54.

74 For more on the Children of the Queen's Revels' move to Whitefriars, see Munro, *Children of the Queen's Revels*, 23–25.

75 See Tiffany Stern, "Taking Part: Actors and Audience on the Stage at the Blackfriars," in *Inside Shakespeare: Essays on the Blackfriars Stage*, ed. Paul Menzer (Cranbury, NJ: Associated University Presses, 2006), 35–53. Scholars disagree about what space within the Whitefriars complex, a former refectory, was used as the theater; for an overview of the possibilities (both substantially smaller than Blackfriars), see Lucy Munro, "The Whitefriars Theatre and the Children's Companies," in *Ben Jonson in Context*, ed. Julie Sanders (Cambridge: Cambridge University Press, 2010), 116–23, esp. 117–18.

76 For more on the visual effects of candlelight in the hall theaters, see Sarah Dustagheer, *Shakespeare's Two Playhouses: Repertory and Theatre Space at the Globe and the Blackfriars, 1599–1613* (Cambridge: Cambridge University Press, 2017), 123–38.

77 For more on the practice of the night watch, see David Cressy, *Birth, Marriage, and Death: Ritual, Religion, and the Life-Cycle in Tudor and Stuart England* (Oxford: Oxford University Press, 1997), 425–32; and Marshall, *Beliefs and the Dead*, 132-36.

78 Cited in Marshall, *Beliefs and the Dead*, 134. Marshall also notes that the use of candles during the day veered into the territory of popish ritual, a sign of the attempt to influence the trajectory of the loved one's soul as it languished in the purgatory that had officially ceased to exist in post-Reformation England.

79 John Aubrey, "Remaines of Gentilisme and Judaisme," in *Three Prose Works*, ed. John Buchanan-Brown (Carbondale, IL: Southern Illinois University Press, 1972), 126–304, esp. 173.

80 Garner, *Bodied Spaces*, 1.

81 Jesus's hunger is one of the means by which he demonstrates his resurrection to the astonished apostles in the New Testament; as the King James translation of Luke 24:41–43 renders it, "And while they yet believed not for joy, and wondered, he said unto them, Have ye here any meat? And they gave him a piece of broiled fish, and of an honeycomb. And he took *it*, and did eat before them."

82 The text quoted comes from the 1559 edition of the Prayer Book, in *The Book of Common Prayer: The Texts of 1549, 1559, and 1662*, ed. Brian Cummings (Oxford: Oxford University Press, 2011), 172.

83 As Judith Maltby puts it, "theologically, the rite was offensive, because it implied that *any* deceased person might be 'asleep in the Lord'." See Maltby, *Prayer Book and People in Elizabethan and Early Stuart England* (Cambridge: Cambridge University Press, 1998), 61.

84 It is impossible, of course, to know how often and to what extent people in this period wondered and worried about their own salvation. Peter Marshall suggests that "there appears to have been a broad cultural presumption in later Reformation England that salvation was widely accessible," though there are extreme examples of people who, believing themselves to be reprobate,

despaired and sought spiritual treatment. There would have been innumerable levels of anxiety in between these two extremes, many of which could have been represented in the playhouse on any given afternoon. See Marshall, *Beliefs and the Dead*, 201. On spiritual treatment, see Michael MacDonald, *Mystical Bedlam: Madness, Anxiety, and Healing in Seventeenth-Century England* (Cambridge: Cambridge University Press, 1981), 217–23.

85 Garner, *Bodied Spaces*, 44.

86 Maurice Merleau-Ponty, *The Visible and the Invisible*, trans. Alphonso Lingis (Evanston, IL: Northwestern University Press, 1968), 254.

87 Snap's fears are not unfounded: as Erika T. Lin notes, in this period "changes in the physical conditions of everyday life were also seen as having very real consequences in the spiritual realm." See Lin, *Shakespeare and the Materiality of Performance* (New York: Palgrave Macmillan, 2012), 75.

88 On the indebtedness of this moment to Ben Jonson's *Epicene*, see Hyland, *Disguise on the Early Modern English Stage*, 20–21; and Maxwell, "The Date of Fletcher's *The Night Walker*," 490–92.

89 William Cartwright, "Upon the Report of the Printing of the Dramaticall Poems of Master John Fletcher," in *Comedies and Tragedies by Francis Beaumont and John Fletcher* (London: Humphrey and Humphrey Mosley, 1647), D2r.

90 *Dramatic Records in the Declared Accounts of the Treasurer of the Chamber 1558–1642*, ed. David Cook and F. P. Wilson (Oxford: Oxford University Press, 1961), 56.

91 Line numbers follow Francis Beaumont and John Fletcher, *The Captain*, vol. 1 of *The Dramatic Works in the Beaumont and Fletcher Canon*, ed. L. A. Beaurline. (Cambridge: Cambridge University Press, 1966).

92 Michael Neill, "'Wits most accomplished Senate': The Audience of the Caroline Private Theaters," *Studies in English Literature* 18.2 (1978): 341–60, esp. 353.

93 Gordon McMullan, "'The Neutral Term?': Shakespearean Tragicomedy and the Idea of the 'Late Play'," in *Early Modern Tragicomedy*, ed. Subha Mukherji and Raphael Lyne (Rochester, NY: D. S. Brewer, 2007), 115–32, esp. 117.

94 Claire M. L. Bourne, "'High Designe': Beaumont and Fletcher Illustrated," *ELR* 44.2 (2014): 275–327, esp. 284.

95 Thomas Jordan, "To his friend the Author," in *The Plays and Poems of Philip Massinger*, ed. Philip Edwards and Colin Gibson, vol. 2 (Oxford: Oxford University Press, 1976), 296.

96 John Dryden, "Heads of an Answer to Rymer," in *The Works of John Dryden*, ed. Samuel Holt Monk, A. E. Wallace Maurer, and Vinton A. Dearing, vol. 17. (Berkeley: University of California Press, 1971), 189.

97 While most of these laudatory descriptions of Fletcherian tragicomedy refer to its ingenious plotting, John Berkenhead seems particularly to recognize the theatrical pleasures of apparent deaths and surprising resurrections in his dedicatory poem in the 1647 Beaumont and Fletcher folio. "FLETCHER, arise" he writes, as if to resurrect the playwright from the stage where he lies, only seemingly dead. See Berkenhead, "On the Happy Collection of Master Fletcher's Works, Never Before Printed," in *Comedies and Tragedies Written by Francis Beaumont and John Fletcher*, E1v.

98 Homer Swander suggests that "through the presence of a corpse, the staged events are alive with new possibilities." In this chapter, I have argued for a more expansive sense of his statement: the early modern stage corpse was more than the bodily version of Chekhov's gun, demanding attention to theatrical possibility within the frame of a single play; beyond that frame, it worked to shape spectators' sense of theatrical possibility across the dramatic landscape more broadly. See Swander, "No Exit for a Dead Body: What to Do with a Scripted Corpse?," *Journal of Dramatic Theory and Criticism* 5.2 1991: 139–52, esp. 141.

99 Act, scene, and line numbers follow William Shakespeare, *Much Ado About Nothing*, ed. Claire McEachern (London: Bloomsbury Arden Shakespeare, 2016).

100 As Howard Felperin beautifully puts it, "Shakespeare in *King Lear* repeatedly holds out hope with his left hand only to take it back with his right; raises romantic expectations only to defeat them with tragic actualities. The play is full of false dawns." *Shakespearean Romance* (Princeton: Princeton University Press, 1972), 117–18.

101 Ellen MacKay, *Persecution, Plague, and Fire: Fugitive Histories of the Stage in Early Modern England* (Chicago: University of Chicago Press, 2011), 132.

CHAPTER 2

Time

Dramatic Suspense, the History Play, and the Elizabethan Succession Crisis

The engraving on the 1619 title page of Francis Beaumont and John Fletcher's *A King and No King* is a tableau of interrupted gestures (Figure 2.1).[1] The titular king (and no king) in question, Arbaces, stands with his arms outstretched as a hand reaches down from the heavens to place a crown on his head – or, more disconcertingly, to remove it. "Gesture," as John Bulwer wrote in 1644, is the means "whereby the Body, instructed by Nature, can ... communicate a thought."[2] But as a theatrical snapshot– a single instant of time, that is, plucked from their successive flow in performance– the image does not so much communicate as confound. Palms upward, Arbaces seemingly reacts with delight to the divine action taking place just above him: To "RAISE OUR HANDS TO HEAVEN," Bulwer writes, is "a signe of amazement," the acknowledgment of "the Hand and Finger of God."[3] The crown is being put on. As Bulwer explains elsewhere, however, "both Hands" are "extended out forward together" by those who mean to "*submit, invoke, doubt, speak* to, *accuse, or call by name, implore or attest.*"[4] The crown is being taken off. Arbaces's upturned hands suggest admiration; his outstretched arms convey his dismay. The static image casts the actor as the "doble dealing ambodexter" that the antitheatricalists feared him to be, his frozen gesture inviting uncertainty in its thwarted attempt to transpire through time.[5]

The title page of *A King and No King* is also a snapshot of a relatively late moment in the commercial theater's history, the point by which the twists and turns of tragicomic plotting had become definitive of dramatic suspense. In the previous chapter, I identified the vital stillness of the theatrical corpse as a key resource for creating such suspense: the breathing actor, playing dead, embodied a narrative equally poised to tumble toward or veer away from tragedy; the uncertainty generated by such moments defined

Figure 2.1   Francis Beaumont and John Fletcher, *A King and No King* (London: Thomas Walkley, 1619), A2r. Call #: STC 1670.

spectators' phenomenological connection to the unfolding stage action. In this chapter, I want to build out the account of how theater practitioners crafted dramatic suspense by attending to a genre in which spectators' uncertainty was especially difficult to achieve: the history play. Scholarship on the genre is divided in response to the question of where Elizabethan playgoers stood in interpretive relation to these fictionalized depictions of the past, many of which dramatized eminently familiar events of English history. In line with work from Phyllis Rackin and Marjorie Garber that foregrounds spectators' proleptic relation to stage chronicle, Brian Walsh suggests that history plays cultivated the knowingness that followed from "a general consciousness of how [historical] narratives are generated."[6] David Scott Kastan, by contrast, argues that the new dramatic genre, invented by Shakespeare and his contemporaries through the 1580s and 1590s, radically reoriented the closed determination of tragedy toward the open-endedness of history, seizing on the contingency of possibility as a defining feature of dramatic action.[7] This chapter charts a middle way between the extremes of these two positions: to experience the contingent open-endedness of history's flow in performance, I will suggest, spectators were required to *unknow* what they already knew about the events displayed before them. To attend to this phenomenological process is to follow the critical move from, as Paul Yachnin and Myrna Selkirk describe it, "an interest in what the plays mean to a focus on what they do," but it is also to suggest that what history plays did could be at odds with what they meant.[8] What looked like providence in a play often felt like uncertainty in the playhouse: the measure of a history play's theatrical success was its phenomenological and epistemological strain against the self-evidence of the very narrative it sought to bring into being.

That strain had to be deliberately achieved, for at a basic level history and drama were understood in early modernity to be formally akin.[9] History recounted, in George Puttenham's estimation, "the good and exemplarie things and actions of the former ages," while drama, in the Aristotelian conception of tragedy that still held sway at the end of the sixteenth century, was the "imitation of an action."[10] Putting historical events onstage, however, bound the sequential unfolding of those past actions to the forward onrush of time as it was experienced, with acute awareness of its evanescence, in the playhouse.[11] On the stage, the unfolding of *action* – the events that together make up the dramatic *plot* – always occurs in dynamic relation to both narrative and theatrical time. Within the world of the play, disruptions to what Paul Ricoeur identifies as "the ordinary representation of time as a linear succession of instants" facilitated large temporal jumps – as when John Webster's *The Duchess of Malfi* skips the birth of the Duchess's two children or Shakespeare's *The Winter's Tale* "slide[s] / O'er" sixteen years (4.1.5–6).[12] Philip Sidney complained that such disruptions filled the dramatic narrative with more events than theatrical time could compass: "Now of time, they [playwrights] are much more liberall. For ordinarie it is, that two yoong Princes fall in loue, after many trauerses she is got with childe, deliuered of a faire boy: he is lost, groweth a man, falleth in loue, and is readie to get an other childe, and all this in two houres space: which howe absurd it is in sence, euen sence may imagine."[13] Theater, in Sidney's estimation, is not just "something happening," but *too much*.[14]

   Sidney might have been relieved to know that practitioners also crafted the opposite theatrical effect. I will argue in this chapter that in the commercial theater, so often denigrated in the period as a site of frenzied action rather than lofty poetry, playwrights also strategically attempted to make *nothing* occur – to stop narrative time, thus cleaving it from time's continued theatrical advance – and, even more daringly, to make the absence of dramatic action theatrically exciting.[15] These plays deploy a range of techniques to halt their own happening, though they are united by their aim to divert spectators' attention from their involvement in the process definitive of early modern performance: the continual, and thus necessarily future-oriented, imaginative construction of the theatrical present. It is no accident that *Henry V*'s famous injunction to "Think, when we talk of horses, that you see them / Printing their proud hoofs i'th' receiving earth" asks spectators to conjure the animals' movement, in time with the gallop of the speaker's iambs, across the stage (Prologue.26–27). The dramatic action that early modern spectators helped conjure into being was synonymous with performance's forward momentum.[16] For precisely this reason, then, these attempts to sunder narrative and theatrical time were bound to fail, though it was in that very failure that history plays were able to approximate, even momentarily, the tense, ambiguous stasis that the title page of *A King and No King* so effortlessly achieves.[17] Operating at the margins of theatrical form, these plays constructed dramatic suspense from the phenomenological experience of temporal suspension.

   These experimental attempts to halt the flow of dramatic action were especially potent at the end of the sixteenth century, for they gave shape to the uncertain present in which Elizabethan playgoers remained confined as they anxiously awaited their aging queen's successor. The preacher of a 1602 sermon reported that "some fickle headed amongst us are wery of the state ... and cry give us a kinge."[18] The complaint echoed Alexander Nowell's address before Parliament nearly forty years earlier, which described Elizabeth's lack of successor as "a plague unto us."[19] If Elizabeth's refusal to name a successor threatened to produce a political crisis, the popular wish for a new monarch was experienced by her subjects as a desire for change – for the promise, that is, of a successive moment in time that could be clearly differentiated from those that had come just before it.[20] The existence of a royal successor offered a glimpse of the future, the ability to see where time was going. Instead, Elizabethans were required to wait for the future to arrive, and the extended present to which they were confined produced both rampant anxiety and fevered speculation.[21] "What trouble shall we be in," Nowell reported hearing subjects cry, "for the succession is so uncertain, and such division for religion! Alack! what shall become of us?"[22] John Harington, court gossip and godson of the Queen, divulged that preacher Matthew Hutton once warned Elizabeth that "the uncertainty of succession gave hopes to Forreiners to attempt fresh invasions and breed feares in many of her Subjects of new Conquest."[23] The 1571 Treasons Act intended to quash speculation about Elizabeth's successor by rendering it unlawful "to affirm the right in succession of the crown in some other than the Queen," though it merely sent such speculation underground; as Leonard Tennenhouse notes, "envision[ing] … narratives" about succession was popular both within and outside of Elizabeth's court.[24] A self-evident dilemma with vast ramifications, the succession crisis was an unusually democratized form of political uncertainty at the end of the sixteenth century: just as it stoked the fears of those who preached to the Queen herself, it fired the imaginations of those furthest from the center of political power.

History plays, as Marissa Nicosia aptly observes, "traffic[ked] in the drama of succession."[25] But by straining against their temporal affordances, they also *enacted* it, inviting spectators to inhabit the stasis of a future that refused to arrive. Put another way, history plays refigured the vexing suspension of waiting – for theatrical spectacle, for monarchical succession – from a state merely to be endured into the pleasurable object of spectators' attention. If, as Kenneth Burke described it, form is nothing more than the satisfaction of expectation, then a key facet of the early modern theater's experimental innovation was its ability to keep what counted as expectations and their satisfactions in flux.[26] In this theater, the repeated diversion of spectators' attention from denouement to the uncertain interim preceding it turned their anticipation, paradoxically, into its own fulfillment. Plays that rendered temporal stasis spectacular transformed the tense uncertainty over the question of Elizabeth's successor into theatrically pleasurable experiences. History plays cultivated conditional thinking by giving spectators a truthful baseline from which their minds were encouraged to wander; they were training grounds in speculation. Amid the forward onrush of performance, depictions of the past licensed the entertainment of what could be and what could have been otherwise, setting spectators' imaginative participation in the proliferation of possibility against the satisfaction produced by the completion of a narrative arc. Thomas Wilson claimed in 1600 that the heart of England "beates extreamely" for succession.[27] The theater allowed spectators to feel the pleasure of possibility in that pulse.

The Multiple Futures of Edward II

Christopher Marlowe's *Edward II* opens by casting what will be in terms of what might have been:

> 'My father is deceased; come, Gaveston,
> And share the kingdom with thy dearest friend.'
> Ah, words that make me surfeit with delight!
> What greater bliss can hap to Gaveston,
> Than live and be the favourite of a king?
> Sweet prince, I come; these, these thy amorous lines
> Might have enforced me to have swum from France,
> And, like Leander, gasped upon the sand,
> So thou wouldst smile and take me in thy arms.
> The sight of London to my exiled eyes
> Is as Elysium to a new-come soul;
> Not that I love the city or the men,
> But that it harbours him I hold so dear,
> The King, upon whose bosom let me die,
> And with the world be still at enmity.   (1.1–15)[28]

Succession proceeds here so swiftly that it has already taken place when the play begins, offering Gaveston the promise of a return to London from his native France, where he has been exiled. Yet just when the soliloquy seems to settle comfortably into exposition, Gaveston veers into allusion, imagining himself as a Leander who has arrived safely in the arms of his Hero. The lines obliquely acknowledge the tragic ending of the Ovidian myth while simultaneously reimagining death as sexual consummation; in cutting Leander's story short, the king and his favorite, Gaveston asserts, will "be still."[29] The tragic determinism of the myth becomes a conduit for the open action; it is not that Gaveston *is* or is *like* Leander, but that he makes his way to an entirely new place by means of the mythical character's reimagined trajectory. The conditional form of the initial comparison – Gaveston "might have" swum to Edward in England – infuses the past with a sense of future-oriented possibility that is transformed, two lines later, into the celeritous immediacy of the present: "The sight of London to my exiled eyes / Is as Elysium." In his mind, Gaveston has already traveled to England.

The Ovidian allusion necessarily involves spectators in the construction of the incipient vector of possibility that Gaveston brings about with his thought alone. In the early modern theater, dramatic openings bore heavy responsibility as phenomenological solicitations; in the absence of detailed sets and backdrops, they forged, largely through verbal description, the link between stage and spectator that propelled the dynamic process of performance and enabled the fictional realization of onstage worlds. But what is striking about Gaveston's speech is that it does not invite spectators to conjure the world of the play itself, but the one of Gaveston's own imagining. "Once framed in the attention," Bert O. States writes of performance, "possibilities arise"; musing that might be relegated to the background of the fictional world in a realist theatrical environment is an ontological threat to Elizabethan spectacle.[30] Leander's journey across the Hellespont traces a narrative trajectory that interferes with the theatrical presentation of Gaveston's imminent journey back to England, at once contextualizing and contesting the action that unfolded for spectators on the Theater's minimally accoutered stage.

That tension is exacerbated as Gaveston makes plans for his role as the king's favorite:

> I must have wanton poets, pleasant wits,
> Musicians, that with touching of a string
> May draw the pliant King which way I please.
> Music and poetry is his delight;
> Therefore I'll have Italian masques by night,
> Sweet speeches, comedies, and pleasing shows;
> And in the day when he shall walk abroad,
> Like sylvan nymphs my pages shall be clad,
> My men like satyrs grazing on the lawns
> Shall with their goat-feet dance an antic hay.   (1.50–59)

Wanton poets, sweet speeches, pleasing shows: Gaveston's theatrically minded fantasy invites spectators to conjure the leisurely delights of his theater alongside the very show being presented to them onstage. The friction between real and imagined spectacle increases as he continues:

> Sometime a lovely boy in Dian's shape,
> With hair that gilds the water as it glides,
> Crownets of pearl about his naked arms,
> And in his sportful hands an olive tree

> To hide those parts which men delight to see,
> Shall bathe him in a spring; and there hard by,
> One like Actaeon peeping through the grove,
> Shall by the angry goddess be transformed,
> And running in the likeness of an hart,
> By yelping hounds pulled down, and seem to die.   (1.60–69)

The "lovely boy in Dian's shape" that Gaveston envisions taking part in a dramatic rendering of the Actaeon myth could be an actor in the Rose; as a function of his imagination, the metatheatrical oscillation between character and actor that occurred so often in the early modern theater takes place at a decorous remove, as if it remains, like the boy actor's body, hidden. Gaveston again relies on the representational power of the theater itself to rewrite the tragedy of classical myth: in his staging of the story, Diana's hunter will, of course, only "*seem* to die." Like the dismembered Actaeon, dead and not dead, the play's singular temporal trajectory suddenly splinters into two; the narrative succession of present moments onstage – what *is* happening – is paused in order to entertain Gaveston's confident supposition about what *shall*. The moment might be characterized as "polychronic," to borrow a term from Jonathan Gil Harris, though it does not create a palimpsest of the past, but of the future: theatrical action and Gaveston's speculation intertwine in the present immediacy of performance, in the process generating a multitemporal fantasy of what could be.[31]

In a play in which male-male desire eventually poses a threat to dynastic succession, the honeyed entertainments evoked by the king's favorite tempt the theater's sodomitical dangers.[32] As antitheatricalist Stephen Gosson described it, "the sweete numbers of Poetrie flowing in verse … might slippe downe in suger by this intisement, for that which delighteth neuer troubleth our swallow."[33] The ease with which iambic sugar moves through the throat produces a dangerously languid sense of stasis: to attend plays is to spend "good howers in euill exercise," Gosson cautions, to "clappe any leade to our heeles … when wee shoulde runne forwardes still."[34] To experience theatrical pleasure is to lose track of time, and to lose track of time is to give what could be equal credence to what is.[35] *Edward II* invites spectators to dwell in suspended time not simply by dilating the present– "such a day tomorrow" is not, as in Polixenes's nostalgic dream of eternal boyhood with Leontes in *The Winter's Tale*, "as today" (1.2.64)– but by multiplying it. A vision of Lee Edelman's "no future" is rejected in favor of more futures than the single stage could compass.[36] The linear unfolding of theatrical action intermingles with

Figure 2.2   Henry Peacham, *Minerua Britanna* (London: Wa: Dight, 1612), 13.
Call #: STC 19511.

the surfeit, in Gaveston's unfixed "sometime," of what might be; the
sense of multitudinous, countervailing temporality that results is akin to
a tree on which several newly formed branches have just begun to grow.
    Laurie Shannon has shown that the emblem of Edward and Gaveston's
relationship is a tree with its branches twined together; I would suggest
that the play's is akin to the one that Henry Peacham would apply to
Queen Anne in 1612: an olive tree, "with braunches faire dispred ...
Which thus I *ghesse*, shall with their outstretcht armes, / In time o'respread
Europa's continent" (Figure 2.2).[37] Peacham's confidence stems from the
comfortable certainty of the Jacobean settlement, yet the unknowingness
acknowledged in his laudatory conjecture ironically evokes the opacity
of the future at the end of the Elizabethan era. At the time of *Edward
II*'s first performance, Elizabeth I neared age sixty; speculation about her
possible suitors had ceased in favor of rumors about her viable succes-
sors. By that time, James VI of Scotland was a leading candidate for the
throne, though he was by no means the only reasonable contender. In
1601, Thomas Wilson identified twelve possible "Competitors that gape
for the death of that good old Princess the now Queen."[38] The authors
of *A Conference about the Next Succession to the Crowne of Ingland* (1595)
offered up sixteen possible future monarchs. The text's stated aim of
emphasizing "the wonderful ambiguity and doubtfulness" of the succession is best realized not on the 500-page tract itself but the diagram that
accompanies it, which displays the genealogical line of England's monarchs and "pretenders" linked to it by branches – not a single family tree
but, as *A Conference* claims, "A perfect and exact Arbor" (Figure 2.3).[39]
The Ramist sensibility of the diagram is contested by its organic style:
winding branches, dotted with leaves, are accompanied by names inside

Figure 2.3   *A Conference about the Next Succession to the Crowne of Ingland*
(Antwerp: A. Conincx, 1595). Call #: STC 19398.

bud-like circles; those circles belonging to monarchs are topped with
flower-like crowns. The ornamentation artfully underscores information
strictly unnecessary to the text's purpose: descendants of various familial
lines who are not claimants to the throne are included with those who
are, and the sixteen candidates are not visually identified as such. To find
them, the reader is required repeatedly to trace the meandering paths of
the branches, following the individual arguments for succession one by
one. Yet it is precisely the stillness of the print image, aesthetically coherent in its confusion, that allows the several possibilities for England's
future comfortably to coexist. The diagram captures, that is, what *Edward
II* has to strain against its own formal principles to enact; in immersing
spectators in multiple narratives vying for priority at the moment of their
emergence, Marlowe's play marshals the temporal stillness of suspension
toward dramatic suspense.

This suspension would seem eventually to succumb to the linear track of historical chronicle. Speaking on behalf of Mortimer and the other rebels, a herald demands that Edward rid himself of another favorite: "Remove / This Spencer, as a putrefying branch / That deads the royal vine" (11.161–63). The branches preserving the manifold possibility of Edward and Gaveston's futures are cut away, one by one, in favor of a single, determined history, which Mortimer himself imagines as he plots to kill the king:

> How easily might some base slave be suborned
> To greet his lordship with a poniard,
> And none so much as blame the murderer,
> But rather praise him for that base attempt,
> And in the chronicle enroll his name
> For purging of the realm of such a plague.   (4.265–70)

Gaveston's role as the play's theatrical architect of futurity is eliminated, too, taken over and transformed by the Queen. In her first soliloquy, she similarly describes her journey from France in mythological terms, though her lines are devoid of the conditional possibility that shapes Gaveston's imagination:

> O miserable and distressèd Queen!
> Would when I left sweet France and was embarked,
> That charming Circes, walking on the waves,
> Had changed my shape, or at the marriage-day
> The cup of Hymen had been full of poison,
> Or with those arms that twined about my neck
> I had been stifled, and not lived to see
> The King my lord thus to abandon me.   (4.170–77)

The Queen's wish that Circes had changed her shape, or that Hymen had filled her cup with poison on her wedding day, or that Edward himself had strangled her on their wedding night, is the tragic counter to Gaveston's assertion that, like Leander, he might have swum from France. Rather than conjure the impossible possibility of a future that might have been, she offers multiple rewritings of a past that has already been irrevocably determined. Her regret tips the temporal orientation of the play from the multifarious futurity of Gaveston's fantasies to the tragic determination of history. Even her haunting prophecy – "Like frantic Juno will I fill the earth / With ghastly murmur of my sighs and cries" (4.178–79), she promises – devolves almost immediately into defeated resignation: "I must entreat him [Edward], I must speak him fair" (4.183). For the Queen, there is only one way forward.

Yet even as the play adopts the determined trajectory of historical chronicle, its realization onstage continues to offer spectators a vision of what could have been. As the king's son and sucessor, Prince Edward embodies the forward march of history. But as Jeffrey Masten has noted, the eventual Edward III becomes the former king's double, adopting Edward II's sugary rhetoric in his final farewell: "Sweet father" (25.99).[40] Playing his father's part, Edward III orders the death of the rebellious Mortimer Junior, realizing the future that Edward II himself desires but does not live to see. "If I be England's king," Edward II earlier asserts of his unsteady hold on the throne, "in lakes of gore / Your headless trunks, your bodies will I trail, / That you may drink your fill and quaff in blood" (11.135–37). The play's final scene makes a spectacle of the former king's fantasy, staging a Lord's entrance with the head of the dead Mortimer Junior, his uprising undone. The show of unrealized possibility is exacerbated when Edward II's hearse is crowded onto the stage with Edward III and Mortimer Junior's head. In this moment, spectators in the Theater may have witnessed the reappearance of the former monarch himself: if, as Thomas P. Anderson has compellingly argued, the Pembroke's Men referenced the famous account of the historical Edward II's death by staging the hearse with an effigy, the actor who played Edward II likely reappeared in the final scene to act the part of the dead king's funereal representation.[41] Alongside the inert prop representing Mortimer Junior's head, the comparative liveliness of the actor as effigy would have finally recalled Gaveston's Actaeon, dead and not dead.[42] Marlowe fashions a narrative that dutifully adheres to the linear chronicle of history, though one ultimately at odds with the theatrical technologies that must bring it about; the final scene both narrates Edward II's succession and offers, as if through a glass darkly, the vision of a counterfactual past in which he lived.[43] With its opening lines, *Edward II* entertains what might be; its conclusion materializes what could have been. It is theater that operates, as Richard Schechner put it, "in the subjunctive mood."[44] The staging of the historical chronicle is thus a claim for the power of theater to manifest the possibilities that history has already foreclosed. In the process of performance, spectators are invited to dwell in the pleasurable uncertainty of unrealized possibility, even as the future makes itself unequivocally, singularly known.

The Uncertain Present of Richard II

By 1595, Shakespeare's *Richard II* had joined *Edward II* in London's theatrical marketplace, offering spectators the opportunity to see the

Chamberlain's Men take on the tragic downfall of a weak king.[45] Shakespeare himself had likely become acquainted with Marlowe's play as a member of the Pembroke's Men in 1593; in modeling his tragedy after Marlowe's, he allowed intertheatricality to assert its own pull on history, providing an origin for the effeminate, ineffective Richard from within the theater itself.[46] But the parallels between the two plays are not absolute. While *Edward II* is theatrically defined by the fulsomeness of its polychronicity, *Richard II* might be set in contrast by what it lacks: crucially, both a favorite and a son, and, as a consequence, the capacious futurity that these figures together enable. "Cozening Hope ... is a flatterer, / A parasite, a keeper-back of Death" (2.2.69–70), as the Queen acerbically puts it.[47] If the languid idleness of imagining daydreams up what might be in *Edward II*, Shakespeare's syntactically difficult play – it has been described as "frustrating ... to listen to," generating "a dramaturgy of discomfort" – refuses to let its spectators' minds wander so easily.[48] To be sure, the highly formal poetry of *Richard II*, one of just four that Shakespeare wrote entirely in verse, is everywhere metaphorical, though the comparisons used to describe Richard, rather than branching in manifold directions, are notably inert. When he sees the king on the walls of Flint Castle, Bolingbroke comments that "Richard doth himself appear, / As doth the blushing discontented sun / From out the fiery portal of the east," while the Duke of York replies with a simple dismissal, "Yet looks he like a king," before attempting a simile of his own: "Behold, his eye, / As bright as is the eagle's, lightens forth / Controlling majesty" (3.3.62–64, 68–70). These comparisons, a microcosm of the temporal experience of the play, merely circle around the divinity of kingship, glancing sidelong at the stage spectacle that remains suspended in inaction for as long as it is described. *Richard II* dilates rather than multiplies time; where Marlowe's play manifests the ambient possibilities produced by mental wandering, Shakespeare's, at arguably greater formal risk, simply makes its spectators wait.

On the opening of *Richard II*, critics agree, as if with teeth set on edge, about two things: first, that nothing keeps happening; second, that Richard is the source of that inaction. Responsible for first delaying the conflict between Mowbray and Bolingbroke over the death of Gloucester and then aborting it entirely, Richard, Stephen Booth writes, is "gloriously, self-indulgently, volubly, extravagantly, ineffectual."[49] The king is "infuriating," according to Leonard Barkan, wielding an "almost flippant self-possession that suggests he is deaf and blind to the passions around him."[50] Describing the interrupted jousting match between Bolingbroke

and Mowbray, Phyllis Rackin knits together the two grievances: "the anti-
climactic effect is nicely calculated to make the audience resent Richard,
since it is he who deprives them of the spectacle they have been waiting
since the opening scene to see."[51] But if spectators arrive at the play wish-
ing for the action to rush headlong toward the excitement of spectacular
conflict, it is also true that *Richard II* makes them complicit in the phenomenological construction of the play's anticlimax. Take, for example,
another moment in which the play comes obtrusively to a halt. The visual
spectacle that defines the tension on the first scene – Bolingbroke's thrown
gage, taken up by Mowbray – is reanimated just before Richard's deposition, stalling the play's movement toward that climactic event: after
Aumerle, accused of involvement in Gloucester's death, challenges Bagot
by throwing down his gage, a total of seven more gages are thrown in the
course of forty lines. So many challenges are issued in this short space that
Aumerle is forced to borrow the last gage he throws. The experimental
oddness of this repetition invites comparisons to the materiality of more
recent media: akin to a broken record, the play briefly appears stuck, try-
ing and failing to jolt itself forward.[52] Shakespeare in part constructs this
spectacle from Raphael Holinshed's account of the noblemen who supported Fitzwater's challenge to Aumerle: "There were .xx. other Lordes
also that threw downe there hoodes, as pledges to proue ye like matter
against the duke of Aumerle."[53] To produce onstage the deluge of thrown
gages described by Holinshed, the scene invites spectators to buffet their
participatory engagement from attention to stage spectacle to imagined
recollection and back again; a pile of literal and virtual gages accumu-
lates in the process, an ontologically hybrid obstacle to the play's forward
momentum. The performance approaches stillness in its recollective circuit through the immediate and imagined.

This imaginative workout is merely preparation, however, for the temporal seizure that precedes Richard's deposition. The suspenseful wait for
succession takes shape as a visual paradox, rendering the very anticlimax
that plagues the first act into the theatrical high point of the play. "Here,
cousin, seize the crown. Here, cousin," Richard beckons Bolingbroke,
"On this side my hand, and on that side thine" (4.1.182–83). The static
image of two opposing hands grasping the "deep well" of the crown is
iconographic in its indeterminacy (4.1.184), refiguring the crown's circular
resonance with the endurance of monarchy into a symbol of uncertainty
itself.[54] If, as is likely, the lines served as embedded stage directions for
Richard Burbage and Augustine Phillips, who may have played Richard
and Bolingbroke, the tension of that ambiguity could have been prolonged

for nearly fifteen lines, through Richard's "two buckets" speech and his subsequent exchange with Bolingbroke.⁵⁵ The scene grinds narrative time to a halt at precisely the moment of monarchical transition, resulting in the spectacular explosion of impossible possibility: there are two kings of England at this moment and, simultaneously, none. The spectacular paradox transforms the charged wait for succession – what James Calderwood evocatively terms "unmoving movement or inactive action" – into the very object of spectators' anticipation.⁵⁶ Scholars have long understood the absence of this scene from the play's early quarto editions as evidence of its political subversiveness.⁵⁷ But depicting the transfer of the crown was not politically risky simply because it staged Richard's deposition, a historical fact with which many of the play's spectators would have been familiar before they ever walked into the playhouse. More crucial is the formal means by which that transfer takes place. In pausing the forward trajectory of its own action, the play makes time for spectators' speculative participation in the performance – exactly the theatrically minded mode of Gaveston's own thought process in *Edward II*. What if there *were* multiple kings of England? What if there were none? *Richard II* enables political thinking by encouraging the imaginative speculation that underwrites it.

In the midst of this uncertain pause, Bolingbroke attempts to prod time ahead with his question to Richard: "Are you contented to resign the crown?" (4.1.200). But Richard's chiastic response – "Ay, no. No, ay." (4.1.201) – continues to resist the play's forward momentum. His indecision catches spectators in the temporal sway of succession, as Richard unkings himself with his affirmation before changing his mind and kinging himself again. If the spectacle of Bolingbroke's and Richard's hands on the crown attempts to stop time, Richard's uncertainty yet more audaciously strives to reverse the play's forward progression, enacting succession and undoing it. "How long a time lies in one little word!" Bolingbroke exclaims after Richard banishes him (1.3.213). The little words that express Richard's mental wavering are experienced in the theater not merely as the dilation of time but its very vacillation. Spectators in the theater who were frustrated through the opening act by Richard's repeated interruption of the play's action, who were disgusted by his cold-hearted corruption, may have already felt their sympathies changing after witnessing the king's arrival back to English soil and his eloquent recognition of his own undoing. But any kinship spectators felt with Richard through his indecision – a wash of relief or a surge of excitement, even momentary, at seeing the king pull the crown back toward himself – was necessarily experienced as a wish for time itself to remain in suspension. *Richard II* succeeded as a

temporal experiment by shaping the wait for succession into riveting theater – by transforming dramatic suspense into the very object of spectators'
anticipation. The play managed the uncertainty of Elizabethans' unknown
future by involving spectators in the desire to hold that future, if only
temporarily, in continued abeyance.

Waiting for James

As they watched the events of Shakespeare's tragedy unfold in the theater, spectators would have inhabited the spectacular interim between
monarchs in *Richard II* only momentarily. But the play's depiction of
England's past at once unraveled a vision of what would be, acting as an
unwitting precis of the prolonged period that would separate Elizabeth's
departure out of London after her death on March 24, 1603, and James's
corresponding royal entry into the city nearly a year later. Plague, which
claimed the lives of a fifth of London's population that summer, was
responsible for the long wait for James, and accounts of the city during
this period emphasize its empty stillness. "In this pitiful or rather pitiless
perplexity stood London," Thomas Dekker writes in *The Wonderful Year*,
his prose pamphlet describing the effects of the disease, "forsaken like a
lover, forlorn like a widow and disarmed of all comfort."[58] "Where are
our solemne meetings, and frequent assemblies," William Muggins asked
that summer: "Men stand a farre off: the Streates and high wayes mourne:
trafficke ceaseth."[59] Writing to mark the occasion of James's royal entry
in *The Magnificent Entertainment* the next year, Dekker noted the joyful contrast of the streets, packed with spectators, that had been "emptie
and vntroden" during the summer of 1603.[60] "Powles grows very thin, for
every man shrinckes away and I am half ashamed to see myself left alone,"
John Chamberlain admitted in a letter to Dudley Carleton in July.[61] The
elaborately detailed arches for the royal entry, erected over the course of
six weeks in April and May, were not dismantled until the end of August,
standing that summer as a ghostly reminder of the consequential moment
that Londoners could not mark.[62] These accounts evoke London brought
to a standstill, the city's ritualized choreography of gathering and procession paused for a duration of uncertain length.[63] As Dekker describes this
suspension, "the tedious minutes of the night stretch out the sorrows of
ten thousand."[64] Absent the patterning that organizes its regular sequencing, time stalls in the loneliness of an interminably prolonged night.

The absence of such patterning also meant, of course, the cessation of
theatrical performance, though I want to argue that Dekker used his plague
pamphlets as a substitute for the stage, offering playgoers an alternative

form of entertaining waiting while they waited for the plague to end, for James to enter, and for the theaters to reopen. In *The Wonderful Year*, the uneasy suspension of the plague picks up where the uncertain stasis of the succession crisis left off, producing precisely the chaos that Elizabethans had feared would follow from the Queen's death. "Who did expect but ruin, blood, and death," Dekker asks,

> To share our Kingdom and divide our breath?
> Religions without religion
> To let each other blood; Confusion
> To be next Queen of *England*.[65]

He goes on to describe fears of a grimly carnivalesque world in which sons brutally kill their fathers and servants steal from their masters. Dekker largely keeps this nightmarish vision of an inverted social hierarchy confined to the conditional mode, for the proclamation of James as king "cur[es] ... that fever" of Elizabeth's death.[66] But the surprising arrival of the plague in the city – Dekker compares it to a Trojan horse – is the unwanted epilogue to the story that was supposed to conclude with James's accession, and it realizes deadly possibilities even worse than those anxiously imagined while Elizabeth still lived. Dekker treats the "ghastly visages" of plague victims as his muses, calling on them directly before turning to his description of the pestilence: "You desolate hand-wringing widows, that beat your bosoms over your departing husbands, you woefully distracted mothers that with dishevelled hair are fallen into swoons, whilst you lie kissing the insensible cold lips of your breathless infants, you outcast and down-trodden orphans, that shall many a yeare hence remember, more freshly to mourn."[67] This bleak accounting of "emptied families" lacks the fanciful quality of the social inversions imagined to follow Elizabeth's death; the plague layers an unthinkable reality on top of what Elizabethans had conditionally feared, materializing the horrifying chaos of possibility during the unexpected prolonging of suspended time.[68]

Dekker repeatedly relies on the theater to make sense of such unspeakable horror. Direct references to tragedy appear ten times in the text, while death is compared to a "stalking Tamburlaine," Elizabeth's funeral to a "dumb show," and sighs of lament to "a Chorus to the tragedy."[69] Tragedy's narrative insistence on its own violent end, as Michael Neill and others have argued, was a form of therapeutic ethics in the period, giving shape and structure to the blank meaninglessness of death itself.[70] Coming on the heels of James's accession, the plague itself should occupy the position of just such an ending – the final "tragical act," as Dekker puts it, of Elizabethan suspension in uncertainty over succession.[71] But its deaths simply refuse to cease: "before the jewel of the morning be fully set in silver, a hundred hungry graves stand gaping [...] Before dinner in the same gulf are twice so many more devoured. And before the sun takes his rest those numbers are doubled."[72] The plague does not respect tragedy's formal constraints, which construct the finality of death as an end to time itself – its last recorded syllable. But there was no putting a stop, either formally or practically, to the river of death that still raged as *The Wonderful Year* was published. Dekker's characterization of the plague as a tragedy begins with references to drama and gradually morphs into the newer, more abstract sense of the word to describe suffering and death on a large scale.[73] If playwrights pushed theatrical form to its limits in the attempt to capture the temporality of the succession crisis, Dekker depicts the failure of tragedy to mold the endlessness of the ongoing epidemic into meaningful shape.

The Wonderful Year eventually retreats into a form that more successfully accommodates the awful, unending arrest of the plague: the jest. The collection of "twice-told tales" that follows Dekker's grisly description of the epidemic actively resists any sense of forward momentum or narrative finality.[74] Dekker produces a sense of suspension evacuated of suspense, in other words, by relying on the endless circularity that he evokes elsewhere in *The Wonderful Year*. Elizabeth's life, he explains, was "dedicated to virginity, both beginning and closing up a miraculous maiden circle"; when he calls on plague victims for inspiration, he asks them to "join all your hands together and with your bodies cast a ring about me."[75] "Narrative's insistence upon ending," Neill writes, "answers the fear of mere shapeless chronicity by gratifying the desire for significant form."[76] But *The Wonderful Year* captures the plague's ongoing flow of death by turning to a narrative form that avoids its own end; jests simply pile up in *The Wonderful Year* like "a heap of carcases" until they are arbitrarily put to a stop: "I could fill a large volume and call it the Second Part of *The Hundred Merry Tales* only with such ridiculous stuff as this," Dekker assures the reader after the final story.[77] When time is held in suspension, *The Wonderful Year* recognizes, there is no end, even to death itself.

The severity of the 1603 plague bore out Dekker's suppositions: outbreaks would continue intermittently through 1610, though they eventually slowed enough to allow festive gathering by early 1604. On March 15, four days before the opening of Parliament and three weeks before the opening of the playhouses, James finally made his royal entry into the city.[78] To mark out the new king's procession, the triumphal arches that had been constructed and torn down the year before were rebuilt along the route that began at the Tower and ended at Temple Bar. These temporary structures were the defining feature of James's royal entry, though their formal contribution to the procession has been given less attention than the theatricality of the pageants, composed by Thomas Dekker and Ben Jonson, that were staged on them.[79] Acting as an emblematic tether of London's ancient Roman origins and England's burgeoning imperialist designs, the arches enabled James's sequential path through the city; in so doing, they materialized the passage of time that had for so long been held at a standstill. If presuccession plays captured temporal stasis by interrupting the forward momentum of theatrical action, the arches stood as monuments to the flow of time itself.[80]

The elaborate structures had roots in the pageant stages that had long dotted the routes of civic processions in London (Figure 2.4). Through architect Stephen Harrison's vision – Dekker refers to him as the "Sole Inuentor of the Architecture" – those platforms were transformed into passageways.[81] William MacDonald explains that the freestanding arch "fuse[s] localities while suggesting division," both "invit[ing] passage and suggest[ing] the presence beyond of a place different from that before it, of an experience in contrast to that of the present, near side."[82] The arches produced and reproduced succession: over the course of nearly six hours, James passed through seven arches, emerging on the other side, again and again, not only to a new place but a new moment in dynastic time. In *The Wonderful Year*, Dekker marvels at the sudden license that Elizabeth's death granted to the distinction of one moment from another: "Upon Thursday it was treason to cry 'God save King James, King of England!' and upon Friday high treason not to cry so. In the morning no voice heard but murmurs and lamentation; at noon nothing but shouts of gladness and triumph."[83] The arches materially enabled precisely this crucial distinction. "Arches are architectural forms that grant permission to proceed along a particular line," MacDonald writes; those along the royal entry route legitimized James's kingship by tracing out the singularly sanctioned passage of time.[84] While it is unlikely that most spectators followed James's passage through each or even many of these arches, the collective effect of this insistence on temporal passage can grasped in *The Magnificent Entertainment*, Dekker's account of the civic procession. Dekker attempts to control readers' movement through the text, rushing them along so that James himself may continue moving. "Wee haue held his Maiestie too long from entring this third Gate of his *Court Royall*," he chastises: "It is now hie time, that those eyes, which on the other side ake with rolling

Figure 2.4   Stephen Harrison, *The Arch's of Triumph Erected in Honor of the High and Mighty Prince. Iames* (London: Stephen Harrison, 1604), C2r. Call #: STC 12863a.

vp and downe for his gladsome presence, should inioy that happinesse. Beholde, hee is in an instance passed thorough."[85] Dekker posits a set of viewers eagerly awaiting James's appearance from within the text, giving readers an indirect vantage on the king from the other side of the arch. *The Magnificent Entertainment* envisions James's passage through the arch from both sides at once, as if offering fulsome satisfaction to readers who, having been suspended for so long in the uncertainty of the succession crisis, cannot get enough of witnessing time spurred into motion once again.

Waiting on Macbeth

When the King's Men debuted *Macbeth* in 1606, England's political future at last appeared secure: the country finally had both a successor to Elizabeth and, in Prince Henry, a beloved heir. It has long been recognized that *Macbeth* was a thoroughly Jacobean play because it dramatized James's own obsessive preoccupations; I want to suggest, however, that it also cultivated a Jacobean theatrical experience by formally accommodating playgoers who could finally see down the line of succession.[86] Rather than requiring its spectators to dwell in the charged uncertainty of the present, *Macbeth* allowed them, as Dekker might have put it, to behold the future in an instance. *Macbeth* (and Macbeth) proceeds with striking celerity; unlike *Edward II* and *Richard II*, Shakespeare's postsuccession succession play involves spectators in its own swiftness by making future imagining not an impediment or alternative to the action unfolding onstage, but a necessary condition of the flow of performance itself. The theatrical present that *Macbeth* encouraged its spectators to imagine into being was one in which the future's certainty had already arrived.

Macbeth's opening storm is a spectacle of imminence, semiotically responsible both for infusing the first scene with a sense of place and, as was conventional in the commercial theater, announcing the impending arrival of supernatural beings – in this case, of course, the Witches.[87] The anonymous *Locrine* (1595), another play that begins with a storm, makes this twinned process explicit. At the signal of "thunder and lightning," the monster Ate enters; a dumb show featuring a lion and a hunter moves across the stage before she speaks her first lines:

> A Mightie Lion ruler of the woods,
> Of wondrous strength and great proportion,
> With hideous noyse scarring the trembling trees,
> With yelling clamors shaking all the earth,
> Trauerst the groues, and chast the wandring beasts.
> Long did he raunge amid the shadie trees,
> And draue the silly beasts before his face,
> When suddeinly from out a thornie bush,
> A dreadfull Archer with his bow ybent,
> Wounded the Lion with a dismall shaft,
> So he him stroke that it drew forth the blood,
> And fild his furious heart with fretting yre.[88]

This recapitulation of the dumb show fills the fictional world with locational detail – "woods," "trembling trees," "groues," "shadie trees," "thornie bush" – while the storm itself becomes an atmospheric expression of the lion's "hideous noyse" and "yelling clamors shaking all the earth." The Witches' opening exchange in *Macbeth* would seem similarly to reinforce the aural and visual generation of onstage place. "When shall we three meet again? / In thunder, lightning, or in rain?" one asks, before demanding more locational detail: "Where the place?" "Upon the heath," another responds (1.1.1, 6).⁸⁹ Yet unlike Ate's verbal conjuration of trees and bushes, the Witches discuss not where they are, but where they are going. The stormy opening marshals the immediacy of theatrical performance toward a clear-eyed vision of the future; even before the first appearance of the eponymous character who will attempt to "o'er-leap" time (1.4.49), *Macbeth* is already ahead of itself.⁹⁰

The brief first scene closes with the Witches' ambiguous intonation of their exit: "Fair is foul, and foul is fair, / Hover through the fog and filthy air" (1.1.9–10). If "hover," as seems most likely, is meant to be taken as an imperative, then the Witches command their own locomotion, but the word itself, which suggests stasis or suspension, is an odd expression of departure. Equally strange is the preposition accompanying the verb: In the sixteenth- and seventeenth-century examples of the verb's usage in the Oxford English Dictionary, nouns hover in, above, with, and over – all implying unmoving movement – but not through.⁹¹ Shakespeare likely spotted the unusual pairing of verb and preposition in a particularly moody passage of Book 6 of *The Faerie Queene*, in which readers are told that "darkenesse dred and daily night did houer / Through all the inner parts" of the "hollow caues" where the Brigants take Pastorella, in which "continuall candlelight" creates "A doubtfull sense of things, not so well seene, as felt" (6.10.42).⁹² In Spenser's account, it is darkness itself that does the hovering; the atmosphere, swathing everything in uncertainty, is everywhere at once. But Shakespeare produces a "doubtfull sense of things" in the theater by making the Witches hoverers, rather than the fog and filthy air, suggesting that the mysterious, possibly supernatural creatures have already arrived at the place to which they are traveling. In imaginatively conjuring the fictional present of the play's opening scene from the verbal detail given to them, spectators are at once made to "feel now / The future in the instant" (1.5.57–58).

In getting ahead of itself, the play simultaneously keeps spectators one step ahead of Macbeth, for they learn that he has been named Thane of Cawdor before he does. Much of Act 1, scene 2 is, from a strictly expositional standpoint, unnecessary: there is no dramatic reason why spectators should not learn that Macbeth has been granted the new title at the same moment he does, in the very next scene. But staging Duncan's transfer of the title in 1.2 does mean that when spectators arrive on the heath at the opening of 1.3 and hear the Witches' prophecy, they already know that the first part of it not only "stands ... within the prospect of belief" (1.3.74), but that it is true. This dramatic irony functions temporally; spectators are placed in an interpretive position superior to Macbeth and Banquo because they have already been granted the ability to "look into the seeds of time" (1.3.58). Put another way, the play makes spectators into phenomenological "harbinger[s]" (1.4.45), those officers who set off ahead of the monarch in the midst of travel in order to prepare the royal household. This is, of course, the designation Macbeth gives himself when he learns that Duncan intends to visit the Macbeth's castle in Inverness, but spectators beat Macbeth there, too, arriving as Lady Macbeth reads her husband's letter aloud. It is spectators' proleptic relationship to the unfolding stage action that makes the Witches' prophecy theatrically manifest.

In the early scenes of the play, then, spectators experience the onstage world by waiting for Macbeth. Waiting *on* him, however, might be the better description, since Macbeth arrives to a world in the opening act that spectators have imaginatively readied for his first appearance. To be a spectator of *Macbeth*, and in the early modern theater more broadly, required an interpretive readiness not only to respond to the fictional world onstage, but, as Macbeth says of time itself, to "anticipat[e]" that world's "dread exploits" (4.1.143) – to make them possible by giving them imaginative structure and form. When Lady Macbeth hears of the Witches' prophecy, she commands "spirits / That tend on moral thoughts" to fill her "from the crown to the toe, top-full / Of direst cruelty" (1.5.40–43). The play's host makes herself into a receptacle of cruelty, both receiving and shaping the distillation of Macbeth's ambition in a bid to assist his seizure of Duncan's throne. Yet the spirit of collaboration that Lady Macbeth evokes in her incantation, which transports her "beyond / The ignorant present" (1.5.56–57), is simultaneously an account of the imaginative and interpretive labor of spectatorship, for it is playgoers who anticipate the vision of the future that is always in the process of coming into being on the stage. *Macbeth* recognizes that the spectatorial capacity for reception necessarily places playgoers ahead of the theatrical present; to interpret staged presentation necessitates their interpretive running ahead.

Think, for example, of Macbeth's dagger. This time, it is Macbeth himself who asks after the reality of his immediate surroundings: "Is this a dagger which I see before me, / The handle toward my hand?" (2.1.33–34). Like the spectacle of Richard and Bolingbroke's hands on the crown, this moment resists the onrush of performance through the temporal drag of suspense. Unlike the earlier play, however, it is a *character's* uncertainty, rather than spectators', that is responsible for the phenomenological slack. But Macbeth's doubt facilitates spectators' interpretive and imaginative engagement with the stage spectacle. He would seem to ask

himself for confirmation of the dagger's reality if not for his next move:
"Come, let me clutch thee" (2.1.34). The attempt to grasp the dagger
necessitates that the actor extend his hand forward, toward the audience;
the gesture reaches after communication along with the weapon.[93] The
embedded stage direction in the soliloquy suggests that when Richard
Burbage kinesthetically interpreted these lines in 1606, he accompanied
a reach for the dagger with bent fingers grasping at the air. The effect – a
hand surrounding a void where a dagger should be – creates, as Andrew
Sofer suggests, an impression of the object as "charged *negative space*."[94]
The emptiness of the gesture invites spectators' imaginative engagement
to outline the missing weapon. The theatrical effect of Macbeth's uncertainty is deictic – "Is *this* a dagger?" functions in the same way that "*this*
is the Forest of Arden" does (2.4.13, emphasis mine) – but it is Macbeth's
own uncertainty that makes spectators' proleptic participation in the
process of performance explicit; they conjure the dagger in answer to
his question.[95] The moment also makes clear that if narrative suspense
works by isolating the instant of time that spectators inhabit from those
adjacent to it, the phenomenological experience of those instants in turbulent succession can crucially vary. Rather than being thrust toward the
new moment in narrative time, as when the crown finally comes to rest
in Bolingbroke's "unlineal hand" (3.1.62), spectators bridge the temporal
divide of *Macbeth*'s suspense by imaginatively pulling the would-be murderer toward themselves.

   Macbeth's account of criminality traces the transformation of thoughts
into things, "horrible imaginings" into the "sorry sight" of a corpse (1.3.140,
2.2.20). Yet in this the play and its criminal are aligned with the process of
performance, for giving local habitations to airy nothings was precisely the
business of the early modern theater.[96] Spectators' anticipatory contribution to the materials of staged representation in this theater might, then,
be better described as accommodation.[97] Julia Reinhard Lupton has compellingly shown that *Macbeth* dramatizes a phenomenology of hospitality;
I mean to suggest that the theatrical component of that phenomenology is
the imaginative work of spectatorship itself.[98] In giving shape to a future
that existed, at the moment of the dagger speech, merely in the realm
of Macbeth's mind, spectators in the Globe "marshall'st [him] the way
that [he] was going" and handed him the weapon for which he clutched
(2.1.42). Waiting on Macbeth exposes the phenomenology of hospitality
as nothing other than imaginative complicity.

   No one more generously accommodates Macbeth's vision of Banquo's
ghost, after all, than the play's spectators. ("[T]he ghoste of Banco came

and sate down in his [Macbeth's] cheier be hind him," Simon Forman dutifully noted when he saw the play in 1610.)[99] The scene staging the spectral visitation is crowded with characters – "MACBETH, LADY, ROSS, LENNOX, Lords *and Attendants*" – to whom Macbeth makes a show of inviting to the table: "You know your own degrees, sit down" (3.4.1). At the risk of stating the blatantly obvious: the scene necessitates several chairs. The banquet is crowded not just with actors but with stage furniture that, in materializing accommodation itself, creates ghost-like impressions of the bodies that will soon occupy them.[100] The most local of habitations, the chair is a prop ahead of itself: in a scene that dwells on Banquo's absence from the banquet, the excessive materiality of the multiple chairs onstage emits a surrounding aura of negative space not unlike Macbeth's hand grasping for the dagger, magnified to the scale of the crime Macbeth has now committed. "The table's full" (3.4.43), Macbeth protests, not yet recognizing Banquo, when he is urged to sit down. The ghost makes a nightmarish spectacle of theatrical spectatorship; in this scene, playgoers' prescient work of filling in the void bodies forth an actual spirit.

The arrival of Banquo's ghost is the first signal that spectators' proleptic relation to the present tense of performance is a position of certainty, though not necessarily a comfortable one. But it is not until the Witches' show of kings – the monarchical line that would culminate in James himself – that *Macbeth* unequivocally stages the spectatorial consequences of occupying the knowing side of dramatic suspense: phenomenological passivity. The moving stillness of all eight kings standing together onstage – what Macbeth calls a "horrible sight," evoking the early sense of "horror" as the suspended motion of shuddering, shivering, or rippling (4.1.121) – upends earlier spectacles of present stasis toward the capture of a single future instant in time.[101] The display evokes the certain legitimacy of James's eventual rule with such a degree of totality that the decorous removal of Mary, Queen of Scots from the lineup goes easily unnoticed.[102] Nor does a representation of James appear on the stage, though rather than simply inviting spectators to infer his presence imaginatively, a material technology (likely a magic glass) is supplied to conjure him.[103] Macbeth's own response to the vision yet further diminishes spectators' involvement in performance:

> From this moment
> The very firstlings of my heart shall be
> The firstlings of my hand. And even now,
> To crown my thoughts with acts, be it thought and done. (4.1.145-48)

In the rush toward his own destruction, Macbeth promises an instantaneous progression from thought to action, effectively eliminating the doubtful suspension in which spectators may be imaginatively involved. If the opening of *Macbeth* constructs a phenomenology of prophecy, placing spectators ahead of the theatrical present that they work dynamically to bring into being, the action immediately following the Witches' vision counteractively enacts the experience of lagging behind – a habitation in the present that, in relation to the apocalyptic inevitability of total certainty, has already become the past. Marjorie Garber has argued compellingly that early modern spectators' proleptic relation to the events staged in the English history play made them "in effect Cassandras," ever aware of the play's future because it belonged to their past and present.[104] Written after the history play had begun to decline in popularity in the commercial theater, *Macbeth* does not simply dramatize the horrors of knowledge for Macbeth alone, but acts as a meditation on the theatrical consequences of dramatic narrative that, in remaining tethered to history, adheres to "the inexorable teleology of ... prophecy."[105] The simple act of beholding is the culmination of spectators' knowing relation to the unfolding stage action for much of the play. It is also their relegation to the sidelines of performance itself.

In producing spectators' theatrical certainty as their phenomenological impotence, the scene creates the conditions for an endorsement of the opposite experience: a return to the dramatic suspense and epistemological opacity of ends that remain unrevealed. That wish, if implicitly evoked in *Macbeth*, is stated plainly in Shakespeare and Fletcher's *Henry VIII*, another history play that concludes with a prophetic revelation of an anterior future: the birth of Elizabeth I. Displayed onstage for her christening, the infant holds the promise of the age through which spectators in the Globe had already lived:

> She shall be loved and feared. Her own shall bless her;
> Her foes shake like a field of beaten corn,
> And hang their heads with sorrow. Good grows with her.
> [...]
> Nor shall this peace sleep with her, but as when
> The bird of wonder dies, the maiden phoenix,
> Her ashes new create another heir
> As great in admiration as herself,
> So shall she leave her blessedness to one,
> When heaven shall call her from this cloud of darkness,
> Who from the sacred ashes of her honour
> Shall star-like rise as great in fame as she was.   (5.4.30–32, 39–46)[106]

Like the vision of Scotland's kings, this speech confirms what Jacobeans already knew. Still, though, mystery remains. The crisis of uncertainty that the question of Elizabethan succession produced is transformed in this description into a spectacle of "wonder," the suspense about the outcome condensed to the appositive phrase that separates James's emergence, against all reason, from the ashes of "the maiden phoenix" Elizabeth. "Wonder occurs," Philip Fisher writes, "at the horizon line of what is potentially knowable, but not yet known."[107] In reinscribing Elizabethan succession as a quasi-divine mystery of resurrection – an attractive enigma that conveniently obscures the widespread anxiety that marked the end of the Elizabethan era – *Henry VIII* draws spectators back from their knowing Jacobean vantage to the horizon line of wonder. The speech is an activation of nostalgia for the lost Golden Era of Elizabeth, though it is equally an advertisement for the spectacular force of theater, which reconfigured the anxious suspension of uncertainty into the pleasures of dramatic suspense. By contrast, *Macbeth*'s show of kings is a warning about the stultifying result when, in the rush toward the clarity of the future, all suspense is left behind.

Historical Contingency and Counterfactual Thought: Perkin Warbeck

Up to now, I have suggested that the conditional mode of the history play in performance oriented the past toward playgoers' own futures, offering license in speculation and practice in charting possible paths through the opaque unknown. These modes of thought would remain relevant as the Jacobean era reliably offered up its own surprises. As if in confirmation of *Henry VIII*'s alternate title – *All is True* – the Globe burned to the ground during a performance of the play in 1613, prompting Ben Jonson to express his own astonishment at the speed with which the playhouse disappeared: "Ere thought could urge, 'This might have been!' (136)."[108] The Globe's destruction occurred just a few months after the shocking death of Prince Henry, which left the sickly Prince Charles in place of the beloved heir. The need for ways of transforming the uncertainty of the future into present entertainment remained even after Elizabethan succession, I would suggest, though what I have so far offered is a necessarily incomplete formal and phenomenological account about the sort of thinking that history plays made *possible*, not a historical account of the effect that they *had*. In the absence of detailed accounts from playgoers of the period, we simply cannot know the ways and extent to which spectators responded to playwrights' experiments with dramatic suspense, though at a fundamental level the success of the commercial theater suggests that many must have enjoyed them. But one superlative instance of proof that the plays engaged their spectators in conditional modes thought, and that such thinking had material effect, is worth pausing over. Ambitious and well-connected, John Ford was not only a playwright but an avid consumer of drama. When he arrived in London as a student at the Middle Temple in 1602, he would have been able to attend plays with the other Inns of Court students to whom the nearby Blackfriars catered, ushering him into a community of theatergoers who not only went to see plays regularly, but who came to understand their own critical responses to commercial drama as culturally valuable.[109] Ford's theatrical fluency is everywhere evident in his own plays, which are stuffed with references and allusions to older drama.[110] But it is *Perkin Warbeck*, Ford's paean to the history plays of the 1590s, that is the clearest creative evidence of his engagement with the kinds of speculative thinking that those plays made possible.

Ford's play stages the imposture of the historical Perkin Warbeck, a pretender to the English throne who claimed to be Richard, Duke of York, one of Edward IV's two sons whom their uncle Richard, Duke of Gloucester, likely had imprisoned in the Tower and killed in 1483. The play brought a new facet of the Wars of the Roses to the theater after several decades during which new composition of history plays had almost entirely ceased, focusing on the contested reign of Henry VII and the marriages, Henry to Elizabeth of York and James I to Margaret Tudor, that would link the royal houses of Scotland and England and pave the way for the Stuart line. Warbeck's claim that he was the rightful heir of Edward IV, which Ford gleaned from recently published accounts written by Thomas Gainsford and Francis Bacon, would have placed him neatly between Henry VI and Richard III, the two kings whose reigns make up Shakespeare's first tetralogy. The play is thus as much a deliberate reimagining of the history play as the revival of the "out of fashion" genre it somewhat apologetically announces itself to be (Prologue.2).[111] Indeed, as Marissa Nicosia has convincingly demonstrated, the entirety of *Perkin Warbeck* is a thought experiment in the conditional vein: "what if," she describes the play to ask, "the princes in the tower had lived?"[112] Not only does Ford make a pretender to the throne rather than a monarch his titular character (one who resembles, as has often been noted, Shakespeare's Richard II); he also transforms the speculative mode that frustrates presuccession history plays' forward momentum into the essential impetus of dramatic action. No longer a mere distraction or fleeting fantasy, in *Perkin Warbeck* the attempt to graft a wayward branch onto the tree of English succession becomes the main object of spectators' theatrical attention.

Yet in the process of theatrically engaging spectators' speculation, Ford's play just as insistently models the calibration of expectation.[113] Only the English King Henry has perfect foreknowledge, achieving the union of thought and action for which Macbeth strives: "Wise Henry / Divines aforehand of events; with him / Attempts and execution are one act" (4.4.66–68). Characters without the divine anointment of kingship's knowing perspective are instead forced to hone their hopes for the future, and they constantly encourage one another to raise or lower their expectations. The Earl of Huntley, father of the Scottish princess Katherine Gordon, encourages his daughter to reject the wealthy Daliell's proposal because he believes she can set her sets higher, possibly even with the aim of becoming the Scottish King James's heir. "My Lord of Daliell, young in years" he cautions her,

> is old
> In honours, but nor emiment in titles
> Or in estate that may support or add to
> The expectation of thy fortunes.   (1.2.115–18)

When James gives Katherine to Perkin as a wife, Daliell complains that his "hopes are in their ruins" (2.3.102). Perkin's supporters, reflecting on his bid for James's support, differ in their assessment: "Here's entrance / Into a certainty above a hope," Frion confidently asserts, to which Heron dismissively replies that "hopes are but hopes" (2.3.107–09). Perkin himself, confident to the end, cannot be convinced to temper his own expectations, though his fellow counterfeiter Lambert Simnel pleads with him to "confess, and hope for pardon!" (5.3.51). This language of expectation permeates the playtext: variations on "hope" appear thirty-three times, "fortune" thirty, "wish" thirteen, "expect" twelve, "doubt" eleven. The characters of *Perkin Warbeck* live in the world of speculative thinking into which Ford theatrically inculcates his own spectators.

And despite the historical distance separating Henrician and Caroline England, the play's characters and spectators collectively occupy the point at which these worlds overlap, for it is in theater, above all, that Ford depicts as the site in which expectations may be voiced, considered, and tested. After Perkin arrives at James's court, a masque is put on in his honor. Ford stages the observations of the women who await Perkins' arrival as eagerly as they do the inset performance:

> Come ladies, here's a solemn preparation
> For entertainment of this English prince.
> The king intends grace more than ordinary;
> 'Twere pity now if 'a should prove a counterfeit.   (2.1.1–4)

In qualifying her own expectations of the supposed English prince, the countess imbricates the impending stage show with Perkin's own trial as royalty. But what is striking about the expression of her hope is the wish that Perkin's performance will be *good*. The indisputable proof of Perkin's imposture will be less entertaining, she implicitly suggests, than the necessarily ambiguous display of kingship's convincing performance.[114] The women who await Perkin's arrival wish to be held in suspense, hoping that the uncertainty of his legitimacy will be kept alive.

For Caroline playgoers, the link posited in these lines between uncertainty and entertainment was confirmed by their own presence in the Cockpit Theater. The commercial theater made the consideration of possibility into a pleasure worth paying for; it gave uncertainty a satisfyingly speculative outlet. At the height of the Elizabethan succession crisis, the theater did not offer a refuge from the circulation of doubt about the Queen's successor; rather, history plays gave spectators myriad ways of imagining possible futures at a moment when England's dynastic present remained at a standstill. The plays encouraged speculative thinking at odds with the relentless forward momentum of performance by redirecting spectators' imaginative energies from what *was* happening on the stage to what *could*. But not all plays so accommodatingly engaged playgoers' participatory involvement in performance. The ambiguity of spectacular display frustrated playgoers' attempts to participate in the imaginative realization of as often as it encouraged them, and I will turn to that frustration in the next chapter.

Notes

1 On the ways that this image captures the surprising twists and turns of *A King and No King*'s plot, see Claire M. L. Bourne, "'High Designe': Beaumont and Fletcher Illustrated," *ELR* 44.2 (2014): 275–327. On the title page's evocation of emblematic imagery, see Zachary Lesser, *Renaissance Drama and the Politics of Publication: Readings in the English Book Trade* (Cambridge: Cambridge University Press, 2004), 157–225.

2 John Bulwer, *Chirologia, or, The Naturall Language of the Hand Composed of the Speaking Motions, and Discoursing Gestures Thereof* (London: R. Whitaker, 1644), 1. Bulwer links the rhetorical effects of gesture to the theater, noting

that embodied communication is an art "inlarged by Actors, the ingenious counterfeiters of mens manners." *Chirologia*, 24.

3 Bulwer, *Chirologia*, 30.

4 Bulwer, *Chirologia*, 55.

5 Phillip Stubbes, *The Anatomie of Abuses* (London: Richard Jones, 1583), L.v.v.

6 Brian Walsh, *Shakespeare, the Queen's Men, and the Elizabethan Performance of History* (Cambridge: Cambridge University Press, 2009), 68. See also Phyllis Rackin, *Stages of History: Shakespeare's English Chronicles* (Ithaca: Cornell University Press, 1990); and Marjorie Garber, "'What's Past Is Prologue': Temporality and Prophecy in Shakespeare's History Plays," in *Renaissance Genres: Essays on Theory, History, and Interpretation*, ed. Barbara Kiefer Lewalski (Cambridge, MA: Harvard University Press, 1986), 301–31.

7 David Scott Kastan, *Shakespeare and the Shapes of Time* (Hanover, NH: University Press of New England, 1982).

8 Paul Yachnin and Myrna Wyatt Selkirk, "Metatheater and the Performance of Character," in *Shakespeare and Character: Theory, History, Performance, and Theatrical Persons*, ed. Paul Yachnin and Jessica Slights (New York: Palgrave Macmillan, 2009), 139–57, esp. 141.

9 In this regard, I share Kastan's sense that "more obviously than any other literary form, the drama, as it unfolds in time, provides an analogy to and an experience of the flow of history," though in this chapter I am interested in what stopping the temporal unfolding of drama does to the phenomenological experience of the flow of history. See Kastan, *Shakespeare and the Shapes of Time*, 3–4.

10 George Puttenham, *The Arte of English Poesie* (London: Richard Field, 1589), 32; Aristotle, *Poetics*, trans. James Hutton (New York: W. W. Norton and Company, 1982), 50. This is not to claim that there was a unified sense of what history was or was meant to accomplish in the late sixteenth century, but merely to suggest that at a very basic level both history and drama took the representation of action as their objects. For an overview of changing conceptions of the nature of history and its purposes in the period, see Rackin, *Stages of History*, 1–39.

11 On the clashes between theatrical and historical time in the period, see Walsh, *The Elizabethan Performance of History*, 49–53. On the early modern English theater's preoccupation with its own disappearance, see Ellen MacKay, *Persecution, Plague, and Fire: Fugitive Histories of the Stage in Early Modern England* (Chicago: University of Chicago Press, 2011).

12 Paul Ricoeur, "Narrative Time," *Critical Inquiry* 7.1 (1980): 169–90, esp. 170; act, scene, and line numbers follow William Shakespeare, *The Winter's Tale*, ed. John Pitcher (London: Arden Shakespeare, 2010).

13 Philip Sidney, *The Defence of Poesy* (London: William Ponsonby, 1595), H4v.

14 Bernard Beckerman, *Dynamics of Drama: Theory and Method of Analysis* (New York: Drama Book Specialists, 1979), 6.

15 The tumultuousness of stage action was often associated with the rough-and-tumble Red Bull, where by the Jacobean period, the perceived vulgarity of stage battles and loud sound effects were the norm. In the prologue to

Two Merry Milkmaids, the Red Bull's spectators are warned not to expect the frenzy of action conventional to the playhouse: "This Day we entreat All that are hither come, / To expect no noyse of Guns, Trumpets, nor Drum, / Nor Sword and Targuet; but to heare Sence and Words, / Fitting the Matter that the Scene affords. / So that the Stage being reform'd, and free / From the lowd Clamors it was wont to bee, / Turmoyl'd with Battailes; you I hope will cease / Your dayly Tumults, and with vs wish Peace." See *A Pleasant Comedie, Called the Tvvo Merry Milke-maids* (London: Lawrence Chapman, 1620), A2v.

16 Act, scene, and line numbers follow William Shakespeare, *King Henry V*, ed. T. W. Craik (London: Arden Shakespeare, 1995).

17 In her account of the intertwined histories of theater and print, Julie Stone Peters shows how print images of performance simultaneously displayed distinct dramatic events – and, therefore, moments of theatrical time – offering "a model for an alternative theatricality, stopped in the instant." I point in this chapter to moments when the commercial theater's own practice of experimental innovation led it, albeit imperfectly, toward just such a model. Peters, *Theatre of the Book 1480–1880: Print, Text, and Performance in Europe* (Oxford: Oxford University Press, 2000), 199.

18 Quoted in Arnold Hunt, "The Succession in Sermons, News, and Rumour," in *Doubtful and Dangerous: The Question of Succession in Late Elizabethan England*, ed. Susan Doran and Paulina Kewes (Manchester: Manchester University Press, 2014), 155–72, esp. 166. Hunt's excellent essay has informed much of my thinking about the widespread social and psychological effects of the succession crisis.

19 Alexander Nowell, "Mr. Noel's Sermon at the Parliament Before the Queen's Majestie," in *A Catechism Written in Latin by Alexander Nowell*, ed. G. E. Corrie (Cambridge: Cambridge University Press, 1853), 223–9, esp. 228.

20 As Susan Doran and Paulina Kewes explain, the question of Elizabeth's successor was not resolved after the execution of Mary Stuart, nor was James VI of Scotland's claim to the throne universally seen as inevitable. See Doran and Kewes, "Introduction: A Historiographical Perspective," in *Doubtful and Dangerous*, 3–19.

21 In 1593, Jesuit Robert Parsons captured this feeling of the crisis as a temporal dilation when he commented that the "obscure and doubtfull" succession gave competitors for the throne "tyme euery man to prepare his frendes & worke his cause vnderhand." Parsons, *Nevves from Spayne and Holland* (Antwerp: A. Conincx, 1593), 40.

22 Nowell, "Mr. Noel's Sermon," 228.

23 John Harington, *A Briefe View of the State of the Church of England as it Stood in Q. Elizabeths and King James his Reigne* (London: Joseph Kirton, 1653), 188.

24 Danby Pickering, *The Statutes at Large*, vol. 6 (London: Charles Bathurst, 1763), 257; Leonard Tennenhouse, *Power on Display: The Politics of Shakespeare's Major Genres* (London: Methuen, 1986), 86.

25 Marissa Nicosia, "'To Plant Me in Mine Own Inheritance': Prolepsis and Pretenders in John Ford's *Perkin Warbeck*," *Studies in Philology* 115.3 (2018): 580–97, esp. 581.

26 As Burke explains it, "If, in a work of art, the poet says something, let us say, about a meeting, writes in such a way that we desire to observe that meeting, and then, if he places that meeting before us – that is form." See Burke, *Counter-Statement* (Berkeley: University of California Press, 1931), 31. The idea that form can be reduced to the satisfaction of expectation suggests, as Colleen Rosenfeld explains, that form itself is a "centripetal, consolidating force," a "logic that underwrites [poetic] figuration and determines its semantic range." My own argument proceeds from the premise that the very instability of early modern theatrical form – a centrifugal rather than centripetal force – produced the capaciousness of conditional imagining in which history plays engaged their spectators. See Colleen Ruth Rosenfeld, "The Queen's Conceit in Shakespeare's *Richard II*," *SEL* 60.1 (2020): 25–46, esp. 27.

27 Thomas Wilson, *The State of England Anno Dom. 1600*, ed. F. J. Fisher, in *The Camden Miscellany*, vol. 16 (London: The Camden Society, 1936), 2.

28 Act, scene, and line numbers follow Christopher Marlowe, *Edward II*, ed. Martin Wiggins and Robert Lindsey (London: Methuen Drama, 2005).

29 In her reading of *Titus Andronicus*, J. K. Barret argues that the play critiques the *Ovide moralisé* tradition by showing how "Ovid's narrative attention to sequence ... curb[s] the potential for new narrative." If, as Barret rightly suggests, the *Metamorphoses* "pretends that we live in a world of endings, where natural objects mark the *result* of a story," Gaveston keeps alive the possibility for new narrative by simply cutting Ovid's conclusion from his appropriation of Hero and Leander's story. See Barret, *Untold Futures: Time and Literary Culture in Renaissance England* (Ithaca: Cornell University Press, 2016), 127.

30 Bert O. States, *The Shape of Paradox: An Essay on "Waiting for Godot"* (Berkeley: University of California Press, 1978), 30.

31 Jonathan Gil Harris, *Untimely Matter in the Time of Shakespeare* (Philadelphia: University of Pennsylvania Press, 2009), *passim*.

32 On the sugary rhetoric of *Edward II*, see Jeffrey Masten, *Queer Philologies: Sex, Language, and Affect in Shakespeare's Time* (Philadelphia: University of Pennsylvania Press, 2016), 172–73. On the gradation of endorsed male–male friendship into illicit male–male desire, see Alan Bray, "Homosexuality and the Signs of Male Friendship in Elizabethan England," *History Workshop* 29.1 (1999): 1–19.

33 Stephen Gosson, *Playes Confuted in Fiue Actions* (London: Thomas Gosson, 1582), D8v.

34 Gosson, *Playes Confuted*, E1v, G2r.

35 In a practical as well as experiential sense, it would have been difficult, as Tiffany Stern has shown, to keep track of time in the playhouse. Spectators would have been able to hear the chiming of London's clocks, but playhouses likely did not have any sort of clock on display, and personal timekeeping devices such as watches and sundials were notoriously unreliable. See Stern,

"Time for Shakespeare: Hourglasses, Sundials, Clocks, and Early Modern Theatre," *British Academy Lectures 2014–15*, ed. Janet Carsten and Simon Frith (Oxford: Oxford University Press, 2016), 1–34.

36 Lee Edelman, *No Future: Queer Theory and the Death Drive* (Durham: Duke University Press, 2004).

37 Henry Peacham, *Minerua Britanna* (London: Wa: Dight, 1612), 13 (emphasis mine). See Laurie Shannon, *Sovereign Amity: Figures of Friendship in Shakespearean Contexts* (Chicago: University of Chicago Press, 2002), 156–84.

38 Wilson, *The State of England*, 2.

39 *A Conference about the Next Succession to the Crowne of Ingland* (Antwerp: A. Conincx, 1595), 10–11, 268. Despite its emphasis on the doubtfulness of Elizabeth's successor, the text was widely understood to endorse the Infanta Isabella of Spain. Thomas Wilson acknowledged in 1600 that "there is a father fryar called Robt. Parsons, in Spayne, who hath lately made a booke whereby, they say, he proves her [the Infanta] to be the next undoubted heyre to the King of England." Wilson, *The State of England*, 5. For more on the genealogical argument in support of the Infanta, see Catherine Grace Canino, *Shakespeare and the Nobility: The Negotiation of Lineage* (Cambridge: Cambridge University Press, 2007), 6.

40 Masten, *Queer Philologies*, 172–73. See also Marie Rutkoski's suggestion that "the imprisoned king finds, instead of another Gaveston in himself, another Edward in Edward" in "Breeching the Boy in Marlowe's *Edward II*," *SEL* 46.2 (2006): 281–304, esp. 287.

41 Thomas P. Anderson, "Surpassing the King's Two Bodies: The Politics of Staging the Royal Effigy in Marlowe's *Edward II*," *Shakespeare Bulletin* 32.4 (2014): 585–611.

42 I treat the liveliness of actors playing dead bodies at length in Chapter 1.

43 The long title of the play in quarto, which crowds together *Edward II*'s main characters, pays homage to the multiple paths that *Edward II* cuts through time. The title lengthens with subsequent printings of the quarto, its longest version appearing in 1598: Christopher Marlowe, *The Troublesome Raigne and Lamentable Death of Edward the Second, King of England with the Tragicall Fall of Proud Mortimer: and Also the Life and Death of Peirs Gaueston, the Great Earle of Cornewall, and Mighty Fauorite of King Edward the Second* (London: William Jones, 1598).

44 Richard Schechner, *Between Theater and Anthropology* (Philadelphia: University of Pennsylvania Press, 1985), 37.

45 On the likelihood that *Richard II* and *Edward II* were performed in repertory concurrently, see Roslyn L. Knutson, "The History Play, *Richard II*, and Repertorial Commerce," in *"Richard II": New Critical Essays*, ed. Jeremy Lopez (London: Routledge, 2012), 74–94.

46 On Shakespeare's likely membership in the Pembroke's Men, see Terence G. Schoone-Jongen, *Shakespeare's Companies: William Shakespeare's Early Career and the Acting Companies, 1577–1594* (Burlington, VT: Ashgate, 2008), 135–45.

47 Act, scene, and line numbers follow William Shakespeare, *King Richard II*, ed. Charles R. Forker (London: Arden Shakespeare, 2002).

48 Stephen Booth, "Syntax as Rhetoric in *Richard II*," *Mosaic: An Interdisciplinary Critical Journal*, 10.3 (1977): 87–103, esp. 87; Brian Walsh, "The Dramaturgy of Discomfort in *Richard II*," in *"Richard II": New Critical Essays*, 181–201, esp. 182.

49 Booth, "Syntax as Rhetoric," 96.

50 Leonard Barkan, "The Theatrical Consistency of *Richard II*," *Shakespeare Quarterly* 29.1 (1978): 5–19, esp. 7.

51 Phyllis Rackin, "The Role of the Audience in Shakespeare's *Richard II*," *Shakespeare Quarterly* 36.3 (1985): 262–81, esp. 263.

52 Long recognized as having an especially "close relationship ... between the action of the play and its iterative imagery," *Richard II* has prompted other comparisons to contemporary forms of media. See, in particular, Alice Dailey, who argues that the play deploys the logic of the photographic image by embedding the theatrical present within fixed images of the past. While Dailey attends compellingly to the ways the play creates snapshots of Richard, my own focus is on the ways that the theatrical creation of stilled images affects the phenomenological experience of the play's temporality. Dailey, "Little, Little Graves: Shakespeare's Photographs of Richard II," *Shakespeare Quarterly* 69.3 (2018): 141–66; and Arthur Suzman, "Imagery and Symbolism in *Richard II*," *Shakespeare Quarterly* 7.4 (1956): 355–70, esp. 355.

53 Raphael Holinshed, *The Firste Volume of the Chronicles of England, Scotlande, and Irelande* (London: John Hunne, 1577), 1120.

54 On the relationship between the material crown and its signification, see Ernst Kantorowicz's classic account in *The King's Two Bodies: A Study in Medieval Political Theology*, (Princeton: Princeton University Press, 1957), 336–83.

55 The "Richard II" episode of *The Hollow Crown* series stages the moment this way: Ben Whishaw, playing Richard, and Rory Kinnear, playing Bolingbroke, both maintain their grasp on the crown until Whishaw pulls it toward himself at the second "no" of Richard's vacillation at 4.1.201. See *The Hollow Crown*, episode 1, "Richard II," directed by Rupert Goold, aired June 30, 2012, on BBC Two.

56 James L. Calderwood, "Ways of Waiting in *Waiting for Godot*," *Modern Drama* 29.3 (1986): 365–75, esp. 366.

57 It is not clear whether the scene is a later edition to the play or whether it was censored from the original playtext. On the ambiguity of the evidence, see Cyndia Susan Clegg, "'By the choise and inuitation of al the realme': *Richard II* and Elizabethan Press Censorship," *Shakespeare Quarterly* 48.4 (1997): 432–48.

58 Thomas Dekker, *The Wonderful Year*, in *Selected Prose Writings*, ed. E. D. Pendry (London: Edward Arnold, 1967), 23–64, esp. 48.

59 William Muggins, *Londons Mourning Garment* (London: Ralph Blower, 1603), D3v.

60 Thomas Dekker, *The Magnificent Entertainment* (London: Thomas Man, 1604), B3v.

61 John Chamberlain, *The Letters of John Chamberlain*, ed. Norman Egbert McClure (Philadelphia: The American Philosophical Society, 1939), 195.

62 Venetian ambassador Giovanni Carlo Scaramelli reports ongoing discussions through the summer of 1603 about what to do with the arches. See *Calendar of State Papers and Manuscripts, Relating to English Affairs, Existing in the Archives and Collections of Venice*, ed. Horatio F. Brown, vol. 10, *1603–1607* (London: H. M. Stationary Office, 1900), 67–68.

63 As Ian Munro puts it, "the advent of the plague means the death of the festive life of the city: pageants and ceremonies are canceled, theaters closed, fairs suppressed, and the gathering of crowds forbidden." See Munro, *The Figure of the Crowd in Early Modern London: The City and Its Double* (New York: Palgrave MacMillan, 2005), 176.

64 Dekker, *The Wonderful Year*, 44.

65 Dekker, *The Wonderful Year*, 35.

66 Dekker, *The Wonderful Year*, 39.

67 Dekker, *The Wonderful Year*, 43.

68 Dekker, *The Wonderful Year*, 43.

69 Dekker, *The Wonderful Year*, 46, 34, 56.

70 Michael Neill, *Issues of Death: Mortality and Identity in English Renaissance Tragedy* (Oxford: Oxford University Press, 1997).

71 Dekker, *The Wonderful Year*, 34.

72 Dekker, *The Wonderful Year*, 44.

73 "tragedy, n.4a." OED Online. June 2020. Oxford University Press. www.oed .com/view/Entry/204352?redirectedFrom=tragedy (accessed August 17, 2020).

74 Munro, *The Figure of the Crowd*, 188.

75 Dekker, *The Wonderful Year*, 37, 43.

76 Neill, *Issues of Death*, 204.

77 Dekker, *The Wonderful Year*, 64.

78 For a timeline of closures and reopenings during the 1603–04 plague outbreak, see Leeds Barroll, *Politics, Plague, and Shakespeare's Theater: The Stuart Years* (Ithaca: Cornell University Press, 1991), 70–116.

79 As David M. Bergeron notes, "No English pageant ... so depend[ed] on triumphal arches as this one." See Bergeron, *English Civic Pageantry, 1558–1642* (Tempe, AZ: The Arizona Center for Medieval and Renaissance Studies, 2003), 76. Janette Dillon draws attention to the temporal sequencing of civic processions – "approach, arrival, pause and departure" – though without theorizing their formal effect. See Dillon, *The Language of Space in Court Performance, 1400–1625* (Cambridge: Cambridge University Press, 2010), 28.

80 On the proverbial, theological, and dramatic association of time and truth in the period, see Leslie Thomson, *Discoveries on the Early Modern Stage: Contexts and Conversations* (Cambridge: Cambridge University Press, 2018), 38–80.

81 Dekker, *The Magnificent Entertainment*, I4r.

82 William L. MacDonald, *The Architecture of the Roman Empire*, vol. 2 (New Haven: Yale University Press, 1986), 75. Though James's procession drew on its conventions, "royal entry" is something of a misnomer for the civic performance, since the procession did not actually include a ceremonial entrance into London at all. The 1603 entry was intended to have included a battle between Saint George and Saint Andrew outside Bishopsgate, which James's arrival would have resolved peacefully. Some material from the entry performance, which was written by Dekker, seems to have been recycled for the performance at Fenchurch Street in 1604, though it is worth noting that the staging of a mock battle at one of the city's gates reinforces the demarcation of two distinct spaces – within and without the city – in a way that the arches do not. For more on the mock battle, see Anne Lancashire, "Dekker's Accession Pageant for James I," *Early Theatre* 12.1 (2009): 39–50, esp. 44–45.

83 Dekker, *The Wonderful Year*, 39.

84 MacDonald, *Architecture*, 77.

85 Dekker, *The Magnificent Entertainment*, D4r.

86 On the play's historical contexts, see Arthur F. Kinney, *Lies like Truth: Shakespeare, Macbeth, and the Cultural Moment* (Detroit: Wayne State University Press, 2001). On the play and James's interest in demonology, see Stephen Greenblatt, "Shakespeare Bewitched," in *Shakespeare and Cultural Traditions*, ed. Tetsuo Kishi, Roger Pringle, and Stanley Wells (Newark: University of Delaware Press, 1994), 17–42. On the play's sensory connections to the Gunpowder Plot, see Harris, *Untimely Matter*, 119–39.

87 As Leslie Thomson has shown, theatrical storms transformed the increasingly contested belief in the supernatural into a reliable theatrical convention; in the playhouse, where there was thunder and lightning, witches were not far behind. See Thomson, "The Meaning of 'Thunder and Lightning': Stage Directions and Audience Expectations," *Early Theatre* 2 (1999): 11–24.

88 *The Lamentable Tragedie of Locrine* (London: Thomas Creede, 1595), A3r-A3v.

89 Act, scene, and line numbers follow William Shakespeare, *Macbeth*, ed. Sandra Clark and Pamela Mason (London: Arden Shakespeare, 2015).

90 On Macbeth's preoccupation with his own belatedness and his attempts to get ahead of time, see Donald W. Foster, "*Macbeth*'s War on Time," *English Literary Renaissance* 16.2 (1986): 319–42.

91 "hover, v.1-3." OED Online. June 2020. Oxford University Press. www.oed .com/view/Entry/88986?rskey=IzoLI7&result=3&isAdvanced=false (accessed August 04, 2020).

92 Book, canto, and stanza numbers follow Edmund Spenser, *The Faerie Queene*, ed. Thomas P. Roche (London: Penguin, 1978).

93 Kevin Curran, in a reading of the ways *Macbeth* stages a phenomenology of intentionality, notes that the Latin root of intention, *intendere*, "mean[s] literally to stretch out, to reach toward." See Curran, "Feeling Criminal in *Macbeth*," *Criticism* 54.3 (2012): 391–401, esp. 395.

94 Andrew Sofer, "Spectral Readings," *Theatre Journal* 64.3 (2012): 323–36, esp. 335.

95   Act, scene, and line numbers follow William Shakespeare, *As You Like It*, ed.
      Juliet Dusinberre (London: Bloomsbury Arden Shakespeare), 2006.

96   As Bernard Beckerman puts it, in slightly different terms, "The presentation of
      drama is a presentation of an *imagined* act." See Beckerman, *Dynamics of Drama:
      Theory and Method of Analysis* (New York: Drama Book Specialists, 1979), 18.

97   Michael Goldman makes a similar claim when he argues that as Macbeth proj-
      ects the imagined dagger "outward into the world around him," he locates it in
      "a deceptively objectified future – the 'business' he must soon perform." What
      I mean to suggest more particularly, however, is that the play's spectators cre-
      ate the conditions of that future, for within the context of the entire soliloquy,
      their interpretive participation in Macbeth's own uncertainty creates a dagger
      "in form as palpable" as the one Macbeth eventually goes on to draw (2.1.40).
      Goldman, "Language and Action in *Macbeth*," *Focus on "Macbeth*," ed. *John
      Russell Brown* (London: Routledge, 1982), 140–52, esp. 147–48.

98   See Julia Reinhard Lupton, *Shakespeare Dwelling: Designs for the Theater of
      Life* (Chicago: University of Chicago Press, 2018), 85–116.

99   Simon Forman, *Bocke of Plaies and Notes Thereof*, MS Ashmole 208, fol.
      207v, Bodleian Library, Oxford.

100   My claim here in part depends upon the supposition that the furniture
      onstage, as plausible impressions of seated human bodies, were chairs with
      backs. Such a supposition is not certain, though, I believe, reasonable. Later
      in the scene, both Lady Macbeth and Macbeth refer to the objects as "stools,"
      a word that in the early modern period could refer generally to seats with or
      without backs. "Cheier [chair]," the word Simon Forman used to name the
      object in his account of the play, has referred to a seat with a back since its
      introduction to the English language. Evidence gleaned from the theatrical
      practices of the period is somewhat more suggestive. Alan Dessen notes that
      actors playing monarchs were raised and lowered from the upper level of the
      playhouse while seated; actors playing sick monarchs were regularly carried
      on and off the stage while seated. Both of these methods of transportation
      would have been made substantially easier (and safer, though that does not
      always seem to have been a chief concern of the commercial theater) by chairs
      with backs against which actors could stabilize their own bodies; at the very
      least, these practices suggest the presence of chairs in the tiring house, if not
      the certainty of their use in this scene. See Dessen, *Recovering Shakespeare's
      Theatrical Vocabulary* (Cambridge: Cambridge University Press, 1995),
      109–26; and "Early Modern Staging of Throne Scenes," *Theatre Notebook*
      71.3 (2017): 190–93. See also "stool, n.1a." OED Online. June 2020. Oxford
      University Press. www.oed.com/view/Entry/190864?rskey=G1pqOd&result
      =1&isAdvanced=false (accessed August 27, 2020); and "chair, n.1a." OED
      Online. June 2020. Oxford University Press. www.oed.com/view/Entry/302
      15?rskey=XiPKoD&result=1&isAdvanced=false (accessed August 27, 2020).

101   See "horror, n.2a-b." OED Online. June 2020. Oxford University Press.
      www-oed-com.ezproxy.cul.columbia.edu/view/Entry/88577?rskey=6jy9cG
      &result=1&isAdvanced=false (accessed September 03, 2020).

102 On the complexity of the spectacle's seeming endorsement of Jacobean ideology, see Rhodri Lewis, "Polychronic *Macbeth*," *Modern Philology* 117.3 (2020): 323–46.

103 A. R. Braunmuller suggests that the glass refers to a "magic crystal permitting visions of the future." See *Macbeth*, ed. Braunmuller (Cambridge: Cambridge University Press, 2008), 212n110. Tiffany Stern suggests that when the play was performed at court, a mirror may have been used to capture James's reflection onstage. See Stern, *Making Shakespeare: From Stage to Page* (London: Routledge, 2004), 32–33.

104 Garber, "Temporality and Prophecy," 331.

105 Garber, "Temporality and Prophecy," 320.

106 Act, scene, and line numbers follow William Shakespeare and John Fletcher, *King Henry VIII (All is True)*, ed. Gordon McMullan (London: Arden, 2000).

107 Philip Fisher, *The Vehement Passions* (Princeton: Princeton University Press, 2002), 2.

108 Line number follows Ben Jonson, "An Execration upon Vulcan," ed. Colin Burrow, in *The Cambridge Edition of the Works of Ben Jonson*, ed. David Bevington, Martin Butler, and Ian Donaldson, vol. 7, *1641* (Cambridge: Cambridge University Press, 2012), 165–79.

109 See Leo Salingar, "Jacobean Playwrights and 'Judicious' Spectators," *Renaissance Drama* 22 (1991): 209–34.

110 On the saturation of Ford's work with dramatic convention, see Allison K. Deutermann, *Listening for Theatrical Form in Early Modern England* (Edinburgh: Edinburgh University Press, 2016), 152–67.

111 Act, scene, and line numbers follow John Ford, *Perkin Warbeck*, in *"Tis Pity She's a Whore" and Other Plays*, ed. Marion Lomax (Oxford: Oxford University Press, 1995).

112 Nicosia, "Prolepsis and Pretenders," 597.

113 Of *Perkin Warbeck*'s depiction of patriarchal rule and divinely anointed monarchy, ideologically under stress by the early Caroline period, Jean Howard has argued that "one sees the nostalgic recreation of a representational system anticipating its own supersession." I mean to identify the phenomenology of this nostalgic anticipation of a future unknown. Jean Howard, "'Effeminately Dolent': Gender and Legitimacy in Ford's *Perkin Warbeck*," in *John Ford: Critical Re-Visions*, ed. Michael Neill (Cambridge: Cambridge University Press, 1988), 261–79, esp. 277.

114 The play's preoccupation with the performance of kingship has long been recognized; see, for example, Jonas Barish, "*Perkin Warbeck* as Anti-History," *Essays in Criticism* 20.2 (1970): 151–71; Michael Neill, "'Anticke Pageantrie': The Mannerist Art of *Perkin Warbeck*," *Renaissance Drama* 7 (1976): 117–50; and Mario DiGangi, "John Ford," in *A Companion to Renaissance Drama*, ed. Arthur F. Kinney (Oxford: Blackwell, 2004), 567–83.

PART II

Playhouse Structure

CHAPTER 3

Props

Staging the Minuscule in the Jacobean Theater

Much less remarked on than that most famous of Shakespeare's handkerchiefs is the one rather ambiguously evoked by Pisanio in Act 1, scene 4 of *Cymbeline*. After her husband Posthumus's forced departure from Britain by ship, Imogen asks Pisanio whether Posthumus "wav'd his handkerchief" in farewell (1.4.6). He replies that

> For so long
> As he could make me with this eye, or ear,
> Distinguish him from others, he did keep
> The deck, with glove, or hat, or handkerchief,
> Still waving, as the fits and stirs of's mind
> Could best express how slow his soul sail'd on,
> How swift his ship.   (1.4.8–14)[1]

The image Pisanio describes is the result of looking at the very limits of his vision. Posthumus flourished something in his hand, but whether it was a "glove, or hat, or handkerchief" Pisanio could not discern. Yet that visual indeterminacy is also crucially inconsequential: Pisano equates the waving object, whatever it may have been, with the "fits and stirs" of Posthumus's mind, the clarity of "and" that yokes the two mental states together replacing supplanting the ambiguity of the twice-stated "or" in the list of objects. A strand of the scholarship on the handkerchief in *Othello* focuses on the prop's misleading evocation of events unstaged and therefore unseen in the play; the handkerchief displayed on the stage comes to represent what both Othello and the spectators might imagine, but are never shown.[2] But in its ambiguity, Posthumus's handkerchief (or glove, or hat) produces for Pisanio a different kind of frustrated visual experience, the one that this chapter takes as its subject: the attempt to see an object clearly at the very moment it disappears from view.

The gap between the early modern theater's material resources and the representations it sought to bring into being produced drama that was, as Katharine Eisaman Maus explains, "radically synecdochic, endlessly referring the spectators to events, objects, situations, landscapes that [could not] be shown them."[3] That reliance on synecdoche is most often explained in relation to the problem of staging spatial immensity; unable to display "the vasty fields of France" (Prologue.12), the theater settled for describing what it could not compass.[4] Tim Fitzpatrick identifies in this practice a "semiotic threshold" that governed the literal or verbal staging of material objects:

> Below that threshold there is no problem in representing a particular visual object both visually and verbally. The two communication codes are complementary, and we hear the world 'handkerchief' and see the object in question on stage. But above the threshold this complementarity breaks down, and the verbal code must substitute for the visual.[5]

This "verbal code" was the basic technology by which the early modern theater enlisted its spectators' imaginative participation to create fictional worlds on its largely bare stages.[6] But the problem of what could not be shown on the platform stage was one of smallness as well as vastness, and on the small end of the semiotic spectrum, I will argue, the theater possessed an unsettled relationship to conventional codes of material and figurative representation. Not content simply to name minuscule objects into existence, plays repeatedly – even paradoxically – insisted that spectators look directly on what they quite literally could not see.[7]

The plays I take as case studies in this chapter – *Cymbeline* (1610), Philip Massinger's *The Picture* (1629), and Shakespeare's *Antony and Cleopatra* (1606) – all displayed vanishingly small objects in both of the theaters used by the King's Men after 1608: the large outdoor Globe and the small indoor Blackfriars.[8] So while the intimate conditions of the exclusive hall theaters might seem to have offered a welcome home for the small prop, the regular restaging of plays in repertory means that the practice cannot simply be attributed to the increasing use of indoor playhouses by the second decade of the seventeenth century.[9] Such an account glosses over what we know about early modern performance practices, but it also makes the broader assumption that this theater was uniformly interested in the unambiguous conveyance of meaning from stage to audience. Sarah Dustagheer has convincingly shown that the King's Men crafted what she calls "combined practices" to "produce plays suitable in different but parallel ways for both their theatres."[10] Our sense of what counted as "suitable" for production in this period should take into account the commercial theater's exuberant commitment to innovation and experimentation – or what we might term, with regard to the staging of tiny props, its program of spectator harassment.[11] By displaying objects onstage too small for spectators to see clearly or, even more audaciously, directing their visual attention to objects not there at all, these plays variously enacted in both the Globe and the Blackfriars the strained, ambiguous experience of seeing that Pisanio describes in *Cymbeline*.

All three plays share, too, a motivation for the staging of small props: The objects are deployed as evidence intended to resolve the epistemological and erotic crises produced by the perceived inscrutability of women's bodies. The central question of both *Cymbeline* and *The Picture*, the plays to which the chapter will give the most sustained attention, is whether a woman's chastity can be known for certain. In a literary context, such a question is nearly synonymous with doubt itself, serving as one of the key formulations of skepticism that, in the late sixteenth and early seventeenth centuries, reconsidered the classical skepticisms of Sextus Empiricus, Cicero, and others.[12] In these reimaginings, men doubt, and women are doubted. Stanley Cavell crystallizes the perceived gender essentialism of skepticism – from an ahistorical perspective, though his focus is on Shakespeare's plays – when he claims that *"so far* as skepticism is representable as the doubt whether your children are yours, skepticism is not a feminine business" before somewhat speculatively driving the point further: "It may be that skepticism on the feminine side is representable as doubt over one's relation to an object other than a child, say a woman's doubt over the identity of the father of her child."[13] Cavell is careful to suggest initially that skepticism is determined by gender only in this precisely limited regard, though much of *Disowning Knowledge* nevertheless explores representations of men's doubt about women more broadly, foregoing attention to the specific issue of questioned paternity.[14] Scholarship that seeks to link the philosophical questions raised by skepticism to early modern drama, whether it agrees with Cavell's essentialist framework or not, tends to conform to it, focusing on the representation of men's doubt and women's fundamental inscrutability.[15] It is certainly true that in this period, within the playhouse as well as outside it, representations of male doubt were inextricably tied to questions about female chastity. But the drama is more imaginatively capacious than this essentialist skeptical framework implies. Concentrating solely on the representations of male doubt in the theater loses sight of moments in which women themselves express uncertainty: in *The Picture*, Sophia doubts her husband's chastity, and in *Cymbeline*,

Imogen's irresolution is a direct response to being doubted by her husband. These moments deserve attention, for, together with the frustrated theatrical experiences produced by the hard-to-see objects onstage, they actively refigure for spectators the very threat of women's inscrutability into the comparatively harmless, if no less fascinating, mystery of interiority. Spectators are undone, that is, in a manner parallel to the plays' jealous husbands: while Posthumus and Mathias are made to confront their wrongheaded assumptions about their wives, playgoers are exposed to their interpretive limitations with regard to the very workings of theater itself.

At the same time, *Cymbeline*, *The Picture*, and *Antony and Cleopatra* all discover the theater as an alternative to the misleading knowledge offered by the evidentiary metonym. It is well known that by the early seventeenth century, English legal and natural philosophical discourses had begun to develop new ways of mitigating uncertainty and, in the process, producing new knowledge: forensic investigation, empiricist methodologies, and probabilistic thought all offered the possibility of arrival of satisfactory certainty, if not absolute truth.[16] As many recent pathbreaking readings of early modern drama have shown, the commercial theater did not simply respond to these new ideas and practices, but existed with them in "a mutually sustaining network."[17] This scholarship indisputably demonstrates that the early modern theater cultivated modes of thinking and imagining in dynamic relation to its epistemologically cognate domains. But it is also true that the theater positioned itself, in concert with its etymological origin as "a place for viewing," as a site for the discovery of knowledge and the revelation of truth.[18] To varying degrees, *The Picture*, *Cymbeline*, and *Antony and Cleopatra* entangle their spectators in experiences of frustrated perception only to posit the spectacular abundance of stage show as the means by which incomplete evidentiary knowledge might be supplanted. More specifically, theatrical moments that insistently call attention to the technologies of their representation – precisely the same spectacles, that is, that so often invite spectators' uncertainty or confusion – are offered up in these plays as the source of the commercial theater's phenomenal and epistemological plenitude. It is not just that theatrical representation is revelatory, in other words, but that what can be seen on the stage is abundant in its very ambivalence. Theatrical truths, these plays recognize, do not last, for performance is inherently an act of disappearance. But in the fulsomeness of its ephemerality, the theater poses a challenge to the incomplete knowledge granted by the evidence, left behind, that lasts.[19]

Minuscule Evidence in The Picture

The Picture's picture is a metonymic tool of surveillance, its presence in the world of the play occasioned by Mathias's departure from his home to join the Hungarian army in its fight against the Turks. His fear that his wife Sophia will be unfaithful to him while he is gone is temporarily allayed when the necromancer Baptista presents him with a magical miniature of her. Baptista tells Mathias that the tiny portrait is "So punctually observed that had it motion / In so much 'twere herself" (1.1.169–70).[20] But the miniature is not just an extremely lifelike representation of Sophia, for Baptista also promises that the portrait will offer Mathias signs of her infidelity:

> Carry it still about you and, as oft
> As you desire to know how she's affected,
> With curious eyes peruse it. While it keeps
> The figure it now has, entire and perfect,
> She is not only innocent in fact
> But unattempted; but if once it vary
> From the true form, and what's now white and red
> Incline to yellow, rest most confident
> She's with all violence courted but unconquered.
> But if it turn all black, 'tis an assurance
> The fort by composition or surprise
> Is forced or with her free consent surrendered. (1.1.174–85)

Baptista's speech is an instruction, for Mathias and spectators both, in how to scrutinize the miniature in lieu of scrutinizing Sophia herself. *The Picture*'s miniature seemingly becomes a technology of surveillance by means of its very resources as an aesthetic object; as Nicholas Hilliard suggested, these intimate portraits could "catch thosse lovely graces wittye smilings, and those stolne glances which sudainely like light[n]ing passe and another Countenance taketh place."[21] In its ability to capture the outward displays of inwardness that otherwise evade the observer's notice – "wittye smilings" and "stolne glances" – Hilliard's miniature is no less magical than Mathias's. Yet, as Lorna Hutson has observed, Massinger is careful to downplay the power of the miniature as it is described in his source material for the play, in which the miniature-wielding magician assures the jealous husband that his wife's intentions are unambiguously discoverable: "If perchaunce she meane to abuse hir honesty, the [portrait] wil waxe pale. And, indeede committing that filthy fact, sodainly the colour will bee blacke."[22] Baptista, by contrast, cautions Mathias that he cannot "dive into / [Sophia's] hidden thoughts" and that the miniature will not offer a clear narrative about her potential infidelity (1.1.155–56); it will change colors whether she is "forced *or* with her free consent surrendered." "Consequently, there is almost no difference," Hutson writes, "between the supernatural device Mathias acquires and the simple mental habit of conjecturing vivid likelihoods by probable reasoning."[23] The miniature's failure as a tool of surveillance is apparent from its first appearance onstage.

Massinger's decision to rework his source material is even more remarkable when we consider that the conditions of the tiny object's staging in the Globe and Blackfriars would have amplified, to opposite extremes, the miniature's diegetic faultiness. More obvious is the problem of the small object in the outdoor amphitheater: some spectators, sitting or standing around thirty feet from the stage, would have strained to apprehend the miniature in any detail at all.[24] But crowded together in the smaller Blackfriars, they would have been invited to gaze on the handheld object with a scrutiny that paralleled Mathias's own.[25] We might assume – in accordance with the Blackfriars's general emphasis, both on the stage and in the playhouse, on visual display – that the prop was fashioned for performance in the hall theater with some care.[26] If the portrait were painted with the metallic tones characteristic of actual miniatures, the theater's candlelight would have glinted and glistered off its limned brushstrokes.[27] Yet however impressive the display might have been in the theater, in imitating Hilliard's lightning strikes of inward feeling, the brandished miniature inescapably announces itself as a prop. The magical miniature is a self-conscious optical illusion, or, to adapt language from another play metatheatrically preoccupied with "glittering" (1.2.203), a piece of counterfeit gold: "art essentially made" (2.4.479).[28] In the playhouse, the miniature's limitation as an evidential tool is synonymous with its deceptive failure as a theatrical property: spectators are invited to search for a visual confirmation of Sophia's chastity that, in the Globe, is not actually there, and in Blackfriars, can only be fraudulently realized.[29]

To put this another way, in the theater the miniature does not simply break down as a tool of surveillance on its own merits, but somewhere along the phenomenological line that tethers audience members to stage performance. Spectators' sensory response to the prop theatrically exacerbates its diegetic defectiveness. Yet that collaborative failure pointedly absolves Sophia herself from bearing the burden of her perceived opacity; spectators are not made to surveil and interpret Sophia's outward behavior as they are, for example, Hermione's interactions with Polixenes in *The Winter's Tale*. Outside the playhouse, such absolution rarely occurred:

within a culture that viewed women's infidelity as an ever-present threat, the preservation of chastity was their particular mandate.[30] "Let [women] indevor to ... above all imbrace chastitie," Edmund Tilney advised in the popular *Flower of Friendship* (1568), "for the happinesse of matrimonie, doth consist in a chaste matrone."[31] Despite this widespread emphasis on women's need to maintain their chastity, other authors stress the need for their surveillance by men, which produces something of a logical double bind: they are quick to emphasize that women's inscrutability is absolute, though they simultaneously insist on the inevitably futile attempt to penetrate it.[32] As Joseph Hall noted in 1631, "There is more mischiefe in a secret infidelity, *which the world either cannot know, or cares not to censure*, then in the foulest adultery."[33] The possibilities Hall poses alternately place the burden of women's dangerous opacity on women themselves and the men who, presumably, do not care to police it. Who is rightly to blame? Jacques Olivier raises the possibility that the problem of women's inscrutability may be a failure of the male observer even as he proposes the opposite in his virulently misogynist *A Discourse of Women* (1662): "A Woman is a creature so difficult to be known, that *the most ingenuous spirit in the world knows not certainly to define her*, she hath about her so many cabinets, such back-shops, so many secret holes, such cunning warehouses, that one knows not wherein to trust her."[34] The list of variously sized openings in Olivier's sentence evokes for the reader the process of discovering cavern after cavern in a woman's body, conjuring an unnerving image of endless genital multiplicity. In Olivier's formulation, the "perfidious and shifting ... female sex" is at once opaque and hollow, riddled with unseen voids for which, one supposes, the husband's single phallus will never be enough.[35] That implicit admission of inadequacy is brought closest to the surface of Olivier's tirade in his insistence that women are not categorically illegible, but that they evade even the most brilliant of investigators. Embedded in Olivier's formulation is an ideological fissure, an unwitting shift of the epistemological burden of women's inevitable opacity onto the men incapable of perceiving them with clarity.

In *The Picture*, the displacement of Sophia's threatening opacity onto the faulty miniature widens that ideological fissure to a semiotic gap. Yet readings of the play nevertheless tend to proceed from the assumption that it works within its culture's binary of male doubt and female illegibility, even as they suggest that, because she is innocent, the play ultimately comes to Sophia's defense.[36] This argument suggests that *The Picture* presents Sophia as a mystery, an object of both her husband's and the audience's doubt. But while I agree that the play deliberately keeps spectators in the dark about Sophia's intentions at key moments – a feature of the play essential to its phenomenological reconfiguration of spectators' perceptions, and topic about which I will say more below – it is also true that *The Picture* does not present her as entirely inscrutable. Sophia's many long speeches, including three soliloquies, are the most nuanced of the play, serving at once to occlude her intentions and to disclose her unsettled consciousness to the audience. If Massinger deliberately exaggerates the miniature's failure to lay bare Sophia's hidden thoughts, in other words, he does so in order to offer up the soliloquy as a key theatrical means by which her mind might be successfully accessed.[37]

In these ruminations Sophia repeatedly gives voice to her own uncertainty, and though she is troubled by her own reciprocal desire to confirm that Mathias has remained faithful to her, she is more often propelled into irresolution far beyond anything that has to do with her husband. When the courtiers Ubaldo and Ricardo appear at her home with a casket of jewels that they falsely tell her are from Mathias, Sophia cautiously unfolds her doubts about how her husband obtained them:

> I find myself
> Strangely distracted with the various stories
> Now well, now ill, then doubtfully by my guests
> Delivered of my lord. And like poor beggars
> That in their dreams find treasure by reflection
> Of a wounded fancy make it questionable
> Whether they sleep or not, yet, tickled with
> Such a fantastic hope of happiness,
> Wish they may never wake, in some such measure,
> Incredulous of what I see and touch,
> As 'twere a fading apparition, I
> Am still perplexed and troubled; and when most
> Confirmed 'tis true, a curious jealousy
> To be assured by what means and from whom
> Such a mass of wealth was first deserved, then gotten,
> Cunningly steals into me.   (3.6.8–23)

As the line break between "I" and "am" midway through her speech suggests, Sophia is here of two minds, even two selves. Conjuring an image of herself poised precariously on the boundary of sleeping and waking, she is unsure to which state she actually belongs; unlike the beggars who find treasure in their dreams and wish never to wake, Sophia touches the box of jewels "as 'twere a fading apparition," hoping a spectral visitation is withdrawing from her. With her note of "a wounded fancy" that then gives way to the question of whether or not she is dreaming, Sophia's romantic uncertainty opens her up to a broader epistemological wavering. The dreamlike blurring of contemplation and fantasy renders the experience of doubt as an unsettled wandering among various affective states in search of quiescence.

Sophia describes the anxiety of irresolution in another soliloquy much earlier in the play, right after Mathias has left for battle: "I was flattered once I was a star, but now / Turned a prodigious meteor, and, like one, / Hang in the air between my hopes and feares" (2.1.37–9). Caught between hope and fear, Sophia's uncertainty both prefigures and synthesizes the wild sets of possibilities posited by the miniature: "by composition or surprise," "forced or with her free consent." Unlike the miniature, however, Sophia's soliloquized uncertainty wedges itself into the space between alternatives, theatrically manifesting the inwardness that the object cannot materialize. Again alone onstage after the courtiers successfully deceive Sophia into believing Mathias has been unfaithful to her, Sophia ventures,

> I begin
> To waver in my faith, and mark it doubtful
> Whether the saints that were canonized for
> Their holiness of life sinned not in secret,
> Since my Mathias is fallen from his virtue
> In such an open fashion.   (3.6.130–35)

Sophia's own articulations of doubt are not distinct in kind from Mathias's, as Cavell would have it, but take as their starting point the very same desire to confirm another's infidelity, only to transform that sexual doubt into spiritual doubt. Her anxious sense that her faith wavers – that is, that the very foundation of the "self" identified in her earlier speech is crumbling beneath her – makes possible the simultaneous emergence and obfuscation of her interior life for the audience during this soliloquy.[38] As has often been pointed out, the soliloquy functions as a dramatic device by sublimating the exchange of dramatic dialogue into the pensive tension of a single mind in conflict with itself; in Sophia's case the interrogative process of speaking alone manifests the contradictions that make up her uncertainty without resolving them into a unified whole.[39] If the tool of Mathias's surveillance seeks and fails to settle on one of several mutually exclusive alternatives, Sophia's soliloquies wander freely among them, offering a portrait of an interior life that wavers and hangs in the balance of possibility. In her work on the history of privacy, Lena Cowen Orlin describes the ways that in early modernity

"interiority [was] constituted in resistance" to a widespread cultural prerogative on surveillance, one which was imbricated with the material
conditions of domestic life that kept families, servants, and neighbors
constantly within eyesight and earshot.⁴⁰ Sophia's soliloquies are the dramatic manifestation of that cultural resistance. What they collectively
accomplish is not an endorsement of broader anxieties about women's
deceptiveness but a reconfiguration of her dangerous inscrutability –
Olivier's "back-shops" and "so many secret holes" – into what Mathias
will eventually term the "cabinet" of Sophia's "rich mind" (5.3.186): interiority itself.

Theatrically, however, the soliloquies are at once an interpretive trap,
the means by which Massinger lures spectators into a false sense of confidence that they, unlike Mathias, *can* dive into Sophia's hidden thoughts.
The play exploits that confidence, eventually revealing the full measure of
spectators' thwarted expectations through a dazzling spectacular display. It
does so by first dispensing with the doubt that characterizes the play's early
scenes. Sophia resolves her uncertainty by deciding to commit adultery as
a vengeful response to Mathias's apparent infidelity – "Chastity / Thou
only art a name, and I renounce thee," she declares (3.6.157–58) – before
changing her mind just two scenes later, adamantly disavowing her presence among the "vast numbers" of the unfaithful (4.2.1). Newly resolved,
she announces that she has a plan to rid herself of her guilt about even
considering "wantonness":

> Howe'er my lord offend it is no warrant
> For me to walk in his forbidden paths.
> What penance then can expiate my guilt
> For my consent—transported then with passion—
> To wantonness? The wounds I give my fame
> Cannot recover his, and though I have fed
> These courtiers with promises and hopes
> I am yet in fact untainted. And I trust
> My sorrow for it, with my purity
> And love to goodness for itself made powerful,
> Though all they have alleged prove true or false,
> Will be such exorcisms as shall command
> This fury, jealousy, from me. What I have
> Determined touching them I am resolved
> To put in execution.   (4.2.10–24)

Sophia's language echoes Baptista's reading of the miniature, assuring the
audience that though she has considered infidelity, she remains "in fact
untainted." What is opened up as a mystery by the end of her speech is not

the status of her chastity, then, but what she plans to do to the courtiers in order to exorcise her own jealousy. And while Sophia does not make those plans clear, upon hearing the announcement of a woman's desire to preserve her chastity and rid herself of unwanted suitors, Caroline theatergoers would have almost certainly known what to expect next: a bed trick, or in this case, two of them.⁴¹ Regularly deployed through every decade of the commercial theater's operation, the bed trick offered playwrights a remarkable amount of narrative freedom because the convention was premised upon the perceived interchangeability of women's bodies; female characters get into or out of proposed sexual arrangements simply by standing in for one another.⁴² Within the broader constellation of the early modern commercial theater, Sophia's reticence about how exactly she will maintain her chastity nevertheless offered the play's Caroline spectators an apparently clear signal of *The Picture*'s impending action. The unmediated access to the mysterious workings of Sophia's *mind*, in other words, is intertheatrically construed as the correct anticipation of the play's *plot*.

But a double bed trick is *not* what happens next. Instead, Sophia convinces the courtiers separately to undress, steals their clothing, and replaces it with an "old woman's biggin for a nightcap" for Ubaldo and "a clown's cast suit" for Ricardo (4.2.137, 154). She does not recruit two different women to sleep with each of them, that is, but substitutes both courtiers for herself, efficiently combining what would have been two separate sex acts into a single trick. In the process, spectators' interpretive errors are rendered theatrically spectacular. Sophia's prank relies on elements of the playhouse structure shared by the Globe and Blackfriars to construct the scene as an inset performance: along with *The Picture*'s spectators, she watches from the platform as Ubaldo and Ricardo separately enter the upper gallery. The stage directions specify that their entrances are accompanied by "*great noise*," as Ubaldo enters with the "*clapping [of] a door*," and Ricardo, likely having entered from the trapdoor of the heavens, crashes onto the gallery floor, "*as fallen*" (4.2.130sd, 145sd). Both register their confusion in a series of frantic cries as Sophia watches from below:

RICARDO. Wither am I fallen? Into hell?
UBALDO. Who makes that noise there?
                         Help me if thou art a friend!
RICARDO. A friend? I am where
    I cannot help myself. Let me see thy face. (4.2.146–49)

The spectacle of the courtiers' disoriented befuddlement is a theatrical in-joke, for playgoers would have been well aware that Hell in the playhouse cosmos resided below the platform, not above it. The sight of the two undressed men, moreover, assigned the roles of peasant and old woman by Sophia through the clothing she has given to them, is a parody of a sexual assignation in which she has pointedly not participated. That comic vision was magnified by the actors in *The Picture*'s original staging: Ubaldo, clutching his woman's cap and crying, "This comes of our whoring" (4.2.205), was played by Thomas Pollard, a skilled comic actor who in 1629 had been a member of the King's Men for over a decade.[43] He likely joined the company as an apprentice of comic impresario John Shank when the older actor moved to the King's Men around 1613; Pollard, by then age fifteen or sixteen, would likely have played women's parts, and John Astington conjectures that if the talented young actor trained directly under Shank "in his own specialty as a low comic" Pollard may even have played "such roles as the Nurse or Mistress Quickly."[44] In that case, the sight in 1629 of Pollard playing Ubaldo, cast in the inset spectacle as a woman, would have activated Caroline spectators' memories of Pollard's long career with the King's Men. In multiple ways, then, the scene comically engages playgoers' deep familiarity with the history of the commercial theater. Yet it does so, I want to emphasize, not as a platitude to spectators' expertise but for precisely the opposite reason: as a means to foreground their thwarted dramatic expectations. The juxtaposition of the thirty-two-year-old Pollard and the sixteen-year-old John Honeyman, who played Sophia, would have visually exaggerated the scope of spectators' interpretive error.[45] *This*, the spectacle seems to say, is what you thought was going to happen?

Set in relief to the miniature, the blatant theatricality of Massinger's surprise denouement is calibrated to the scale of the playhouse; it thus makes unequivocally plain what the tiny prop cannot. But *The Picture*'s two spectacular foci share a common purpose. If Mathias is drawn into a series of mistaken suppositions about his wife, his misplaced jealousy exacerbated each time he notices a change in the miniature's colors, spectators' interpretive assurance in the smooth operation of dramatic convention is the theatrical equivalent of that reliance on faulty evidence. Mathias's fearful speculation is driven to wildness when he learns not that Sophia *has* been unfaithful to him, but that she *will*; when he sees that the miniature has been tinged with "yellow / That does assure she's tempted" and covered in "lines / Of a dark color that disperse themselves / O'er every miniature of her face," he is assured by Baptista that Sophia is false "in her consent and wishes … but not in fact *yet*" (4.1.32–35, 39, emphasis mine).[46] Spectators are similarly lured into a false sense of confidence about the inevitability of actions that have yet to unfold. And the miniature's excessive failure as an evidentiary metonym and prop is essential to spectators' misplaced confidence, for Mathias's assurance in the obviously faulty object seems to set their comparative interpretive acuity in relief. The upendings on the stage and in the playhouse aim for a corresponding end; while Mathias comes finally to trust in his wife, audience members are finally invited to behold the complex capaciousness of Sophia's interior life. Her manipulation of the bed trick convention turns the perceived interchangeability of women's bodies on its head, foregrounding instead the undifferentiated, prosthetic construction of the male courtiers' identities.[47] Stripped of the visual signs of their masculinity and wealth, the courtiers have no discernible identities left: "I am now," Ubaldo claims, "I know not what" (5.3.136). But the fullness of Sophia's subjectivity – at once outwardly visible and hidden from view – stands out in individual relief next to the superficial trappings of the duped men. The soliloquies and manipulation of the bed trick convention preserve the singularity of Sophia's identity as well as her interiority, which emerges by this scene through a complex mixture of display and concealment, revelation and mystery. The dramatic structuring of this characterological transformation is *The Picture*'s final scheme: spectators are invited to accept the benign opacity of Sophia's interiority at exactly the moment it is revealed she has deceived them.

The Picture's tragicomic turn, then, is not simply an effect of its narrative structure. The veer away from tragedy is theatrically dependent upon spectators' sensory frustration and the spectacular confrontation with their upended expectations, generated through gestures to conventional semiotic systems that the play roundly overturns. And that interpretive unsettling accords with *The Picture*'s conclusion, which protracts Sophia's own uncertainty even after she has purged Mathias of his doubt: "Suppose I pardon / What's past," Sophia proposes to the group gathered onstage in the final scene, "who can secure me, he'll be free / From jealousy hereafter?" (5.3.208–10).[48] If a version of doubt essentialized by gender is offered in *The Picture*, perhaps it is here, when Sophia provides something of an answer to Cavell's speculation about what form women's uncertainty takes. Even by the end of the play, when the mistaken impressions have been resolved and husband and wife restored to one another, Sophia cannot be sure that Mathias will never doubt her again.

Invisible Evidence in Cymbeline

As in *The Picture*, to see in *Cymbeline* is to squint. Shakespeare's tragicomedy imagines a world plagued by sexual jealousy, misperception, and visual strain: Posthumus wrongly suspects Imogen of infidelity; Imogen herself dies a false death and misidentifies Cloten's dead body; eye-strings are described as "crack[ing]" in their attempt to see beyond their ability (1.4.17).[49] The play embroils spectators in this disoriented and disorienting world. And while *The Picture* foregrounds the miniature's faultiness before separately luring spectators into a false sense of confidence about their dramatic expectations, *Cymbeline* knits these two evidentiary threads together, showing the process by which entirely innocuous objects are made to serve as the bits and pieces of a dangerously false narrative. Theater itself comes to the rescue: after entangling spectators in their own experience of frustrated, incomplete seeing, *Cymbeline* depicts Imogen's own deliberate unknowing as the self-consciously theatrical strategy by which she is able to rebuke Posthumus's mistaken judgements about her and bring about the successful reunion of her father and brothers. The joyful recognitions that take place in the final scene of the play become a kind of corrective lens for looking in *Cymbeline*, one that frees its characters – and its spectators – from the search for certainty by making the limitations of vision ultimately insignificant.

The act of surveillance in *Cymbeline* originates not from an object but a wager. After hearing Posthumus praise Imogen's chastity, Iachimo bets that he can break it; in order to prove he has succeeded, Iachimo promises to bring back "sufficient testimony" that he has slept with her (1.5.145). The scene that stages Iachimo's evidentiary process entangles spectators in conflicting registers of theatrical seeing. After gaining access to the sleeping Imogen's bedroom by hiding in a trunk, he verbally guides spectators' apprehension of the scene by alerting them that their imaginative participation in the illusory realization of the fictional bedroom is about to be engaged: "To note the chamber: I will write all down" (2.2.24). The details Iachimo goes on to narrate are all features of the room that would not have materially appeared on the Globe or Blackfriars stage, but which must be figuratively brought into being by spectators themselves: "Such, and such pictures: there the window, such / Th' adornment of her bed; the arras, figures, / Why, such, and such" (2.2.25–27). It might be protested that spectators are not given much detail to work with in these lines. But the repeated "such" functions as a deictic gesture in exactly the same way that "*there* the window" does; Iachimo not only names the details of the room into existence, but points them, one by one, into place.[50] The lines are a figurative orchestration of fictional place; they guide spectators in a collaborative, choreographed process of imaginative looking.[51]

On its own, there is nothing out of the ordinary about this mode of theatrical seeing; it is the most basic representational technology of the early modern theater. But what *is* unusual about Iachimo's speech, I would argue, is also what is most obvious about it: three lines into noting the imaginary details of the room, Iachimo turns to register Imogen's body. In the midst of Iachimo's ekphrastic narration, what erupts suddenly into spectators' field of vision is at once materially present on the stage. The speech crosses the semiotic threshold from figurative to mimetic representation, in the process requiring spectators to shift from imaginative looking to literal surveillance:

> Ah, but some natural notes about *her body*
> Above ten thousand meaner moveables
> Would testify, t'enrich mine inventory.
> O sleep, thou ape of death, lie dull upon her,
> And be her sense but as a monument,
> Thus in a chapel lying. Come off, come off;
> As slippery as the Gordian knot was hard.
> *'Tis mine, and this will witness outwardly,*
> As strongly as the conscience does within,
> To th' madding of her lord. *On her left breast*
> *A mole cinque-spotted:* like the crimson drops
> I' th' bottom of a cowslip.   (2.2.28–39, emphases mine)

The remainder of the speech stays within a register of literal seeing: Iachimo notes Imogen's body and removes her bracelet before finally letting his eyes fall on the mole, "cinque-spotted," on her breast. Yet this final direction is one that spectators cannot follow, for it is an order to look on what is not there. As Ann Rosalind Jones and Peter Stallybrass put it, by giving the mole "a precise but imaginary location upon the body of the boy actor," spectators are "forced to confront the absences which mark the boy actor's body."[52] The self-conscious attention to the actor's body deliberately sets the two modes of spectatorial seeing – imaginative and literal – in conflict with one another. Simon Forman's 1611 account of seeing *Cymbeline* in the Globe bears out the impossibility of Iachimo's direction even as it suggests that Forman attempted to follow it: "the Italia*n* [...] vewed her in her bed and the markes of her body. & toke a wai her braslet."[53] Forman's summary reorders the progression of Iachimo's narration, noting Imogen's presence onstage and glossing over the mole itself as "markes of her body" before moving back into the comfortable register of literal looking – "her braslet" – as if the invisible is too unstable a realm in which to remain for much longer than an instant.

But the order of that unfolding matters to the phenomenological experience of the speech. Once engaged in literal looking rather than imaginative seeing, spectators' very ability to participate in the manifestation of the fictional world before them is strained, and eventually, surpassed. The speech is a verbal enactment of diminution: Iachimo first zeroes in on Imogen's body and registers her bracelet ("*this* will witness outwardly" implies a brandishing of the prop), then the boy actor's absent breast, then the mole – an imagined pinprick that disappears into invisibility. As they directed their attention to the boy actor's body and the forensic metonyms that will eventually come to stand for Imogen in turn, spectators were entangled in a visual experience that theatrically replicated Pisanio's relayed attempt to apprehend Posthumus's handheld object as it receded from him. The comparison to Sebastiano Serlio's diagrams of single point perspective theatrical scenes in *The First Booke of Architecture*, translated into English the same year that Forman saw *Cymbeline* at the Globe, is inviting.[54] But if the aim of Serlio's designs, visually stuffed with all of the architecture and objects that the English stage could only speak into being, is to situate spectators within the "formal tension between unity and heterogeneity" of fictional space, Iachimo's verbal evocation does the opposite.[55] The clash between figurative and literal registers of seeing does not orient them within the fictional world of the play itself but deliberately frustrates their relation to the tools of theatrical representation. "Sit in a full Theater, and you will thinke you see so many lines drawne from the circumference of so many eares, whiles the *Actor* is the *Center*," the author of "An Excellent Actor" claimed in 1615.[56] Iachimo's narration traces these lines into invisibility, phenomenologically producing exactly the visual strain that Imogen herself describes after hearing about Posthumus's departure from Britain:

> I would have broke mine eye-strings, crack'd them, but
> To look upon him, till the diminution
> Of space had pointed him sharp as my needle:
> Nay, followed him, till he had melted from
> The smallness of a gnat, to air: and then
> Have turn'd mine eye, and wept.   (1.4.17–22)

With the attention to material evidence at once minuscule and invisible, the scene theatrically constructs Iachimo's act of invasive scrutiny as the failed attempt to register what resides at the vanishing point of spectators' vision – ever receding, as if a ship on the horizon, permanently from view.

   At almost exactly the same moment that perspectival representation was beginning to take hold in England through the elaborate visual scenery and stage machinery of Jacobean court performance, then, *Cymbeline* verbally constructed perspectival seeing on the public stage as an act of disappearance, one that called the very reliability of spectators' vision into question.[57] Elsewhere in Shakespeare's work, the verbal organization of space by means of the techniques of perspectival representation is synonymous with deception itself, and *Cymbeline* is no different.[58] The mixture of figurative and literal seeing in which spectators are entangled becomes, in Iachimo's account of Imogen's infidelity, a narrative trompe l'oeil; the false show is laced with evidential details that make his story to Posthumus more convincing by further undercutting spectators' already frustrated visual experience.[59] Imogen's room takes on a more fulsome reality as the details fit together into Iachimo's story: the "window," "figures," and "such, and such" become tapestries that depict "Proud Cleopatra, when she met her Roman," a chimney cut with figures of "Chaste Dian, bathing" and a ceiling fretted with "golden cherubins" (2.4.70, 82, 88). The story punishes spectators most devoted to the process of performance, for those who had been intimately engaged in the imaginative construction of the bedroom would have likely been required to reevaluate what they had conjured into being just two scenes earlier. Iachimo's narrative to Posthumus is not false simply because it is a lie, but because it undermines spectators' visual confirmation of what unequivocally did *not* occur in Imogen's bedroom: adultery. For Posthumus, these individual evidential details gain force as they find their place in Iachimo's narrative, eventually accumulating as, to borrow a phrase Shakespeare coined in *Othello*, the "foregone conclusion" of women's infidelity (3.3.430).[60]

Shakespeare redoubles this turbulent visual experience back into the world of the play when he figures Imogen's response to being doubted by her husband as geographic disorientation – as the very destruction, that is, of her own orientation within space itelf. Pisanio reveals that Posthumus, deceived into believing that Imogen has been unfaithful to him, plans to have her killed; the only way to save herself, Pisanio advises, is to escape. Imogen's speculative response points to Britain's ambiguous location in the wider world:

> Where then?
> Hath Britain all the sun that shines? Day? Night?
> Are they not but in Britain? I' th' world's volume
> Our Britain seems as of it, but not in't:
> In a great pool, a swan's nest: prithee think
> There's livers out of Britain. (3.4.137–42)

Imogen's questions conjure the world's vastness, rendering Britain not the repository of "all the sun that shines" but merely one remote part of "th' world's volume."[61] Her home country becomes a false metonym for the entire world, a mere mole or pinprick on what Shakespeare elsewhere terms "the great globe itself" (4.1.153): "In a great pool, a swan's nest."[62] No longer the vanishing point by which Imogen's own spatial orientation is governed, Britain's sudden unfixity prevents her from finding firm epistemological footing. Unanchored, the place she chooses to go – Milford Haven – is, as Huw Griffiths points out, itself indistinct, ambiguously both part of Britain and separate from it.[63] Posthumus's doubt about Imogen, like Mathias's about Sophia, is precisely focused on her sexual fidelity; but Imogen's reciprocal uncertainty, like Sophia's, is more capacious, pertaining to her place within the entire world. While Sophia asks who she is, Imogen asks *where* she is, mapping her radical epistemological doubt onto the world's expanse.[64] On Imogen, the effect of being doubted is nothing less than world-altering.

Cymbeline points to the uncertainty brought on by the extreme limits of vision, both in diminution to the point of vanishing and in the ambiguity brought on by the vastness of geographical expanse. But somewhere in between the invisibly minuscule and incomprehensibly immense is the Globe – in other words, the theater. Pisanio offers to Imogen that she will be able to remain "full of view" if, rather than disappearing into hiding, she disguises herself as a boy (3.4.149). The insistent metatheatricality of the crossdressing plot, so familiar on the early modern stage, resists the perspectival promise of mimetic disappearance into illusion. After unknowingly being forced to submit to Iachimo's sexual scrutiny of her body, Imogen's disguise allows her simultaneously to withdraw into safety while refusing to vanish from view entirely. In order to put her plan into action, Pisanio explains, Imogen "must forget to be a woman" (3.4.156). To forget deliberately, in this sense, becomes Imogen's own means of "disowning knowledge," to borrow Cavell's phrase – an embrace of the disorienting effect of being doubted as a means to right the wrongs of the play. Indeed, Imogen interrupts Pisanio's explanation, claiming she already understands his intent: "Nay, be brief: / I see into thy end, and am almost / A man already" (3.4.167–69). "Almost / A man," Imogen finds a comfortable home in the ambivalence of the theatricality cultivated by the commercial playhouse, through which audiences were invited to revel in the prismatic doubleness of spectacles that refused to resolve into illusionistic coherence. The employment of this theatricalized unknowing adds Pisanio's epistemological vantage to her perspective: "I see into *thy* end," she assures him.

Imogen's strategic harnessing of educed effacement does not immediately extinguish fallible vision from the world of *Cymbeline*, for it is only after she assumes her disguise that she mistakes Cloten's dead body for

Posthumus's; the sight of the corpse prompts her to admit, "Our very eyes / Are sometimes like our judgments, blind" (4.2.301–02).[65] Her decision to disguise herself, however, does become the catalyst for the play's reestablishment of mutual relations: Imogen stumbles on her brothers Guiderius and Arviragus, a reunion that leads to Cymbeline's recovery of his lost sons. The fulsome reality that these recognitions bring into being is enabled by nothing other than a mole on Guiderius's neck; the bodily mark that earlier allowed Iachimo to delude Posthumus about his wife's fidelity is transformed from a "stain" to a "mark of wonder" in the play's final scene (5.5.366), a "natural stamp" that links Imogen to her biological brothers (5.5.367). Rather than acting as evidence for a false narrative, Guiderius's mole confirms for spectators what they already know by other means: that the brothers are "sons to th' king," as Belarius reveals during the first scene in which they appear (3.3.80). The mole on Guiderius's neck is no more visible to spectators than the one on Imogen's breast, but like the ambiguous object Posthumus waves during his departure from Britain, its indiscernibility at last becomes inconsequential.

This change in what the mole represents works to reshape not only what both spectators and characters onstage see, but how they see. The mutual recognitions of the play's final scene, in Cymbeline's account, alleviate his own incomplete knowledge. "How liv'd you?" he asks his daughter, incredulous:

> And when came you to serve our Roman captive?
> How parted with your brothers? how first met them?
> Why fled you from the court? and whither? These,
> And your three motives to the battle, with
> I know not how much more, should be demanded
> And all the other by-dependances,
> From chance to chance. But nor the time nor place
> Will serve our long inter'gatories. See,
> Posthumus anchors upon Imogen;
> And she (like harmless lightning) throws her eye
> On him: her brothers, me: her master hitting
> Each object with a joy: the counterchange
> Is severally in all.
>   (5.5.385–98)

The king's desire to learn of Imogen's travails is briefly stopped when he notices the "harmless lightning" of looking that ricochets among the reunited family members onstage, creating a reciprocity greater, and more manifold, than the sum of its parts: "severally in all." There will be a time and place for interrogation. But for the moment, the forensic pressures of the evidentiary metonym are released in favor of the mutual exchanges of recognition – the joyful immensity of "counterchange." The prismatic plenitude of collective looking that ends the play is a safeguard against what exceeds the understanding, allowing it temporarily to slip, unnoticed, out of sight.

Disappearance in Antony and Cleopatra

Up to this point I have argued that the theater's staging of small objects entangled spectators in the epistemological limitations of evidentiary metonyms. The unpredictable patterns of disclosure and occlusion, unambiguous revelation and false expectations, into which spectators were thrust alternately reinforced and weakened their phenomenological tether to stage performance. But though The Picture and Cymbeline exacerbate the inherently faulty presentation of small objects in the theater, they also represent the theater itself as a site of spectacular abundance – as a replacement, that is, for the partial, misleading knowledge offered by evidence alone. The revelatory possibilities and limitations of the theater are synthesized, I want now to suggest, in Antony and Cleopatra. The play is simultaneously Shakespeare's most full-throated defense of the theater's capacity for spectacular disclosure and clearest acknowledgement of the essential impermanence of the truths it displays.

Cleopatra's own "infinite variety" is put on display just before her suicide (2.2.246), when she is dressed by her women in the robe, crown, and jewels she will wear to meet Antony after death.[66] The scene carries with it the commercial theater's ever-present risk of failure, inviting spectators to bring into focus the materials of theatrical representation when the boy actor playing Cleopatra draws the asp to his nonexistent breast.[67] But the Egyptian queen's transformation into the ephemeral stuff of nature – "I am fire and air" (5.2.288), she asserts – is also made theatrically possible only by inviting spectators to acknowledge directly what she so emphatically insists cannot capture her: the imagined Roman actor who will only serve to "boy [her] greatness" (5.2.219). "We must accept [the boy actor's] verisimilitude," Phyllis Rackin writes, "before we can appreciate the force of Cleopatra's charge that it is a poor parody of the greatness she possesses."[68] Spectators witness that transcendence at the moment of her death, for if Cleopatra "beggar[s] all description" (2.2.208), it is precisely the acknowledgement of the limitations of stage representation that allow theatrical spectacle to make up for the words that fail her. Peggy Phelan describes the process of performance that *Antony and Cleopatra* endorses when she suggests that "theatrical spectators … see what they believe to be false – and in attempting to account for that falsity, they see the truth of disguise and discover the need to augment the real itself."[69] The theater finally becomes a site of unambiguous disclosure when its verbal and visual technologies intertwine and surpass illusionistic verisimilitude – when what should exceed the capacity of representation becomes, in the immediacy of performance, what is.[70] In these moments, the theater, to borrow Enobarbus's characterization of Cleopatra herself, "make[s] defect perfection" (2.2.241); it does not just stand in for "an imagined act," but stands beyond it.[71]

Cleopatra relies on this capacity for transcendence as a means to resolve, finally, her own uncertainty. The anxieties that dominate *The Picture* and *Cymbeline* are absent from *Antony and Cleopatra*, for the threat of infidelity does not lurk at the margins of this particular love story, anxiously evoked though never seen; the torrid affair between Cleopatra and Antony instead constitutes the play's central action. Yet Cleopatra still doubts: not who she is, as Sophia does, or where she is, as Imogen does, but where Antony is, when he is not with her. Early on in the play, Cleopatra demands to know her lover's whereabouts:

CLEOPATRA. Saw you my lord?
ENOBARBUS. No, lady.
CLEOPATRA. Was he not here?
CHARMIAN. No, madam.
CLEOPATRA. He was disposed to mirth, but on the sudden
          A Roman thought hath struck him. Enobarbus!
ENOBARBUS. Madam?
CLEOPATRA. Seek him and bring him hither. (1.2.83–90)

Antony is retrieved, and enters, just five lines after her initial inquiry. The episode is repeated a scene later, with the same celeritous progression from Cleopatra's doubt to Antony's presentation to her sight. These repeated episodes create a binary between onstage presence and offstage absence that is oddly small in scale compared to the movement between the two far-flung fictional locations that otherwise shape the play's action.[72] But Cleopatra characterizes Antony's absence in exactly these immense terms; he is gone because he has been struck by a "Roman thought," though he appears merely to be in the next room.[73] Cleopatra resolves her persistent doubt about her lover's whereabouts in a manner that entirely outmatches its spatial insignificance. And by the end of the play, she finds a way to join Antony in death by being, quite simply, everywhere at once.

The play's intensification of Antony's absence from Cleopatra when they are not so very far apart at all reaches its poetic apex in Enobarbus's famous report of their first meeting on the river Cydnus – a spectacle that, according to Plutarch, Cleopatra arranged in "mock[ing]" response to Antony's solicitations that she come to him:[74]

> For her own person,
> It beggared all description: she did lie
> In her pavilion, cloth-of-gold of tissue,
> O'erpicturing that Venus where we see
> The fancy outwork nature. On each side her
> Stood pretty dimpled boys, like smiling cupids,
> With divers-colored fans, whose wind did seem
> To glow the delicate cheeks which they did cool,
> And what they undid did.   (2.2.207–15)

Jonathan Gil Harris has detailed the ways that Enobarbus's report of Cleopatra's spectacular display on the barge, in its careful description of the details surrounding the queen, produces her as the very void that nature itself was proverbially believed to abhor.[75] Yet I would suggest that another gap is produced by the description of Cleopatra's separation from Antony:

> The city cast
> Her people out upon her, and Antony,
> Enthroned i'th' market-place, did sit alone,
> Whistling to th'air, which, but for vacancy,
> Had gone to gaze on Cleopatra, too,
> And made a gap in nature.   (2.2.223–28)

It is not Antony alone who, "whistling to th' air," sits and waits for his queen as "her people" rush toward her; the air itself waits with him. At the moment of her death, Cleopatra's transformation into the very substance that grazes Antony's lips as he waits for her in Tarsus ensures that the void between them she so abhors will no longer be allowed to persist. "Husband," she cries, "I come!" (5.2.286).

Yet this process of transformation is, like performance itself, at once an act of disappearance.[76] Though Cleopatra's body remains onstage after her death, clearly visible to both the onstage Roman investigators and the audience in the playhouse, it is inscrutable, showing no outward signs of the way that she died. "She looks like sleep," Caesar observes (5.2.345). Cleopatra herself has found her way elsewhere, to Antony, and the Romans strain to look on what eludes them.[77] When Caesar arrives, having just missed Cleopatra's suicide, Dolabella casts him as a spectator of Cleopatra's death, warning him, "Thyself art coming / To see performed the dreaded act" (5.2.329–30). What proceeds, however, is not an inset performance but a forensic investigation, as Caesar and his attendants piece together a "most probable" narrative about Cleopatra's death with the materials left available to them (5.2.352).[78] But the very nature of the evidence he arranges into the story of her suicide gestures to the spectacle that has nevertheless escaped him. The hauntingly gossamer evidence that Dolabella and the guard register – "a vent of blood," "something blown," "an aspic's trail," "fig leaves [with] slime upon them" (5.2.348, 348, 350, 350–51) – is barely substantial, merely pointed to on the stage rather than materially presented. These materials pass into invisibility even as they preserve the manner of Cleopatra's disappearance. In the guard's description, "leaves" fixes that paradox of permanent departure as the word slips from noun to verb in its repetition: "This is an aspic's trail, and these fig leaves / Have slime upon them such as th'aspic leaves / Upon the caves of Nile" (5.2.350–52). This evidence acts not as a failed or deceptive representation of unseen narratives, as it does in *Cymbeline* and *The Picture*, but merely a lackluster version of the same story told through theatrical spectacle. As they observe Caesar's evidentiary narrative come solidly into view, spectators simultaneously witness the spectacle of Cleopatra herself recede and diminish until she is "scant to be discerned," as Thomas North translates Plutarch's description of the bites on her arm.[79] Just as she does description, Cleopatra beggars all evidence. At the close of *Antony and Cleopatra*, the material detritus of Cleopatra's suicide creates for spectators, in the frustrated experience of visual strain, the paradoxical display of what is lost when only probable knowledge remains.[80]

Antony and Cleopatra has aptly been characterized as a "contest between narrative and drama, text and performance."[81] But the play's depiction of the ways that Egyptian theatricality wins out against the reductive narrative the Romans construct to interpret it captures the epistemological program of the commercial theater more broadly. All three of the plays examined in this chapter variously stage just such a contest between the unstable wholeness of theatrical spectacle and the enduring incompleteness of evidence. As its culture moved in fits and starts toward an epistemology heavily dependent on the probable certainties offered by eyewitness testimony, evidential narrative, and experiment, the theater offered itself up as a site of capacious and complex, if ultimately fleeting, revelation. Theatrical spectacle, in all its abundant immediacy, takes place at the vanishing point.

Notes

1 Act, scene, and line numbers follow William Shakespeare, *Cymbeline*, ed. J. M. Nosworthy (London: Arden Shakespeare, 2007).

2 See, for example, Kenneth Burke, "*Othello*: An Essay to Illustrate a Method" in "*Othello*": *Critical Essays*, ed. Susan Snyder (New York: Garland, 1988), 127–68; Lynda Boose, "Othello's Handkerchief: 'The Recognizance and Pledge of Love'," *English Literary Renaissance* 5.3 (1975): 360–74; Susan Frye, *Pens and Needles: Women's Textualities in Early Modern England* (Philadelphia: University of Pennsylvania Press, 2010), 160–90; Michael Neill, "Unproper Beds: Race, Adultery, and the Hideous in *Othello*," *Shakespeare Quarterly* 40.4 (1989): 383–412; and Katharine Eisaman Maus, *Inwardness and Theater in the English Renaissance* (Chicago: University of Chicago Press, 1995), 104–27.

3 Maus, *Inwardness*, 32.

4 Act, scene, and line numbers follow William Shakespeare, *King Henry V*, ed. T. W. Craik (London: Arden Shakespeare, 1995).

5 Tim Fitzpatrick, *Playwright, Space and Place in Early Modern Performance: Shakespeare and Company* (New York: Routledge, 2011), 27–61, esp. 30.

6 For work on language as a theatrical technology for the representation of place in the early modern theater, see Alan C. Dessen, *Elizabethan Stage Conventions and Modern Interpreters* (Cambridge: Cambridge University Press, 1984), 84–104; Bert O. States, *Great Reckonings in Little Rooms: On the Phenomenology of Theater* (Berkeley: University of California Press, 1985), 48–70; and Robert Weimann, *Author's Pen and Actor's Voice: Playing and Writing in Shakespeare's Theatre* (Cambridge: Cambridge University Press, 2000), 180–215.

7 Related to my object in this chapter is Andrew Sofer's elucidation of what he terms "dark matter" in the theater: that which "*is materially unrepresented onstage but un-ignorable.*" I aim to attend, though, to objects that *are* materially represented on the stage but remain impossible to apprehend completely. See Sofer, *Dark Matter: Invisibility in Drama, Theater, and Performance* (Ann Arbor: University of Michigan Press, 2013), 4.

8 Dating follows Martin Wiggins, *British Drama 1533–1642: A Catalogue*, vols. 5, 6, and 8 (Oxford: Oxford University Press, 2015). The title page of *The Picture*'s 1630 quarto indicates that the play was staged at both the Globe and the Blackfriars. Neither *Cymbeline* nor *Antony and Cleopatra* were printed in quarto, though the Lord Chamberlain's records of 1669 indicate

that both plays were "formerly acted at the Blackfryers." See Allardyce Nicoll, *A History of Restoration Drama 1660–1700* (Cambridge: Cambridge University Press, 1923), 315–16. Indirect evidence for *Cymbeline*'s performance at the Globe comes from Simon Forman's account of seeing the play in 1611, likely in late April. He does not indicate where he saw the play, though his description of *Cymbeline* is surrounded by descriptions of three other plays he saw at the Globe. See Gāmini Salgādo, *Eyewitnesses of Shakespeare: First Hand Accounts of Performances, 1590–1890* (New York: Barnes and Noble Books, 1975), 32. *Antony and Cleopatra* very likely debuted at the Globe. It was entered in the Stationer's Register on May 20, 1608, just over a month before the King's Men acquired the Blackfriars via a lease from Richard Burbage and over a year before the company was able to perform in their new playhouse, having been kept out of it due to an outbreak of the plague.

9 For this argument, see Tiffany Stern, "'Taking Part': Actors and Audience on the Stage at Blackfriars," *Inside Shakespeare: Essays on the Blackfriars Stage*, ed. Paul Menzer (Selinsgrove, PA: Susquehanna University Press, 2006), 35–53. The many plays that stage miniatures are too numerous to name here, though it is worth registering that such staging occurs throughout the period, in outdoor amphitheaters as well as indoor halls. In Marlowe's *Edward II* (1592), for example, Gaveston and Edward exchange miniatures: "Here, take my picture and let me wear thine" (4.127); Bassanio finds Portia's portrait in the lead casket in *The Merchant of Venice* (1596); in *Twelfth Night* (1601) Olivia gives Cesario her miniature as a gift: "Here, wear this jewel for me: 'tis my picture" (3.4.203). All of these plays were originally staged in outdoor theaters – *Edward II* and *The Merchant of Venice* at the Theatre, *Twelfth Night* at the Globe – which would have actively frustrated spectators' ability to see the tiny portraits. Tourneur's *The Atheist's Tragedy* (1610), a slightly later play, exacerbates this frustration to an even greater degree by including the exchange of a miniature in a ring. Act, scene, and line numbers follow Christopher Marlowe, *Edward II*, in *The Complete Plays*, ed. Frank Romany and Robert Lindsey (London: Penguin, 2006); and William Shakespeare, *Twelfth Night*, ed. Keir Elam (London: Arden Shakespeare, 2008). For a comprehensive list of plays that stage miniatures and portraits, see Emanuel Stelzer, *Portraits in Early Modern English Drama: Visual Culture, Play-Texts, and Performances* (New York: Routledge, 2019).

10 Sarah Dustagheer, *Shakespeare's Two Playhouses: Repertory and Theatre Space at the Globe and the Blackfriars, 1599–1613* (Cambridge: Cambridge University Press, 2017), 7.

11 This phrase is adapted from Stanley Fish, who details "Milton's programme of reader harassment" in *Surprised by Sin: The Reader in "Paradise Lost,"* 2nd ed. (Cambridge, MA: Harvard University Press, 1998), 4.

12 In François Rabelais's *Tiers Livre* (1546), for example, when Panurge goes on a journey to determine whether or not he should marry, he encounters the skeptical philosopher Wordspooler. "Will she be modest and chaste? That's the only point I'm after," Panurge asks. "I doubt it," the skeptic responds. Rabelais, *Gargantua and Pantagruel*, trans. Burton Raffel

(New York: W. W. Norton and Company, 1990), 336. Rabelais's own engagements with Pyrrhonian skepticism and Erasmian skeptical fideism have been well-documented; see, for example, M. A. Screech's classic study, *The Rabelaisian Marriage: Aspects of Rabelais's Religion, Ethics, and Comic Philosophy* (London: Edward Arnold, 1958); and Martha M. Houle, "The Marriage Question, or, the *Querelle des hommes* in Rabelais, Molière and Boileau," *Dalhousie French Studies* 56 (2001): 46–54.

13 Stanley Cavell, *Disowning Knowledge in Seven Plays of Shakespeare* (Cambridge: Cambridge University Press, 2003), 16.

14 Mark Breitenberg helpfully characterizes the problem with Cavell's essentialist, ahistorical approach: "By positioning philosophical knowledge in a pure, abstract realm apart from and prior to its sexualized enactment, Cavell relies upon and perpetuates a theory of philosophical knowledge which is assumed to be male. Furthermore, since 'philosophical skepticism' is central to those humanistic models of interpretation originating in the Renaissance, Cavell is trapped in a kind of historical circularity in which his own interpretive method is guaranteed by the historical period under scrutiny." See Breitenberg, *Anxious Masculinity in Early Modern England* (Cambridge: Cambridge University Press, 1996), 179.

15 See, for example, Katharine Eisaman Maus, "Horns of Dilemma: Jealousy, Gender, and Spectatorship in English Renaissance Drama," *English Literary History* 54.3 (1987): 561–83; Patricia Parker, *Shakespeare from the Margins: Language, Culture, Context* (Chicago: University of Chicago Press, 1996), 229–72; and Karen Cunningham, *Imaginary Betrayals: Subjectivity and the Discourses of Treason in Early Modern England* (Philadelphia: University of Pennsylvania Press, 2002), 40–76. On sexual jealousy as an "inevitable constituent of masculine identity," see Breitenberg, *Anxious Masculinity*, 176.

16 On the emergence of "constructive scepticism" as an antecedent to empirical modes of thought that would gain traction in the seventeenth century, see Richard Popkin, *The History of Scepticism from Savonarola to Bayle* (Oxford: Oxford University Press, 2003), esp. 112–27. On the origins of the experimental method in individual experience, see Peter Dear, *Discipline and Experience: The Mathematical Way in the Scientific Revolution* (Chicago: University of Chicago Press, 1995). On the development of the experimental method in the later seventeenth century, see Simon Schaffer and Steven Shapin, *Leviathan and the Air-Pump: Hobbes, Boyle, and the Experimental Life* (Princeton: Princeton University Press, 1985). On the conjectural practices that would eventually become codified as probabilistic modes of thought, see Ian Hacking, *The Emergence of Probability: A Philosophical Study of Early Ideas about Probability, Induction and Statistical Inference*, 2nd ed. (Cambridge: Cambridge University Press, 2006). On the emergence of the modern concept of "fact" in legal discourse, specifically with regard to eyewitness testimony, see Barbara J. Shapiro, *A Culture of Fact: England, 1550–1720* (Ithaca, NY: Cornell University Press, 2003).

17 Howard Marchitello, "Science Studies and English Renaissance Literature," *Literature Compass* 3.3 (2006): 341–65, esp. 355. On the inferential forensic and modes of thought cultivated in the theater, see Lorna Hutson, *The Invention of Suspicion: Law and Mimesis in Shakespeare and Renaissance Drama* (Oxford: Oxford University Press, 2007); and Subha Mukherji, *Law and Representation in Early Modern Drama* (Cambridge: Cambridge University Press, 2006). On the literary response to the emergence of new, counterintuitive ways of describing the natural world, see Mary Thomas Crane, *Losing Touch with Nature: Literature and the New Science in Sixteenth-Century England* (Baltimore: Johns Hopkins University Press, 2014). On early modern science and literature as acts of making, see Elizabeth Spiller, *Science, Reading, and Renaissance Literature: The Art of Making Knowledge, 1580–1670* (Cambridge: Cambridge University Press, 2004). On the indebtedness of the theater's spatial practices to mathematical and scientific modes of thought, see Henry S. Turner, *The English Renaissance Stage: Geometry, Poetics, and the Practical Spatial Arts 1580–1630* (Oxford: Oxford University Press, 2006).

18 Theater practitioners, to be sure, frequently described the playhouse as a site of *moral* revelation in this period; Thomas Heywood, for example, describes several instances of playgoers revealing their own secret truths and admitting to misdeeds as a result of seeing them displayed on the stage. I give attention in this chapter, however, not to how practitioners talked about the theater, but what the theater did – the formal means, that is, by which it cultivated both spectatorial uncertainty and knowingness through its stage practices. See Heywood, *An Apology for Actors* (London: Nicholas Okes, 1612).

19 My argument about the fulsome ephemerality of stage show in this chapter bears some affinity to debates in performance studies about disappearance and persistence: scholars such as Herbert Blau and Peggy Phelan have characterized the central feature of live performance as the necessity of its ephemerality; others, such as Rebecca Schneider and Diana Taylor, have challenged these suppositions, pointing to, in Schneider's words, performance as "the *act* of remaining and as a means of re-appearance." This chapter does not engage directly in this theoretical debate because it follows the concerns about the lively immediacy of performance expressed in early modern drama itself. Within that archive, there is a persistent recognition that stage spectacle disappears. See Schneider, *Performing Remains: Art and War in Times of Theatrical Reenactment* (New York: Routledge, 2011), 101. See also Blau, *Take Up the Bodies: Theater at the Vanishing Point* (Urbana, IL: University of Illinois Press, 1982); Phelan, *Unmarked: The Politics of Performance* (New York: Routledge, 1993); and Taylor, *The Archive and the Repertoire: Performing Cultural Memory in the Americas* (Durham, NC: Duke University Press, 2003).

20 Act, scene, and line numbers follow Philip Massinger, *The Picture*, ed. Lucy Munro, in *The Routledge Anthology of Early Modern Drama*, ed. Jeremy Lopez (New York: Routledge, 2020).

21 Nicholas Hilliard, *Art of Limning*, ed. Arthur F. Kinney (Boston: Northeastern University Press, 1983), 77.

22 Lorna Hutson, "Probable Infidelities from Bandello to Massinger," in *Staging Early Modern Romance: Prose Fiction, Dramatic Romance, and Shakespeare*, eds. Valerie Wayne and Mary Ellen Lamb (New York: Routledge, 2008), 219–35. Massinger's source, William Painter's "The Lady of Boeme," takes great pains to emphasize the unambiguous veracity of the miniature: it is said to be a "certaine secrete experiment" and to offer "certaine signes," "sure knowledge," and "sure evidence." See *Italian Tales from The Age of Shakespeare*, ed. Pamela Benson (London: Everyman, 1996), 149–74, esp. 156–57.

23 Hutson, "Probable Infidelities," 228. Joanne Rochester similarly suggests that "because [the miniature] is the physical product of Mathias' doubts and jealousies, the process of being reassured by it feeds the fears it is designed to combat." See Rochester, *Staging Spectatorship in the Plays of Philip Massinger* (Burlington, VT: Ashgate, 2010), 114.

24 Historians have debated the Globe's size for decades, its partial excavation in 1989 both confirming and unsettling suppositions made prior to that date. For an attempt to account for the theater's size based on both contractual records for the building of the Fortune Theater (overseen by Peter Street, the same architect who managed the Theater's dismantling and rebuilding as the first Globe) as well as evidence from the excavation, see Tim Fitzpatrick, "The Fortune Contract and Hollar's Original Drawing of Southwark: Some Indications of a Smaller First Globe," *Shakespeare Bulletin* 14.4 (1996): 5–10. Fitzpatrick concludes that the Globe's yard measured sixty feet in length, with a stage extended halfway through it, which is where my estimation of thirty feet originates.

25 Thomas Dekker satirically notes the proclivity for this sort of scrutiny in the hall theaters when he advises would-be gallants to purchase a seat on the playhouse stage, the better to (among other things) "examine the play-suits lace." See Dekker, *The Guls Horne-booke* (London: R. S., 1609), 29.

26 Dustagheer, *Shakespeare's Two Playhouses*, 123–38.

27 Farah Karim-Cooper's suggestion, in her work on stage cosmetics, that "the use of silver, gold, or pearl would allow the face of the actor to glisten in dimly lit halls" provides an apt comparison to the limned portrait as a mimetic substitute for Sophia. See Karim-Cooper, *Cosmetics in Shakespearean and Renaissance Drama* (Edinburgh: Edinburgh University Press, 2006), 162.

28 Act, scene, and line numbers follow William Shakespeare, *King Henry IV, Part 1*, ed. David Scott Kastan (London: Arden Shakespeare, 2002).

29 This attention to the conditions of performance gives phenomenological texture to a thematic reading of the portrait. As Mukherji rightly puts it, "as a mimetic, cognitive, and legal instrument, 'the artifice of signs' meets with its most systematic rejection in [*The Picture*]"; I am suggesting that spectators experience those failures as a theatrical failure. See Mukherji, *Law and Representation*, 53–54.

30 As Laura Gowing explains, "Women's honesty was defined by their sexuality, men's by that of the women connected with them." See Gowing, *Domestic Dangers: Women, Words, and Sex in Early Modern London* (Oxford: Clarendon Press, 1996), 112.

31 Edmund Tilney, *The Flower of Friendship: A Renaissance Dialogue Contesting Marriage*, ed. Valerie Wayne (Ithaca, NY: Cornell University Press, 1992), 128. The text went through seven editions between 1568 and 1587. In her introduction, Wayne connects this expressed need for women's chastity to paternity: "Since a woman's virtue is also connected with her husband's paternity and their children's parentage, the wife's primary virtue is her chastity: virginity before marriage and fidelity after it." See Introduction, *The Flower of Friendship*, 52.

32 For more on the language of secrecy with regard to women's anatomy, see Parker, *Shakespeare from the Margins*, 234–38. On the illegibility of the female reproductive body, see Sara D. Luttfring, *Bodies, Speech, and Reproductive Knowledge in Early Modern England* (New York: Routledge, 2016); and Mara Amster, "Frances Howard and Middleton and Rowley's *The Changeling*: Trials, Tests, and the Legibility of the Virgin Body," in *The Single Woman in Medieval and Early Modern England: Her Life and Representation*, ed. Laurel Amtower and Dorothea Kehler (Tempe: Arizona Center for Medieval and Renaissance Studies, 2003), 211–32. For more on the "secrets of women" tradition in medieval natural philosophical and medical discourses, see Katharine Park, *Secrets of Women: Gender, Generation, and the Origins of Human Dissection* (New York: Zone Books, 2006); and Monica H. Green, *Making Women's Medicine Masculine: The Rise of Male Authority in Pre-modern Gynaecology* (Oxford: Oxford University Press, 2008). On the early modern social history of women's vernacular bodily knowledge, see Laura Gowing, *Common Bodies: Women, Touch and Power in Seventeenth-Century England* (New Haven: Yale University Press, 2003).

33 Joseph Hall, *Occasionall Meditations* (London: Nathaniel Butter, 1631), 235 (emphasis mine).

34 Jacques Olivier, *A Discourse of Women, Shewing Their Imperfections Alphabetically* (London: Henry Brome, 1662), 41 (emphasis mine).

35 Olivier, *A Discourse of Women*, 42.

36 As Subha Mukherji puts it, for example, both Mathias and the play's audience "learn that the flowing stream of intentionality cannot be captured in an isolated, momentary representation." Mukherji, *Law and Representation*, 53. See also Marina Hila, "'To heighten your desire': Sexual Politics in Massinger's *The Picture* (1629)," *Cahiers Élisabéthains: A Journal of English Renaissance Studies* 92.1 (2016): 68–81. Focusing mostly on the miniature, Erin V. Obermueller is largely concerned with the ways it "disarms and subsumes" Sophia, though she does turn briefly to her "verbal prowess [as an] instance of female fashioning of male subjectivity". See Obermueller, "'On Cheating Pictures': Gender and Portrait Miniatures in Philip Massinger's *The Picture*," *Early Theatre* 10.2 (2007): 87–107, esp. 98, 102.

37 By 1629, the soliloquy was an eminently familiar theatrical device. It is worth noting, however, that the sixteenth-century emphasis on the soliloquy's self-reflexive qualities paved the way for the knotty, uncertain ruminations characteristic of its later appearances onstage. On the Tudor origins of the dramatic soliloquy, see Raphael Falco, "Tudor Transformations," in *Shakespeare and the Soliloquy in Early Modern English Drama*, ed. A. D. Cousins and Daniel Derrin (Cambridge: Cambridge University Press, 2018), 29–42.

38 Hutson characterizes Sophia's suspension as "a hauntingly memorable expression of the self-annihilating horror of contemplating opposing probabilities"; I would suggest that while the *psychological* effect of the lines may be the threat of self-annihilation, their *theatrical* effect is precisely the opposite. See Hutson, "Probable Infidelities," 231.

39 See, for example, Karen Newman, *Shakespeare's Rhetoric of Comic Character: Dramatic Convention in Classical and Renaissance Comedy* (New York: Routledge, 1985), 63–64. On the soliloquy as a process of self-interrogation, see Rachel Eisendrath, "The Long Nightwatch: Augustine, *Hamlet*, and the Aesthetic," *ELH* 87.3 (2020): 581–606.

40 Lena Cowen Orlin, *Locating Privacy in Tudor London* (Oxford: Oxford University Press, 2007), 323.

41 For more on various iterations of the bed trick as a theatrical convention, see Marliss C. Desens, *The Bed Trick in English Renaissance Drama: Explorations in Gender, Sexuality, and Power* (Newark: University of Delaware Press, 1994).

42 On the ideological premise of the bed trick, see Janet Adelman, *Suffocating Mothers: Fantasies of Maternal Origin in Shakespeare's Plays, "Hamlet" to "The Tempest"* (New York: Routledge, 1992), 78.

43 Pollard, born in 1597, became a sharer in the King's Men by 1624. On the comic repertoire of Pollard's later career, see Lucy Munro, "Comedy, Clowning and the Caroline King's Men: Manuscript Plays and Performance," in *Early British Drama in Manuscript*, ed. Tamara Atkin and Laura Estill (Turnhout: Brepols Publishers, 2019), 213–28.

44 John Astington, *Actors and Acting in Shakespeare's Time: The Art of Stage Playing* (Cambridge: Cambridge University Press, 2010), 87.

45 John Honeyman, born in 1613, was also apprenticed to John Shank; he moved to playing male roles for the rest of his brief career after his performance as Sophia in 1629. See Astington, *Actors and Acting*, 201–2.

46 This unusual use of "miniature" to mean "lineament" or "feature," it is worth noting, transforms each element of the portrait into a metonym for the portrait itself, as if Mathias's attempt to discern Sophia's intentions has caused her to recede yet further from his grasp. The OED cites only *The Picture* and another Massinger play, *The Great Duke of Florence*, as uses of the word in this way. "miniature, n. 2." OED Online. November 2018. www.oed.com/view/Entry/118826 (accessed November 2, 2018).

47 As Joanne Rochester points out, "The technique [of the bed trick] works because both men's nobility and putative virility lies in their exteriors – their clothing and manners – rather than their characters." See *Staging Spectatorship*, 120.

48 This is not to say that the play does not work hard to find comic closure: Mathias tells Sophia in the final scene that he will "set no watch upon you, and for proof of't / This cursèd picture I surrender up / To a consuming fire" (5.3.213–15), a promise that may well have been accompanied by the miniature's fiery destruction onstage. But Sophia's (eventually abandoned) declaration that she "desire[s] a separation from [Mathias's] bed" keeps her irresolution alive through *The Picture*'s final lines (5.3.180), so that the play's conclusion approaches a tonal ambivalence closer to the so-called problem play than a comedy.

49 For more on misperception in *Cymbeline*, see, for example, Cynthia Lewis, "'With Simular Proof Enough': Modes of Misperception in *Cymbeline*," *SEL* 31.2 (1991): 343–64; and Nancy Simpson-Younger, "'The garments of Posthumus': Identifying the Non-Responsive Body in *Cymbeline*," in *Staging the Blazon in Early Modern English Theater*, ed. Deborah Uman and Sarah Morrison (Burlington, VT: Ashgate, 2013), 177–88.

50 The question of whether Shakespeare's stage was actually populated with the objects that Iachimo describes in this scene has generated fervent debate. For the suggestion that the scene includes the stage furniture Iachimo names, see Peggy Muñoz Simonds, *Myth, Emblem, and Music in Shakespeare's "Cymbeline": An Iconographic Reconstruction* (Newark: University of Delaware Press, 1992), 95. For the argument that the commercial theater regularly employed imagistic tapestries and hangings as part of its settings, see Mariko Ichikawa, "'What Story Is That Painted Vpon the Cloth?': Some Descriptions of Hangings and Their Use on the Early Modern Stage," *Theatre Notebook* 70.1 (2016): 2–31. Ichikawa's argument is compelling, though in the case of *Cymbeline*, it does not account for the way Iachimo describes the details of the tapestries: he only does so in 2.4, *after* he has left Imogen's room. In both 2.2 and 2.4, then, I would argue that Iachimo's verbalization of the room's details is ekphrastic rather than a repetition of furniture and decoration on the stage. For a similar argument, see Lois Potter, *The Life of William Shakespeare: A Critical Biography* (Oxford: Wiley Blackwell, 2012), 372; and Keir Elam, *Shakespeare's Pictures: Visual Objects in the Drama* (London: Bloomsbury, 2017), 73–82.

51 For more on the performative power of Iachimo's language, see Christy Desmet, "Shakespearean Comic Character: Ethos and Epideictic in *Cymbeline*," in *Acting Funny: Comic Theory and Practice in Shakespeare's Plays*, ed. Frances N. Teague (Rutherford, NJ: Fairleigh Dickinson University Press, 1994), 123–41; and Bruce Smith, "Eyeing and Wording in *Cymbeline*," *in* *Knowing Shakespeare: Senses, Embodiment and Cognition*, ed. Lowell Gallagher and Shankar Raman (New York: Palgrave Macmillan, 2010), 50–64. See also J. K. Barret's argument that Iachimo's narrative in the bedroom keeps in view

"what *might be*," and afterward, "what *might have been*" in "The Crowd in Imogen's Bedroom: Allusion and Ethics in *Cymbeline*," *Shakespeare Quarterly* 66.4 (2015): 440–62, esp. 447.

52　Ann Rosalind Jones and Peter Stallybrass, *Renaissance Clothing and the Materials of Memory* (Cambridge: Cambridge University Press, 2000), 212, 213.

53　Simon Forman, *Bocke of Plaies and Notes Thereof*, MS Ashmole 208, fol. 206r, Bodleian Library, Oxford.

54　Sebastiano Serlio, *The First Booke of Architecture* (London: Robert Peake, 1611).

55　Peter Womack, "The Comical Scene: Perspective and Civility on the Renaissance Stage," *Representations* 101.1 (2008): 32–56, esp. 40. For more on the representation of perspective on the English stage, see Henry S. Turner, *The English Renaissance Stage*, 163–70; and Leonard Barkan, "Making Pictures Speak: Renaissance Art, Elizabethan Literature, Modern Scholarship," *Renaissance Quarterly* 48.2 (1995): 326–51.

56　Thomas Overbury, *New and Choise Characters* (London: Laurence Lisle, 1615), M5v.

57　As John Peacock points out, "the first surviving design for a thoroughgoing perspective set comes in … *Prince Henry's Barriers*," a masque by Ben Jonson performed at Whitehall in 1610, the same year of *Cymbeline*'s first performance. Inigo Jones's set designs for the court entertainment are, akin to Serlio's drawings, stuffed with architectural details that conjure the ruins of Roman Britain. See Peacock, *The Stage Designs of Inigo Jones: The European Context* (Cambridge: Cambridge University Press, 1995), 165.

58　The paradigmatic Shakespearean example of verbal perspective deployed as deception is Edgar's description of the Cliffs of Dover in *King Lear*. On the way that the speech verbally organizes space, see Turner, *The English Renaissance Stage*, 163–69. On the deceptive qualities of perspective art as a paradigm for all theatrical representation, see Stephen Orgel, "Shakespeare Imagines a Theater," *Poetics Today* 5.3 (1984): 549–61.

59　Iachimo's account thus both foregrounds and questions the increased reliance on eyewitness testimony, by the opening of the seventeenth century, in the assimilation of evidence in common law trials – a reliance that laid the groundwork for the establishment of a formal law of evidence. Lorna Hutson argues that as a consequence of such dependence on testimony, lay people were increasingly encouraged in this period to take part in the legal process of constructing evidentiary narratives. As a result, she suggests, they were "acquainted with ways of thinking about how to present or evaluate narratives as evidence at the same time as some popular drama was … encouraging the development of a similar kind of awareness." But *Cymbeline* demonstrates that even as drama responded to this shift in the legal system, the theater did not simply replicate for its spectators the experience of evaluating witness testimony in a legal setting. In the theater, spectators were not only encouraged to perform such evaluation, but their attempts to do so were often deliberately exploited and subsequently revealed as wrong. Hutson, *The Invention of Suspicion*, 88. For more on the emergence of a formal law of evidence in this period, see Barbara Shapiro, *Probability and Certainty in Seventeenth-Century England: A Study of the Relationships Between Natural Science, Religion, History, Law, and Literature* (Princeton: Princeton University Press, 1983); and more recently, "Beyond Reasonable Doubt: The Evolution of a Concept," in *Fictions of Knowledge: Fact, Evidence, Doubt,* eds. Yota Batsaki, Subha Mukherji, and Jan-Melissa Schramm (New York: Palgrave Macmillan, 2012), 19–39. Though John H. Langbein has argued against earlier contentions that traces of a law of evidence appear in the English legal system from the sixteenth century onwards, he does allow that the formalization of witness testimony during the same period laid the groundwork for later conceptions of the law of evidence. See Langbein, "Historical Foundations of the Law of Evidence: A View from the Ryder Sources," *Columbia Law Review* 96.5 (1996): 1168–202.

60 Act, scene, and line numbers follow Shakespeare, *Othello*, ed. E. A. J. Honigmann (London: Arden Shakespeare, 1997). The cumulative effect of Iachimo's narration mattered in a world that existed on the cusp of Aristotelian, inductive reasoning, which sought to explain universal knowledge supported by general experience (that heavy bodies tend to fall toward the earth, for example), and knowledge constructed through the particularized experience of the experiment. A singular event could no longer act as vivid confirmation of commonplace knowledge; the event of the experiment could only make up part of the collection of evidence used to arrive at a more general truth. In other words, as Peter Dear has shown, "the singular experience could not be *evident*, but it could provide *evidence*." See Dear, *Discipline and Experience*, 25.

61 As J. M. Nosworthy notes, this ambiguity appears in Holinshed's *Chronicles*, as well: "And some other authors not vnwoorthie to be read and perused, it is not certeine vnto which portion of the earth our Ilands … should be ascribed, bicause they excluded them (as you sée) from the rest of the whole earth." See Nosworthy, *Cymbeline*, 97 n140. Raphael Holinshed, *The First and Second Volumes of Chronicles* (London: John Harison, George Bishop, Rafe Newberie, Henrie Denham, and Thomas Woodcocke, 1587), 2.

62 Act, scene, and line numbers follow William Shakespeare, *The Tempest*, ed. Virginia Mason Vaughan and Alden T. Vaughan and (London: Arden Shakespeare, 1999).

63 Huw Griffiths, "The Geographies of Shakespeare's *Cymbeline*," *English Literary Renaissance* 34.3 (2004): 339–58, esp. 345.

64 For more on the ways that *Cymbeline* stages threats to a sense of place – specifically, the home – see Heather Dubrow, "'I would I were at home': Representations of Dwelling Places and Havens in *Cymbeline*," in *Shakespeare and Historical Formalism*, ed. Stephen Cohen (Burlington, VT: Ashgate, 2007), 69–93.

65 See, however, Maurice Hunt's argument that Imogen's mistake "represent[s] a first step in the reconstitution of the British body politic." Hunt, "Dismemberment, Corporal Reconstitution, and the Body Politic in *Cymbeline*," *Studies in Philology* 99.4 (2002): 404–31, esp. 418.

66 Act, scene, and line numbers follow Shakespeare, *Antony and Cleopatra*, ed. John Wilders (London: Bloomsbury Arden Shakespeare, 1995).

67 Jones and Stallybrass note that, as he does in *Cymbeline*, Shakespeare amends his source material seemingly in order to draw attention to the body of the boy actor at this moment of *Antony and Cleopatra*: "In Plutarch, Cleopatra attaches an asp to her *arm*. Shakespeare retains this, but only after she has already placed an asp on her *breast*." Jones and Stallybrass, *Renaissance Clothing and the Materials of Memory*, 212.

68 Phyllis Rackin, "Shakespeare's Boy Cleopatra, the Decorum of Nature, and the Golden World of Poetry," *PMLA* 87.2 (1972): 201–12, esp. 211.

69 Phelan, *Unmarked*, 116.

70 Jonathan Gil Harris points to these limits of theatrical representation when he suggests that Cleopatra's "very vividness is shown to be the effect of a Roman desire for her presence, prompted by the gaps and absences that repeatedly afflict the play's attempts to represent her." It is at the moment that Cleopatra takes the matter of her representation into her own hands, I argue, that spectators – though, notably, *not* the Romans – are finally granted with her presence. See Harris, "'Narcissus in thy Face': Roman Desire and the Difference it Fakes in *Antony and Cleopatra*," *Shakespeare Quarterly* 45.4 (1994): 408–25, esp. 417.

71 Bernard Beckerman, *Dynamics of Drama: Theory and Method of Analysis* (New York: Drama Book Specialists, 1979), 18.

72 I treat various theatrical uses of this spatial binary in greater detail in Chapter 4.

73 As Gillian Knoll points out, Cleopatra's questions about Antony's whereabouts continue after he has left for Rome. See Knoll, "Binding the Void: The Erotics of Place in *Antony And Cleopatra*," *Criticism* 58.2 (2016): 281–304.

74 Plutarch, *The Lives of the Noble Grecians and Romanes*, trans. Thomas North (London: Thomas Vautroullier and John Wight, 1579), 981.

75 See Harris, "Narcissus," 417–18. For the proverb that "nature abhors a vacuum," see R. W. Dent, *Shakespeare's Proverbial Language: An Index* (Berkeley, CA, 1981), 180, N42.

76 As Phelan puts it, "live performance plunges into visibility – in a maniacally charged present – and disappears into memory, into the realm of invisibility and the unconscious where it eludes regulation and control." See Phelan, *Unmarked*, 148. For an account of the early modern English theater's preoccupation with its own disappearance, see Ellen MacKay, *Persecution, Plague, and Fire: Fugitive Histories of the Stage in Early Modern England* (Chicago: University of Chicago Press, 2011).

77 Mary Thomas Crane casts this elusiveness in terms of a division between Egyptian and Roman worldviews, suggesting that Shakespeare ultimately endorses the earthy theatricality of Egypt: "If Egypt can't be clearly seen or firmly touched, it seems difficult to know or conquer it with any certainty." See Crane, *Losing Touch*, 163.

78 Tara E. Pedersen rightly points out that from an audience perspective, this scene is entirely redundant: "The audience knows what killed Cleopatra; in the final act, we watch it happen before our eyes. Why then is Shakespeare

not precluded from staging a mystery to which we already seem to know the answer?" Pedersen's question is the same one that motivates my own reading of the play's final moments, and I agree with her suggestion that Cleopatra endorses the manifold possibility of performance that evidential narrative cannot compass. Yet I would argue that the play is ultimately more ambivalent about its own resources than Pedersen allows, for the very act of Cleopatra's suicide acknowledges that the aftereffect of staged plenitude is disappearance. See Pedersen, *Mermaids and the Production of Knowledge in Early Modern England* (Burlington, VT: Ashgate, 2015), 102.

79 Plutarch, *Lives*, 1010.

80 Ania Loomba argues of the play that "the Roman theatre takes over from the volatile Egyptian one"; I would suggest that in this final scene, Shakespeare enacts such a transformation only to expose the limitations of a Roman forensic perspective. See Loomba, *Gender, Race, Renaissance Drama* (Manchester: Manchester University Press, 1989), 130.

81 W. B. Worthen, "The Weight of Antony: Staging 'Character' in *Antony and Cleopatra*," *SEL* 26.2 (1986): 295–308, esp. 297. For more on the ways *Antony and Cleopatra* sets Roman historiography against Egyptian theatricality, see Alan Stewart, *Shakespeare's Letters* (Oxford: Oxford University Press, 2008), 94–114.

CHAPTER 4

Space

Dramatic Impersonation, Playgoing Community, and the Amphitheater

Through the last quarter of the sixteenth century, as theater practitioners introduced the tropes, representational technologies, and genres that would eventually calcify into the conventions defining Jacobean drama, the outdoor playhouses in which those formal experiments were staged underwent significant changes themselves. Recent archaeological evidence has demonstrated that London's Elizabethan amphitheaters were more architecturally varied than was once thought. The 1576 Theater was circular – a multi-sided polygon – though the 2016 excavation of the 1587 Curtain showed that the playhouse, once believed to be Shakespeare's "Wooden O," was rectangular.[1] In 1592, Philip Henslowe had the fourteen-sided Rose enlarged; the reshaped structure approximated a rounded rectangle.[2] The circular Swan was built in 1595, while the rectangular Boar's Head was converted from an already-extant innyard in 1598. That same year, the Theater was dismantled and, in the spring of 1599, reconstructed south of the Thames as the Globe.[3] In 1600, the square Fortune took the circular Globe as its model.[4] What united these variously shaped playhouses was the opportunity not only to see "everything well" but to "be seen," as Thomas Platter noted when he visited the new Globe in September 1599.[5] In the uniform lighting of the outdoor amphitheater, the Elizabethan playgoers who frequented these suburban playhouses with increasing regularity would have been made inescapably aware of the different ways they had been placed in relation not only to the spectacles unfolding before them, but to each other. The early modern theater industry was enabled by a single architectural feature: an entrance at which to charge spectators admission.[6] But the London theater *scene* – the broader sphere of activity that included playhouse performances as well as their extratheatrical circulation by self-identified playgoers – gradually emerged amid the construction and reconstruction, imagining and reimagining, of playhouse space.[7]

The doors of those permanent playhouses made possible, for the first time in London's history, a theatrical public – what Michael Warner defines as "a relation among strangers" within "an ongoing space of encounter for discourse."[8] Much-needed revisions to Jürgen Habermas's formative account of the public sphere have emphasized, in the context of the early modern theater, the openness of the public as a social concept. Publics are the enactment of shared attention; they are open-ended and expansive; they promote "affective-critical" as well as "rational-critical" debate.[9] By these standards, the commercial theater obviously qualified as a public, and not just because the playhouses welcomed anyone with the price of admission in hand. Playgoers became aware of their membership in theatrical publics by occupying spaces that kept them in full view of one another.[10] But even as the theater industry expanded to accommodate a larger and larger public – a series of associations among playgoing individuals that were more or less fleetingly confined to the span of a performance – it is also true that playgoing produced the smaller, more durable subset of theatrical *community*.[11] This collective was comprised of spectators who found a shared affinity in stage plays, who ascribed cultural value to their critical responses to commercial drama, and who were deeply familiar with the theater's conventions at the same time that they were invested in continually retracing the horizons of their own theatrical knowledge. They were comprised, in other words, of *playgoers*: spectators for whom playgoing had become not just an occasional or habitual participation in a theatrical public, but an ongoing category of identity. Yet the earliest terms applied to playgoers – "assemblyes," "multitudes," "applauding croud" – emphasize the collective publicity of theatrical spectatorship, but they do not describe an individual affiliation with that collective beyond the occasion of performance itself.[12] Playgoers, including the very word to describe them, were not an immediate consequence of playgoing. By the first decade of the seventeenth century, however, the narrower, more rigid borders of theatrical community were being drawn within London's ever-expanding theatrical public, for playgoers began consciously to take ownership – through commonplacing in the theater, critical responses, amateur performances in alehouses and inns, and the composition of their own dramatic work – of the material they consumed in the playhouse.[13]

Membership in a community asks more of its participants than membership in a public, for communality requires the tense, contradictory resolution of the one and the many, the individual and the crowd; a community is not just a *relation*, but an acknowledged *affinity*, among strangers.[14] That affinity is most identifiable in elements of playgoing culture pertaining to the fashionable, elite clientele who attended the small, expensive hall theaters through the mid-Jacobean and Caroline eras – indoor playhouses that became "meeting-place[s] of the nobility and gentry."[15] A range of contemporary accounts offer portraits of "the twelvepenny-stool gentlemen" who made fashionable spectacles of themselves onstage and voiced their praise or censure of plays (3.157), becoming, in Thomas Dekker's tongue-in-cheek guide to gallantry, instantly recognizable even outside the playhouse: "The simplest dolt in the house snatches vp your name, and when he méetes you in the streets ... héele cry, Hees such a Gallant."[16] But if it was something of a truism in this period that all gallants were playgoers, it was not the case that all playgoers were recognizable as gallants. This chapter offers a phenomenological prehistory of theatrical community before the presence of the hall theaters inevitably narrowed its borders, seeking it at the moment of its emergence among the larger, more socially diverse crowds who gathered in the outdoor amphitheaters.[17] In what did these playgoers begin to discover their collective commonality during the experimental late-Elizabethan, early-Jacobean years of the theater industry?[18] How, in other words, did spectators identify one another as playgoers at a moment when the theater was still actively deciding what its plays looked like? That playgoing was a new kind of activity at the end of the sixteenth century, one that cut across traditional hierarchical social boundaries, should remind us that the embrace of communal identity is neither straightforward nor automatic. *The Comedy of Errors*, to take just one dramatic example, describes the absorption of the self into a wider social world as a terrifying annihilation rather than a welcome means of belonging. "I to the world am like a drop of water," Antipholus of Syracuse claims as he sets out in search of his long-lost twin, "That in the ocean seeks another drop; / Who, falling there to find his fellow forth, / Unseen, inquisitive, confounds himself" (1.2.35–38).[19] While the architecture of the early modern playhouse enabled the mutual recognition required of collectivity, the spatial dynamics of stage representation, I will suggest, obliged spectators skeptically to draw and redraw the shifting borders of belonging that circumscribed their theatrical community.

That is to say, if our knowledge of early modern playgoers has up to now been constituted by the discursive evidence of their existence – how they talked about themselves and were understood by their contemporaries – this chapter explicates the ways those communities were actualized in the outdoor amphitheaters by the process of performance.[20] The theatrical resolution of the one and the many found its dramatic counterpart in the Elizabethan trope that modeled it more insistently than any other: the impersonation play.[21] A subset of the ubiquitously popular disguise plot, impersonation plays proceed from a devilishly simple premise: they inject the inherent duplicity of theatrical presentation into the dramatic world by replicating within it a character who already exists there. The double manifestation of the actor's embodied identity – onstage, he is "both character and performer" at once, a "composite" figure – both fascinated practitioners and spectators in this period and typified antitheatricalist resistance to stage playing as old as the Western theatrical tradition itself.[22] As Rebecca Schneider puts it, "The threat of theatricality is … the threat of the imposter status of the copy, the double, the mimetic, the second, the surrogate, the feminine, or the queer."[23] The "common Player," as a 1615 satirical description put it, "is, *A dayly Counterfeite*: Hee hath been familiar so long with out-sides, that hee professes himselfe, (beeing vnknowne) to bee an apparant Gentleman."[24] The copy threatens because it exposes the perceiver's inability to parse false from true, original from reproduction.[25] From the antitheatricalist's perspective, then, impersonation is a representational nightmare: the trope gleefully accedes to the danger of the copy, allowing the replicative theatrical technology to infiltrate the fictional world of the play itself. At the same time, the trope complicates Andrew Gurr's contention that disguise plots allowed Elizabethan audiences growing increasingly familiar with company players to see more roles, more costumes, more variety, over the course of a single play.[26] Impersonation multiplies, but it does so recursively – thereby creating the play's fictional world as a series of reflections, the relationality of identity to be grasped in the mirror.

It might be protested that impersonation plots were theatrically harmless because they were not interpretively destabilizing for playgoers; what spectator, after all, suffers any sustained confusion about the identities of *Twelfth Night*'s Viola and Sebastian or shares the Duke's inability to tell the Antipholus twins apart ("Stay, stand apart; I know not which is which" [5.1.364])? But playwrights managed formally to produce the experience of partial knowledge, I will argue, through a series of spatial manipulations, arranging plots of mistaken identity within the bifurcated structure of the enclosed playhouse. With doors leading to unseen elsewheres beyond the stage, the early modern theater created worlds that were never fully present to playgoers' view. In formally depicting the intersubjectivity of identity as a spatial relation – the identity of the Antipholus *here* can only be comprehended in relation to the Antipholus *there* – impersonation plots produced the experience of limited knowledge that the plays themselves depict. Yet that experience, I will contend, also redoubled beyond the stage itself. As they watched (and watched each other watch) these Elizabethan experiments with impersonation unfold in the playhouse, spectators were bound together by their searching production of themselves as imperfect copies of one another. These mutual relations forged from skeptical acknowledgement were acts of making, constructions of shared fictions paralleling the performances that unfolded on the theater's stages.[27] The playgoers who gazed upon each other in the theater's hall of mirrors were reflections all.

Onstage Presence, Offstage Absence, and the Construction of Counterfeited Copies

In the early modern theater, impersonation was, at the most basic level, a spatial trope. To take an example of an impersonation plot that is not often recognized as one: in *The Merchant of Venice*, Portia's counterfeiting performance as a lawyer involves the navigation of space as much as it does her costume. As part of her scheme to save Antonio, she orders her servant Balthazar to fetch "notes and garments" from her cousin, a lawyer named Bellario (3.4.51).[28] Once alone with her waiting-woman Nerissa, Portia divulges her plan to play the part of a lawyer herself, promising to "speak between the change of man and boy / With a reed voice, and turn two mincing steps / Into a manly stride" (3.4.66–68). The temporal gap between boy and man becomes a spatial expanse traversed by a single substantial step.[29] The scene ends, accordingly, with Portia ushering Nerissa offstage, in a rush to cover a great distance: "Haste away / For we must measure twenty miles today" (3.4.83–4). Portia's transformation takes her places. Spectators witness the fruits of her travail just two scenes later, when Portia enters the courtroom wearing her cousin's robes. Yet the name given to introduce the "young doctor of Rome" – Balthazar – conjures for spectators not the Mantuan lawyer himself, but the servant ordered to fetch the clothing from him (4.1.152).[30] The denomination has a specific theatrical consequence: Portia's identification of herself as her servant creates an embodied referent for her performance as the lawyer. She is not just in disguise but undertaking an impersonation, and the servant whom the audience has likely last seen exiting the stage – dutifully running or anxiously sprinting or disgruntledly jogging, depending on how the actor interprets Balthazar's promise to go "with all convenient speed" to Mantua (3.4.56) – becomes a standard against which Portia's own manly strides can be measured during her juridical masquerade. As Autolycus says, having traded clothes with Florizell in *The Winter's Tale*, "hath not my gait in it the measure of the court?" (4.4.736).[31] The theatrical success of imper-sonation depends on more than just costume. Phenomenologically, it is apprehended as a function of the counterfeiter's movement through space.

These examples point to the ways that the theater transforms into a spatiotemporal process the duplicative danger of imposture, for the very existence of similarity suggests the lurking presence of deceit. Leontes's interrogation of his son Mamillius in *The Winter's Tale* crystallizes the perceived danger of such likeness. "Art thou my boy?" Leontes asks, before again questioning his son: "What? Hast smutched thy nose? / They say it is a copy out of mine. Come, captain, / We must be neat – not neat, but cleanly, captain" (1.2.120, 121–23). In wiping a nose that is effectively his own, an action proverbially associated with being cheated in the period, Leontes actively, if unconsciously, produces himself as a cuckold.[32] (He will later do so consciously: "You had a bastard by Polixenes, / And I but dreamed it," he says to Hermione [3.2.81–82].) Difference and similarity work together in a circularly toxic combination as Leontes appraises his son; the very presence of visual likeness demands the closer inspection that discovers the stain of difference.

Yet the destabilizing uncertainty sparked by apparent verisimilitude did not transfer seamlessly from the world of the play to the early modern playhouse. Spectators in the Globe in 1611 would likely not have perceived Mamillius as an exact copy of his father, for though it is reported that the two are "almost as like as eggs" (1.2.130), the actors who originally played father and son presumably bore, at best, a passing resemblance to one another.[33] That difference is not a source of confirmation for Leontes's sus-picions as much as an obvious technological limitation of stage representa-tion, one that had a material effect on the plays written for the commercial theater: Ben Jonson reportedly abandoned his plan for a play about twins because "he could never find two so like others that he could persuade the spectators they were one."[34] Other playwrights were undeterred, however, and in what follows I am going to suggest that they managed to enact the experience of partial knowledge for spectators not by attempting to con-fuse them about the identities of particular characters, but by arranging the mistakings and deceptions of impersonation plots within the play-house's architectural structure. Dramatic impersonation, in other words, was a theatrical exercise in spatial manipulation.

The attachment of the tiring house to the rear of the stage in the com-mercial theater was the spatial solution to companies' need to safeguard stage properties and costumes in permanent, purpose-built playhouses.

But that division of on- and offstage space had phenomenological consequences, for it created fictional worlds that were necessarily incomplete.[35]
Playgoers paid to gaze on the here and now of the theatrical present, as
Samuel Weber puts it, "in a way that c[ould] never simply be seen, because
it [wa]s never fully there."[36] The mistakings of impersonation plots capital-
ize on this spatial incompleteness, which allows a counterfeited character
to be relegated to the tiring house while his false copy wreaks delightful
havoc onstage. The impersonation plays that proliferated at the close of
the Elizabethan era (which I will discuss in more detail below) are evidence that the trope served as a relatively early method of experimentation
with the division of the playing space into onstage presence and offstage
absence.[37] The effect of these theatrical experiments, I will suggest, is the
construction of dramatic identity as a function of the playhouse's bifurcated structure. On the stage, the epistemological impasse produced by
the attempt to measure a duplicitous copy against a counterfeited original
becomes the phenomenological experience of repeated displacement, theatrically managed through the careful interplay of entrances to the visible
fictional location and exits to places offstage – and therefore unknown.

The anonymous *Look About You*, first performed by the Admiral's Men
in 1599, makes for an apt, if overwhelming, case study of Elizabethan dramatic impersonation, for it takes experimentation with the trope's spatial
relationality to a gleeful extreme.[38] *Look About You* includes an astonishing
sixteen total disguises, several of which are direct impersonations of other
characters who exist within the world of the play. Counterfeiters not only
don disguises but trade them in quick succession, even competing, wearing the same clothing, to impersonate the same characters. But the play's
"cheerful excess of contradiction" finds its phenomenological match in
the unseen absence of the tiring house; an insistence on spectators' partial view of the fictional world substitutes for the recognition scenes that
neatly resolve the plots of other late Elizabethan plays featuring mistaken
identity.[39]

Look About You's first con is to unsettle the conventional assumption,
in a theater without scenic backdrops or extensive stage furniture, that
characters can be relied upon to signify their location.[40] "Vpon the back of
that [Rock]," Philip Sidney groused of the commercial stage, "comes out a
hidious monster with fire and smoke, and then the miserable beholders are
bound to take it [the stage] for a Caue."[41] *Look About You* seems to adhere
to this logic. At the play's opening, Robin Hood, having journeyed to a
secluded cell, makes a request of an apparent hermit; as Robin explains, the
notorious rogue Skink must be conjured at court to answer for crimes he

committed before the play's opening. The exchange seemingly functions as exposition, though once Robin departs, the hermit reveals that he is not actually a hermit at all, but Skink himself; after "help[ing] [the hermit] forward" toward death, the rogue explains, Skink donned the hermit's robes and adopted his identity (1.54).[42] The turnabout establishes the topsy-turvy world of disguise and counterfeiting by demanding that spectators revise their foundational judgments about that world almost immediately. Yet if the opening scene lets spectators in on the play's continued site of mistaking – several characters will subsequently seek out the hermit's cell for the knowledge and assurance provided by his powers of prophecy – it simultaneously upends the conventional assumption that dramatic identity and fictional place work together to signify the environment of the onstage world. Instead, *Look About You* sets up a relational system of identity governed by presence and absence, fitted to the bifurcated structure of the playhouse. The theatrical effect of Skink's revelation is akin to what Lady Fauconbridge experiences when she seeks out the hermit in his cell and instead merely finds a "beard," "counterfeited hair," and "garments, and his beads" jumbled together on the ground (11.155–56). The hermit's very presence has been displaced, plucked from his material accoutrement and apparently stashed at an unseen remove; Lady Fauconbridge finds the hollow void of impersonation's absence in precisely the place where she expects to find the hermit himself.

Look About You exploits the theater's spatial relation of presence and absence through Skink's impersonation of Redcap, a foolish tipstaff who has two signature character traits beyond his eponymous cap: a marked stutter, and a habit of running – everywhere. "Wh wh why, le le let me run. I am Re Redcap" (3.61), Skink, in disguise as Redcap, protests to a constable. Redcap's stutter, because it leaves the tipstaff vulnerable to impersonation and largely prevents him from impersonating others, has received more commentary than his tendency to run.[43] But the latter trait is just as formally significant, for it is the key mechanism by which *Look About You* inheres dramatic impersonation within the enclosed playhouse structure. The tipstaff's dashes offstage repeatedly emphasize the fictional incompleteness of the stage space, gesturing to adjacent locations of the dramatic world that spectators cannot apprehend. Successful theatrical impersonation depends upon the dramatic separation of the counterfeited character from his counterfeiter. While the still-disguised Cesario may caution Sebastian, "Do not embrace me till each circumstance / Of place, time, fortune do cohere and jump / That I am Viola" (5.1.247–49), their joint appearance onstage is a signal to spectators that the play's comic resolution approaches.[44] Redcap's continual disappearances, by contrast, make literal space for his multiple counterfeiters.

But impersonation is more than just successful stage management. The inherent recursiveness of the trope – the counterfeiting character's duality which mirrors that of the actor's – foregrounds the vexed transformation of the one into two: only a single Redcap is ever allowed onstage at any given moment. *Look About You* theatrically preserves the *idea* of Redcap's singular identity, that is, even as Skink manages to coopt it. Indeed, for almost the entire play, imposture occurs by trade rather than multiplication. "Off with your coat," the disaffected courtier Gloucester demands of Skink, dressed as Redcap (5.31); the two exchange their clothing, giving both characters a new disguise. When Prince John asks for Gloucester a few lines later, Gloucester, imitating Redcap's stutter, directs him to Skink: "Y y yonder he walks" (5.52). The theatrical joke upholds the singularity of Gloucester's identity to the point of absurdity, for the Gloucester present on the stage, by his own admission, is not there. The play also carefully choreographs characters' entrances and exits so that an imposter and the character he counterfeits never appear onstage at the same time. Twice, Skink, in disguise as Prince John, exits, only for the real Prince John to appear "*at the other door*" (5.114sd); in a later scene, Gloucester enters "*like* FAUCONBRIDGE" immediately after the real Fauconbridge exits (8.29sd). This sequence of identity tradeoffs is dizzying, though the center of its spatial logic holds: there may be more than one Redcap, Skink, Gloucester, or Fauconbridge, but never in the same place and at the same time.[45] The theatrical reach toward the multiplicity suggested by similitude is thwarted by the absence and partial knowledge produced by the architectonics of the playhouse. Early on in the search for the counterfeiting rogue, the King demands that "if ye find Skink, see that you apprehend him" (6.134). The multivalence of "apprehend" is particularly resonant in this context: impersonation locks spectators into a visual pursuit that, confined to the stage side of the bifurcated playhouse, they are bound to lose.

Yet *Look About You* finally tops all of these carefully arranged counterfeitings, in a dazzling denouement of fraudulence, by breaking its own spatial rule. Onstage together, Gloucester and Skink impersonate the dead hermit at the same time. Redcap foolishly struggles to distinguish what he imagines must be the real wizard from his counterfeiter: "To two hermits? I'll ca ca clapperclaw to to t'one of ye for mo mo mocking me, and I d d do not, ha ha hang me. Wh wh which is the fa fa false k k k knave?" (15.152–54). The audience, of course, is in on the joke, though like a skilled spectator in the playhouse, Redcap comes to believe, addressing Gloucester, that he has sorted out his own visual confusion: "Si si sirrah, you are the co counterfeit" (15.166). He attempts to keep the apparent counterfeiter in view by ordering Skink to "sta sta stand still g good man, at that," before threatening Gloucester: "I'll bu bumbaste you I'faith. I'll make you g give the old m m man his gown" (15.166–68). From Redcap's faulty perspective, the visual apprehension of impersonator and impersonated depends upon their stationary isolation, a requirement to which neither Skink nor Gloucester deign to adhere. Anticipating Redcap's assault, Gloucester trips up the heels of the stuttering tipstaff and quickly "*shifts SKINK into his [own] place*" (15.168sd). The acrobatic substitution of one false hermit for another momentarily transforms the segmented, partially visible fictional world into a totalized one; the switch does not occur in an offstage elsewhere that spectators are not allowed to see, but takes place entirely within in their view.[46] The spectacle exposes the magic of theatrical representation as a mere trick by temporarily eliminating the division between on- and offstage space. But that totalizing vision comes with a tradeoff, one that gleefully points up the perceived danger of theatrical duplicity itself. The alternative to a real hermit, sequestered within while his counterfeiters gallivant freely on the stage, is a world populated entirely by false copies.

Most impersonation plots are, admittedly, much less dizzying than *Look About You*'s. But the play is nevertheless a crucial case study for unraveling the spatial conventions which organize the trope and to which other plays adhere. Written within a decade of each other, Shakespeare's *The Comedy of Errors* (1592), *Twelfth Night* (1601), and Marston's *What You Will* (1601) collectively upend the assumption that a counterfeited character relegated backstage is more primary than his imposter, in the process developing a spatial strategy for overcoming what Jonson recognized as the theatrical impossibility of representing absolute likeness. On one level, they verbally train spectators to see likeness where none may exist, as when Orsino explicitly registers the absolute similarity of twins Viola and Sebastian: "One face, one voice, one habit, and two persons: / A natural perspective, that is and is not" (5.1.212–13).[47] But this explicit push toward the perception of similitude is underwritten by a formal strategy that all three plays employ: they withhold the entrance of the character whose identity has been usurped while spectators look, first, on his counterfeiter.[48] The relegation of the impersonated character offstage for much of the opening action invites spectators to evaluate him only in the wake of his imposter's performance, rather than the other way around.[49] These impersonation plots, like the very theatrical form that contains them, give the imposter primacy, establishing the elements of the counterfeiter's performance – clothing, voice, and gait – as the semiotic means by which spectators are required to identify the counterfeited character.[50] As a theatrical trope, impersonation confounds without confusing, obliging spectators paradoxically to rely on fundamentally fraudulent markers of identity as they attempt to sort out the world of the play.

Switching the order in which the Antipholus brothers are introduced to the audience is thus as significant a change to Plautus's *Menaechmi*, Shakespeare's Roman source for *The Comedy of Errors*, as the addition of a second pair of twins. In *Menaechmi*, the hometown Menaechmus appears onstage first, lamenting his restrictive domestic and professional duties before introducing the carnivalesque premise of the play's action: "Hidden from my wife we'll live it up and burn this day to ashes" (152–53).[51] Menaechmus I exits, and just a few lines later, his twin Menaechmus II, in the midst of a far-flung search for his long-lost brother, appears at the opposite entrance. Shakespeare instead stages Antipholus of Syracuse's wary arrival in Ephesus before the Antipholus who lives there ever appears onstage. This spatial orchestration theatrically involves spectators in the psychological horrors produced by annihilated identity; arriving onstage after his brother, the hometown twin can only be perceived as the copy of his itinerant imposter.[52] Shakespeare employs a similar sequence of action in *Twelfth Night*: Sebastian's first appearance in Illyria is sandwiched between two scenes that track Viola's departure from Olivia's home and Malvolio's chase after her on Olivia's orders. Viola's movement across the stage, together with her entrances onto and exits from it, mark out what Patrice Pavis calls the "gestural space" of the performer: "the '*ground*' actors cover with their movements; the 'trail' left in the space in their wake, which marks their taking possession of the territory."[53] Despite her insistence that "him I imitate" (3.4.380), within this sequence of scenes, Viola assimilates Sebastian into her gestural trail, catching him up in the ghostly path she leaves behind after her exit. If impersonation plots work by injecting the theater's "tactical vibration between representation and presentation" into the fictional world of the play, this sequence of action radiates that destabilizing duplicity back to the playhouse.[54] The semiotic subversion produced by fraudulent appearance is not a marker of a *break* in the otherwise seamless "informational circuitry" of performance, but *constitutes* the smooth transmission of meaning from stage to audience.[55]

John Marston's *What You Will*, which depicts an identity deliberately stolen rather than merely misplaced, verbally and spatially orchestrates spectators' semiotic acceptance of fraudulence even more thoroughly. The perfumer Francisco disguises himself as Albano, who, thought to be dead in a shipwreck, does not appear onstage for the first half of the play. By the time Albano returns to Venice, word of the perfumer's deception has already widely spread; as a consequence, Albano is accused of being the imposter himself. Marston puts spectators in mind of the absent Albano from the play's first scene, when Jacomo and Randolfo describe in great detail the appearance of their dear, and apparently departed, friend:

JACOMO.   O, I shall ne'er forget how he went clothed.
             He would maintain 't a base ill-usèd fashion
             To bind a merchant to the sullen habit
             Of precise black.
[...]
RANDOLFO. In a black beaver felt, ash-colour plain,
             A Florentine cloth-of-silver jerkin, sleeves
             White satin cut on tinsel, then long stock.
JACOMO.   French panes embroider'd, goldsmith's work, O God!
             Methinks I see him now how he would walk. (1.1.141–53)[56]

The friends' imagined conjuring of Albano supplies the sartorial and kinetic material for Francisco's impersonation, priming the audience to recognize the imposter when he first appears in disguise. "*Enter* FRANCISO, *half-dressed*," the stage direction specifies, "*in his black doublet and round cap, the rest rich*" (3.1.1.sd). Together, these scenes inhere Albano's clothing and accessories with an emblematic meaning in conflict with their more neutral semantic function as a marker of identity, infusing the clothing donned by the fraudulent perfumer with the stink of imposture.[57] While disguised, Francisco skillfully imitates Albano's stutter, which Matthew Steggle suggests "offers an opportunity to the actor [playing Francisco] for virtuoso comic repetitions, variations, and improvisations."[58] But it also lures spectators into an interpretive trap, inviting them to evaluate the performance of the actor playing Albano, who, in order to personate *his* character credibly, must skillfully match the gestures and vocalizations of the actor playing his counterfeiter. As in *The Comedy of Errors* and *Twelfth Night*, spectators may know that Francisco is a fraud, but that interpretive security is guaranteed only by a reliance on the same fallacious signs of identity that bamboozle the characters onstage. The convention developed in these three plays solves the Jonsonian problem of theatrical unlikeness by neatly circumventing it; in order to maintain their own interpretive balance in the playhouse, spectators must accede to the counterfeiter's terms.

The bait-and-switch does nothing less than transform dramatic fraudulence into semiotic legitimacy.

Staged Frontiers: Entrances, Exits, and the Indeterminate In-between

The spatial orchestration of impersonation plots allowed fraudulence to run wild in the early modern theater, confusing characters and reminding spectators of their interpretive limitations and partial knowledge. At the same time, however, that unsettling produced both mobile spatial imagining on the stage and communal possibility in the playhouse, particularly through a reliance on the indeterminacy of fictional place itself. In theaters with relatively little scenery and stage furniture, the "here" of the stage often did not signify a particular place so much as an undefined setting adjacent to the specific location from which a character, entering the stage, had just come. Though it remains uncertain whether the opening to the discovery space was an actual passing to the tiring house or merely a recessed space that could hold large props – Desdemona and Othello's bed, for instance, or the two coffins that conceal Moll Yellowhammer and Touchwood Junior in *A Chaste Maid in Cheapside* – it is generally agreed that the majority of those entrances and exits took place through the two doors that flanked the central opening.[59] The effect, as Tim Fitzpatrick explains, was to establish "a triangular spatial relationship between the offstage places evoked as lying beyond the doors and the 'in between' place represented by the stage."[60] Lodged between doors that acted as portals to determined, though unseen, fictional locations, the stage itself was structurally defined by its unnamed indeterminacy. The stage materialized, in other words, what Michel de Certeau designates as the narrative boundary or frontier: an "an 'in-between'," "a 'space between'," "a middle place, composed of interactions and inter-views," that is articulated by "having come from the other side."[61] De Certeau's definition of the narrative frontier is useful in this context because it offers a way of understanding the early modern stage's spatial triangulation in concert with the dichotomy of onstage presence and offstage absence. If we conceive of early modern playhouse architectonics according to his schema, the frontier of the commercial playhouse was not comprised of the defined offstage locations suggested by the rear doors, but the indeterminate platform, articulated as such every time an actor crossed over from one of those known, though unseen, realms. The confines of this unknown in-between transformed the threat of the false copy into an indeterminate spatial imagining, one that modeled the emergence of a relational social world.

John Fletcher's *Love's Cure*, written c. 1615 and possibly revised by Philip Massinger after 1625, is a dramatic narrative tailored to the stage as a spatial and social frontier.[62] As a King's Men's play, *Love's Cure* could have been performed at both the outdoor Globe and the indoor Blackfriars, though it draws on the spatial conventions of earlier impersonation plays staged in the amphitheaters. Written just over a decade after the cluster of Elizabethan plays that established the conventions of impersonation – and a point by which, as Bruce Smith has argued, crossdressing plots had become something of a specialty of the King's Men – *Love's Cure* represents a second generation of experimentation with the malleability of dramatic identity.[63] While the play does not feature direct impersonation or make mistaken identity a central theme of its action, the main plot converts the spatial conventions of the trope into social ones, following two characters who construct new identities for themselves by observing and imitating each other. Prior to the play's opening, the young siblings Clara and Lucio were separated following their father's murder of a Spanish aristocrat. Lucio remained in Seville with their mother Eugenia, while Clara followed their father into exile. To protect the children's safety, Eugenia raised Lucio as a girl, while Alvarez brought Clara up as a boy. The action of *Love's Cure* concerns the brother and sister's reunion in adulthood, when they must learn to inhabit the genders of their births. In a play that begins rather than ends with a sibling reunion, neither Clara nor Lucio takes theatrical priority as an imposter; rather, brother and sister mutually imitate each other in order to engage in a coordinated act of doubled gender reversal by the play's end. *Love's Cure* maps the indeterminacy of that process onto the theater's architectural structure, dramatizing the siblings' gradual adoption of a new gender as an orientation within space itself.[64] "Perception," Sara Ahmed writes, "is a way of facing something."[65] The siblings understand themselves through the spatial relation of recognition; they construct their new identities by coming to face one another.

Fitzpatrick's triangular model of stage space suggests that one stage door was generally reserved for "'further inwards' or 'nearby' or 'more private'" locations, while the other represented entrances from or exits to "'further outwards' or 'distant' or 'more public'" locations.[66] When the locations from or to which characters are explained to be traveling in *Love's Cure* are named or evoked, those offstage locations largely map onto a "further inward, further outward" opposition while at once neatly managing traffic to, from, and through the stage.[67] This topographic arrangement sets in motion social as well as spatial relations.[68] The two doors leading offstage constitute a rigid binary opposition between private and public spaces, as well as the genders associated with those spaces; the in-betweenness of the stage space itself, however, inevitably complicates any such easy distinctions.[69] Suspended in the balance of these spatial signi-fiers, the location of theatrical presentation becomes a space in which the semantic opposition of the rear doors may be reimagined and reoriented, as well as reinforced.[70]

Lucio and his mother Eugenia, unsurprisingly, are the homebound pair of the family, and early scenes of the play insistently associate both charac-ters with domestic spaces. In his first speech, dressed in women's clothing, Lucio appears on the stage only to gesture to the fictional places adjacent to the presentational space, ordering his servant Bobadilla to "go fetch [his] [needle]work" (1.2.1), as well as to feed and water the poultry.[71] The scene closes with his mother Eugenia's evocation of her bedroom, as she urges that the space must be readied for her husband's imminent return: "Haste, and take down those black, with which my chamber / Hath like the widow, her sad Mistris, mourn'd," she orders Bobadilla,

> And hang up for it, the rich Persian arras,
> Us'd on my wedding night: for this to me
> Shall be a second marriage: send for Musique,
> And will the cooks to use their best of cunning
> To please the palat.   (1.2.91–97)

Both Lucio and Eugenia's concerns point to locations – the bedroom, the kitchen, and the henhouse – more recessed, and in some cases more pri-vate, than the one in which the action of the present scene unfolds. With this fictional spatial layout mapped onto the stage's structure, *Love's Cure* appears to endorse the mandate, espoused over and over again in wom-en's conduct manuals, that girls and women must be responsible for "the care and management of the home."[72] Edmund Tilney's popular *Flower of Friendship* (1568) warned that household management was at once a source of reputational hygiene: "The chiefest way for a woman to preserve and maintayne this good fame, is to be resident in hir owne house."[73] But even as the scene evokes a map of the house's spatial layout, it also suggests confinement within those spaces. Bobadilla frames Lucio's childhood and gender performance in terms of its immobility: "My Lady your mother … hath brought you up like her daughter, and h'as kept you this twentie year, which is ever since you were born, a close prisoner within dores, yet since you are a man, and are as wel provided as other men are, methinks you should have the same motions of the flesh, as other Cavaliers of us are inclin'd unto" (1.2.21–26). Masculine "motions of the flesh" are here set in opposition to feminine domestic containment; the gender binary

Bobadilla describes is both spatial and kinetic. Yet when this scene closes, Lucio chooses, "with humble gladnesse," to follow in his mother's gestural trail, exiting further inward to help her ready the house (1.2.110).

At the moment that Eugenia and Lucio retreat through the inward door, the other half of their family appears at the outward entrance, an opposition that both practically manages the stage traffic of these entrances and exits and, in the momentary crossover of one scene to the next, establishes the visual binary of mother and feminine son, father and masculine daughter. Like Eugenia and Lucio, Alvarez and Clara's minds are on offstage locations from the first moment they appear, but they verbally extend the fictional world of the play in the opposite direction, evoking further outward, more public spaces through their dialogue as the scene unfolds. In response to Alvarez's inquiry about a companion they lost on their journey into Seville, Clara notes that "he was met / Entring the City by some Gentlemen" and "was compel'd to stay" (1.3.1–2, 5). Her response evokes the city's outskirts, though the father and daughter actually stand just outside their own home. Their sustained attention to a farther-flung metropolitan threshold and the absent companion who remains there conjures the emblematic atmosphere of the distant spatial horizons created by Viola's wash up to the shore of Illyria or Antipholus of Syracuse's wary steps from boat to Ephesian dock. The verbal intensification of Clara and Alvarez's juxtaposed opposition spatially lodges the scene further outward even as the action of the scene itself is pulled in the opposite direction.

The spatial binary set up by their entrance is intensified when Lucio and Eugenia reappear at the inward door through which they previously exited, Eugenia assuring her husband that "I have preserv'd / The Jewell left lock'd up in my womb" (1.3.70–71). Her metaphorical figuration of her womb as a protected space is literalized when the happy family reunion is broken up by Bobadilla's warning that Alvarez's sworn enemy approaches. While Alvarez and Clara are ready to draw their swords, a phallic association the play repeatedly deploys, Lucio wants no part in the fighting: "Oh I am dead with feare! let's flye into / Your Closet, Mother" (1.3.85–86). His plea to Eugenia is a pointedly public declaration of the wish to retreat into the privacy that the household closet provided through its lock and key security.[74] And while Lucio may unwittingly express a wish to fly back into his mother's womb, also tightly battened since her husband's departure, his expressed desire to seek refuge in an inner recess of the house operates topographically as well as psychologically, adding another, yet more private, room to the play's verbalized map of offstage domestic spaces. The general effect of the scene, as Lucio cowers in his dress and Clara rushes toward the attackers with her sword, is to reinforce the opposition that adheres within the stage space's fictionally adjacent offstage structure.

But it is precisely that opposition which leaves open the possibility for a more indeterminate navigation of the stage frontier. When the siblings next appear onstage, they have both enacted their sartorial shift, but their spatial reorientation remains incomplete.[75] Lucio enters as he shooed out of the kitchen by Bobadilla: "What should you doe in the Kitchin, cannot the Cooks lick their fingers without your overseeing?" (2.2.2–4). The dialogue implies that both characters have entered from the further inward door. Clara's boisterous entrance several lines later suggests that she appears from the opposite, further outward door, as she gleefully shouts "ran tan tan ta ran tan ran tan tan, ta ran tan tan-tan" (2.2.66–67). Having crossed over the threshold of the stage doors, the siblings meet in the onstage in-between, and they look to each other in order to navigate their new frontier. Both Clara and Lucio find their new clothing unwelcome because it impedes their movement; despite the earlier commentary emphasizing women's domestic confinement, this scene is replete with language referencing both siblings' impeded gait. Lucio laments that his boots "make me walk stiffe, as if my leggs were frozen" (2.2.15). "This masculine attire," he protests, "is most uneasie, / I am bound up in it: I had rather walke / In folio, againe, loose, like a woman" (2.2.18–20). Bobadilla comments on his restricted gait:

> Oh, how he walkes
> As if he had be-piss'd himself, and fleares!
> Is this a gate for the young Cavalier,
> *Don Lucio*, Sonne and heire to *Alvarez*?
> Has it a corne? or do's it walke on conscience,
> It treads so gingerly?   (2.2.23–28)

Spectators in the Globe or Blackfriars would have almost certainly watched Lucio awkwardly lurch across the stage as Bobadilla narrated his immobility. But Clara does not share Lucio's opinion about the freedom of movement provided by women's skirts: "Brother why are womens hanches only limited," she complains, "confin'd, hoop'd in, as it were with these same scurvy vardingales?" (2.2.69–71). The source of one sibling's confinement is the condition of the other's mobility.

Clara and Lucio confront a world made newly strange to both of them, and in the attempt to situate themselves within it, the siblings begin to imitate each other.[76] Lucio reluctantly adopts the masculine traits he did not possess during the earlier fight, attacking Bobadilla on Clara's orders:

"Kick him, I say, / Or I will cut thy head off" (2.2.113–14). Clara herself, beginning to fall in love with Vitelli, gives her sword to him, an action that not only suggests the relinquishment of her own masculinity but echoes Lucio's earlier refusal to brandish his sword: "I'le not draw," he protests (2.2.38). The scene dramatizes the spatialized construction of a social world at the smallest possible scale; it establishes identity itself as a relation between two people who first come face to face and then begin to mirror one another.

Following the disorientation of these early scenes, both siblings' narrative trajectories are more predictably plotted out according to the heteronormative conventions of comedy. (In a reflection of Clara's marriage plot, Lucio soon falls in love with Vitelli's sister Genevora.) As love gradually prompts the siblings to "cure" their aversion toward the genders of their birth, they correspondingly exchange their modes of entering and exiting the stage. In Clara's very next appearance onstage, she enters from a more inward location in the house, accompanied by Bobadilla; her navigation of the stage space mimics her brother's entrance from the kitchen in 2.2. Lucio, by contrast, begins to inhabit more public offstage places, calling on Genevora at her home at the opening of 5.2; his entrance reflects Clara's arrival, with Alvarez, to the family's home in 1.3. Yet the earlier scenes demonstrate that the successful exchange of the siblings' entrance and exit patterning – the paths that trace out their retreat to gendered norms – requires the indeterminacy of the stage itself, which functions in *Love's Cure* as a kind of spatial mirror in perpetual motion: the siblings enter, discern their own reflections in one another, and are turned out, at the opposite stage door, anew.

The Roaring Girl *and the Production of Theatrical Collectives*

In modeling the formation of relational identities, *Love's Cure* displayed for its Jacobean spectators what the architecture of the commercial amphitheaters enabled: the emergence of a social world – or more precisely, for playgoers, a theatrical community – as a set of spatial relations. Surrounding the thrust stage on three sides, the large, raucous crowds of playgoers who gazed at each other in the uniform lighting of the amphitheater became each other's imperfect reflections. The communal identity produced in the playhouse merely required the perception of likeness or similarity, rather than the exact congruence that constituted successful dramatic impersonation, but the ambivalent social relationality it set in motion was also more durable, continuing on after the conclusion of an individual performance.

In the late sixteenth century, frequenters of plays adopted a new kind of identity in a new kind of place by looking on one another, and identifying in that gaze, a new sort of person. They became playgoers in each other's company.

Middleton and Dekker's *The Roaring Girl* (1611) enacts these parallel theatrical and dramatic processes perhaps more insistently than any other play of the period. The play's spatial orchestration of theatrical community begins onstage, for Moll Cutpurse – the play's titular one-of-a-kind, universal object of fascination – is nowhere more at home than in the center of a crowd.[77] The London marketplace she enters when she first appears onstage choreographs a whirl of activity that remains largely segregated by class and gender. The mistress wives set up shop in a row at the rear of the stage, while the gallants Goshawk and Laxton, after perusing the stalls in succession, gather together downstage.[78] Moll accepts an offer of tobacco from the downstage gallants before approaching the upstage mistresses at each of their stalls; when a nameless man threateningly wielding a long rapier appears, she fights with him until he slinks, beaten, offstage. In this scene crowded with large props and multiple bodies, the only open location in which to stage an extended swordfight, even on the relatively large Fortune stage, was likely midway between the upstage mistresses and downstage gallants.[79] Lodged precisely in the indeterminate middle ground between these two carefully segregated spatial anchors, Moll occupies a singularly privileged place within the play's social world because she is able to chart a path that does not exist prior to her arrival. Whereas counterfeited characters unwittingly follow their impersonators' gestural trails, Moll forges a way through the crowd entirely her own.

Yet Moll's spectacular singularity is more often set in relief to her multivalent duplicity. Characters' near-constant speculation that she is a hermaphrodite – as Sir Alexander puts it, "The sun gives her two shadows to one shape" (2.134) – belies a different kind of theatrical truth: *The Roaring Girl*'s Moll possesses the duplicitous identity of the imposter. She is a fictional copy not of another character within the world of the play, of course, but the notorious cutpurse Mary Frith, who, at some point before, during, or after at least one performance of *The Roaring Girl* at the Fortune in 1611, infamously "sat there upon the stage in the public view of all the people there present in man's apparel & played upon her lute & sang a song."[80] *The Life and Death of Mistresse Mary Frith*, published three years after Frith's death, attests to Frith's own concern for and management of her singularity, going so far as to force a male lookalike to quit her neighborhood:

There was also a fellow a cotemporary of mine, as remarkable as my self, called *Anniseed-water Robin*: who was cloathed very near my Antick Mode, being an Hermaphrodite, a person of both Sexes [...] I think nature owed me a spight in sending that thing into the world to Mate and Match me, that nothing might be without a peer ... but contrariwise it begot in me a naturall abhorrence of him with so strange an Antipathy, that what by threats and my private instigating of the Boyes to fall upon, and throw Durt at him, I made him quit my Walk and Habitation, that I might have no further scandall among my Neighbours, who used to say, *here comes Malls Husband.*[81]

Stephen Orgel suggests that Frith expunges the "version of herself, her mirror image" in order to "preserve her uniqueness, which is ... precisely the uniqueness of her costume."[82] But she is also attentive to her imposter's navigation of social space; Frith's "Match" threatens to steal her "Walk," the word evoking her gait as well as her path. We might recall Portia's manly strides or Redcap's repeated dashes offstage or Lucio's halting steps in his new clothing in comparison; the logic of theatrical impersonation, in this account of Mary Frith's counterfeiter, now permeates the world itself.

The Roaring Girl similarly draws upon the replicative threat of the imposter in its construction of Frith's dramatic persona. The play's thirty-line prologue builds audience expectation for Moll's arrival by withholding it, tantalizing spectators with the promise of her imminent display:

> Yet what need characters, when to give a guess,
> Is better than the person to express?
> But would you know who 'tis? Would you hear her name?
> She is called Mad Moll; her life, our acts proclaim. (Prologue.27–30)

But the character who enters the stage immediately after the conclusion of this prologue is not the Mad Moll whom spectators, likely with some eager anticipation, had paid to see strut across the Fortune stage in 1611. *The Roaring Girl's* romantic heroine, Mary Fitzallard, enters the world of the play both *"disguised like a sempster"* and as an unwitting imposter of the fictional Moll Cutpurse who will not appear until the play's third scene (1.1sd). The long setup of the prologue delivers a cleverly theatrical punchline: the Moll for whom the audience continues to wait in eager anticipation is the *true* imposter, *The Roaring Girl* assures, of the real Mary Frith. Like earlier plays that delay the appearance of counterfeited characters, the opening of *The Roaring Girl* fashions authenticity out of the very fraudulence of dramatic impersonation. The account of Frith's transgressions in the

Consistory of London Correction Book has garnered much speculation about when, how often, and with what amount of endorsement from the Prince's Men she actually appeared on the Fortune stage.[83] But the desire to pinpoint the moments when the real Mary Frith supplanted her imposter submits to the subversive semiotic effects of impersonation that the play itself exploits; the construction of a fictional world that brings an imitation of Mary Frith into immediate view inexorably displaces her real counterpart to the world of the playhouse – that absent elsewhere beyond the stage.

The Roaring Girl recognizes, however, that the slippery relationality of public identity is not a property of Mary Frith or even the theatrical stage alone, but is enabled by the architecture of the playhouse and thus involves its audience. The play's second scene, in which Sir Alexander Wengrave describes the decorative details of his parlor at great length, makes that involvement explicit:

> Nay, when you look into my galleries—
> How bravely they are trimmed up—you all shall swear
> You're highly pleased to see what's set down there:
> Stories of men and women, mixed together
> Fair ones with foul, like sunshine in wet weather.
> Within one square a thousand heads are laid
> So close that all of heads the room seems made;
> As many faces there, filled with blithe looks,
> Show like the promising titles of new books
> Writ merrily, the readers being their own eyes,
> Which seem to move and to give plaudities.
> And here and there, whilst with obsequious ears
> Thronged heaps do listen, a cutpurse thrusts and leers
> With hawk's eyes for his prey—I need not show him:
> By a hanging villainous look yourselves may know him,
> The face is drawn so rarely. Then, sir, below,
> The very floor, as 'twere, waves to and fro,
> And like a floating island, seems to move
> Upon a sea bound in with shore above.   (2.14–32)

The speech collapses the fictional representation with the site of its presentation, the audience members themselves coming to constitute the portraits on Sir Alexander's parlor walls. His closing evocation of the stage as a floating island situates the Fortune's seated spectators on a bounded shore; they are poised on a threshold that, mirroring the boundary that separates stage from tiring house, demarcates the space of performance from the wider world outside the theater. Impersonation plays, of course, take advantage of the thematic redolence of the shore as a brink shimmering with transformational power: it is the place where Antipholus of Syracuse fearfully articulates the porosity of his identity and Viola saves herself by dissolving hers. In inviting *The Roaring Girl*'s audience members to attend metatheatrically to their own collective presence in the playhouse, Sir Alexander activates their dissolution. The description of the doubled eyes on each face, "which seem to move and to give plaudities," blurs the distinction between individual members of the audience, as if the entire crowd shares a single vantage. This is the work of collectivity made explicit; the speech enacts the process by which members of the varied crowd of strangers in the audience could achieve the reflective likeness of theatrical community, and it manifests the crucial role of playhouse architecture in enabling this recognition.

But this resolution of the one and many – the single mass "mixed together, / Fair ones with foul" – is not without tension, for Alexander also cautions spectators of their need to regard each other with suspicion, in so doing evoking yet another version of Moll: the cutpurse who, with a "hanging villainous look," lurks in the audience with his own set of "hawk's eyes," "thrust[ing] and leer[ing]" not at the stage spectacle or even other spectators, but their purses. The warning seems clearly to distinguish a particular spectator from the rest of the unified, multi-eyed group. But the suggestion that audience members shift their eyes from the stage to the crowd does not guarantee that they will hone their attention on the would-be thief.[84] As they craned their necks to isolate the cutpurse's rarely drawn face amid a sea of those less distinctively limned, the 1611 Fortune spectators' eyes presumably met – at which point, of course, they would have discovered each other in the midst of the same task.[85] The suspicious looking prompted by Alexander's direction unexpectedly engenders a mutually skeptical recognition among *The Roaring Girl*'s spectators; it invites them, that is, to perceive themselves as collectively engaged in the very act of rooting out the cutpurse who does not belong in the crowd.[86]

A warning to playgoers from Robert Greene captures the ambiguous difficulty of such surveillance: "At plaies, the Nip standeth there leaning like some manerly gentleman against the doore as men go in, and there finding talke with some of his companions, spieth what euery man hath in his purse."[87] The cutpurse who does not belong in the playhouse is difficult to root out because he successfully impersonates the gentlemen who do.[88] Yet no matter the cutpurse's intent upon entering the playhouse, the most crucial feature of his imposture – payment of the admission that allowed him to pass through the door – was inescapably authentic. As Thomas Dekker writes, "A Foyst nor a Nip shall not walke into a Fayre or a Play-house, but euerie cracke will cry looke to your purses"; the cutpurse may be easily distinguished from the rest of the crowd in this account, but he nevertheless shares their status as a paying playgoer.[89] Other rogue pamphlets blur the distinction between playgoer and cutpurse to an even more extreme extent. In another account by Greene, a cutpurse-in-training goes to see the latest offering at the Red Bull; while there, he steals a playgoer's purse and finds "nothing therein but white counters, a thimble and a broken three pence," the man having created a decoy "to deceiue the cutpurse withall."[90] There is a likeness among these two young men, both at the Red Bull to see a play, both attempting to outwit their fellow playgoers. Greene continues this portrait with the would-be nip's observation of a well-known cutpurse accompanied by a companion. The couple presses into the audience, "where both they might best beholde the playe, and worke for aduantage."[91] Following behind, the young nip sees the cutpurse attempt to hand his companion a stolen purse that she, "being somwhat mindful of the play, because a merriment was then on the stage, gaue no regarde."[92] More successful at watching the play than stealing a purse, the pair fully elides the distinction between spectator and thief. The crowd of playgoing cutpurses in Greene's account transforms the audience of the Red Bull into a community yoked together by their mutual intent to deceive.

The Roaring Girl, by contrast, creates the impression that the cutpurse's presence in the playhouse is recognizably distinct from the intentions of the "honest men" and women there to see the play.[93] But Sir Alexander's very assurance that the spectators will be able to pinpoint the cutpurse – "yourselves may know him" – implies a kind of knowledge that unexpectedly encompasses the ambiguous mutuality inherent to theatergoing itself; the *him* that each spectator recognizes is a possible cutpurse and fellow playgoer at once. This mutual looking was neither part of a broader contest for spectators' attention in the playhouse nor a meditation on playgoers' "individual identit[ies]," then, but an activity in concert with the mode of looking that impersonation encouraged.[94] "Beware of trusting feined beggars or fawninge fellonse," Simon Forman wrote of *The Winter's Tale* after seeing the play at the Globe around the time of *The Roaring Girl*'s first performance; even his much-maligned moral summation looks less "inattentive" with this activity of mutual surveillance in mind.[95] Yet if the major threat of the false copy in *The Winter's Tale* turns out to be false – Mamillius *is* Leontes's son, after all – *The Roaring Girl*'s invocation of impersonation keeps its spectators mired in theatrical uncertainty. How does one distinguish the playgoer from the cutpurse who has paid to pose as one?

By raising this question, I do not mean to suggest that people in this period frequented plays merely to scrutinize potential cutpurses or that their fleeting spectatorial affiliations were not discoverable by any of the great many affective responses that performance inevitably produced. But what *The Roaring Girl*'s emphasis on surveillance makes plain is that the suspicion of an imposter lurking among the throng of spectators – and, more importantly, the difficulty, even impossibility, of pinpointing him – is precisely what makes possible the countervailing recognition of oneself and others as *playgoers*. In the commercial theater, skeptical looking enabled individual strangeness to resolve itself into collective similitude; it was a key tool by which spectators traced the borders of theatrical belonging in the absence of positive affiliations that preceded their entry into the playhouse. Spectators marshalled the artificiality of their communal circumstance in the playhouse to create the shared fiction of collectivity, and the formation of that in-crowd depended upon the exclusion of those whose ongoing membership in such a community was contested or denied. As a communal category of identity, the playgoer stood in relief to not only the cutpurse, but the mere frequenter of plays – even when those occupants of the playhouse were impossible to discern with certainty. Likeness, in this circumstance, was admitted as a set of negative associations.

For seeing and being seen, to return to Thomas Platter's description of the Globe's spatial resources, was not the same thing as knowing and being known. The bifurcated structure of the commercial playhouse, as Richard Preiss has shown, enabled the formation of dramatic interiority as an unfulfilled promise – the suggestion of *something* beneath "the trappings and the suits" constituting a character's surface that would always remain "just out of sight" (1.2.86).[96] That structure was also ideal for the depiction of imposture because it made room – *a* room – for an unseen and therefore unknown elsewhere, in which the very selves that characters so eloquently insist they have could be stolen, traded, and lost. But the promise of total visibility remained in the portion of the playhouse where audience members put themselves on display as they gazed on their fellow playgoers in the bright light of the afternoon. The amphitheater was as public as it got. Yet this, too, was a false promise, for in scrutinizing one another playgoers met with another reality not fully graspable. "Theatre, like the playhouse that framed and obscured it," Preiss writes, "fundamentally resists disclosure or comprehension."[97] So do playgoers. Their opacity in relation to one another was just as fundamental as the mysterious interiority of characters onstage. What substituted for mutual knowledge in the playhouse, then, was acknowledgement: the skeptical recognition

of collective likeness where none, perhaps, existed.[98] The publicity of theatrical acknowledgement was at once the drawing of the boundaries of
belonging, the uncertain creation of a community that faced itself.

Indeed, it is the collective of theatergoers who capture each other's
mutual attention after the play has finished. In a prose tract written not
long after *The Roaring Girl*, Thomas Dekker describes the indeterminate
shift out of the playhouse after the epilogue has been delivered:

> As I haue often scene, after the finishing of some worthy Tragedy, or Catas-
> trophe in the open Theaters, that the Sceane after the Epilogue hath béene
> more blacke (about a nasty bawdy Iigge) then the most horrid Sceane in
> the Play was: The Stinkards speaking all things, yet noman vnderstanding
> any thing; a mutiny being amongst them, yet none in danger: no tumult,
> and yet no quietnesse: no mischife begotten, and yet mischiefe borne: the
> swiftnesse of such a torrent, the more it ouerwhelmes, bréeding the more
> pleasure.[99]

As they make their way out of the playhouse, spectators take over the
presentational activity that was once the occupation of the actors and the
traffic of the stage, impersonating the harmless mischief and pleasurable
torrent of the play that has already passed into absence. And it is in this
very act that playgoers capture the ephemeral duplicity of theatrical performance and the spatial relationality it produces.[100] In Dekker's formulation,
these spectacles add up to something precisely through what they are *not*:
neither tumultuous nor quiet, simultaneously full of mischief and devoid
of it, the act of impersonating stage performance brings into being the
surreal unreality of performance itself. These extratheatrical copies of a
past show are there and not there at once, as if the union of presence and
absence that defines playing and the playhouse space has followed playgoers out of the theater. These "Stinkards speaking all things" collectively
recognize themselves as players without "vnderstanding any thing." It is
this extratheatrical life of dramatic material, its transformation through
acts of remaking on the part of theatrical publics, and the newly pleasurable uncertainties those remakings correspondingly produced in the playhouse, to which I turn in the next chapter.

Notes

1 "Initial Findings from Excavation at Shakespeare's Curtain Revealed,"
   Museum of London Archaeology, May 17, 2016, www.mola.org.uk/blog/
   initial-findings-excavation-shakespeare%E2%80%99s-curtain-theatre-revealed.
2 See Mariko Ichikawa, *The Shakespearean Stage Space* (Cambridge: Cambridge
   University Press, 2013), 3–4.

3 John Orrell, *The Quest for Shakespeare's Globe* (Cambridge: Cambridge University Press, 1983), 156.

4 For an account of how the polygonal Globe may have served as a source for the square Fortune, see Tim Fitzpatrick, "The Fortune Contract and Hollar's Original Drawing of Southwark: Some Indications of a Smaller First Globe," *Shakespeare Bulletin* 14.4 (1996): 5–10.

5 Thomas Platter, *Thomas Platter's Travels in England*, 1599, trans. Clare Williams (London: Jonathan Cape, 1937), 167.

6 Richard Preiss, "Interiority," in *Early Modern Theatricality*, ed. Henry S. Turner (Oxford: Oxford University Press, 2013), 47–70, esp. 49.

7 I adopt the term "theater scene" from Jeffrey S. Doty and Musa Gurnis, "Theatre Scene and Theatre Public in Early Modern London," *Shakespeare* 14.1 (2018): 12–25.

8 Michael Warner, *Publics and Counterpublics* (New York: Zone Books, 2005), 74, 90.

9 Paul Yachnin expands the Habermasian concept of "rational-critical" debate to include the affective responses the theater produced in "Performing Publicity," *Shakespeare Bulletin* 28.2 (2010): 201–19, esp. 216.

10 Warner suggests that "a public can be a crowd witnessing itself in visible space" in *Publics and Counterpublics*, 66.

11 What I identify as theatrical community in this chapter bears some affinity with Victor Turner's influential concept of *communitas*, though I am going to suggest that the collectives formed in the early modern playhouse did not experience a deep sense of mutual recognition that Turner emphasizes. *Communitas*, as Turner describes it, is "a transformative experience that goes to the root of each person's being and finds in that root something profoundly communal and shared." As I will argue, the socially formative moments that produced playgoing communities made space for playgoers' doubt about the very possibility of going to the root of another person's being – a skepticism that the drama itself, as I examine at length in Chapter 3, so often articulates. See Turner, *The Ritual Process: Structure and Anti-Structure* (New York: Routledge, 2017), 138.

12 For "assemblyes" and "multitudes," see Stephen Gosson, *The Schoole of Abuse* (London: Thomas Woodcocke, 1579), 20; for "applauding croud," see Joseph Hall, *Virgidemiarum* (London: Robert Dexter, 1597), 8. For more examples, see Michael West's excellent essay on the emergence of playgoers in the period. His emphasis, however, is on individual identification as a playgoer rather than collectivity. West, "Were There Playgoers During the 1580s?" *Shakespeare Studies* 45 (2017): 68–76, esp. 68.

13 As Charles Whitney puts it, "early modern audiences ventriloquize commercial performances for their own uses." See Charles Whitney, *Early Responses to Renaissance Drama* (Cambridge: Cambridge University Press, 2006), 82. For more on the alehouse as a site for social performance, see András Kiséry, *Hamlet's Moment: Drama and Political Knowledge in Early Modern England* (Oxford: Oxford University Press, 2016), 14–15. For a thorough account of

playgoers who composed their own plays, see Matteo Pangallo, *Playwriting Playgoers in Shakespeare's Theater* (Philadelphia: University of Pennsylvania Press, 2017).

14 Henry S. Turner, "The Problem of the More-than-One: Friendship, Calculation, and Political Association in *The Merchant of Venice*," *Shakespeare Quarterly* 57.4 (2006): 413–42.

15 Gerald Eades Bentley, *The Jacobean and Caroline Stage*, vol. 6, *Theatres* (Oxford: Clarendon Press, 1968), 33.

16 Scene and line numbers follow Thomas Middleton and Thomas Dekker, *The Roaring Girl*, ed. Coppélia Kahn, in *Thomas Middleton: The Collected Works*, ed. Gary Taylor and John Lavagnino (Oxford: Oxford University Press, 2007). Thomas Dekker, *The Guls Horne-booke* (London: R. S., 1609), 30. For more on these elite London communities as they existed both in and outside the playhouse, see Michelle O'Callaghan, *The English Wits: Literature and Sociability in Early Modern England* (Cambridge: Cambridge University Press, 2006); and Adam Zucker, *The Places of Wit in Early Modern English Comedy* (Cambridge: Cambridge University Press, 2011), 54–101.

17 For more on the social composition of theatrical audiences, see Andrew Gurr, *Playgoing in Shakespeare's London* (Cambridge: Cambridge University Press, 1987).

18 To clarify: I do not mean to suggest the theater, at some point, stopped experimenting with its tropes and technologies of representation. That the theater remained innovative up through its closure in 1642, and as a result continually unsettled its spectators' interpretive expectations, is a key contention of this book as a whole. But what I am arguing is that the accumulated, eventually familiar, conventions of Jacobean and Caroline drama made members of the theatrical community more easily recognizable to one another than they were at the end of the sixteenth century; I will treat this later period of the theater's deployment of familiar, recognizable conventions in Chapter 5.

19 Act, scene, and line numbers follow William Shakespeare, *The Comedy of Errors*, ed. Kent Cartwright (London: Bloomsbury Arden Shakespeare, 2017).

20 See, in particular, Amy J. Rodgers, *A Monster with a Thousand Hands: The Discursive Spectator in Early Modern England* (Philadelphia: University of Pennsylvania Press, 2018).

21 This is not to suggest that impersonation plays were not performed in hall theaters; they of course were. My focus in this chapter, however, is on the social manifestation of stage conventions that were practiced at a particular historical moment and under particular structural conditions. The large crowds and the visibility of outdoor lighting that characterized the amphitheaters are central to this claim.

22 Bert O. States, *Great Reckonings in Little Rooms: On the Phenomenology of Theater* (Berkeley: University of California Press, 1985), 119; and Robert Weimann, "The Actor-Character in 'Secretly Open' Action: Doubly Encoded Personation on Shakespeare's Stage," in *Shakespeare and Character: Theory, History, Performance, and Theatrical Persons*, ed. Paul Yachnin and Jessica

Slights (New York: Palgrave Macmillan, 2009), 177–93, esp. 181. The paradigmatic classical example of theatricality as the false copy of the real is Plato's famous description of the cave in the *Republic*. In his foundational definition as explicated in *the Poetics*, Aristotle describes the action of drama as, first and foremost, "imitation," or *mimesis*. See Aristotle, *Poetics*, trans. James Hutton (New York: W. W. Norton, 1982), 1447a. On the long history of Western antitheatricalism, see Jonas Barish, *The Antitheatrical Prejudice* (Berkeley: University of California Press, 1981).

23 Rebecca Schneider, *Performing Remains: Art and War in Times of Theatrical Reenactment* (New York: Routledge, 2011), 30.

24 John Stephens, *Satyrical Essayes Characters and Others* (London: Roger Barnes, 1615), 244.

25 The problem of distinguishing an original from its false copy occupies a prominent place in the long history of skeptical thought. In his *Academica*, Cicero asserts that "no presentation proceeding from a true object is such that a presentation proceeding from a false one might not also be of the same form." In "Of the Lame or Cripple" (an essay that includes several direct quotations of the *Academica*), Montaigne writes, "Truth and falsehood have both alike countenances, their port, their taste, and their proceedings semblable." See Cicero, *Academica*, trans. H. Rackham (Cambridge, MA: Harvard University Press, 1933), II.xxiv.77; and Montaigne, *The Essayes or Morall, Politike and Millitarie Discourses of Lo: Michaell de Montaigne*, trans. John Florio (London: Edward Blount, 1603), 613.

26 Andrew Gurr, *Shakespeare's Opposites: The Admiral's Company 1594–1625* (Cambridge: Cambridge University Press, 2009), 49–53.

27 My thinking about the dynamism of this process has been influenced by Charles Taylor's description of the intersubjective formation of individuals through recognition, which Taylor roots in the Hegelian master-slave dialect. See Charles Taylor, "The Politics of Recognition," in *Multiculturalism: Examining the Politics of Recognition*, ed. Amy Gutmann (Princeton: Princeton University Press, 1994), 25–73. Patchen Markell, following Taylor, describes this process as a "constructive act." See Markell, "The Recognition of Politics: A Comment on Emcke and Tully," *Constellations* 7.4 (2000): 496–506, esp. 496.

28 Act, scene, and line numbers follow William Shakespeare, *The Merchant of Venice*, ed. John Drakakis (London: Arden Shakespeare, 2010).

29 Shakespeare figuratively evokes a spatialized gap between boyhood and manhood in *Twelfth Night*, as well, in Malvolio's assessment of Cesario: " 'Tis with him in standing water between boy and man" (1.5.154–55). Act, scene, and line numbers follow *Twelfth Night*, ed. Keir Elam (London: Arden Shakespeare, 2008).

30 John Drakakis suggests that Portia's assumed identity is not meant to impersonate Bellario, rather that the name "is a perfunctory disguise and is of a piece with such supernumerary characters as Salerio and Salanio." But whatever the intention behind Portia's choice of name, the moment nevertheless works

in the playhouse as a subtle bait-and-switch: spectators are invited to expect Portia-as-Bellario during the trial scene and get Portia-as-Balthazar instead. See *The Merchant of Venice*, 344 n152. For a reading of Portia's disguise as an impersonation, see Alan Stewart, *Shakespeare's Letters* (Oxford: Oxford University Press, 2008), 190.

31 Act, scene, and line numbers follow William Shakespeare, *The Winter's Tale*, ed. John Pitcher (London: Arden Shakespeare, 2010).

32 See Pitcher, *The Winter's Tale*, 160 n122.

33 Eggs were a common example in skeptical treatises demonstrating that similar appearances could cheat the senses. See Sextus Empiricus, *Against the Logicians*, ed. Richard Bett (Cambridge: Cambridge University Press, 2005), I.409; and Cicero, *Academica*, II.xvii.57, which treats eggs and twins together as examples of deceptively similar appearances.

34 William Drummond, "Informations to William Drummond of Hawthornden," ed. Ian Donaldson, in *The Cambridge Edition of the Works of Ben Jonson*, ed. David Bevington, Martin Butler, and Ian Donaldson, vol. 5, *1616–1625* (Cambridge: Cambridge University Press, 2012), 359–91, esp. 380.

35 See Peter Womack, "Off-Stage," in *Early Modern Theatricality*, ed. Henry Turner (Oxford: Oxford University Press, 2013), 71–92, esp. 74.

36 Samuel Weber, *Theatricality as Medium* (New York: Fordham University Press, 2004), 109.

37 The language of the Fortune contract reflects the simultaneous union and separation of on- and off-stage space: the theater was to be built "with a Stadge and Tyreinge howse to be made erected & settupp within the saide fframe [of the playhouse]." See Philip Henslowe, *Henslowe's Diary*, ed. R. A. Foakes (Cambridge: Cambridge University Press, 2002), 308. For more on the construction of the stage and tiring house as distinct structures, see John Orrell, "Beyond the Rose: Design Problems for the Globe Reconstruction," in *New Issues in the Reconstruction of Shakespeare's Theatre: Proceedings of the Conference Held at the University of Georgia, February 16–18, 1990*, ed. Franklin J. Hildy (New York: Peter Lang, 1990), 95–118.

38 Dating follows Martin Wiggins, *British Drama 1533–1642: A Catalogue*, vol. 4 (Oxford: Oxford University Press, 2014). 106.

39 Jeremy Lopez, *Theatrical Convention and Audience Response in Early Modern Drama* (Cambridge: Cambridge University Press, 2003), 123. The limited work on the theatricality of *Look About You* focuses on the sheer number of its disguises, though my point in this chapter is to track the moment-by-moment phenomenological effects of the play's overlapping and competing impersonations. Both Andrew Gurr and Peter Hyland use *Look About You* as evidence of the spectatorial skills of early modern audiences; the play's complex, layered, and manifold disguises prove, they contend, that only audiences well-versed in the theatrical conventions of disguise and doublings would have been able to follow the play's many twists and turns. See Gurr, *Shakespeare's Opposites*, 49–81; and Peter Hyland, *Disguise on the Early Modern English Stage* (Burlington, VT: Ashgate, 2011), 15–36.

40 On "locality [as] a function of characterization," see Russell West, *Spatial Representations and the Jacobean Stage: From Shakespeare to Webster* (New York: Palgrave, 2002), 29. On theatrical place as "perceptual assemblages" of various fragmented stage elements, see Andrew Bozio, *Thinking Through Place on the Early Modern English Stage* (Oxford: Oxford University Press, 2020), 121.

41 Philip Sidney, *The Defence of Poesie* (London: William Ponsonby, 1595), H4v.

42 Scene and line numbers follow *Look About You*, ed. Paul Menzer, in *The Routledge Anthology of Early Modern Drama*, ed. Jeremy Lopez (New York: Routledge, 2020).

43 See Menzer, Introduction to *Look About You*, 267–69, esp. 268. and Hyland, *Disguise on the Early Modern English Stage*, 6.

44 On the ways that Shakespeare conceives of recognition as spatially located and arranged in the theater, see David Bevington, *Action is Eloquence: Shakespeare's Language of Gesture* (Cambridge, MA: Harvard University Press, 1984), 115–18. On the return of an absent character as a signal of imminent comic resolution in Shakespeare's plays, see Anthony Brennan, *Onstage and Offstage Worlds in Shakespeare's Plays* (New York: Routledge, 1989), 80–93.

45 For more on the ways *Look About You* "dilates upon the problem of more-than-one," see Paul Menzer, Introduction, *Look About You*, 267–69, esp. 268. My special focus is on the way duplicity in the play intersects with playhouse architecture.

46 As Paul Ricoeur writes, the "operation of substitution" is constitutive of representation. See *Memory, History, Forgetting*, trans. Kathleen Blamey and David Pellauer (Chicago: The University of Chicago Press, 2004), 230.

47 For more on the ways that plays verbally trained spectators to see likeness among actors, see Erika T. Lin, "'Lord of thy presence': Bodies, Performance, and Audience Interpretation in Shakespeare's *King John*," in *Imagining the Audience in Early Modern Drama, 1558–1642*, ed. Jennifer A. Low and Nova Myhill (New York: Palgrave Macmillan, 2011), 113–33.

48 *What You Will* and *Twelfth Night* were likely both first performed in 1601; *The Comedy of Errors* can be dated to approximately 1592. I follow Wiggins's dating of all three plays in *British Drama 1533–1642: A Catalogue*.

49 Later plays follow this convention, as well; in James Shirley's *The Imposture* (licensed November 10, 1640), for example, Juliana, drawn into a scheme to keep Leonato from marrying Fioretta, impersonates Fioretta before Fioretta herself ever appears onstage.

50 Shakespeare follows this logic in *The Taming of the Shrew*, as well; Vincentio does not appear onstage until spectators have witnessed the merchant's impersonation of him.

51 Line numbers follow Plautus, *The Brothers Menaechmus*, in *Four Comedies*, trans. Erich Segal (Oxford: Oxford University Press, 1996).

52 As Ruth Nevo puts it, *The Comedy of Errors* depicts "identities … lost, split, engulfed, hallucinated, imploded." *Comic Transformations in Shakespeare* (London: Methuen, 1980), 22. For more on the play's representation of twinship as a threat to the psychological stability of the self, see G. R. Elliot,

"Weirdness in *The Comedy of Errors*," *University of Toronto Quarterly* 9.1 (1939): 95–106; Coppélia Kahn, *Man's Estate: Masculine Identity in Shakespeare* (Berkeley: University of California Press, 1981); Barbara Freedman, *Staging the Gaze: Postmodernism, Psychoanalysis, and Shakespearean Comedy* (Ithaca, NY: Cornell University Press, 1991), 78–113; Martine van Elk, 'This Sympathizèd One Day's Error': Genre, Representation, and Subjectivity in *The Comedy of Errors*," *Shakespeare Quarterly* 60.1 (2009): 47–72; and Will Stockton, *Members of His Body: Shakespeare, Paul, and a Theology of Nonmonogamy* (New York: Fordham University Press, 2017): 17–41.

53 Patrice Pavis, *Analyzing Performance: Theater, Dance, and Film* (Ann Arbor: University of Michigan Press, 2003), 152.

54 Daniel L. Keegan, "Performing Prophecy: More Life on the Shakespearean Stage," *Shakespeare Quarterly* 62.3 (2011): 420–43, esp. 426.

55 States, *Great Reckonings*, 12.

56 Act, scene, and line numbers follow John Marston, *What You Will*, in *The Works of John Marston*, vol. 2, ed. A. H. Bullen (London: J. C. Nimmo, 1887).

57 For more on this distinction, see Henry Turner's elaboration of emblematic versus topographic signification in the theater. While his focus is on the realization of fictional place on the stage, the basic dichotomy he outlines applies to Albano's clothing: the signifying materials that would otherwise possess "relatively neutral semiotic value" are given heightened symbolic meaning as a result of Francisco's impersonation. Turner, *The English Renaissance Stage: Geometry, Poetics, and the Practical Spatial Arts 1580–1630* (Oxford: Oxford University Press, 2006), 155–85, esp. 165.

58 Matthew Steggle, "Varieties of Fantasy in *What You Will*," in *The Drama of John Marston: Critical Re-visions*, ed. T.F. Wharton (Cambridge: Cambridge University Press, 2000), 45–59, esp. 56.

59 For explanations of the three-door theory, see Mariko Ichikawa, "Were the Doors Open or Closed? The Use of Stage Doors in the Shakespearean Theatre," *Theatre Notebook* 60.1 (2006): 5–29; Bernard Beckerman, "The Use and Management of the Elizabethan Stage," in *The Third Globe*, ed. C. Walter Hodges, S. Schoenbaum, and Leonard Leone (Detroit: Wayne State University Press, 1981), 151–63; and Andrew Gurr, "Doors at the Globe: The Gulf between Page and Stage," *Theatre Notebook* 55.2 (2001): 59–71. For the two-door theory, see Fitzpatrick, *Playwright, Space and Place*, 39–61.

60 Fitzpatrick, *Playwright, Space and Place*, 143.

61 Michel de Certeau, *The Practice of Everyday Life*, trans. Steven Rendall (Berkeley: University of California Press, 1984), 127.

62 Both the authorship and date of *Love's Cure* are somewhat uncertain; for an account of the debates about both, see Martin Wiggins, *British Drama 1533–1642: A Catalogue*, vol. 6 (Oxford: Oxford University Press, 2015), 465–66.

63 Bruce Smith, "Making a Difference: Male/Male 'Desire' in Tragedy, Comedy, and Tragi-comedy," in *Erotic Politics: Desire on the Renaissance Stage*, ed. Susan Zimmerman (New York: Routledge, 1992), 99–116.

64 Nearly all of the (limited) scholarship on *Love's Cure* operates within the familiar binary of containment and subversion, suggesting that the play either endorses or undercuts the siblings' mandated acceptance of the "natural" genders of their births. A focus on the formal affordances of the theater's architectural structure, I would suggest, helps break the play out of this binary, for it shows how *Love's Cure* stages the phenomenological encounter with gendered identity as a spatial orientation. For arguments that emphasize the play's conservatism, see Simon Shepherd, *Amazons and Warrior Women: Varieties of Feminism in Seventeenth-Century Drama* (New York: Harvester Press, 1981); and Jonathan Dollimore, "Subjectivity, Sexuality, and Transgression: The Jacobean Connection," *Renaissance Drama* 17 (1986): 53–81. For a countervailing account of the play's progressive dramatization of gender as performance, see Anne Duncan, "It Takes a Woman to Play a Real Man: Clara as Hero(ine) of Beaumont and Fletcher's *Love's Cure*," *English Literary Renaissance* 30.3 (2000): 396–407.

65 Sara Ahmed, *Queer Phenomenology: Orientations, Objects, Others* (Durham: Duke University Press, 2006), 27.

66 Fitzpatrick, *Playwright, Space, and Place*, 144. For a compelling account of how the flexibility of the model proposed by Fitzpatrick would have alleviated the burdens on actors charged with memorizing dozens of entrances and exits for the many plays in their repertories, see Evelyn Tribble, *Cognition in the Globe: Attention and Memory in Shakespeare's Theatre* (New York: Palgrave, 2011), 30–44.

67 In his account of staging *Love's Cure*, José A. Pérez Díez notes that many of the play's entrance and exits patterns accord with Fitzpatrick's' model, though he does not go on to explore the implications of that patterning. See Díez, "Editing on Stage: Theatrical Research for a Critical Edition of John Fletcher and Philip Massinger's *Love's Cure, or The Martial Maid*," *Shakespeare Bulletin* 34.1 (2016): 69–88.

68 De Certeau's assertion that space is "actuated by the ensemble of movements deployed within it" implies that space itself is the product of social relations. See de Certeau, *The Practice of Everyday Life*, 117.

69 On the "semantic as well as ... structural importance" of the stage's triangulated structure, see Turner, *The English Renaissance Stage*, 197–209, esp. 197. Turner focuses on the importance of the backstage wall in forming a "topographic sequence" within *Westward Ho*'s dramatic structure; I attend in this section to the ways that the stage doors generate such sequences.

70 In his account of the openness of the Shakespearean marriage plot, Alan Sinfield memorably insisted that "readers do not have to respect closures." In the early modern playhouse, I am suggesting, exits were the spatial equivalent of narrative endings. See Sinfield, *Faultlines: Cultural Materialism and the Politics of Dissident Reading* (Berkeley: University of California Press, 1992), 48.

71 Act, scene, and line numbers follow *Love's Cure*, ed. George Walton Williams, in *The Dramatic Works in the Beaumont and Fletcher Canon*, vol. 3 (Cambridge: Cambridge University Press, 1976).

72 Juan Luis Vives, *The Education of a Christian Woman: A Sixteenth-Century Manual*, ed. Charles Fantazzi (Chicago: University of Chicago Press, 2000), 58.

73 Edmund Tilney, *The Flower of Friendship: A Renaissance Dialogue Contesting Marriage*, ed. Valerie Wayne (Ithaca, NY: Cornell University Press, 1992), 136. The text went through seven editions between 1568 and 1587. For more on the pervasiveness of such advice to women, see Jessica C. Murphy, *Virtuous Necessity: Conduct Literature and the Making of the Virtuous Woman in Early Modern England* (Ann Arbor, MI: University of Michigan Press, 2015). The social and working lives of women in this period were obviously more complex than the deliberately oversimplified *topoi* of the conduct manuals suggest; see, for instance, Jane Whittle and Mark Hailwood, "The Gender Division of Labour in Early Modern England," *Economic History Review* (2020): 3–32.

74 Challenging social histories that seek to explain the rise of the closet in the early modern home as evidence for an emergent modern subjectivity that included the desire for privacy, Lena Cowen Orlin contends that the physical space of the closet arose out of a wish to protect material goods rather than to cultivate the inward self: "Safe storage was the dominant purpose of the room that in early modern England was known interchangeably as a closet or study. Its nature was betrayed by the first of its names: it was a room that was closed (and secured), even during daylight hours." See Orlin, *Locating Privacy in Tudor London* (Oxford: Oxford University Press, 2007), 296–326, esp. 301. Alan Stewart draws attention to the tension, located in the closet, between the desire for privacy and the retreat there as a "very *public* gesture of withdrawal." See Stewart, *Close Readers: Humanism and Sodomy in Early Modern England* (Princeton: Princeton University Press, 1997), 161–87, esp. 168.

75 The power of clothing to transform identity was repeatedly emphasized in antitheatricalist pamphlets, and scholars are right to emphasize it in investigations of early modern imaginings about gender. I mean to suggest that the triangulated structure of fictional place necessarily made the navigation of gendered identity a spatial as well as a sartorial issue. For more on clothing and the remaking of identity, see Stephen Orgel, *Impersonations: The Performance of Gender in Shakespeare's England* (Cambridge: Cambridge University Press, 1996); and Laura Levine, *Men in Women's Clothing: Anti-Theatricality and Effeminization, 1579–1642* (Cambridge: Cambridge University Press, 1994).

76 As Ahmed writes, "the work of inhabiting space involves a dynamic negotiation between what is familiar and unfamiliar, such that it is still possible for the world to create new impressions, depending on which way we turn." See *Queer Phenomenology*, 7–8.

77 As Kelly J. Stage aptly puts it, Moll "must move because she has nowhere to stand." My reading of Moll's navigation of the stage space in 2.1 is dependent upon Stage's argument about Moll's traversal of segregated social spaces. I build from her excellent reading to situate Moll's social competency phenomenologically; the ease with which she navigates various social spheres, I suggest, stems from her skill at apprehending herself as a body in space. See Stage, "*The Roaring Girl*'s London Spaces," *SEL* 49.2 (2009): 417–36, esp. 424.

78 Adam Zucker suggests that the "shop scene is given just enough visual order by the Fortune's stage to render coherent the contentious production of status and social power in London's diversifying marketplaces," though I would argue that it is precisely Moll's *disruption* of these social divisions that make them manifest. See Zucker, "Space and Place," in *A New Companion to Renaissance Drama*, ed. Arthur F. Kinney and Thomas Warren Hopper (Hoboken, NJ: John Wiley and Sons Ltd., 2017), 501–12, esp. 509.

79 On the size of the Fortune stage, see Fitzpatrick, "The Fortune Contract."

80 From the *Consistory of London Correction Book*, quoted in *Renaissance Drama by Women: Texts and Documents*, ed. S. P. Cerasano and Marion Wynne-Davies (New York: Routledge, 1996), 172.

81 "The Life and Death of Mal Cutpurse," in *Counterfeit Ladies*, ed. Janet Todd and Elizabeth Spearing (New York: New York University Press, 1994), 35–36.

82 Orgel, *Impersonations*, 148, 149.

83 See, for example, Mark Hutchings, "Mary Frith at the Fortune," *Early Theatre* 10.1 (2007): 89–108; and Orgel, *Impersonations*, 139–53.

84 On the encouragement of spectators' surveillance of other audience members in the playhouse, see Musa Gurnis, *Mixed Faith and Shared Feeling: Theater in Post-Reformation London* (Philadelphia: University of Pennsylvania Press, 2018), 118–21.

85 As Matthew Hunter aptly puts it, "encounters with other Londoners as anonymous strangers forced one to conceive of one's own self as such an anonymous stranger too." See Hunter, "City Comedy, Public Style," *ELR* 46.3 (2016): 401–32, esp. 404.

86 Craig Dionne's contention that cony-catching pamphlets united a disparate readership, "yet to develop into a coherent form of class solidarity," against a perceived outlaw has influenced my own attention to the formal technologies of community formation in the theater. See Dionne, "Fashioning Outlaws: The Early Modern Rogue and Urban Culture," in *Rogues and Early Modern English Culture*, ed. Craig Dionne and Steve Mentz (Ann Arbor: University of Michigan Press, 2004), 33–61, esp. 40.

87 Robert Greene, *The Second Part of Conny-catching* (London: William Wright, 1591), C4v.

88 On the theatrical techniques employed by rogues in cony-catching pamphlets, see Robert Henke, "Sincerity, Fraud, and Audience Reception in the Performance of Early Modern Poverty," *Renaissance Drama* 36/37 (2010): 159–78.

89 Thomas Dekker, *Lanthorne and Candle-light* (London: John Busby, 1609), D2r.

90 Robert Greene, *The Third and Last Part of Conny-catching* (London: C. Burby, 1592), D4r.

91 Greene, *The Third and Last Part of Conny-catching*, D4r.

92 Greene, *The Third and Last Part of Conny-catching*, D4v.

93 Greene, *The Third and Last Part of Conny-catching*, D4v.

94 See Anthony B. Dawson, "The Distracted Globe," in Dawson and Yachnin, *The Culture of Playgoing in Shakespeare's England: A Collaborative Debate* (Cambridge: Cambridge University Press, 2001), 88–107, esp. 95; and Paul Yachnin, "Eye to Eye Opposed," in *The Culture of Playgoing*, 69–87, esp. 81.

95 Simon Forman, *Bocke of Plaies and Notes Thereof*, MS Ashmole 208, fol. 202r, Bodleian Library, Oxford. Martin Wiggins, "The King's Men and After," in *Shakespeare: An Illustrated Stage History*, ed. Jonathan Bate and Russell Jackson (Oxford: Oxford University Press, 1996), 23–44, esp. 34.

96 Act, scene, and line numbers follow William Shakespeare, *Hamlet*, ed. Ann Thompson and Neil Taylor (London: Bloomsbury Arden Shakespeare, 2006). Preiss, "Interiority," 69.

97 Preiss, "Interiority," 53.

98 Stanley Cavell searchingly traces out the relationship between unknowing and acknowledgement in "The Avoidance of Love: A Reading of *King Lear*," in *Disowning Knowledge in Seven Plays of Shakespeare* (Cambridge: Cambridge University Press, 2003), 39–123.

99 Thomas Dekker, *A Strange Horse-Race* (London: Joseph Hunt, 1613), C4v.

100 As Paul Menzer writes, this moment "blurs the threshold between performance and postperformance," shifting the centerpiece of the action from the stage to the boundary that demarcates the theater from the world beyond it. See Menzer, "Crowd Control," in *Imagining the Audience in Early Modern Drama, 1558–1642*, ed. Jennifer A. Low and Nova Myhill (New York: Palgrave Macmillan, 2011), 19–36, esp. 27.

PART III

Theater History

CHAPTER 5

Audience

Expecting Surprise in the Caroline Theater

The consequence of too frequent indulgence in the theater's pleasures, Richard Brathwaite believed, was nothing short of deadly. In his 1630 conduct manual *The English Gentleman*, Brathwaite cautions that "as I approve of the *moderate* use and recourse which our *Gentlemen* make to *Playes*; so I wholly condemne the daily frequenting of them: as some there be (especially in this Citie) who, for want of better imployment, make it their Vocation."[1] Letting the reader infer causation from correlation, he goes on to tell the story of a young woman who, "being accustomed in her health every day to see one *Play* or other, was at last strucke with a grievous sicknesse even unto death."[2] One of those plays must have been Thomas Kyd's *The Spanish Tragedy*, for Brathwaite reports that the woman, "exhorted by such Divines as were there present, to call upon God," instead cried out, "Oh Hieronimo, Hieronimo, methinks I see thee brave Hieronimo!" before she "fix[ed] her eyes attentively, as if she had seene *Hieronimo* acted," sighed deeply, and died.[3] The woman's voracious appetite for the theater culminates in her own overblown deathbed performance, a display of an embarrassing lack of taste that Brathwaite figures as a sacrilegious lack of discernment. Like the revenger's victims in the dramatic object of her obsession, her devotion to stage fiction brings about her very real demise.[4]

Yet in the very process of excoriating this spectator for worshipping at the wrong altar, Brathwaite is careful to reference a dramatic figure who possessed something close to divine status himself: Hieronimo. First printed in 1592, the year Philip Henslowe records fourteen performances of it, and written as early as 1585, *The Spanish Tragedy* was one of the most performed, printed, and referenced plays of the commercial theater until its closure in 1642.[5] To condemn playgoing in 1630, Brathwaite – himself a playgoer, if not a daily one – deliberately targets the wide swath of readers who can also picture Hieronimo in their minds' eyes; the moral censure's efficacy requires readers who, in recognizing the reference to Kyd's play, recognize themselves in the fatally mistaken spectator.[6] The castigation of an individual playgoer's incomprehension thus inadvertently reveals the contours of a theatergoing community that the extratheatrical circulation of Kyd's play helped to create.

A reference to *The Spanish Tragedy* in 1630 tells us something about the play itself – namely, that it was enduringly popular – but it also tells us something about the theatrical expertise of the seasoned playgoers who would have recognized it. As I have outlined in earlier chapters, over its several decades of operation in London, the commercial theater relied upon the use of recognizable conventions to convey information and meaning to its spectators.[7] These conventions spurred collaborative processes of inter-pretation between audience and performance, working to inculcate the theatrical literacies that helped spectators make sense of stage representa-tion as it unfolded in real time. By the fifth decade of the commercial theater's operation, theater scholars generally agree, Caroline theatergoers regarded the commercial theater as an institution defined by an accumu-lating history and set of recognizable conventions, and they were thereby conscious of the numerous resources they possessed to interpret and judge what they saw and heard on the stage.[8] But the established semiotic sys-tems that governed the phenomenology of the Caroline theater were also highly vulnerable to exploitation by theater practitioners, for every known convention simultaneously offered the opportunity for any number of surprising departures from it. While the long horizons of knowledgeable spectators' expectations allowed them to experience any single moment in the theater as inextricably intertwined with many others – as, that is, deeply and multifariously familiar – it also allowed them the opportunity to experience the new even more potently.[9] While, as Marissa Greenberg suggests, "early modern playgoers paid their pennies in anticipation of a particular dramatic arc and denouement," the experimental volatility of theatrical convention meant that they also paid, paradoxically, in expecta-tion of surprise.[10] It was precisely the theatrical literacy of frequent playgo-ers that attuned them to the delight produced by the unexpected break with convention: the uncertainty produced by the sudden turn into the unknown.

At the same time, these pleasurable experiences of recognition and surprise were more than individual responses to stage action; they also did socially constitutive work. As I showed in the previous chapter, the collective nature of theatrical spectatorship did not immediately create a community out of the strangers who gathered together in London's sub-urbs to watch plays. Only as playgoers began to take elements of stage performance out of the playhouse and into the world beyond it did a theatrical community that persisted beyond the occasion of performance began to establish itself. As Edmund Gayton described these extratheatri-cal practices in 1654, the "expressions and passages" that audience mem-bers heard in the playhouse "with ease insinuate[d] themselves into their capacities," so that a frequent theatergoer might be able to try out some of Hieronimo's best lines in the alehouse, or, as in Brathwaite's anec-dote, on her deathbed.[11] And by in turn depicting amateur performances in their plays, practitioners brought these extratheatrical practices back into the playhouse, making playgoers' dramatic consumption legible to them as part of the theatrical experience.[12] The relentless exploitation of the theatrical conventions introduced by *The Spanish Tragedy* and other early plays did more, that is, than mark out the horizons of spectators' interpretive acuities into the seventeenth century. The interplay of surprise and familiarity, registered in the duration of performance, produced this community as it emerged alongside, and in competition with, the com-mercial theater's mimetic practices.[13] As I will argue in this chapter, the very nature of theatrical experience made those increasingly fluent in its language known to each other not only through their shared acuity, but through their pleasurable, collective confrontations with the limits of their theatrical knowledge.

When it originally appeared in the commercial theater, *The Spanish Tragedy* likely packed its narrative punch through a surprise twist. Hieronimo's "solicit[ations] for justice" having gone unfulfilled (3.7.14), the dutiful public servant takes the matter of revenge into his own hands, murdering his son's killers during a play he has staged for the Spanish King, the Portuguese Viceroy, and their followers.[14] The King's unsuspect-ing adulation in response to the deadly denouement – "This was bravely done" (4.4.67) – misinterprets the stage spectacle for the playhouse audi-ence, suggesting to them that Lorenzo, Balthazar, and Bel-Imperia, lying motionless on the ground, are merely playing dead. The fundamental fic-tion that governs all theatrical representation thus appears to apply to the device of the play-within-the-play. But at precisely the moment that a set of ideational conventions with regard to this particular device might seem to be nascently coalescing in *The Spanish Tragedy*, Hieronimo interrupts to explain that the King has interpreted the spectacle incorrectly. What the audience has just seen, Hieronimo clarifies, is no imitation of deadly violence, but murder itself:

> Haply you think, but bootless are your thoughts,
> That this is fabulously counterfeit
> And that we do as all tragedians do,
> To die today, for - fashioning our scene -
> The death of Ajax, or some Roman peer,
> And, in a minute starting up again,
> Revive to please tomorrow's audience.
> No, princes, know I am Hieronimo,
> The hopeless father of a hapless son,
> Whose tongue is tuned to tell his latest tale,
> Not to excuse gross errors in the play. (4.4.75–85)

Hieronimo's play-within brilliantly exploits the conventional practice of using live actors to imitate dead bodies to murderous ends, presumably keeping first-time spectators of *The Spanish Tragedy*, along with the onstage audience, ignorant about the deadly conflation of a theatrical falsehood with a fictional truth. The uncertainty produced by Hieronimo's cryptic interruption ultimately culminates in the surprise of his confession. His negation of what both audiences perceive as mere mimesis – "No" – homophonically anticipates the revision of their faulty judgments in the same line: "know."[15]

The Spanish Tragedy is a drama of tyrannical authority upended; it operates by correspondingly unsettling its spectators' interpretive authority.[16] Kept in the dark about his plans, spectators feel the force of Hieronimo's theatrical shock to a corrupt political system which refuses to answer his cries for redress; the government official well-versed in judicial display wields, as Ellen MacKay puts it, the "misconceived harmlessness" of the theater to his own unexpectedly violent ends."[17] He continues to sow chaos beyond the surprise of the twist, as the King demands more information from Hieronimo that he refuses to give: "Speak, traitor! Damned, bloody murderer, speak! / For now I have thee, I will make thee speak: / Why hast thou done this undeserving deed?" (4.4.161–63). As several readers of the play have pointed out, the King's frenzied questioning follows directly on the heels of Hieronimo's exhaustive explanation of exactly why he has "done this undeserving deed."[18] What more could there possibly be left to say? But the force of Hieronimo's silence in the face of the King's demands suggests that, somehow, *something* has – an ambiguity that the revenger holds in permanent abeyance by biting out his tongue and stabbing himself with a penknife before *The Spanish Tragedy*'s close. If Hieronimo's vengeance codified revenge tragedy as an act of resistance to an unjust judicial authority, it at once established how that dramatization was phenomenologically experienced in the playhouse: as the repeated confrontation with the limits of one's theatrical knowledge.

It would be tempting to pinpoint *The Spanish Tragedy*'s twist as a crucial source of the play's enduring popularity into the seventeenth century, then, if not for the complication that very endurance introduces: while first-time spectators of Kyd's play are presumably surprised along with Hieronimo's onstage audience, repeat viewers and readers of *The Spanish Tragedy* interpretively leave the King and his followers behind. For those in the know, in the play's final act the prone bodies are dead bodies, and Hieronimo's tongue will soon be bitten out; the roil of revelation ceases to surprise. Why, then, did a play so heavily dependent on pulling the interpretive rug out from under its audiences remain popular long after it could reliably produce those confusions? Or, to put the question another way: what happens to a surprise ending when it no longer remains a surprise? Several of the seventeenth-century references to *The Spanish Tragedy*, including Brathwaite's anecdote, suggest one possible explanation: that the thrill of confusion and the surprising revision of judgment came gradually to be replaced by the knowing delight of recognizing references or allusions to the play. Indeed, following the play's initial onstage success, Hieronimo rapidly became a metonym for Kyd's play, as indicated by Christopher Sly's angry cry of "Go by, Saint Jeronimy" while being kicked out of a tavern (where spectators might have imagined he had been engaged in his own amateur performance of *The Spanish Tragedy*) during Shakespeare's *The Taming of the Shrew* (Ind.1.8),[19] or the assertion in *Cynthia's Revels*, by a playgoer with "more beard than brain," that "'the old *Hieronimo*', as it was first acted, 'was the only, best, and judiciously penned play of Europe'" (Praeludium. 164, 166–67).[20] These references would have invited moments of collective recognition in the playhouse, creating the opportunity not only to display one's own familiarity with *The Spanish Tragedy*, but, through the "smiles, frownes, or distorted faces" that Thomas Carew described playgoers displaying during performances, to discover others likewise in the know.[21] Those spectators who "admire[d], nod[ded], sh[oo]ke the head" in response to these metonymic mentions of *The Spanish Tragedy* made the theatrically literate in-crowd manifest to itself in the midst of performance, distinguishing, in real time, the bonafide playgoers in the audience from those merely attending a play.[22]

Direct references are not the only means, however, of producing such a response, for the more diffuse adoption of Kydian conventions would have similarly made frequent theatergoers known to each other. In the prologue to *No Wit/Help Like a Woman's* (1612), Thomas Middleton

laments the difficulty of pleasing audience members who have come to
the playhouse for various reasons, many entirely unrelated to watching
the play at all: "How is't possible to suffice / So many ears, so many eyes?"
(1–2).[23] Without shared theatrical tastes or literacies, playgoers remain a
"distracted multitude" (4.3.4), as *Hamlet*'s Claudius puts it, rather than
a collective.[24] The inculcation of theatrical fluency through conventional
repetition overcomes this problem, not by orchestrating uniform theatrical
responses from its spectators, but by inviting knowing audience members
to disclose themselves to each other through their recognition of familiar
conventions.[25] If *The Spanish Tragedy*'s status as a blockbuster ruined its
initial theatrical effect, that destructive popularity simultaneously worked
flexibly to produce the very collective of experienced playgoers who found
new ways to react and respond to the intertheatrical echoes of Kyd's play.
Theatrical surprise crossfades into theatrical community.

In what follows, I move forward several decades from *The Spanish
Tragedy*'s debut, using Philip Massinger's *The Roman Actor* as a case
study to explore both the affordances and the limits of theatrical literacy
made collectively visible in the playhouse. First performed in 1626, *The
Roman Actor* takes the pleasures of theatrical familiarity and recognition that *The Spanish Tragedy* made possible at the end of the sixteenth
century to their Caroline extreme; described by Jonathan Goldberg
as a play comprised of "the best-loved moments of Jacobean drama,"
The Roman Actor seems designed to cater to a theatrically literate community at every possible plot twist and turn.[26] Massinger's most self-
conscious rumination on both the political power and impotence of
performance, *The Roman Actor* contains three inset plays; the final one
culminates in an actual murder, a blurring of the boundary between
art and life that many other plays had adopted and adapted from *The
Spanish Tragedy* by 1626 (and about which I will say more below). But
The Roman Actor is more than an intertheatrical anthology. In the same
moments that it rewards frequent playgoing through recognizable references to older drama, it also does precisely the opposite, deliberately
upending its audience's expectations of what they are about to see. If
The Spanish Tragedy provokes its first-time spectators into confusion
by thwarting their theatrical expectations within the scope of a single
play, *The Roman Actor* does so by upending its audience's *intertheatrical* expectations – those produced by experiential familiarity with the
common conventions and repeated dramatic devices that saturated the
Caroline theater. *The Roman Actor* is a play designed to surprise an audience deeply in the know.

Rather than waiting until its conclusion to entangle its spectators in uncertainty, as *The Spanish Tragedy* does, *The Roman Actor* plunges its audience into confusion from its very first lines. The play's opening has long been recognized as an exploitation of the induction, a dramatic device that frames and directly comments upon the main action of the play. Popularized by Ben Jonson at the opening of the seventeenth century, the induction was originally introduced to the collection of conventions that circulated through the commercial theater as a disruption of an even earlier theatrical device: the prologue. Inductions distribute the speech of the prologue into a dialogue among multiple actors who, in advance of enacting the fictional representation, share the time and place of the staged presentation with the audience.[27] Jonson's particular innovation was to heighten the prologue's emphasis on audience judgment, transforming the opening frame into an occasion during which, as Leo Salingar explains, "critical theory and the state of public taste are made the subjects of discussion, and the real spectators are provoked into critical engagement within the play."[28] When Asper expresses his desire that the audience of *Every Man Out of His Humour* will "join their profit with their pleasure, / And come to feed their understanding parts" (Induction.200–01), spectators are implicitly positioned in critical relation to the fiction unfolding before them.[29] These Jonsonian inductions – which were imitated and adapted by other playwrights, especially in plays for the self-consciously parodic children's companies – reinforce the importance of spectators' evaluation at exactly the moment that the commercial theater's in-crowd, defined by their ascription of value to such judgments, was coming into being. Twenty years later, then, the familiar first inklings of an induction would have alerted the frequent playgoers in Blackfriars that their sophisticated theatrical acumen was about to be called upon, their superior discernment catered to.

But what seems a generous invitation is a trap. "What do we act today?" Aesopus asks; "Agave's frenzy, / With Pentheus' bloody end," Latinus answers, before Paris laments that "It skills not what" the company plays (1.1.1–2).[30] In 1626, this opening exchange would have apparently identified Richard Robinson, Curtis Greville, and Joseph Taylor – playing Aesopus, Latinus, and Paris, respectively – as players with the King's Men; as long-standing sharers of the company, Robinson and Taylor, if not Greville, would almost certainly have been immediately recognizable to frequent playgoers.[31] Likely attired in sandals and robes, the actors seemingly readied themselves on the Blackfriars stage to personate Euripides's ancient characters anew.[32] Taylor-as-Paris goes on to clarify his complaint:

"The times are dull, and all that we receive / Will hardly satisfy the day's expense" (1.1.3–4). At the close of 1626, the London theater scene was just beginning to pick up again after a long period of dull times; James's death on March 27, 1625, as well as a virulent plague outbreak, resulted in the closure of the theaters for several months. In just the way a beleaguered player with the King's Men might, the speech comments directly on the extratheatrical world beyond the walls of the playhouse. As the Roman actor continues, however, he complicates the sense that the performers and playgoers occupy a shared here and now:

> The Greeks (to whom we owe the first invention
> Both of the buskined scene and humble sock)
> That reign in every noble family
> Declaim against us; and our amphitheatre,
> Great Pompey's work, that hath giv'n full delight
> Both to the eye and ear of fifty thousand
> Spectators in one day, as if it were
> Some unknown desert, or great Rome unpeopled,
> Is quite forsaken.   (1.1.5–13)

The playhouse walls he evokes – those of Pompey's amphitheater – suddenly reveal that Taylor does not metatheatrically personate himself at all, but the Roman actor Paris, and that the action of the play itself, rather than being framed by an induction, is already underway. Yet despite the wide gulf of time and place now distinguishing their own world from the one represented onstage, the Caroline audience may still have found itself invoked: "*our* amphitheatre" establishes the fictional place of the play deictically, much as Rosalind's designation that "*This* is the Forest of Arden" does (2.4.13, emphasis mine).[33] The gesture outward from the stage – one can imagine Taylor stretching his arms toward the audience as he seems to locate them within Pompey's amphitheater – appears to collapse the location of the fictional representation with the site of the theatrical presentation. If the audience first believed themselves to share with the players onstage the actual time and place of an induction, the here and now of the Blackfriars playhouse, Paris's gesture newly incorporates them into the fictional location of the play. In a span of fewer than ten lines, Massinger establishes, unsettles, and resettles the audience's position in relation to the unfolding representation, in the process apparently metamorphosing the contemporary Blackfriars into an ancient Roman amphitheater.[34]

But almost as soon as the play invites spectators to recognize themselves as part of the collective audience that constitutes Paris's "our," it unsettles their position in relation to the unfolding fiction once more. For while the Caroline spectators would have crowded together in Blackfriars to watch *The Roman Actor*, the vast outdoor amphitheater that Paris invokes is empty. As Joanne Rochester explains the contradiction, "The Blackfriars spectators are the audience for a complaint that there is no audience; they are troped as simultaneously there and not there."[35] Yet I would stress that the complaint is not *quite* simultaneous. A line and a half separate Paris's evocation of Pompey's theater and the lament that it is "quite forsaken." The delay matters. If ever so briefly, the line withholds the clarity of Paris's conclusion, squeezing a doubled simile between "one day" and "forsaken"; spectators thus find that the theater in which they imagine themselves to sit reminds Paris of "some unknown desert" or "great Rome unpeopled" before they learn definitively that it is empty. The similes draw attention not just to the occasion of the performance, but to the yet further sundering, in real time, of the fictional representation from its moment and location of theatrical presentation. In the midst of Paris's similes, spectators discover themselves in the ambiguous overlap of fiction and performance, hovering somewhere between Caroline London and Flavian Rome. This temporal gap foregrounds the audience's experience during the seeming induction as a moment-to-moment dance between recognition and surprise; the constant phenomenological shift between the two positions collectively entangles spectators in interpretive uncertainty about exactly where they are in relation to the spectacle unfolding before them.

The Roman Actor's opening thus refigures the conventional gesture to an audience's *evaluative* judgment in order to expose the limits of their *interpretive* judgment: at the very moment that spectators are seemingly invited to engage their critical responses to the play, Massinger suddenly thwarts their sense of what is happening onstage at all. Massinger's innovation to the induction is deployed, in other words, as the appeal to and subsequent unsettling of spectators' tether to performance. At the same time, the phenomenological effect of the opening registers that, especially for an audience fluent in the commercial theater's conventions, having one's interpretive expectations entirely catered to is simply less entertaining than having them occasionally exploited. Theatrical pleasure is produced by imbricating the recognition of familiar devices with the surprise of unexpected action; part of the fun of playgoing is experiencing the interpretive unsteadiness created by the toggling between both. So while Massinger does not draw directly on *The Spanish Tragedy* during the first scene of *The Roman Actor*, what the close of Kyd's play shares with the opening of Massinger's is an awareness that phenomenological confusion

produces spectatorial satisfaction. In the theater, the disruption of convention is experienced as the jolt of unknowing that interrupts the steadiness
of interpretive security; that unbalancing constitutes the entertainment of
uncertainty itself.

The theatrical force of *The Roman Actor*'s opening is at odds with the
play's more ambivalent representation of the theater's efficacy, dramatized
in the face of rising fears about theatrical censorship in the 1620s.[36] At
the same time, the question of what the theater could do to subvert or
reinforce dominant power structures and ideologies had become especially
pressing by 1626, as rumors flew that the newly crowned, increasingly
absolutist Charles I sought to abolish Parliament.[37] Yet the play itself seems
divided on the issue. While Paris makes an impassioned speech defending
drama as a tool for judicial and moral reformation, *The Roman Actor*'s
inset performances dramatize the troubling ineffectuality of stage show:
the miser made to watch *The Cure of Avarice* refuses to reform; the senators on Caesar's public scaffold decline to react in the way he wishes; the
tyrant's conscripted wife, confusing art with life in much the same manner
as Brathwaite's undiscerning fan of Hieronimo, falls in love with Paris
while watching him onstage in *Iphis and Anaxarete*.[38] While there is no
doubt that many spectators would have understood *The Roman Actor* as a
commentary on the political tensions produced by Charles I's accession,
reading the play solely in this context has trapped critics in the binary of
theatrical power and powerlessness that *The Roman Actor* itself constructs.
This approach overlooks that *The Roman Actor* is just as insistently a commentary on the effects, and effectiveness, of the theatrical history that had
accumulated in the decades preceding this highly anthological play.

As I will suggest in what follows, in parroting outmoded theories about
theatrical power, *The Roman Actor* posits the need for a longer view of the
theater's material efficacy. The power of drama as it is constructed by the
play – that is, its ability to produce affective and interpretive responses
in its spectators – depends upon the upending of their dramatic expectations, an upending that was increasingly hard to pull off for those playgoers who had cultivated their theatrical literacy through knowledge of the
commercial theater's conventional repertory. *The Roman Actor* works on
its spectators not by producing immediate moral or political reform, then,
but by deliberately exploiting the long theatrical history that had, by 1626,
culminated in their deep expertise. And it is in the very process of jos-
tling spectators out of their comfortable interpretive positions, I will argue,
that Massinger also manipulates the dramatic logic of revenge tragedy as
the extrajudicial means to right a wrong more broadly.[39] With his inset

performances, Massinger flips the conventional script of revenge tragedy, staging dramatic action orchestrated not by a loyal political subject barred access to justice – Hieronimo's "broken sighs ... Beat at the windows of the brightest heavens" (3.7.11–13) – but by the tyrant whose hand, akin to Jupiter's, "holds thunder" itself (1.4.55).

It is perhaps not surprising that *The Roman Actor*'s central actor believes in the power of theater. Offered in response to the accusation that he and his fellow actors are "libellers against the state and Caesar" (1.3.34), Paris's passionate defense of the stage recalls Jacobean rejoinders, most clearly Thomas Heywood's *Apology for Actors* (1612), to antitheatricalist discourse that had largely quieted by the opening of the seventeenth century.[40] With his assertion that depicting "vice upon the stage" works as both a moral and judicial force for good, the Roman actor anachronistically counters Elizabethan warnings about theater's corrupting power (1.3.98).[41] But any Caroline spectator familiar with *Hamlet* – which Paris calls to mind when he claims to have seen the "guilty hearer" of a tragedy "forced by the terror of a wounded conscience / To make discovery" of his crimes (2.1.92–94) – already had ample theatrical evidence of the theater's spectacular failure to move the hearts and minds of its audiences: to "catch the conscience" as Hamlet famously puts it (2.2.540), or, as Paris does, to force those guilty audience members to "Cry out 'Tis writ by me'" (1.3.122).[42] Massinger wastes no time in proving Paris wrong, staging the miserly Philargus's refusal to reform in response to *The Cure of Avarice*, the play's first inset performance and his intended theatrical remedy.[43] The inset play is a singularly pointed response to the apologists' claims that the structures of poetry could shape an audience's response toward predefined ends.[44] The failure of this theory about theater's moral power, the scene seems to suggest, is its very premise: when a spectator is theatrically literate enough to discern himself on the stage, there can be no opportunity for any jolt of surprise or possibility for reform. Philargus is admittedly no fan of the theater – he only agrees to go, after all, once he is assured the performance will be free – but while his son asks questions as the action unfolds in order to interpret it, Philargus recognizes himself in the portrait of the onstage miser immediately: "We were fashioned in one mould," he grumbles (2.1.298). Never moved, Philargus remains stubbornly incalcitrant during the moral lesson aimed directly at him, the reparative powers of performance outmatched by his unshaken interpretive abilities.

Yet if *The Roman Actor* conspicuously revives a decades-old theatrical debate about the theater's broader social efficacy, it seemingly does so only to render it moot, for though Paris's play fails to touch Philargus, Domitian himself succeeds, ordering the miser's execution just a few lines after the inset performance concludes. When the audience of a play includes a tyrant who wields a "whirlwind of ... will and power" (3.2.28), questions about the efficacy of performance would seem beside the despotic point. To suggest that the scene constructs performance as either disappointingly ineffectual or merely unnecessary, however, disregards its intertheatrical context, for the entire display, from Philargus's recalcitrance to Caesar's command, is a rewriting of the familiar conventions of revenge tragedy.[45] Unlike Philargus, Caesar is an enthusiastic playgoer, and he betrays a taste for the kind of action usually reserved for those without recourse to justice, let alone tyrannical authority: revenge.[46] As James J. Condon has pointed out, the revenger's gradual interchange with the villain against whom he plots conventionally entails his appropriation of "various facets of political power ... considered exclusively the prerogative of royalty."[47] By starting instead in the tyrant's place, Caesar can only trade down. In self-consciously adopting the role of a theatrical revenger, Domitian opens himself up to the vulnerability of theatrical surprise – a vulnerability that will eventually be shared by *The Roman Actor*'s audience itself.

Caesar's proclivity for revenge first begins to threaten his grasp on absolute power when the emperor attempts publicly to torture two senators already sentenced to death for betraying him. His advisors are alert to the unwieldy effects of performance, whether judicial or theatrical: "'Tis doubted," Parthenius warns, "That the sad object may beget compassion / In the giddy rout, and cause some sudden uproar / That may disturb you" (3.2.21–24). Yet Caesar persists in the punishment that he imagines will extend even beyond death, promising the senators to "afflict your souls, / And force them groaning to the Stygian lake" (3.2.52–53). The senators' Stoic refusal to display a response, which prompts Caesar to plead with them to "for my sake roar a little / And show you are corporeal" (3.2.84–85), is unexpected; to his dismay, Domitian discovers that their souls are beyond his reach. The senators, by contrast, know exactly what to expect from the event: "Give us leave / To die, fell tyrant" (3.2.51–52), Sura implores. The senators' Stoicism inures them to their grisly fate because it shapes death itself into a set of conventions that can be known and therefore managed. As Rusticus explains, "To guilty men / It [death] may bring terror; not to us that know / What 'tis to die" (3.2.59–61). The familiarity that inculcates expectation, weaponized by Philargus as stubborn recalcitrance, is transformed by the senators into an existential anesthetic. Only Caesar is caught off guard. Frustrated that the senators will not display their anguish, he rails, "I am tortured / In their want of feeling torments" (3.2.88–89). Despite embodying in his own person the state's power over torture itself, Caesar suddenly finds himself grasping at the vengeful logic of the powerless private subject, reaching for what is beyond his recourse even as he orders the senators' annihilation.

In a shift that narrows the scope of Domitian's own purview yet further, it is a personal rather than a political wrong that ultimately signals his wholehearted identification as a revenger. Caesar suffers, like revengers Vindice, Hamlet, and Hieronimo before him, a familial loss over which he has no control – though it comes in the form of betrayal rather than murder. When his advisors report that Domitia has begun an affair with Paris, he becomes a cuckolded husband. Incredulous at the possibility of his wife's infidelity, Domitian nevertheless decides to hear more, agreeing with his advisors to

> put off
> The deity you labour to take from me,
> And argue out of probabilities with you,
> As if I were a man. (4.1.132–35)

Playing the part of a mere man, Domitian's strategy both recalls and reworks those of other wronged husbands: he moves quickly from probabilities to the ocular proof that that Othello and Leontes so desperately want, spying Domitia kissing Paris before confronting them both. In revenge for an offense so wicked that even Paris admits "if a private man should sit down with it, / Cowards would baffle him" (4.2.196–97), Caesar secretly plans to kill the Roman actor during a performance of *The False Servant*, in which Caesar himself will play "a lord suspecting his wife's constancy" (4.2.213). Such a plan, including Caesar's silence about it until after he murders Paris, is also utterly conventional; the violence that explodes beyond the borders separating art from life in *The False Servant* is perhaps Massinger's most direct echo of *The Spanish Tragedy*. Yet rather than appropriating the power of a corrupt state that has refused his calls for justice, as Hieronimo does, in taking Paris's role as an actor for himself, *The Roman Actor*'s emperor changes places with the lowliest of his many targets of revenge. The broad arc of Massinger's play thus brings Domitian down from his cosmic heights by degrees, winnowing not only the scope of Caesar's power but his problems; the tyrant turned cuckold ultimately chooses to redress the sexual wrong against him through means reserved for those who have no recourse to justice at all. Jupiter's equal finally loses his grasp on absolute power by taking the stage as a revenger.

For *The Roman Actor*'s Caroline spectators, Paris's death during an inset play would have come as no surprise. By 1626, the shocking rupture in the conventional border dividing art from life had been contained as a dramatic device in its own right, fully merged with the smooth transfer of meaning from performance to audience. Like the induction, moreover, the fatal play-within-the-play became conventional in the commercial theater not simply through the device's repeated staging, but as a deliberate appeal to the interpretive expertise of the playhouse spectators, who, in seventeenth-century deployments of the device, are often prepared for carnage by being set against an unsuspecting onstage audience. The final scene of Middleton's *The Revenger's Tragedy* (1606) takes the semiotic force of the device to an extreme, staging a deluge of murderous inset performances. Vindice puts on a masque in order to take his intended victims by surprise: "When they think their pleasure sweet and good, / In midst of all their joys they shall sigh blood" (5.2.21–22).[48] Just after he exits, having stabbed Lussurioso, a competing group of murderers enters, planning to stage their own fatal show. For all of its chaos, the final act of Middleton's early seventeenth-century revenge tragedy unfolds as a meticulous set of instructions in how to anticipate and interpret inset performance in this generic context. Later plays delight in exposing the gap between ignorant onstage spectators and the knowing audience in the playhouse. In Middleton's *Women, Beware Women* (1621), the unknowing Duke and Frabritio watch a masque and register their confusion about murders that they take to be harmless stage action. "What's the conceit of that?" the Duke wonders (5.1.157), as Isabella falls down, dead, during the show; spectators are no longer aligned with the unsuspecting onstage royal spectator, as they are in *The Spanish Tragedy*, but invited to distinguish their expertise from his unknowing.[49] Not all onstage spectators are so unsuspecting: *Hamlet*'s Claudius cannot be faulted for possibly believing he is in grave danger when, during *The Mousetrap*, his nephew announces that the character about to murder the Player King is "Lucianus, nephew to the King" (3.2.237).[50] The dramatic expectations produced by the device of the fatal play-within eventually became so familiar that they could be entirely evacuated of their corresponding dramatic content without any loss of meaning: in Webster's *The White Devil* (1612), Lodovico announces, in disguise, "We have brought you a masque" (5.6.169), before getting straight to the business of murdering without actually staging one.[51] To a Caroline audience, Hieronimo's request that his soon-to-be victims "play a part" in the tragedy he has written would have no longer been a source of interpretive misdirection (4.1.81), but a clear signal that at least one unsuspecting character was soon to end up dead.

Indeed, in the action leading up to Paris's murder, *The Roman Actor* preemptively engages that theatrical familiarity by repeatedly hinting at the deadly events to come. Massinger gives spectators a backstage glimpse at Caesar's preparations for his performance in *The False Servant*, as he removes his robes and dons a cloak and hat in costume. Rebecca Bushnell notes that the action "effect[s] a change from Roman trappings to 'realistic' contemporary dress"; after the opening's careful attempt to measure out the distance from contemporary London to ancient Rome, the sartorial switch brings the violent immediacy of the coming action back up close.[52] Despite changing his clothing, however, Caesar refuses to substitute his sword for a prop foil, one with its "point and edge rebated" (4.2.229). "In jest or earnest this parts never from me" (4.2.232), he protests. The extended attention to his sword narrows spectators' focus on the prop's status *as* a prop in Blackfriars in order to give it newly menacing meaning within the world of *The Roman Actor*, as if sharpening its dull point to a deadly one before spectators' eyes. Massinger alerts his audience to Paris's imminent death by offering a straightforward instruction in the contradictory semiotics of theatrical seeing: the prop sword held by the actor playing Domitian is not a prop.

Domitian further drives home that murder is on his mind by acknowledging his amateur status as an actor just before *The False Servant* begins: "Though but a new actor," he admits, "When I come to execution you shall find / No cause to laugh at me" (4.2.237–39). The pun on "execution," combined with the extended attention to Domitian's sword, one could reasonably say, rewards the theatrical acuity of *all* spectators; there is no need to have seen *The Spanish Tragedy* or any other revenge tragedy to understand the implication of Caesar's double meaning. But the line is also a company joke, one designed precisely to appeal to those theatergoers who regularly frequented the Blackfriars. In 1626, the pun would have been uttered by John Lowin, by that year the longest-serving member of the King's Men. Caesar's admission of his lack of skill thus self-consciously assigns amateur status to the company's most expert player during his very personation of a character type that regular spectators would have been used to seeing him play onstage. Some may have recognized Lowin, a player of remarkable range, from his performance as Bosola in *The Duchess of Malfi* or as Falstaff in *1 Henry IV*.[53] Still others may have recalled when the actor, much earlier in his career, had played himself during the induction of Marston's *The Malcontent*, and could have entwined that metatheatrical moment with Domitian's reference to himself as an actor before *The False Servant* begins. Caesar again highlights his own amateur status at the moment he fatally wounds Paris with the sword he earlier refused to give up: "I have forgot my part. But I can do: / Thus, thus, and thus" (4.2.282–83). Where Caesar's memory fails, however, experienced Caroline spectators are again invited to fill in the gaps, for in 1626 Lowin would have struck his prop sword at Joseph Taylor's Paris, the gesture replicating Lowin-as-Bosola murdering Taylor-as-Ferdinand in Webster's *The Duchess of Malfi* a decade earlier (and likely many other plays for which casting lists do not survive). The repeated, explicit attention to Domitian's lack of skill does more than alert the audience to a crucial plot point: it simultaneously makes the Caroline theatrical community visible to itself by exposing the single fictional representation to the history of the commercial theater, thereby inviting the play's spectators to share in their own knowledge of that accumulated theatrical past.

Caesar's intertheatrically inflected stage murder culminates in a confession that sounds out an echo of the early modern theater's primal revenger. Whether or not spectators recognized Hieronimo in Caesar's oration, spoken as Paris lies dying on the ground before him, its deep familiarity would have emerged from its diffuse reverberation with Hieronimo's lengthy speech admitting to his own crime. Caesar speaks like a revenger because he speaks like those who speak like Hieronimo. "See here my show, look on this spectacle" (4.4.88), Hieronimo cries. "I do glory yet, / That I can call this act mine own" (5.6.292–93), Lodovico likewise gloats, standing over the pile of dead bodies before him in *The White Devil*. Middleton similarly upholds the conventional dictates of the revenger's confession in *The Revenger's Tragedy*, even as they frustrate the play's narrative credibility. Unable to keep his revenge a secret, Vindice brings about his own demise, as well as his accomplice's, by needlessly confessing to the crime: "'Twas we two murdered him" (5.3.98). Multiple murderers clamor for the revenger's title in *Antonio's Revenge*, competing with each other to take credit for the act:

I SENTATOR. Whose hand presents this gory spectacle?
ANTONIO. Mine.
PANDULFO. No, mine!
ALBERTO. No, mine! (5.3.115–18)[54]

Domitian conforms to convention even as he goes off *The False Servant*'s script, relishing in the act of revenge as he confesses directly to his dead victim: "'Twas my plot that thou / Shouldst die in action" (4.2.297–98).[55] Tethered to Kyd's play less by any direct inheritance than by his presence in an intertheatrical constellation of revenge tragedy, Massinger's Paris becomes the "Roman peer" who will not "revive to please tomorrow's audience," as Hieronimo puts it during his own confession (4.4.79, 81). *The False Servant*'s bloody conclusion spectacularly realizes lines from *The Spanish Tragedy* that audience members may well have been able to recall from past performances of the play, whether in the playhouse or the tavern, as they sat in Blackfriars. Through both his murder of Paris and his bombastic confession to it, the emperor turned amateur revenger self-consciously dredges up a theater with a long history.

Of course, these intertheatrical echoes of *The Spanish Tragedy* and other earlier plays are not determinative of the collective Caroline playgoing experience; avid theatergoers in Blackfriars could surely have experienced the moment of Paris's murder beyond the singular frame of *The Roman Actor* in any number of distinctively overlapping or divergent ways. But what I want to emphasize is that *The Roman Actor* seems most consciously to gesture beyond itself and toward the history of the commercial theater at precisely the moment that Caesar admits he has forgotten his part. Into the discursive vacuum Caesar produces onstage as he stabs Paris, *The Roman Actor*'s Caroline spectators are encouraged to place the various theatrical memories, allusions, and references they necessarily always brought with them into the playhouse.[56] The emphasis on Domitian's amateur acting ability is not simply ironically juxtaposed with Lowin's professional skill, but is at once countered by spectators' own theatrical expertise that extends beyond the dramatic frame of *The Roman Actor* entirely. The staged moment is an anthology of past performances made legible by the Caroline theatrical community's spectatorial participation in the fictional representation unfolding before them. In constructing the moment in this fashion, Massinger places the conventional logic of revenge tragedy partly in the hands of spectators themselves. John Kerrigan has shown that *The Spanish Tragedy* ties revenge to memory; *The Roman Actor* rewrites Hieronimo's remembrance of his son, nearly forty years later, as the collective theatrical memory of the Caroline playgoers in the audience.[57] The remembrance that spurs and contextualizes revenge becomes an attribute of neither the fictional revenger nor the play, but the property of the playhouse community watching the action unfold; their spectatorial acumen imbues the stage spectacle with the collective memorial texture of a shared theatrical history when Domitian forgets his lines.

Nor would spectators have acquired the theatrical acuity which produced the thick legibility of Caesar's murder though their time spent in the playhouse alone. Imbricated with the history of the commercial theater that contextualizes the violence of Caesar's gesture and the self-assured grandeur of his confession afterward is the extratheatrical circulation of those dramatic sources themselves. One form that circulation took was amateur performance in public gathering places outside the playhouse, as Edmund Gayton details in his mid-seventeenth century recollection of the commercial theater's heyday:

> Humours are sodainly imitated, especially if there be any life and fancy in 'um. Many have by representation of strong paisions been so transported, that they have gone weeping, some from Tragedies, some from Comedies; so merry, lightsome and free, that they have not been sober in a week after, and have so courted the Players to re-act the same matters in the Tavernes, that they came home, as able Actors as themselves.[58]

As a locus for the display and performance of cultural competence more broadly, the tavern here becomes a site beyond the playhouse for the professional replaying of beloved dramatic material. In 1600 Samuel Rowlands similarly called to mind the gallants who, "like Richard the usurper, swagger, / That had his hand continuall on his Dagger," consciously emulated Shakespeare's Machiavellian hero.[59] The lesson in personation supplied by the actors offered playgoers the opportunity to try out their own acting skills.[60]

Yet these amateur imitations of memorable performances were not merely responses to beloved plays and characters; they also actively shaped the ever-evolving conventions of the commercial theater. Theatrical depictions of amateur performers – from Drugger's donning of "Hieronimo's old cloak, ruff, and hat" in *The Alchemist* (4.7.71), to Pistol's corrupted delivery of *Tamburlaine* in *2 Henry IV*, to Rafe's personation of a picaresque hero in *Knight of the Burning Pestle* – knit the diffuse set of practices that constituted the early modern theatrical community into onstage characters, in the process reformulating theatrical convention as a dramatic answer to those practices.[61] As much as he belongs to the commercial theater's infamous cadre of revengers, Domitian is also an example of this distinctly late-Jacobean, early-Caroline stock character created by frequent playgoers: the amateur actor. If Caesar struck spectators as familiar at the moment he reveals his act of deadly violence against Paris, then, that recognition was formed in part by the theatrical community's practice of assimilating dramatic material into the wider world of London. Caesar, akin to a spectator "sodainly" immersed in the performance he has just seen, does his best imitation of a dramatic revenger even as he forgets his lines. As they watched Domitian swaggering and clutching his dagger, audience members would have been reminded of Hieronimo or Bosola or Richard III. But, just as crucially, they also would have been reminded of themselves. As he does with the seeming induction that opens the play, Massinger here again unsettles spectators' positions in relation to the unfolding stage spectacle, this time thwarting their dramatic expectations by offering them a familiar portrait of their theatrically inflected actions outside the playhouse. In its upending of the traditional portrait of the theatrical revenger, *The Roman Actor* cuts the tyrant down to size by aligning him with the playhouse audience who takes account of his actions. That equation makes manifest the extratheatrical circulation of dramatic material that constituted the Caroline theatrical community, but it simultaneously reveals the role of that circulation in shaping dramatic convention. By means of their very consumption of dramatic material, playgoers gradually made dramatic revengers look and sound more like themselves.

The emergence of a theatrical community fundamentally reshaped, in turn, the phenomenological effects of performance as it unfolded onstage. Domitian is legible as an amateur performer doing his best Hieronimo because Massinger's direct references to *The Spanish Tragedy* and other revenge tragedies merge inextricably with the more diffuse, extratheatrical circulation of Kyd's dramatic material; the two distinct forms of theatrical influence intertwine in the playhouse. Massinger's portrait of Domitian thus embodies the circuitous efficacy of performance that had by then been at work in London for decades: performance seeped into the world beyond the playhouse in the bodies and minds of its spectators, gathered those playgoers into a community, and brought the effects of that collection back to the stage. William Prynne's 1633 antitheatrical screed – which exaggerates Brathwaite's story about the overzealous theatergoer's deathbed performance to include, akin to playgoers at the alehouse pleading for actors to repeat their stage performances, her direct demand for Hieronimo's appearance: "Hieronimo, Hieronimo; *O let mee see* Hieronimo *acted*" – provides a map of this social circumlocution:[62]

> For who more luxurious, ebrious, riotous or deboist, then our assiduous Actors and Play-haunters? Who greater Taverne, Ale-house, Tobacco-shop, Hot-water house haunters, &c? who greater, stouter drinkers, health-quaffers, Epicures, or good-fellowes, then they? What walke more usuall then from a Play-house to a Taverne, to an Ale-house, a Tobacco-shop, or Hot-water Brothel-house; or from these unto a Play-house? where the Pot, the Can, the Tobacco-pipe are alwayes walking till the Play be ended; from whence they returne to these their former haunts.[63]

Prynne's depiction of the actors and playgoers who, "alwayes walking," perambulate from the theater, to the tavern, to the brothel and back, offers a literal model of the cultural circulation of dramatic material that makes its way out of the playhouse and into the social haunts of the city before eventually being returned to the playhouse where it originated. The theatrical history that makes Caesar's murder of Paris deeply legible in the moment of performance is not so much linear as triangulated, jutting outward from the Elizabethan Rose and the Caroline Blackfriars to incorporate London's theatergoing community.[64] By displaying the social circulation of theatrical material in *The Roman Actor*, Massinger offers a distinctly Caroline perspective on the indirect, though powerfully cumulative, efficacy of the commercial theater. Itself a dramatic anthology, the play closes this circuit with the deadly immediacy of an amateur murder that explicitly recalls the climactic action of a blockbuster from a bygone theatrical era.

The play does not end, however, on this recognizably emulative note, for *The Roman Actor*'s conclusion takes an unconventional turn beyond the norms of revenge tragedy that shape the play's first four acts. Massinger's dramatic anthology finally departs from its evocation of Kyd's runaway hit after Paris's murder, concluding not with the death of the Roman actor, but with that of Caesar himself. By the final act of the play, the tyrant turned actor scrambles desperately for control over his own fate, going so far as to keep a list of his potential murderers whom he plans to have killed before they can commit the act – in order, as he puts it, to "free [him] of [his] doubts and fears" (5.1.98). He finds certainty only at the moment of his own murder, when his former allies, including his wife, stab him to death in the final scene of the play. The exact nature of their machinations remains unclear until the moment of the ambush. Caesar's advisor Parthenius cryptically assures the other conspirators, "I have conceived a way, / And with the hazard of my life I'll practice it" (5.2.16–17), before, in the familiar style of the revenger, adopting the false persona of the loyal subject at the sight of Caesar's final entrance: "All happiness, / Security, long life, attend upon / The monarch of the world!" (5.2.43–45). But if Massinger hints to spectators through these series of actions that Domitian is in danger, the culminating effect of his assassination remains one of both violent excess and swiftly brutal surprise:

STEPHANOS.   Make the door fast. – Here,
          A messenger of horror.
CAESAR.   How! Betrayed?
DOMITIA. No; taken, tyrant.
CAESAR.   My Domitia,
          In the conspiracy! (5.2.66–69)

The series of shared lines suggest the speed at which the seizure occurs, as well as Caesar's own unpreparedness for the attack; he lags, fatally, half a line behind the conspirators. Together his advisors stab him to death, then stab his dead body in turn, as if sharing in their collective identity as revengers even beyond the villain's own death. As several scholars have noted, *The Roman Actor*'s spectators may have recognized this culminating murder as an echo of Shakespeare's *Julius Caesar*, but the allusion, deployed concurrently with the chaos of the fatal attack, comes into focus only in the moment of Domitian's assassination; even knowing spectators are prevented from getting ahead of the play's curve.[65] Coincident with Caesar's death, clarity comes too late. At this crucial climactic moment, *The Roman Actor* frees its audience of their own uncertainties about the plot's next turn at precisely the same instant Caesar himself is fatally released from doubt. Massinger exposes the limits of theatrical familiarity as an interpretive resource even as he throws out a reference his spectators are likely to catch.

It is also worth noting that, for all of its shocking spectacle, Caesar's sudden demise could not possibly be more dramatically conventional, even beyond its close connection to Shakespeare's depiction of the murder of a Roman emperor. The very ritualistic excess of Caesar's assassination paradoxically emphasizes the spectacle's status as fictional, and thus harmless, imitation; it contains none of the danger marking the apparently inset murders of both *The Roman Actor* and *The Spanish Tragedy*, in which representation pushes violently beyond its borders. On the commercial stage in 1626, Caesar's murder would have been wholly unremarkable, a display of violence no different from those avid theatergoers could have seen on their sojourns to the playhouse any (or every) other afternoon that week. The theatrical force of Massinger's ending comes into focus only when considered in relation to what has come before it in *The Roman Actor*: set against three plays-within that blur the boundary between imitation and action, it is precisely the representational containment of Caesar's murder that unexpectedly stands out.

By following a series of indeterminate inset performances with the semiotic straightforwardness of Caesar's assassination, Massinger transforms an otherwise dramatically familiar action into something newly surprising. *The Roman Actor* does not simply exploit its audience's expectations by breaking established theatrical conventions and pushing forward into unexplored dramatic territory; rather, it does essentially the opposite, thwarting knowing Caroline playgoers by strategically deploying an otherwise mundanely familiar kind of stage action. After the accumulation of nearly five decades of dramatic convention and five acts of references to a whole host of familiar plays, *The Roman Actor* throws its most experienced spectators off course by making the eminently conventional entirely new. Massinger's play imparts to spectators a shock akin to that invited by *The Spanish Tragedy* at just the moment it seems to push past Kyd's play completely, frustrating the expectations of its most in-the-know spectators by giving them precisely what they should know best. The accumulated theatrical history of the Caroline era allows ruptures in the conventional deployment of theatrical information to come full circle; it is, paradoxically, the extensive theatrical acumen of these spectators that allows a deeply recognizable stage action to metamorphose, without warning, into its inverse.

The dramatic arc of *The Roman Actor* thus encourages spectators to make sense of the world of the play with the interpretive tools so crucially withheld from them in *The Spanish Tragedy*, only to thwart, ultimately, precisely that attempt. This appearance of a spectacle on the stage that would have looked very much like Kyd's play, though crucially deviating from it, is just one example of how *The Spanish Tragedy* itself, much like its play-within, bled into the broader world early modern drama, appearing again and again in the commercial theater as it was repeatedly staged, parodied, and referenced. To be alert to these reappearances of plays one had already seen on the stage, as they merged and blurred with other performances, was to experience the boundaries between distinct theatrical frames as porous – to allow past performances to seep into and complicate new ones. The unpredictable effects of *The Spanish Tragedy* were not limited to Hieronimo's famous collapse of the boundary between play and play-within; understood intertheatrically, *The Spanish Tragedy*'s material effect was its infiltration of the very world of the commercial theater – a world, at once fictional and real, that produced the community comprised of London's most knowing playgoers.

Intertheatricality breaks apart the clear link between prediction and repetition; the reappearance of a familiar line, costume, or gesture on the stage is not a guarantee of what will follow but the radical opening up of unknown possibility. The power of the early modern theater lay in its ability to thicken a single performance with "remembrance of things past" (1.3.139), to borrow a phrase from *The Roman Actor*, while simultaneously opening up new, as-yet-unrealized possibilities for the future.[66] And yet those possibilities did not simply set surprise in increasingly precise relief to the familiar; they also transformed the familiar *into* the surprising. At this late moment in the commercial theater's heyday, the Caroline theatrical community was bound together by its responses to staged representation that had begun to turn back on itself. *The Roman Actor* calls back to *The Spanish Tragedy* while at once departing from it, and in so doing, it invites the audience's shock in response to a spectacle of violent action that is unambiguously contained within the world of the play. What was astonishing in 1587 had coalesced into a cluster of dramatic convention by 1626, and *The Roman Actor* exploits the commonplace blurring of the world of play and play-within by neatly reestablishing the boundary between them. More entangled, the play shows, are the playhouse and the London theatrical community beyond its walls. *The Roman Actor*'s conclusion enacts the unpredictability of performance dramatized by its inset plays, becoming in the process a microcosm of the commercial theater's broader cultural power. The effects of performance as they radiated from the stage, into the minds and bodies of theatergoers, and back again were recognizable, though unpredictable and ever-expanding. If Massinger's play finally offers a model of the theater's ability to strike out with material force into the world beyond the stage, it is one that goes decidedly beyond the immediately efficacious accounts described in Elizabethan and Jacobean defenses of the stage and deployed to theatrical failure in *Hamlet*. The very anthological quality of performance is an accretive process tending toward combustion; put together in the right combination, even the theater's most familiar tropes and conventions have the potential to explode, without warning, into spectacular surprise.

To know a play as a theatergoer in early modern London was to be at once familiar with it and open to its next unpredictable, transformed appearance on the stage – to recognize familiar elements of *The Spanish Tragedy* during *The Roman Actor* while simultaneously remaining attuned to Massinger's transformations and deformations of Kyd's play. This openness to possibility was thus an openness to uncertainty, for the unpredictability of performance that so torments *The Roman Actor*'s tyrant was a key source of entertainment in the early modern commercial theater. In the playhouse, where even the expectations of the most adept playgoers could be deftly exploited, the pleasure brought about by intimate familiarity with dramatic convention was countered by the awareness of not knowing exactly how that convention would be transformed the next time one walked into the theater. Henry Harington's Interregnum characterization of reading plays was exacerbated by the experience of watching those plots unfold in the playhouse: spectators are "*glad* to be deceiv'd," he explains, "finding thy [the playwright's] Drift / T'excell our guess and every turn, and shift."[67] Evacuated of its material consequence, the repeated confrontation with the limits of one's own knowledge in the theater was form of recreation and an occasion for collective pleasure.

Such pleasures have serious ends. The openness to uncertainty cultivated by the commercial theater was a crucial social and cultural resource though early modernity's epistemological upheaval. We might imagine playgoer John Davies, for instance, watching the Ghost lumber onstage during the opening scene of *Hamlet*, intrigued by the sense that the play had rendered spectacular the very questions he had recently asked in his own poetic rumination on uncertainty: "What can we know? or what can we discerne?"[68] Or John Donne, "great frequenter of Playes," heading into a Bankside playhouse with the expectation that the company's offering might transform his frustration with uncertainty and paradox – "Oh, to vex me contraries meet in one," he complained – into enjoyable entertainment.[69] How might friends and fellow playgoers Edward Dering and John Hobart, one an eventual royalist, the other from a family of Parliamentary supporters, have collectively responded to *The Roman Actor*'s portrayal of a theater-loving tyrant?[70] What scenes might they have discussed or replayed after seeing that or another show?[71] In what ways was playgoer Anne Newport's religious ambivalence, which culminated in her evening conversion to Catholicism following an afternoon at the Cockpit in 1637, shaped by the spectacular contradictions she was asked to apprehend in the theater?[72] Through an era that simultaneously demanded and frustrated intellectual, religious, and political resolve, the commercial theater licensed the collective suspension in unknowing for these playgoers and untold others like them.

The distinctiveness of English early modernity is traditionally defined by the range and intensity of its inducements to uncertainty, the epistemological clashes produced as emergent and established modes of thought came to exist uneasily alongside one another. This book has suggested, however, that the exuberant precision with which the theater formally aligned itself with those tensions was just as significant. Uncertainty was the definitive mode of early modern theatrical phenomenology; at once enabling and frustrating spectators' imaginative involvement in stage fiction, unknowing fueled the process of performance in the playhouses that dotted London's outskirts by the close of the sixteenth century. The commercial theater's spectacles were realized through a profoundly uneven mixture of technologies: no scenic backdrops, little stage furniture, elaborate costumes, scores of conventions, and endless words. That combination often produced, simultaneously, too little and too much information – or, to put the effect another way, too little and too much theatricality.

"The chief faults of ours," Richard Flecknoe complained of the commercial theater's plays in 1664, "are our huddling too much matter together ... we imagining we never have intrigue enough, till we lose our selves and Auditors, who shu'd be led in a Maze, but not a Mist."[73] Moment to moment, parsing this theater's "density of signs and sensations," to use Roland Barthes's phrase, required interpretive work; the early modern stage did not so much display fictional worlds to its spectators as require them to participate, continually, in their contingent coming into being.[74] That phenomenological experience could not replicate the experience of confronting one's own doubts about the afterlife or the legitimacy of monarchy or the order of the cosmos, but it did *conform* to them, inviting spectators to inhabit multiple possibilities at once as they worked to participate imaginatively in stage performance. The theater's drive toward the self-conscious display of its own innovation held through the first half the seventeenth century, even as the emergence of a theater industry helped codify conventions and stabilize the transmission of meaning from stage to audience. The vantage point of the Caroline era, on the cusp of the English Civil War and the commercial theater's closure, offers a glimpse of the social force of that multi-decade experimentation in an increasingly politically uncertain world. "All stand wondering how / The thing will be," wrote William Cartwright of the spectators gathered together in the early modern theater, "untill it is."[75] Outside the playhouse as well as within it, the theater's entertaining uncertainties so moved playgoers to stand in eager anticipation of an unknown future about to arrive.

Notes

1 Richard Brathwaite, *The English Gentleman* (London: John Haviland, 1630), 195.

2 Brathwaite, *The English Gentleman*, 195.

3 Brathwaite, *The English Gentleman*, 195.

4 James Shapiro notes that the story is constructed to make the woman a victim of Hieronimo's deliberate, and deadly, blurring of life and art; see "'Tragedies naturally performed': Kyd's Representation of Violence," in *Staging the Renaissance: Reinterpretations of Elizabethan and Jacobean Drama*, ed. David Scott Kastan and Peter Stallybrass (New York: Routledge, 1991), 99–113, esp. 108.

5 *The Spanish Tragedy* has been described by theater scholars as "the first commercial blockbuster of the early modern stage" as well as its "most influential play." See Richard Preiss, "Interiority," in *Early Modern Theatricality*, ed. Henry S. Turner (Oxford: Oxford University Press, 2013), 47–70, esp. 61; and Emma Smith, "Author v. Character in Early Modern Dramatic

Authorship: The Example of Thomas Kyd and *The Spanish Tragedy*," *Medieval and Renaissance Drama in England* 11 (1999): 129–42, esp. 129. William N. West summarizes that "diligent scholarship has counted about 120 clear verbal references to the play across nearly 70 different works." See West, "Intertheatricality," in *Early Modern Theatricality*, 151–72, esp. 162. For more references to *The Spanish Tragedy*, see Emma Smith, "Hieronimo's Afterlives," in *The Spanish Tragedie with the First Part of Jeronimo*, ed. Emma Smith (London: Penguin, 1998), 133–59. The remarkable influence of Kyd's play was not confined to England; on adaptations of *The Spanish Tragedy* on the Continent, see Lukas Erne, *Beyond the Spanish Tragedy: A Study of the Works of Thomas Kyd* (Manchester: Manchester University Press, 2001), 119–30. I follow Martin Wiggins's conjectures about *The Spanish Tragedy*'s date; he suggests a date range for composition of 1585–91, with a best guess of 1587. The play was entered in the Stationer's Register on October 6, 1592. See Wiggins, in association with Catherine Richardson, *British Drama 1533–1642: A Catalogue*, vol. 2 (Oxford: Oxford University Press, 2012), 369.

6 Andrew Gurr, *Playgoing in Shakespeare's London*, 3rd ed. (Cambridge: Cambridge University Press, 2004), 225.

7 See Jeremy Lopez, *Theatrical Convention and Audience Response in Early Modern Drama* (Cambridge: Cambridge University Press, 2003).

8 For more on Caroline connoisseurship as an awareness of theatrical history, see also Adam Zucker and Alan B. Farmer, "Introduction," in *Localizing Caroline Drama: Politics and Economics of the Early Modern English Stage, 1625–1642*, ed. Adam Zucker and Alan B. Farmer (New York: Palgrave Macmillan, 2006), 1–16; and Michael Neill, "'Wits most accomplished Senate': The Audience of the Caroline Private Theaters," *Studies in English Literature* 18.2 (1978): 341–60. For more on Caroline audiences, see Martin Butler, *Theatre and Crisis 1632–1642* (Cambridge: Cambridge University Press, 1984), 100–40.

9 West, "Intertheatricality," 152. As Gina Bloom, Anston Bosman, and William N. West rightly put it in their discussion of intertheatricality, "even the best of innovations are only recognized *as* innovations because they develop or over-turn something that is, on some level, familiar." While their aim is to press the familiarity inculcated by intertheatricality, mine is to investigate the other side of the coin – to ask what theatrical possibilities are presented by mak-ing something new out of the conventionally familiar. See Bloom, Bosman, and West, "Ophelia's Intertheatricality, or, How Performance Is History," *Theatre Journal* 65.2 (2013): 165–82, esp. 181. I borrow the term "horizon of expectations" from Hans Robert Jauss, *Toward an Aesthetic of Reception*, trans. Timothy Bahti (Minneapolis: University of Minnesota Press, 1982), 23.

10 Marissa Greenberg, "Crossing from Scaffold to Stage: Execution Processions and Generic Conventions in *The Comedy of Errors* and *Measure for Measure*," in *Shakespeare and Historical Formalism*, ed. Stephen Cohen (Burlington, VT: Ashgate, 2007), 127–46, esp. 129. For more on the expectation of sur-prise, especially in tragicomedy, see Claire M. L. Bourne, "'High Designe': Beaumont and Fletcher Illustrated," *ELR* 44.2 (2014): 275–327.

11 Edmund Gayton, *Pleasant Notes upon Don Quixot* (London: William Hunt, 1654), 271.

12 See Jeffrey S. Doty and Musa Gurnis's contention that "instead of thinking of embedded examples of reception in plays as removed from what they indirectly record, we might instead think of these theatrical imitations of amateur imitations as rich evidence of recursive exchange" in "Theatre Scene and Theatre Public in Early Modern London," *Shakespeare* 14.1 (2018): 12–25, esp. 17.

13 On the competitive relationship of early modern audiences to stage performance, see Richard Preiss, *Clowning and Authorship in Early Modern Theatre* (Cambridge: Cambridge University Press, 2014).

14 Act, scene, and line numbers follow Thomas Kyd, *The Spanish Tragedy*, ed. Clara Calvo and Jesús Tronch (London: Bloomsbury Arden Shakespeare, 2017).

15 For more on the theatrical confusion created by this stage moment for Elizabethan audiences, see William N. West, "'But this will be a mere confusion': Real and Represented Confusions on the Elizabethan Stage," *Theatre Journal* 60.2 (2008): 217–33, esp. 229.

16 Kyd's play arguably sparked the English theatergoing public's decades-long obsession with revenge as the dramatization of political resistance. Linda Woodbridge has argued that early modern revenge tragedy staged the dramatic search for fairness as a cultural response to economic inequality in the period, though the genre has long been understood to dramatize the extrajudicial redress of wrongs in the absence of justice itself. See Woodbridge, *English Revenge Drama: Money, Resistance, Equality* (Cambridge: Cambridge University Press, 2010).

17 Ellen MacKay, *Persecution, Plague, and Fire: Fugitive Histories of the Stage in Early Modern England* (Chicago: University of Chicago Press, 2011), 17.

18 See, in particular, Preiss, "Interiority," 65–67.

19 Act, scene, and line numbers follow William Shakespeare, *The Taming of the Shrew*, ed. Barbara Hodgdon (London: Arden Shakespeare, 2010).

20 Act, scene, and line numbers follow Ben Jonson, *Cynthia's Revels*, ed. Eric Rasmussen and Matthew Steggle, in *The Cambridge Edition of the Works of Ben Jonson*, ed. David Bevington, Martin Butler, and Ian Donaldson, vol. 1, *1597–1601* (Cambridge: Cambridge University Press, 2012), 429–548.

21 Thomas Carew, "To my worthy Friend, M. D'AVENANT, Vpon his Excellent Play, *The Iust Italian*," in William Davenant, *The Just Italian* (London: John Waterson, 1630), A3v.

22 Carew, "To my worthy Friend," A3v. In his work the social relations of early modern city comedy, Adam Zucker helpfully characterizes the material manifestation of the in-crowd as those actions that allow particular people "to exist in a privileged relation to the spaces and materials of a given environment." To this argument I would add that references to *The Spanish Tragedy* not only allowed spectators to inhabit a privileged position with regard to their fellow audience members in the playhouse, but also actively to recognize each other as collective members of such an in-crowd. See Zucker, *The Places*

of Wit in Early Modern English Comedy (Cambridge: Cambridge University Press, 2011), 3.

23 Act, scene, and line numbers follow Thomas Middleton, *No Wit/Help Like a Woman's*, ed. John Jowett, in *Thomas Middleton: The Collected Works*, ed. Gary Taylor and John Lavagnino (Oxford: Oxford University Press, 2007), 779–832. The prologue goes on to list the various reasons the theatergoers seek out the playhouse in the prologue: "Some in wit, some in shows / Take delight, and some in clothes; / Some for mirth they chiefly come, / Some for passion, for both some / Some for lascivious meetings, that's their errand, / Some to detract, and ignorance their warrant" (3–8).

24 Act, scene, and line numbers follow William Shakespeare, *Hamlet*, ed. Ann Thompson and Neil Taylor (London: Bloomsbury Arden Shakespeare, 2006).

25 For more on the openness of collective response, see Musa Gurnis, *Mixed Faith and Shared Feeling: Theater in Post-Reformation London* (Philadelphia: University of Pennsylvania Press, 2018), 53.

26 Jonathan Goldberg, *James I and the Politics of Literature: Jonson, Shakespeare, Donne, and Their Contemporaries* (Baltimore: Johns Hopkins University Press, 1983), 203.

27 As Tiffany Stern explains, inductions and prologues were often tied to the first performances of plays, emphasizing the present time and place of performance in the process of registering anxiety or uncertainty about an audience's response to new work. See Stern, *Documents of Performance in Early Modern England* (Cambridge: Cambridge University Press, 2009), 82–97.

28 Leo Salingar, "Jacobean Playwrights and 'Judicious' Spectators," *Renaissance Drama* 22 (1991): 209–34, esp. 215.

29 Act, scene, and line numbers follow Ben Jonson, *Every Man Out of His Humour*, ed. Randall Martin, in *The Cambridge Edition of the Works of Ben Jonson*, ed. David Bevington, Martin Butler, and Ian Donaldson, vol. 1, *1597–1601* (Cambridge: Cambridge University Press, 2012), 233–428.

30 Act, scene, and line numbers follow Philip Massinger, *The Roman Actor*, ed. Martin White (Manchester: Manchester University Press, 2007).

31 Richard Robinson was made a sharer in the King's Men around 1619, having begun performing with the company by 1611 as a boy actor; Joseph Taylor joined the company in 1619 and inherited most of Richard Burbage's roles. Curtis Greville was a hired man. See Gerald Eades Bentley, *The Profession of Player in Shakespeare's Time, 1590–1642* (Princeton: Princeton University Press, 1984), 251.

32 The sole surviving contemporary illustration of an early modern play in performance is Henry Peacham's 1595 pen-and-ink drawing of a scene from Shakespeare's *Titus Andronicus*, which includes actors in Renaissance as well as Roman dress. For more on the illustration, see R. A. Foakes, *Illustrations of the English Stage 1580–1642* (Stanford, CA: Stanford University Press, 1985), 48. A key bit of textual evidence from *The Roman Actor* also lends support to the supposition that the actors would have worn robes when the play began: when Caesar changes into costume to personate a scorned lover in

the inset drama *The False Servant*, he orders, "Off with my robe and wreath" (4.2.224).

33 Act, scene, and line numbers follow William Shakespeare, *As You Like It*, ed. Juliet Dusinberre (London: Bloomsbury Arden Shakespeare, 2006).

34 In my reading of Paris's opening speech, then, Massinger does more than simply prevent the audience, as Bill Angus argues, from "plac[ing] the opening statements in any authoritative, interpretive framework." It is precisely by inviting spectators apparently to recognize their own position in relationship to the unfolding action that Massinger is then able to unsettle not only that position, but the audience's sense of familiarity regarding the use of the dramatic device at hand. See Angus, "*The Roman Actor*, Metadrama, Authority, and the Audience," *Studies in English Literature* 50.2 (2010): 445–64, esp. 448.

35 Joanne Rochester, *Staging Spectatorship in the Plays of Philip Massinger* (Burlington, VT; Ashgate, 2010), 22.

36 David A. Reinheimer, for example, calls *The Roman Actor* Massinger's "condemnation of the practice and the politics of censorship from the practical concerns of the performer." See "*The Roman Actor*, Censorship, and Dramatic Autonomy," *Studies in English Literature* 38.2 (1998): 317–32, esp. 317. See also Annabel Patterson, *Censorship and Interpretation: The Conditions of Writing and Reading in Early Modern England* (Madison: University of Wisconsin Press, 1984).

37 For a detailed account of Charles I's almost immediately contested relationship with Parliament after assuming the throne, see Kevin Sharpe, *The Personal Rule of Charles I* (New Haven: Yale University Press, 1992), 1–62.

38 This ambivalence has inspired widely divergent readings: Patricia Thomson, for instance, claims that Massinger "undoubtedly has faith in Paris's and his own profession," while Anne Barton suggests that "there is a sense in which *The Roman Actor* is more pessimistic about the power of art to correct and inform its audience than any other play written between 1580 and 1642." See Thomson, "World Stage and Stage in Massinger's *Roman Actor*," *Neophilologus* 54.4 (1970): 409–26, esp. 425; and Barton, "The Distinctive Voice of Massinger," *The Times Literary Supplement* (1977): 623–24, esp. 623.

39 In her reading of *The Roman Actor*, Marissa Greenberg suggests, as I will, that Domitian takes on for himself the role of "cathartic authority." But where she traces that assumption of authority to English legal history that ties poetic catharsis to justice, I tie Caesar's assumption of theater's perceived power to English theatrical history; as the vengeful substitute for justice itself, Hieronimo's ability to manipulate the reactions of his audience through the careful deployment of unexpected stage action can be understood as the deliberate assumption of cathartic authority. See Greenberg, *Metropolitan Tragedy: Genre, Justice, and the City in Early Modern England* (Toronto: University of Toronto Press, 2015), 89.

40 See Amy J. Rodgers, *A Monster with a Thousand Hands: The Discursive Spectator in Early Modern England* (Philadelphia: University of Pennsylvania Press, 2018), 49.

41 For more on the connection of *The Roman Actor* to these antitheatrical tracts, see Stephen Orgel, "The Play of Conscience," in *Performativity and Performance*, ed. Andrew Parker and Eve Kosofsky Sedgwick (New York: Routledge, 1995), 133–51.

42 For more on the links between *The Roman Actor* and *Hamlet*, see T. A. Dunn, *Philip Massinger: The Man and the Playwright* (London: Thomas Nelson, for The University College of Ghana, 1957), 243–45. Ellen MacKay also cites parallels between *Hamlet* and *The Roman Actor* in her explication of the theater's tyrannical ambitions to apprehend the consciences of its spectators. See MacKay, *Persecution, Plague, and Fire*, 72–73.

43 For more on the failure of performance to move Philargus, see Marissa Greenberg, *Metropolitan Tragedy*, 91–92.

44 On early modern (most notably Philip Sidney's) claims for the "singularly efficacious" quality of poetry, see Stephen Cohen, Introduction, *Shakespeare and Historical Formalism*, ed. Stephen Cohen (Burlington, VT: Ashgate, 2007), 1–27, esp. 9.

45 MacKay suggests that the scene depicts performance's "fail[ure] to ignite any spark of conscience from audiences in need of rebuke," while Jonathan Goldberg maintains that it displays the tyrant's ability to "[make] sure that *The Cure of Avarice* works." See MacKay, *Persecution, Plague, and Fire*, 73; and Goldberg, *James I and the Politics of Literature*, 207.

46 MacKay aptly describes him as the theater's "most notorious fan"; see *Persecution, Plague, and Fire*, 74.

47 James J. Condon, "Setting the Stage for Revenge: Space, Performance, and Power in Early Modern Revenge Tragedy," *Medieval and Renaissance Drama in England* 25 (2012): 62–82, esp. 62.

48 Act, scene, and line numbers follow Thomas Middleton, *The Revenger's Tragedy*, ed. MacDonald P. Jackson, in *Thomas Middleton: The Collected Works*, ed. Gary Taylor and John Lavagnino (Oxford: Oxford University Press, 2007), 543–93.

49 Act, scene, and line numbers follow Thomas Middleton, *Women, Beware Women*, ed. John Jowett, in *Thomas Middleton: The Collected Works*, ed. Gary Taylor and John Lavagnino (Oxford: Oxford University Press, 2007), 1488–541.

50 The attention to Hamlet's seemingly deliberate botching of his theatrical experiment has a long history. For psychological treatments of Hamlet's seeming equation of himself with Lucianus, see, for example, Eileen Z. Cohen, "*Hamlet* and *The Murder of Gonzago*: Two Perspectives," *Revue belge de Philologie et d'Histoire* 61.3 (1983): 543–56; and Charles Edelman, "'The very cunning of the scene': Claudius and the Mousetrap," *Parergon* 12.1 (1994): 15–25. For the argument that the experiment unfolds exactly as Hamlet plans, see Alfred Mollin, "On Hamlet's Mousetrap," *Interpretation: A Journal of Political Philosophy* 21.3 (1994): 353–72. For arguments that his interference renders the results of the experiment inconclusive, see John Kerrigan, *Revenge Tragedy: Aeschylus to Armageddon* (Oxford: Oxford University Press, 1996), 79; and Rhodri Lewis, *Hamlet and the Vision of Darkness* (Princeton: Princeton University Press, 2017), 214–19.

51 Act, scene, and line numbers follow John Webster, *The White Devil*, ed. Benedict S. Robinson (London: Arden, 2019).

52 Rebecca Bushnell, *Tragedies of Tyrants: Political Thought and Theater in the English Renaissance* (Ithaca, NY: Cornell University Press, 1990), 182.

53 See John Astington, *Actors and Acting in Shakespeare's Time: The Art of Stage Playing*. (Cambridge: Cambridge University Press, 2010), 37.

54 Act, scene, and line numbers follow John Marston, *Antonio's Revenge*, in "*The Malcontent" and Other Plays*, ed. Keith Sturgess (Oxford: Oxford University Press, 1997).

55 Hamlet's inability to take credit for Claudius's murder sets Shakespeare's manipulations of the conventions of revenge tragedy in relief to these examples that conform to the confessional expectations of the genre: "Had I but time (as this fell sergeant Death / Is strict in his arrest) – O, I could tell you – / But let it be." (5.2.320–22). Just as he is unable, for so much of the play, to take up the central role of the genre in which he finds himself, Hamlet dies without offering the revenger's conventional confession, instead shifting that responsibility to Horatio.

56 Joseph Roach describes such a process as "surrogation," or the collective cultural attempt to fill "actual or perceived vacancies ... in the network of relations that constitutes the social fabric." His emphasis on the messiness of such a process – "the intended substitute either cannot fulfill expectations, creating a deficit, or actually exceeds them, creating a surplus" – helps characterize, in a theatrical context, the diverse phenomenological that would have characterized this particular moment, as spectators with various and competing theatrical associations supplied what Domitian himself lacked. See Roach, *Cities of the Dead: Circum-Atlantic Performance* (New York: Columbia University Press, 1996), 2.

57 John Kerrigan, *Revenge Tragedy*, 170–92. The theater and memory, of course, are yoked together beyond Hieronimo and revenge tragedy: Marvin Carlson, in particular, has shown that the theater at its most basic level "is as a cultural activity deeply involved with memory and haunted by repetition." While I share his sense that the theater always operates as memory machine, I mean to draw attention here to the specific self-consciousness the Caroline period brought to the theater as an institution with an accumulated history – precisely the history, that is, that made Caroline theatrical publics recognizable as a community. See Carlson, *The Haunted Stage: The Theatre as Memory Machine* (Ann Arbor: The University of Michigan Press, 2003), 11.

58 Gayton, *Pleasant Notes upon Don Quixot*, 140.

59 Samuel Rowlands, *The Letting of Humours Blood in the Head-vaine* (London: W. F., 1600), A2r. See also Jean E. Howard's reading of these lines, which attends to their ambivalence: it is not clear whether the gallants emulate Richard III, Richard Burbage, or some combination of actor and character. Howard, "Stage Masculinities, National History, and the Making of London Theatrical Culture," in *Center or Margin: Revisions of the English Renaissance in Honor of Leeds Barroll*, ed. Lena Cowen Orlin (Cranbury, NJ: Associated University Press, 2006), 199–214, esp. 210.

60 For more on these extratheatrical sites of amateur performance, see Michelle O'Callaghan, *The English Wits: Literature and Sociability in Early Modern England* (Cambridge: Cambridge University Press, 2006); and András Kiséry, *Hamlet's Moment: Drama and Political Knowledge in Early Modern England* (Oxford: Oxford University Press, 2016), 14–15.

61 For more on the evidence of amateur performance practices that escape the historical record, see Charles Whitney, *Early Responses to Renaissance Drama* (Cambridge: Cambridge University Press, 2006), 82–91; and Pamela Allen Brown, *Better a Shrew than a Sheep: Women, Drama, and the Culture of Jest in Early Modern England* (Ithaca, NY: Cornell University Press, 2003), 56–82. Act, scene, and line numbers follow Ben Jonson, *The Alchemist*, ed. Peter Holland and William Sherman, in *The Cambridge Edition of the Works of Ben Jonson*, ed. David Bevington, Martin Butler, and Ian Donaldson, vol. 3, *1606–1611* (Cambridge: Cambridge University Press, 2012), 541–710.

62 William Prynne, *Histrio-Mastix* (London: Michael Sparke, 1633), 556.

63 Prynne, *Histrio-Mastix*, 511.

64 My argument about theatrical and extratheatrical circulation of dramatic material is indebted to Stephen Greenblatt's formative model of what he terms "the circulation of social energy." Yet I depart from his approach, which consistently emphasizes the shaping work of the theater in appropriating and transforming the sources of social energy that existed outside the playhouse, by focusing here on the active work of spectators themselves in both disrupting and reshaping the conventions that governed the plays they saw onstage. At the same time, for all of his investment in the particularities of early modern English culture, Greenblatt's notion of social energy depends crucially upon the lasting quality of Shakespeare's plays through to our own time; my own focus, locally concentrated on the theatrical community in Caroline England, deliberately takes a much shorter view. See Greenblatt, *Shakespearean Negotiations: The Circulation of Social Energy in Renaissance England* (Berkeley: University of California Press, 1988), 1–20.

65 For readings that compare this moment of *The Roman Actor* to *Julius Caesar*, see Rochester, *Staging Spectatorship*, 15–51; and Greenberg, *Metropolitan Tragedy*, 96.

66 The phrase itself may have conjured the very act of remembering on the part of audience members. It originates in Wisdom of Solomon 11:12, rendered in the King James version as "For a double grief came upon them, and a groaning for the remembrance of things past," and also appears widely in texts of the period, from Cornelius Agrippa's *Vanity of the Arts and Sciences* (1530) to Shakespeare's Sonnet 30 (1609). The biblical citation refers to *The Bible: Authorized King James Version with Apocrypha* (Oxford: Oxford University Press, 1997).

67 Henry Harington, "To the incomparable Mr. Fletcher, upon his excellent play, *The Wild-Goose Chase*," in John Fletcher, *The Wild-Goose Chase* (London: Humphrey Mosley, 1652), A2r (emphasis mine).

68 John Davies, *Nosce Teipsum* (London: John Standish, 1599), 3.

69 Richard Baker, *Chronicles of the Kings of England* (London: Daniel Frere, 1643), 156; Donne, "Sonnet: 'Oh, to vex me'," in *The Complete Poems of John Donne*, ed. Robin Robbins (New York: Routledge, 2013), 495.

70 See T. N. S. Lennam's transcription of Dering's "Booke of expences," which notes that he attended a play with Hobart on November 20, 1623: "Sir Edward Dering's Collection of Playbooks, 1619–1624," *Shakespeare Quarterly* 16.2 (1965): 145–53, esp. 150.

71 Dering was an avid collector of playbooks and occasionally bought multiple copies of single plays, suggesting that they were intended for private performance. Lennam, "Sir Edward Dering's Collection of Playbooks," 148.

72 Thomas Wentworth, *The Earle of Strafforde's Letters and Dispatches*, ed. William Knowler, vol. 2 (London: William Bowyer, 1729), 128.

73 Richard Flecknoe, "A Short Discourse of the English Stage," in *Love's Kingdom* (London: Richard Flecknoe, 1664), G4r–G8r, esp. G5v.

74 Roland Barthes, "Baudelaire's Theater," in *Critical Essays*, trans. Richard Howard (Evanston: Northwestern University Press, 1972), 25–31, esp. 26.

75 William Cartwright, "Upon the Report of the Printing of the Dramaticall Poems of Master John Fletcher," in *Comedies and Tragedies Written by Francis Beaumont and John Fletcher* (London: Humphrey Robinson and Humphrey Mosley, 1647), d2r.

Coda
Frame

Resolution in the Restoration Theater

A narrative of the early modern English theater's relentless formal experimentation – its insistent attention to the materials of stagecraft, its regular upending of established conventions – is at once a narrative of continuity. This theater's ability to test the interpretive horizons of its spectators well into the seventeenth century, sounding out the limits of even its most seasoned playgoers' theatrical acuity, was enabled by its relatively unimpeded operation from the late-sixteenth to the mid-seventeenth century. Closures due to the plague were frequent, but every time the playhouses reopened, companies managed to pick up, more or less, where they had left off. The commercial theater's conventions remained recognizable because the interplay between familiarity and surprise remained continuous for several straight decades. Yet it is worth acknowledging that the history of the early modern English theater is as famous for its marked *discontinuity* as it is for this remarkable outpouring of dramatic verse and experimental practice. Through the eighteen-year rupture of the Interregnum, but for irregular illicit performances in the theaters that had once staged plays six days a week, all playing ground to a halt. What changed when the theaters came back?

Arguably, not much.[1] Indeed, the drama itself did not initially change at all, for the new repertory's full slate of plays had already graced the stage in the years prior to 1642.[2] This immediate return to pre-Interregnum drama was, in part, practical: having been granted "full power and authoritie to erect Two Companys of Players" by Charles II on August 21, 1660, Thomas Killigrew and William Davenant got their theaters up and running quickly by mounting extant plays.[3] Over a decade later, however, pre-Interregnum revivals still made up over half of the London repertory.[4] The seeming nostalgia of the post-1660 embrace of familiar plays had been articulated well before the theaters' reopening. "Then shall Learn'd *Johnson* reassume his Seat," Aston Cokaine mused, writing in 1653,

Revive the *Phoenix* by a second heat
Create the Globle [*sic*] anew, and people it,
By those that flock to surset on his *Wit*.
Judicious *Beaumont,* and th' Ingenious Soule
Of *Fletcher* too may move without controule.
Shakespeare (most rich in *Humours*) entertaine
The crowded *Theaters* with his happy veine.[5]

Cokaine imagines the very return to a lost dramatic world that the restoration of commercial playing realized.

His vision of London's resurrected playhouses, however, was mistaken. The Second Globe, dismantled in 1644, was never rebuilt, while the Phoenix, Fortune, and Salisbury Court were "pulled downe" by Cromwell's soldiers in 1649.[6] After receiving Charles II's charter, Killigrew used the surviving Red Bull for just three performances before moving his King's Players to another temporary venue, the Vere Street Theater, adapted from a covered tennis court. On May 7, 1663, he opened the new Theater Royal in Drury Lane. Davenant reoutfitted Salisbury Court's empty shell for performance in 1660, but his Duke's Players acted there only while he installed changeable scenery in a new playing space; the company began performing at the Lincoln's Inn Fields Theater, also an adapted tennis court, in June 1661. Restoration theater practitioners may have been eager to return to the drama of an earlier theatrical era, but they were just as eager to leave behind the playhouses in which that drama had once been staged.

Dramatically familiar, then, the Restoration theater was architecturally new. The accommodation of Continental and courtly theatrical conventions and practices, including machinery and perspective scenery, required extensive changes to the shape and arrangement of the playing space itself. In the Theater Royal and Dorset Garden, the thrust stage of the pre-Interregnum amphitheaters, which allowed the audience to surround the playing platform on three sides, was reduced in favor of a smaller forestage extending just beyond a proscenium frame. As Edward A. Langhans explains, "performers appearing on it [the forestage]... could, if they wished, move back and use the scenery as an environment instead of a decorative background."[7] In privileging spectators' interaction with performers, the thrust had also privileged their imaginative involvement in the construction of dramatic worlds; the proscenium frame and smaller forestage, by contrast, encouraged actors' interaction with the visual scenery on the stage itself. By the end of the seventeenth century, the forestage had been reduced yet further; as a result, actor Colley Cibber complained, "the Actors … are kept so much more backward from the main Audience, than they us'd to be."[8]

Changes to English drama followed quickly on the heels of these architectural shifts. Heroic drama was the first genre that the Restoration theater could claim as its own, and it had no more enthusiastic proponent than John Dryden. The genre dramatized, with great intensity, the urgency of choice: caught between "Love and Valour," as Dryden characterized heroic drama's essential conflict, the hero must determine his allegiance.[9] *The Conquest of Granada*'s hero Alamanzor is the quintessential embodiment of such resolve. Bombastic, self-assured, and bold – "I alone am King of me" (1.1.206), he asserts early on – Almanzor substitutes decision for doubt, action for thought. His very first lines register his inability to tolerate hesitation; having stumbled into the middle of a factional conflict within the Moorish army, he immediately chooses a side: "I cannot stay to ask which cause is best; / But this is so to me because opprest" (1.1.128–29). Stuffed with turns, counterturns, and returns, Dryden's heroic plays make the hero's rapid-fire oscillation between possibilities the engine of their action; Almanzor and others do not vacillate so much as – confidently, repeatedly, blithely – pivot.[10]

Heroic drama found a welcome home in London's new theaters, I want to suggest, because they similarly aimed to compel the imaginative conviction of their spectators. Even as he professes his adherence to his predecessors, Dryden foregrounds the emergence of this new theatrical phenomenology in his defense of heroic drama. "To those who object my frequent use of Drums and Trumpets; and my representations of Battels," he writes, "I answer, I introduc'd them not on the *English* stage, *Shakespear* us'd them frequently: and, though *Jonson* shows no Battel in his *Catiline*, yet you hear from behind the Scenes, the sounding of Trumpets, and the shouts of fighting Armies."[11] What he has taken from these earlier playwrights, Dryden goes on to explain, is a formal technique by which to subdue the imaginations of his audience:

> These warlike Instruments, and, even the representations of fighting on the Stage, are no more than necessary to produce the effects of an Heroick Play; that is, to raise the imagination of the Audience, and to perswade them, for the time, that what they behold on the Theater is really perform'd. The Poet is, then, to endeavour an absolute dominion over the minds of the Spectators.[12]

Earlier accounts of stage performance similarly extol its ability to convince spectators that what they were seeing was "really perform'd," though Dryden amplifies that power as the total domination of spectators' imaginations; he construes the spectator as a passive witness to stage show, not involved in the process of performance but over-taken by it.[13] The increasing demarcation of audience and stage in the new Restoration theaters enabled this changing view of spectatorship. Julie Stone Peters writes that stages filled with perspective scenery and framed by the proscenium "entailed, ideally, perfect control of the gaze of the spectator"; as Dryden puts it, they encouraged spectators simply to "behold" what was displayed before them.[14] These phenomenological changes continued into the mid-eighteenth century, by which point, as Pannill Camp has suggested, the proscenium frame would come to be associated "with the window frame – a transparent boundary that promised candid access to a stage that seemed like an actual segment of contemporary reality."[15] That promise of unambiguous transparency was enabled by the spatial severance of the interpretive link between spectator and stage that had defined the process of performance in the commercial theaters up to 1642.[16] Dryden's particular innovation as a practitioner was to match his heroic drama, itself defined by confident resolution, to a theatrical phenomenology that newly compelled specta-tors' imaginative clarity.

As part of his insistence on heroic drama's continuity with the past, Dryden may have intended his defense to sound out an echo of the Prologue to Shakespeare's Prologue *Henry V*, in which talk of armies similarly gives way to talk of the imagination; their comparison is illustrative. "Let us, ciphers to this great account," *Henry V*'s speaker requests,

> On your imaginary forces work.
> Suppose within the girdle of these walls
> Are now confined two mighty monarchies,
> Whose high upreared and abutting fronts
> The perilous narrow ocean parts asunder.
> Piece out your imperfections with your thoughts.
> Into a thousand parts divide one man
> And make imaginary puissance.
> Think, when we talk of horses, that you see them
> Printing their proud hoofs i'th' receiving earth. (Prologue.17–27)[17]

Spectators are asked to imagine horses because the early modern the-ater could not present them; indeed, though horses are mentioned and described with striking frequency in the drama of this period, they never appeared onstage. That changed after the Restoration. On July 11, 1668, Samuel Pepys recorded his attendance at the Theater Royal: "After dinner, to the King's playhouse to see an old play of Shirly's called *Hide parke*, the first day acted – where horses are brought upon the stage."[18] *Hyde Park* was originally licensed for performance in 1637, a moment by which, as William N. West suggests, horses had come to stand in as "an elaborate shared theatrical joke" about the limitations of the commercial theater's representational technologies.[19] Separated from that bygone theatrical culture by the eighteen years of the Interregnum, the Restoration theater was no longer in on it.

Another moment from *Henry V* makes clear what was lost in the Restoration theater's embrace of a phenomenology that aimed to control what its spectators saw. "Thus with imagined wing our swift scene flies / In motion of no less celerity / Than that of thought," the speaker of the Prologue claims halfway through the play, as the king's soldiers board the ships that will take them across the English Channel to France:

> Suppose that you have seen
> The well-appointed King at Hampton pier
> Embark his royalty, and his brave fleet
> With silken streamers the young Phoebus fanning.
> Play with your fancies, and in them behold
> Upon the hempen tackle ship-boys climbing;
> Hear the shrill whistle which doth order give
> To sounds confused; behold the threaden sails,
> Borne with th'invisible and creeping wind,
> Draw the huge bottoms through the furrowed sea,
> Breasting the lofty surge. O do but think
> You stand upon the rivage and behold
> A city on th'inconstant billows dancing,
> For so appears this fleet majestical,
> Holding due course to Harfleur.   (3.0.1–17)

Suppose, play, behold, behold, think, behold: the speech's imperatives suggest a Drydenian aim to dominate spectators' imaginations, but as each line progresses, the commands themselves become increasingly difficult to follow. The opening casts the imagination as the "wing" with which spectators will move from England to France, though the metaphor is quickly appropriated as a literal image of the ships' "threaden sails"; spectators are now meant to conjure the material detail into being, along with the fleet's other elements: silken streamers, the hempen tackle, climbing ship-boys. Yet just as the imagined picture seems to reach its verbal completion, the lines suddenly jump ship, moving to the shore: "O do but think / You stand upon the rivage and behold / A city on th'inconstant billows dancing." This is an odd request. From a new vantage, spectators are asked to deceive themselves into believing that the ships they have just constructed in their minds' eyes are actually a city bobbing on the swelling waves. The visual metaphor of the opening lines, replaced by the order to imagine a literal image, eventually transforms into the impossible demand to see that image for precisely what it is *not*, as if the lines appropriate the very fleet dutifully conjured by spectators as the technology for another representation entirely. The speech challenges spectators' ability to imagine with any clarity at all: what do ships mistaken for a city from the perspective of the shore look like, exactly? Despite the speaker's insistence, there is no beholding happening here. The result is a thoroughly ambiguous piece of imagined stage furniture: an amalgamation of city and ship, land and sea, conjured out of words and thin air.

The Restoration stage could not brook such ambiguity. Dryden's endeavor to take "absolute dominion" over his spectators' minds was made possible by a stage framed by a proscenium and organized by perspective scenery; the unified clarity of its images aimed to produce contained and singular visions, overwhelming in magnificence but rid of the duplicity that characterized the self-conscious spectacles of the early modern stage. The Restoration theater broke from its progenitor, in short, by allowing its spectacles to come uniformly into focus. In the midst of an era defined by epistemological clash, commercial theater came to thrive in London by suspending its spectators in pleasurable uncertainty – by freeing them from the need, that is, to make a choice. Yet after the war that had forced many people to do just that – to turn away, and return, from one allegiance to another – playgoers came back to a theater newly invested in compelling their imaginative resolution. This is not to suggest that Charles II's ascension to the throne ushered his subjects into a newly quieted age, though that is exactly what his own propaganda declared.[20] Uncertainty did not disappear after the Restoration. What changed was the theater's ability to compass it.

Notes

1 A narrative of continuity across the "long seventeenth century," which does not privilege 1642 and 1660 as moments of rupture, has been a key consequence of revisionist and postrevisionist historiography of this period. See, for instance, Thomas Cogswell, Richard Cust, and Peter Lake, "Revisionism and its Legacies: The Work of Conrad Russell," in *Politics, Religion, and Popularity in Early Stuart Britain: Essays in Honour of Conrad Russell*, ed. Thomas Cogswell, Richard Cust, and Peter Lake (Cambridge: Cambridge University Press, 2002), 1–17, esp. 15.

2 On this "all-revival repertory," see Michael Dobson, "Adaptations and Revivals," in *The Cambridge Companion to English Restoration Theatre*, ed. Deborah Payne Fisk (Cambridge: Cambridge University Press, 2000), 40–51, esp. 41.

3 Davenant's draft of the joint warrant is reproduced in Leslie Hotson, *The Commonwealth and Restoration Stage* (Cambridge, MA: Harvard University Press, 1928), 199–200.

4 The 1674–75 season included twenty-nine plays written since 1660 and twenty-five written before the 1642 closure; see Dobson, "Adaptations and Revivals," 41.

5 Aston Cokaine, "A Praeludium to Mr. *RICHARD BROMES* Playes," in Richard Brome, *Five New Playes* (London: Humphrey Moseley, Richard Marriot, and Thomas Dring, 1653), A2r.

6 Quoted in Hotson, *The Commonwealth and Restoration Stage*, 43.

7 Edward A. Langhans, "The Theatre," in *The Cambridge Companion to English Restoration Theatre*, 1–18, esp. 8.

8 Colley Cibber, *An Apology for the Life of Mr. Colley Cibber* (London: Colley Cibber, 1740), 241.

9 John Dryden, *The Conquest of Granada, Part 1*, in *The Works of John Dryden*, ed. John Loftis, David Stuart Rodes, and Vinton A. Dearing, vol. 11 (Berkeley: University of California Press, 1978), 10.

10 As Stuart Sherman puts it, "what Dryden most conspicuously offered his audiences was a sequence of quick turns among opposite probabilities, wherein what was often most hypnotic was not the choice but the choosing." See Sherman, "Dryden and the Theatrical Imagination," in *The Cambridge Companion to John Dryden*, ed. Steven N. Zwicker (Cambridge: Cambridge University Press, 2004), 15–36, esp. 17.

11 Dryden, *The Conquest of Granada*, 13.

12 Dryden, *The Conquest of Granada*, 13–14.

13 See, in particular, Thomas Heywood's assertion that history plays had the power to make spectators regard an actor "as if [he] were the man Personated." See *An Apology for Actors* (London: Nicholas Okes, 1612), B4r.

14 Julie Stone Peters, *Theatre of the Book, 1480–1880: Print, Text, and Performance in Europe* (Oxford: Oxford University Press, 2000), 187.

15 Pannill Camp, *The First Frame: Theatre Space in Enlightenment France* (Cambridge: Cambridge University Press, 2014), 16.

16 See Peters's compelling suggestion that "framed, unifed perspective" produces "a general aspiration towards scenic magnificence protected from audience incursion." *Theatre of the Book*, 186, 187.

17 Act, scene, and line numbers refer to William Shakespeare, *King Henry V*, ed. T. W. Craik (London: Arden Shakespeare, 1995).

18 Samuel Pepys, *The Diary of Samuel Pepys*, ed. Robert Latham and William Matthews, vol. 9, *1668–1669* (London: Harper Collins, 1995), 260.

19 William N. West, "Intertheatricality," in *Early Modern Theatricality*, ed. Henry S. Turner (Oxford: Oxford University Press, 2013), 151–72, esp. 169.

20 His Declaration of Breda, for instance, "ordain[ed] that henceforward all Notes of discord, separation and difference of Parties, be utterly abolished among all our Subjects, whom we invite and conjure to a perfect Vnion among themselves under our Protection." See *King Charls II. His Declaration to All His Loving Subjects of the Kingdome of England* (London: John Playford, 1660), 4.

Bibliography

Adelman, Janet. *Suffocating Mothers: Fantasies of Maternal Origin in Shakespeare's Plays, "Hamlet" to "The Tempest."* New York: Routledge, 1992.

Ahmed, Sara. *Queer Phenomenology: Orientations, Objects, Others.* Durham: Duke University Press, 2006.

Altman, Joel. *The Tudor Play of Mind: Rhetorical Inquiry and the Development of Elizabethan Drama.* Berkeley: University of California Press, 1978.

Amster, Mara. "Frances Howard and Middleton and Rowley's *The Changeling*: Trials, Tests, and the Legibility of the Virgin Body." In *The Single Woman in Medieval and Early Modern England: Her Life and Representation*, edited by Laurel Amtower and Dorothea Kehler, 211–232. Tempe: Arizona Center for Medieval and Renaissance Studies, 2003.

Anderson, Thomas P. "Surpassing the King's Two Bodies: The Politics of Staging the Royal Effigy in Marlowe's *Edward II*." *Shakespeare Bulletin* 32.4 (2014): 585–611.

Anglicus, Bartholomeus. *Batman Vppon Bartholome His Booke: De Proprietatibus Rerum.* London: Thomas East, 1582.

Angus, Bill. "*The Roman Actor*, Metadrama, Authority, and the Audience." *Studies in English Literature* 50.2 (2010): 445–464.

Annas, Julia and Jonathan Barnes. *The Modes of Scepticism: Ancient Texts and Modern Interpretations.* Cambridge: Cambridge University Press, 1985.

Archer, Ian W. *The Pursuit of Stability: Social Relations in Elizabethan London.* Cambridge: Cambridge University Press, 1991.

Aristotle. *Poetics.* Translated by James Hutton. New York: W. W. Norton and Company, 1982.

Astington, John. *Actors and Acting in Shakespeare's Time: The Art of Stage Playing.* Cambridge: Cambridge University Press, 2010.

Attie, Katherine Bootle. "Passion Turned to Prettiness: Rhyme or Reason in *Hamlet*." *Shakespeare Quarterly* 63.3 (2012): 393–423.

Aubrey, John. "Remaines of Gentilisme and Judaisme." In *Three Prose Works*, edited by John Buchanan-Brown, 126–304. Carbondale: Southern Illinois University Press, 1972.

Bacon, Francis. *The New Organon.* Edited by Lisa Jardine and Michael Silverthorne. Cambridge: Cambridge University Press, 2000.

Baker, Richard. *Chronicles of the Kings of England*. London: Daniel Frere, 1643.

Barber, Charles Laurence. *Shakespeare's Festive Comedy: A Study of Dramatic Form and Its Relation to Social Custom*. Cleveland: Meridian Books, 1959.

Barish, Jonas. "*Perkin Warbeck* as Anti-History." *Essays in Criticism* 20.2 (1970): 151–171.

Barish, Jonas. *The Antitheatrical Prejudice*. Berkeley: University of California Press, 1981.

Barkan, Leonard. "Making Pictures Speak: Renaissance Art, Elizabethan Literature, Modern Scholarship." *Renaissance Quarterly* 48.2 (1995): 326–351.

Barkan, Leonard. "The Theatrical Consistency of *Richard II*." *Shakespeare Quarterly* 29.1 (1978): 5–19.

Barlow, William. *Psalmes and Hymnes of Praier and Thanksgiuing*. London: John Beale, 1613.

Barret, J. K. "The Crowd in Imogen's Bedroom: Allusion and Ethics in *Cymbeline*." *Shakespeare Quarterly* 66.4 (2015): 440–462.

Barret, J. K. *Untold Futures: Time and Literary Culture in Renaissance England*. Ithaca, NY: Cornell University Press, 2016.

Barroll, Leeds. *Politics, Plague, and Shakespeare's Theater: The Stuart Years*. Ithaca, NY: Cornell University Press, 1991.

Barthes, Roland. "Baudelaire's Theater." In *Critical Essays*, translated by Richard Howard, 25–36. Evanston, IL: Northwestern University Press, 1972.

Barton, Anne. "The Distinctive Voice of Massinger." The Times Literary Supplement (May 20, 1977): 623–624.

Beaumont, Francis and John Fletcher. *The Captain*. Vol. 1 of *The Dramatic Works in the Beaumont and Fletcher Canon*, edited by L. A. Beaurline. Cambridge: Cambridge University Press, 1966.

Beaumont, Francis and John Fletcher. *A King and No King*. London: Thomas Walkley, 1619.

Beckerman, Bernard. *Dynamics of Drama: Theory and Method of Analysis*. New York: Drama Book Specialists, 1979.

Beckerman, Bernard. "The Use and Management of the Elizabethan Stage." In *The Third Globe*, edited by C. Walter Hodges, S. Schoenbaum, and Leonard Leone, 151–163. Detroit: Wayne State University Press, 1981.

Bell, Millicent. *Shakespeare's Tragic Scepticism*. New Haven: Yale University Press, 2002.

Bell, Thomas. *The Woefull Crie of Rome Containing a Defiance to Popery*. London: William Welby, 1605.

Bellarmine, Robert. *Iacob's Ladder Consisting of Fifteene Degrees or Ascents to the Knowledge of God by the Consideration of His Creatures and Attributes*. London: Henry Selle, 1638.

Bentley, Gerald Eades. *The Jacobean and Caroline Stage*. 7 vols. Oxford: Clarendon Press, 1968.

Bentley, Gerald Eades. *The Profession of Player in Shakespeare's Time, 1590–1642*. Princeton: Princeton University Press, 1984.

Bergeron, David M. *English Civic Pageantry, 1558–1642*. Tempe, AZ: The Arizona Center for Medieval and Renaissance Studies, 2003.

Berkenhead, John. "On the Happy Collection of Master Fletcher's Works, Never Before Printed." *In Comedies and Tragedies Written by Francis Beaumont and John Fletcher*. London: Humphrey Robinson and Humphrey Mosley, 1647.

Bevington, David. *Action Is Eloquence: Shakespeare's Language of Gesture*. Cambridge, MA: Harvard University Press, 1984.

Bevington, David, Martin Butler, and Ian Donaldson, eds. *The Cambridge Edition of the Works of Ben Jonson*. 7 vols. Cambridge: Cambridge University Press, 2012.

The Bible: Authorized King James Version with Apocrypha. Oxford: Oxford University Press, 1997.

Bishop, T. G. *Shakespeare and the Theatre of Wonder*. Cambridge: Cambridge University Press, 1996.

Blau, Herbert. *Take Up the Bodies: Theater at the Vanishing Point*. Urbana: University of Illinois Press, 1982.

Bloom, Gina. *Gaming the Stage: Playable Media and the Rise of English Commercial Theater*. Ann Arbor: University of Michigan Press, 2018.

Bloom, Gina, Anston Bosman, and William N. West. "Ophelia's Intertheatricality, or, How Performance Is History." *Theatre Journal* 65.2 (2013): 165–182.

Bly, Mary. "The Boy Companies 1599–1613." In *The Oxford Handbook of Early Modern Theatre*, edited by Richard Dutton, 136–150. Oxford: Oxford University Press, 2009.

Bly, Mary. *Queer Virgins and Virgin Queans on the Early Modern Stage*. Oxford: Oxford University Press, 2000.

The Book of Common Prayer: The Texts of 1549, 1559, and 1662. Edited by Brian Cummings. Oxford: Oxford University Press, 2011.

Boose, Lynda. "Othello's Handkerchief: 'The Recognizance and Pledge of Love'." *English Literary Renaissance* 5.3 (1975): 360–374.

Booth, Stephen. "On the Value of *Hamlet*." In *Reinterpretations of Elizabethan Drama: Selected Papers from the English Institute*, edited by Norman Rabkin, 137–176. New York: Columbia University Press, 1969.

Booth, Stephen. "Syntax as Rhetoric in *Richard II*." *Mosaic: An Interdisciplinary Critical Journal*, 10.3 (1977): 87–103.

Bourne, Claire M. L. "'High Designe': Beaumont and Fletcher Illustrated." *English Literary Renaissance* 44.2 (2014): 275–327.

Bozio, Andrew. *Thinking through Place on the Early Modern English Stage*. Oxford: Oxford University Press, 2020.

Bradshaw, Graham. *Shakespeare's Scepticism*. Ithaca, NY: Cornell University Press, 1987.

Brathwaite, Richard. *Anniversaries Upon His Panarete Continued*. London: Robert Bostock, 1635.

Brathwaite, Richard. *The English Gentleman*. London: John Haviland, 1630.

Bray, Alan. "Homosexuality and the Signs of Male Friendship in Elizabethan England." *History Workshop* 29.1 (1999): 1–19.

Brecht, Bertolt. "Alienation Effects in Chinese Acting." In *Brecht on Theatre: The Development of an Aesthetic*, edited and translated by John Willett, 91–99. New York: Hill and Wang, 1964.

Breitenberg, Mark. *Anxious Masculinity in Early Modern England*. Cambridge: Cambridge University Press, 1996.

Brennan, Anthony. *Onstage and Offstage Worlds in Shakespeare's Plays*. New York: Routledge, 1989.

Briggs, Julia. "*The Lady's Tragedy*: Parallel Texts." In *Thomas Middleton: The Collected Works*, edited by Gary Taylor and John Lavagnino, 833–838. Oxford: Oxford University Press, 2007.

Bristol, Michael. *Carnival and Theater: Plebeian Culture and the Structure of Authority in Renaissance England*. New York: Routledge, 1985.

Brome, Richard. *The Queen's Exchange. Vol. 7 of The Dramatic Works of Richard Brome*, edited by John Pearson. New York: AMS Press, Inc., 1966.

Brown, John Russell, ed. *Focus on "Macbeth."* London: Routledge, 1982.

Brown, Pamela Allen. *Better a Shrew than a Sheep: Women, Drama, and the Culture of Jest in Early Modern England*. Ithaca, NY: Cornell University Press, 2003.

Bulwer, John. *Chirologia, or, The Naturall Language of the Hand Composed of the Speaking Motions, and Discoursing Gestures Thereof*. London: R. Whitaker, 1644.

Burke, Kenneth. *Counter-Statement*. Berkeley: University of California Press, 1931.

Burke, Kenneth. "*Othello*: An Essay to Illustrate a Method." In *"Othello": Critical Essays*, edited by Susan Snyder, 127–168. New York: Garland, 1988.

Bushnell, Rebecca. *Tragedies of Tyrants: Political Thought and Theater in the English Renaissance*. Ithaca, NY: Cornell University Press, 1990.

Butler, Martin. *Theatre and Crisis 1632–1642*. Cambridge: Cambridge University Press, 1984.

Calderwood, James L. *Metadrama in Shakespeare's Henriad: "Richard II" to "Henry V."* Berkeley: University of California Press, 1979.

Calderwood, James L. "Ways of Waiting in *Waiting for Godot*." *Modern Drama* 29.3 (1986): 365–375.

Calendar of State Papers and Manuscripts, Relating to English Affairs, Existing in the Archives and Collections of Venice. 38 vols. London: H. M. Stationary Office, 1864–1940.

Calvin, John. *The Sermons of M. Iohn Caluin Upon the Fifth Booke of Moses Called Deuteronomie*. Translated by Arthur Golding. London: George Bishop, 1583.

Camp, Pannill. *The First Frame: Theatre Space in Enlightenment France*. Cambridge: Cambridge University Press, 2014.

Canino, Catherine Grace. *Shakespeare and the Nobility: The Negotiation of Lineage*. Cambridge: Cambridge University Press, 2007.

Carew, Thomas. "To my worthy Friend, M. D'AVENANT, Vpon his Excellent Play, *The Iust Italian*." In *The Just Italian*. London: John Waterson, 1630.

Carlson, Marvin. *The Haunted Stage: The Theatre as Memory Machine*. Ann Arbor: The University of Michigan Press, 2003.

Cartwright, William. "Upon the Report of the Printing of the Dramaticall Poems of Master John Fletcher." In *Comedies and Tragedies Written by Francis Beaumont and John Fletcher*. London: Humphrey Robinson and Humphrey Mosley, 1647.

Cavell, Stanley. *Disowning Knowledge in Seven Plays of Shakespeare*. Cambridge: Cambridge University Press, 2003.

Cerasano, S. P. and Marion Wynne-Davies, eds. *Renaissance Drama by Women: Texts and Documents*. New York: Routledge, 1996.

Certeau, Michel de. *The Practice of Everyday Life*. Translated by Steven Rendall. Berkeley: University of California Press, 1984.

Chamberlain, John. *The Letters of John Chamberlain*. Edited by Norman Egbert McClure. Philadelphia: The American Philosophical Society, 1939.

Charles II. *King Charls II. His Declaration to All His Loving Subjects of the Kingdome of England*. London: John Playford, 1660.

Cibber, Colley. *An Apology for the Life of Mr. Colley Cibber*. London: Colley Cibber, 1740.

Cicero. *Academica*. Translated by H. Rackham. Cambridge, MA: Harvard University Press, 1933.

Clark, Stuart. *Vanities of Eye: Vision in Early Modern European Culture*. Oxford: Oxford University Press, 2007.

Clegg, Cyndia Susan. "'By the choise and inuitation of al the realme': *Richard II* and Elizabethan Press Censorship." *Shakespeare Quarterly* 48.4 (1997): 432–48.

Clubb, Louise. *Italian Drama in Shakespeare's Time*. New Haven: Yale University Press, 1989.

Clubb, Louise. "Italian Stories on the Stage." In *The Cambridge Companion to Shakespearean Comedy*, edited by Alexander Leggatt, 32–46. Cambridge: Cambridge University Press, 2002.

Cogswell, Thomas, Richard Cust, and Peter Lake, eds. *Politics, Religion, and Popularity in Early Stuart Britain: Essays in Honour of Conrad Russell*. Cambridge: Cambridge University Press, 2002.

Cohen, Eileen Z. "*Hamlet* and *The Murder of Gonzago*: Two Perspectives." *Revue belge de Philologie et d'Histoire* 61.3 (1983): 543–56.

Cohen, Stephen, ed. *Shakespeare and Historical Formalism*. Burlington, VT: Ashgate, 2007.

Cokaine, Aston. "A Praeludium to Mr. *RICHARD BROMES* Playes." In Richard Brome, *Five New Playes*. London: Humphrey Moseley, Richard Marriot, and Thomas Dring, 1653.

Condon, James J. "Setting the Stage for Revenge: Space, Performance, and Power in Early Modern Revenge Tragedy." *Medieval and Renaissance Drama in England* 25 (2012): 62–82.

A Conference about the Next Succession to the Crowne of Ingland. Antwerp: A. Conincx, 1595.

Cox, John D. *Seeming Knowledge: Shakespeare and Skeptical Faith*. Waco, TX: Baylor University Press, 2007.

Crane, Mary Thomas. *Losing Touch with Nature: Literature and the New Science in Sixteenth Century England*. Baltimore: Johns Hopkins University Press, 2014.

Cressy, David. *Birth, Marriage, and Death: Ritual, Religion, and the Life-Cycle in Tudor and Stuart England*. Oxford: Oxford University Press, 1997.

Crockett, Bryan. *The Play of Paradox: Stage and Sermon in Renaissance England*. Philadelphia: University of Pennsylvania Press, 1995.

Crooke, Helkiah. *Mikrokosmographia: A Description of the Body of Man*. London: William Jaggard, 1615.

Cunningham, Karen. *Imaginary Betrayals: Subjectivity and the Discourses of Treason in Early Modern England*. Philadelphia: University of Pennsylvania Press, 2002.

Curran, Kevin. "Feeling Criminal in *Macbeth*." *Criticism* 54.3 (2012): 391–401.

Curran, Kevin and James Kearney. "Introduction." *Criticism* 54.3 (2012): 353–64.

Dailey, Alice. "Little, Little Graves: Shakespeare's Photographs of Richard II." *Shakespeare Quarterly* 69.3 (2018): 141–66.

Davies, John. *Nosce Teipsum*. London: John Standish, 1599.

Dawson, Anthony B. and Paul Yachnin. *The Culture of Playgoing in Shakespeare's England: A Collaborative Debate*. Cambridge: Cambridge University Press, 2001.

Deák, František. "Structuralism in Theatre: The Prague School Contribution." *The Drama Review* 20.4 (1976): 83–94.

Dear, Peter. *Discipline and Experience: The Mathematical Way in the Scientific Revolution*. Chicago: University of Chicago Press, 1995.

Degenhardt, Jane Hwang and Cyrus Mulready, "Romance and Tragicomedy." In *A New Companion to Renaissance Drama*, edited by Arthur F. Kinney and Thomas Warren Hopper, 417–40. Hoboken, NJ: John Wiley and Sons Ltd., 2017.

Dekker, Thomas. *The Guls Horne-booke*. London: R. S., 1609.

Dekker, Thomas. *Lanthorne and Candle-light*. London: John Busby, 1609.

Dekker, Thomas. *The Magnificent Entertainment*. London: Thomas Man, 1604.

Dekker, Thomas. *A Strange Horse-Race*. London: Joseph Hunt, 1613.

Dekker, Thomas. *The Wonderful Year*. In *Selected Prose Writings*, edited by E. D. Pendry, 23–64. London: Edward Arnold, 1967.

Dent, R. W. *Shakespeare's Proverbial Language: An Index*. Berkeley: University of California Press, 1981.

Desens, Marliss C. *The Bed Trick in English Renaissance Drama: Explorations in Gender, Sexuality, and Power*. Newark: University of Delaware Press, 1994.

Desmet, Christy. "Shakespearean Comic Character: Ethos and Epideictic in *Cymbeline*." In *Acting Funny: Comic Theory and Practice in Shakespeare's Plays*, edited by Frances N. Teague, 123–124. Rutherford, NJ: Fairleigh Dickinson University Press, 1994.

Dessen, Alan. "Early Modern Staging of Throne Scenes." *Theatre Notebook* 71.3 (2017): 190–93.

Dessen, Alan. *Elizabethan Stage Conventions and Modern Interpreters*. Cambridge: Cambridge University Press, 1984.

Dessen, Alan. *Recovering Shakespeare's Theatrical Vocabulary.* Cambridge: Cambridge University Press, 1995.

Dessen, Alan C. and Leslie Thomson. *A Dictionary of Stage Directions in English Drama, 1580–1642.* Cambridge: Cambridge University Press, 1999.

Deutermann, Allison K. *Listening for Theatrical Form in Early Modern England.* Edinburgh: Edinburgh University Press, 2016.

Diehl, Huston. *Staging Reform, Reforming the Stage: Protestantism and Popular Theater in Early Modern England.* Ithaca, NY: Cornell University Press, 1997.

DiGangi, Mario. "John Ford." In *A Companion to Renaissance Drama,* edited by Arthur F. Kinney, 567–83. Oxford: Blackwell, 2004.

Dillon, Janette. *The Language of Space in Court Performance, 1400–1625.* Cambridge: Cambridge University Press, 2010.

Dionne, Craig. "Fashioning Outlaws: The Early Modern Rogue and Urban Culture." In *Rogues and Early Modern English Culture,* edited by Craig Dionne and Steve Mentz, 33–61. Ann Arbor: University of Michigan Press, 2004.

Dobson, Michael. "Adaptations and Revivals." In *The Cambridge Companion to English Restoration Theatre,* 40–51. Cambridge: Cambridge University Press, 2000.

Dollimore, Jonathan. *Radical Tragedy: Religion, Ideology and Power in the Drama of Shakespeare and His Contemporaries.* 3rd ed. Durham: Duke University Press, 2004.

Dollimore, Jonathan. "Subjectivity, Sexuality, and Transgression: The Jacobean Connection." *Renaissance Drama* 17 (1986): 53–81.

Donne, John. *The Complete Poems of John Donne.* Edited by Robin Robbins. New York: Routledge, 2013.

Donne, John. *Fifty Sermons.* London: M. F., J. Marriot, and R. Royston, 1649.

Doran, Susan and Paulina Kewes, eds. *Doubtful and Dangerous: The Question of Succession in Late Elizabethan England.* Manchester: Manchester University Press, 2014.

Doty, Jeffrey S. and Musa Gurnis. "Theatre Scene and Theatre Public in Early Modern London." *Shakespeare* 14.1 (2018): 12–25.

Dramatic Records in the Declared Accounts of the Treasurer of the Chamber 1558– 1642. Edited by David Cook and F. P. Wilson. Oxford: Oxford University Press, 1961.

Drummond, William. "Informations to William Drummond of Hawthornden." Edited by Ian Donaldson. Vol. 5 of *The Cambridge Edition of the Works of Ben Jonson,* 359–391. Cambridge: Cambridge University Press, 2012.

Dryden, John. *The Conquest of Granada, Part 1.* Vol. 11 of *The Works of John Dryden,* edited by John Loftis, David Stuart Rodes, and Vinton A. Dearing. Berkeley: University of California Press, 1978.

Dryden, John. "Heads of an Answer to Rymer." Vol. 17 of *The Works of John Dryden,* edited by Samuel Holt Monk, A. E. Wallace Maurer, and Vinton A. Dearing. Berkeley: University of California Press, 1972.

Dubrow, Heather. "'I would I were at home': Representations of Dwelling Places and Havens in *Cymbeline.*" In *Shakespeare and Historical Formalism*, 69–93. Burlington, VT: Ashgate, 2007.

Duncan, Anne. "It Takes a Woman to Play a Real Man: Clara as Hero(ine) of Beaumont and Fletcher's *Love's Cure.*" *English Literary Renaissance* 30.3 (2000): 396–407.

Dustagheer, Sarah. *Shakespeare's Two Playhouses: Repertory and Theatre Space at the Globe and the Blackfriars, 1599–1613.* Cambridge: Cambridge University Press, 2017.

Eaton, Sara. "'Content with art?': Seeing the Emblematic Woman in *The Second Maiden's Tragedy* and *The Winter's Tale.*" In *Shakespearean Power and Punishment: A Volume of Essays*, edited by Gillian Murray Kendall, 59–86. Cranbury, NJ: Associated University Presses, 1998.

Edelman, Charles. "'The very cunning of the scene': Claudius and the Mousetrap." *Parergon* 12.1 (1994): 15–25.

Edelman, Lee. *No Future: Queer Theory and the Death Drive.* Durham: Duke University Press, 2004.

Eggert, Katherine. *Disknowledge: Literature, Alchemy, and the End of Humanism in Renaissance England.* Philadelphia: University of Pennsylvania Press, 2015.

Eisendrath, Rachel. "The Long Nightwatch: Augustine, *Hamlet*, and the Aesthetic." *English Literary History* 87.3 (2020): 581–606.

Elam, Keir. *The Semiotics of Theatre and Drama.* New York: Routledge, 1980.

Elam, Keir. *Shakespeare's Pictures: Visual Objects in the Drama.* London: Bloomsbury, 2017.

Elk, Martine van. "'This Sympathizèd One Day's Error': Genre, Representation, and Subjectivity in *The Comedy of Errors. Shakespeare Quarterly* 60.1 (2009): 47–72.

Elliott, John R. Jr, Alan H. Nelson, Alexandra F. Johnston, and Diana Wyatt, eds. *Records of Early English Drama: Oxford.* 2 vols. Toronto: University of Toronto Press, 2004.

Empiricus, Sextus. *Against the Logicians.* Edited by Richard Bett. Cambridge: Cambridge University Press, 2005.

Empiricus, Sextus. *Outlines of Scepticism.* Translated by Julia Annas and Jonathan Barnes. Cambridge: Cambridge University Press, 2000.

Enterline, Lynn. *Shakespeare's Schoolroom: Rhetoric, Discipline, Emotion.* Philadelphia: University of Pennsylvania Press, 2012.

Eliot, T. S. *Selected Essays, 1917–1932.* New York: Harcourt, Brace, and Company, 1932.

Elliot, G. R. "Weirdness in *The Comedy of Errors.*" *University of Toronto Quarterly* 9.1 (1939): 95–106.

Erne, Lukas. *Beyond the Spanish Tragedy: A Study of the Works of Thomas Kyd.* Manchester: Manchester University Press, 2001.

Es, Bart van. *Shakespeare in Company.* Oxford: Oxford University Press, 2013.

Falco, Raphael. "Tudor Transformations." In *Shakespeare and the Soliloquy in Early Modern English Drama*, edited by A. D. Cousins and Daniel Derrin, 29–42. Cambridge: Cambridge University Press, 2018.

The Famous Victories of Henry V. In *The Oldcastle Controversy*, edited by Peter Corbin and Douglas Sedge. Manchester: Manchester University Press, 1991.

Felperin, Howard. *Shakespearean Romance.* Princeton: Princeton University Press, 1972.

Ferguson, Margaret W. "*Hamlet*: Letters and Spirits." In *Shakespeare and the Question of Theory*, edited by Patricia Parker and Geoffrey Hartman, 291–307. London: Methuen, 1985.

Fish, Stanley. *Surprised by Sin: The Reader in "Paradise Lost,"* 2nd ed. Cambridge, MA: Harvard University Press, 1998.

Fisher, Philip. *The Vehement Passions.* Princeton: Princeton University Press, 2002.

Fisher, Will. *Materializing Gender in Early Modern English Literature and Culture.* Cambridge: Cambridge University Press, 2006.

Fischer-Lichte, Erika. *The Semiotics of Theater.* Translated by Jeremy Gaines and Doris L. Jones. Bloomington: Indiana University Press, 1992.

Fisk, Deborah Payne, ed. *The Cambridge Companion to English Restoration Theatre.* Cambridge: Cambridge University Press, 2000.

Fitzpatrick, Tim. "The Fortune Contract and Hollar's Original Drawing of Southwark: Some Indications of a Smaller First Globe." *Shakespeare Bulletin* 14.4 (1996): 5–10.

Fitzpatrick, Tim. *Playwright, Space and Place in Early Modern Performance: Shakespeare and Company.* New York: Routledge, 2011.

Flecknoe, Richard. "A Short Discourse of the English Stage." In *Love's Kingdom*, G4r–G8r. London: Richard Flecknoe, 1664.

Fletcher, John. *The Faithful Shepherdess.* Vol. 3 of *The Dramatic Works in the Beaumont and Fletcher Canon*, edited by Cyrus Hoy. Cambridge: Cambridge University Press, 1976.

Fletcher, John. *Love's Cure.* Vol. 3 of *The Dramatic Works in the Beaumont and Fletcher Canon*, edited by George Walton Williams. Cambridge: Cambridge University Press, 1976.

Fletcher, John. *The Night Walker.* Vol 7 of *The Dramatic Works in the Beaumont and Fletcher Canon*, edited by Cyrus Hoy. Cambridge: Cambridge University Press, 1989.

Floridi, Luciano. *Sextus Empiricus: The Transmission and Recovery of Pyrrhonism.* Oxford: Oxford University Press, 2002.

Foakes, R. A. *Illustrations of the English Stage 1580–1642.* Stanford, CA: Stanford University Press, 1985.

Ford, John. *Perkin Warbeck.* In *"Tis Pity She's a Whore" and Other Plays*, edited by Marion Lomax. Oxford: Oxford University Press, 1995.

Forman, Simon. *Bocke of Plaies and Notes Thereof.* MS Ashmole 208. Bodleian Library, Oxford.

Foster, Donald W. "*Macbeth*'s War on Time." *English Literary Renaissance* 16.2 (1986): 319–42.

Foster, Verna A. *The Name and Nature of Tragicomedy*. Burlington, VT: Ashgate, 2004.

Freedman, Barbara. *Staging the Gaze: Postmodernism, Psychoanalysis, and Shakespearean Comedy*. Ithaca, NY: Cornell University Press, 1991.

Frye, Susan. *Pens and Needles: Women's Textualities in Early Modern England*. Philadelphia: University of Pennsylvania Press, 2010.

Fuller, Thomas. *The History of the Worthies of England*. London: Thomas Williams, 1662.

Garber, Marjorie. "'What's Past Is Prologue': Temporality and Prophecy in Shakespeare's History Plays." In *Renaissance Genres: Essays on Theory, History, and Interpretation*, edited by Barbara Kiefer Lewalski, 301–31. Cambridge, MA: Harvard University Press, 1986.

Garner, Stanton B. *Bodied Spaces: Phenomenology and Performance in Contemporary Drama*. Ithaca, NY: Cornell University Press, 1994.

Gayton, Edmund. *Pleasant Notes upon Don Quixot*. London: William Hunt, 1654.

Goldberg, Jonathan. *James I and the Politics of Literature: Jonson, Shakespeare, Donne, and Their Contemporaries*. Baltimore: Johns Hopkins University Press, 1983.

Goold, Rupert, dir. *The Hollow Crown*. Episode 1, "Richard II." Aired June 30, 2012, on BBC2.

Gosson, Stephen. *Playes Confuted in Fiue Actions*. London: Thomas Gosson, 1582.

Gosson, Stephen. *The Schoole of Abuse*. London: Thomas Woodcocke, 1579.

Gottlieb, Christine M. "Middleton's Traffic in Dead Women: Chaste Corpses as Property in *The Revenger's Tragedy* and *The Lady's Tragedy*." *English Literary Renaissance* 45.2 (2015): 255–274.

Gowing, Laura. *Common Bodies: Women, Touch and Power in Seventeenth-Century England*. New Haven: Yale University Press, 2003.

Gowing, Laura. *Domestic Dangers: Women, Words, and Sex in Early Modern London*. Oxford: Clarendon Press, 1996.

Grady, Hugh. *Shakespeare, Machiavelli, and Montaigne: Power and Subjectivity from "Richard II" to "Hamlet."* Oxford: Oxford University Press, 2002.

Graves, R. B. *Lighting the Shakespearean Stage, 1567–1642*. Carbondale: Southern Illinois University Press, 1999.

Green, Monica H. *Making Women's Medicine Masculine: The Rise of Male Authority in Pre-modern Gynaecology*. Oxford: Oxford University Press, 2008.

Greenberg, Marissa. "Crossing from Scaffold to Stage: Execution Processions and Generic Conventions in *The Comedy of Errors* and *Measure for Measure*." In *Shakespeare and Historical Formalism*, 127–146. Burlington, VT: Ashgate, 2007.

Greenberg, Marissa. *Metropolitan Tragedy: Genre, Justice, and the City in Early Modern England*. Toronto: University of Toronto Press, 2015.

Greenblatt, Stephen. *Hamlet in Purgatory*. Princeton: Princeton University Press, 2001.

Greenblatt, Stephen. "Shakespeare Bewitched." In *Shakespeare and Cultural Traditions*, edited by Tetsuo Kishi, Roger Pringle, and Stanley Wells, 17–42. Newark: University of Delaware Press, 1994.

Greenblatt, Stephen. *Shakespearean Negotiations: The Circulation of Social Energy in Renaissance England.* Berkeley: University of California Press, 1988.

Greenblatt, Stephen. *The Second Part of Conny-catching.* London: William Wright, 1591.

Greene, Robert. *The Third and Last Part of Conny-catching.* London: C. Burby, 1592.

Griffiths, Huw. "The Geographies of Shakespeare's *Cymbeline*." *English Literary Renaissance* 34.3 (2004): 339–58.

Gurnis, Musa. *Mixed Faith and Shared Feeling: Theater in Post-Reformation London.* Philadelphia: University of Pennsylvania Press, 2018.

Gurr, Andrew. "Doors at the Globe: The Gulf between Page and Stage." *Theatre Notebook* 55.2 (2001): 59–71.

Gurr, Andrew. *Playgoing in Shakespeare's London.* Cambridge: Cambridge University Press, 1987.

Gurr, Andrew. *Shakespeare's Opposites: The Admiral's Company 1594–1625.* Cambridge: Cambridge University Press, 2009.

Hacking, Ian. *The Emergence of Probability: A Philosophical Study of Early Ideas about Probability, Induction and Statistical Inference*, 2nd ed. Cambridge: Cambridge University Press, 2006.

Hakewill, George. *The Vanitie of the Eie.* Oxford: Joseph Barnes, 1608.

Hall, Joseph. *Occasionall Meditations.* London: Nathaniel Butter, 1631.

Hall, Joseph. *Virgidemiarum.* London: Robert Dexter, 1597.

Hamlin, William. "A Lost Translation Found? An Edition of 'The Sceptick' (c. 1590) Based on Extant Manuscripts [with text]." *English Literary Renaissance* 31.1 (2001): 34–51.

Hamlin, William. *Tragedy and Scepticism in Shakespeare's England.* New York: Palgrave Macmillan, 2005.

Harington, Henry. "To the incomparable Mr. Fletcher, upon his excellent play, *The Wild-Goose Chase*." In John Fletcher, *The Wild-Goose Chase.* London: Humphrey Mosley, 1652.

Harington, John. *A Briefe View of the State of the Church of England as it Stood in Q. Elizabeths and King James His Reigne.* London: Joseph Kirton, 1653.

Harris, Jonathan Gil. "'Narcissus in thy Face': Roman Desire and the Difference it Fakes in *Antony and Cleopatra*." *Shakespeare Quarterly* 45.4 (1994): 408–25.

Harris, Jonathan Gil. *Untimely Matter in the Time of Shakespeare.* Philadelphia: University of Pennsylvania Press, 2009.

Harrison, Stephen. *The Arch's of Triumph Erected in Honor of the High and Mighty Prince. Iames.* London: Stephen Harrison, 1604.

Henke, Robert. "Sincerity, Fraud, and Audience Reception in the Performance of Early Modern Poverty." *Renaissance Drama* 36/37 (2010): 159–78.

Henslowe, Philip. *Henslowe's Diary.* Edited by R. A. Foakes. Cambridge: Cambridge University Press, 2002.

Herman, Peter C. *Destabilizing Milton: Paradise Lost and the Poetics of Incertitude.* New York: Palgrave Macmillan, 2005.

Heywood, Thomas. An *Apology for Actors*. London: Nicholas Okes, 1612.

Hila, Marina. "'To heighten your desire': Sexual Politics in Massinger's *The Picture* (1629)." *Cahiers Élisabéthains: A Journal of English Renaissance Studies* 92.1 (2016): 68–81.

Hilliard, Nicholas. *Art of Limning*. Edited by Arthur F. Kinney. Boston: Northeastern University Press, 1983.

Hillman, David. *Shakespeare's Entrails: Belief, Scepticism, and the Interior of the Body*. New York: Palgrave, 2007.

Hobgood, Allison P. *Passionate Playgoing in Early Modern England*. Cambridge: Cambridge University Press, 2014.

Holinshed, Raphael. *The Firste [Laste] Volume of the Chronicles of England, Scotlande, and Irelande*. London: John Hunne, 1577.

Holinshed, Raphael. *The First and Second Volumes of Chronicles*. London: John Harison, George Bishop, Rafe Newberie, Henrie Denham, and Thomas Woodcocke, 1587.

Holinshed, Raphael. *The Third Volume of Chronicles*. London: John Harison, George Bishop, Rafe Newberie, Henrie Denham, and Thomas Woodcocke, 1586.

"An Homilee of the Resurrection of our Sauiour Iesus Christe." In *The Second Tome of Homilees of Such Matters as were Promised, and Intituled in the Former Part of Homilees*. London: Richarde Jugge, and John Cawood, 1571.

Horne, Robert. *Life and Death Foure Sermons*. London: Francis Burton, 1613.

Hotson, Leslie. *The Commonwealth and Restoration Stage*. Cambridge, MA: Harvard University Press, 1928.

Houle, Martha M. "The Marriage Question, or, the *Querelle des hommes* in Rabelais, Molière and Boileau." *Dalhousie French Studies* 56 (2001): 46–54.

Howard, Jean E. "'Effeminately Dolent': Gender and Legitimacy in Ford's *Perkin Warbeck*." In *John Ford: Critical Re-Visions*, edited by Michael Neill, 261–279. Cambridge: Cambridge University Press, 1988.

Howard, Jean E. "Shakespeare, Geography, and the Work of Genre on the Early Modern Stage." *Modern Language Quarterly* 64.3 (2003): 299–322.

Howard, Jean E. "Stage Masculinities, National History, and the Making of London Theatrical Culture." In *Center or Margin: Revisions of the English Renaissance in Honor of Leeds Barroll*, edited by Lena Cowen Orlin, 199–214. Cranbury, NJ: Associated University Press, 2006.

Howard, Jean E. *Theater of a City: The Places of London Comedy, 1598–1642*. Philadelphia: University of Pennsylvania Press, 2007.

Howell, James. *Epistolae Ho-Elianae*. London: Humphrey Mosley, 1645.

Hunt, Arnold. "The Succession in Sermons, News, and Rumour." In *Doubtful and Dangerous: The Question of Succession in Late Elizabethan England*, edited by Susan Doran and Paulina Kewes, 155–72. Manchester: Manchester University Press.

Hunt, Maurice. "Dismemberment, Corporal Reconstitution, and the Body Politic in *Cymbeline*." *Studies in Philology* 99.4 (2002): 404–31.

Hunter, G. K. "Italian Tragicomedy on the English Stage." *Renaissance Drama* 6 (1973): 123–48.

Hunter, Matthew. "City Comedy, Public Style," *English Literary Renaissance* 46.3 (2016): 401–32.

Husserl, Edmund. *Ideas for a Pure Phenomenology and Phenomenological Philosophy: First Book: General Introduction to Pure Phenomenology*. Translated by Daniel O. Dahlstrom. Indianapolis, IN: Hackett, 2014.

Hutcheon, Linda. *A Theory of Adaptation*. New York: Routledge, 2006.

Hutchings, Mark. "Mary Frith at the Fortune." *Early Theatre* 10.1 (2007): 89–108.

Hutson, Lorna. *The Invention of Suspicion: Law and Mimesis in Shakespeare and Renaissance Drama*. Oxford: Oxford University Press, 2007.

Hutson, Lorna. "Probable Infidelities from Bandello to Massinger." In *Staging Early Modern Romance: Prose Fiction, Dramatic Romance, and Shakespeare*, edited by Valerie Wayne and Mary Ellen Lamb, 219–235. New York: Routledge, 2009.

Hyland, Peter. *Disguise on the Early Modern English Stage*. Burlington, VT: Ashgate, 2011.

Ichikawa, Mariko. *The Shakespearean Stage Space*. Cambridge: Cambridge University Press, 2013.

Ichikawa, Mariko. "Were the Doors Open or Closed? The Use of Stage Doors in the Shakespearean Theatre." *Theatre Notebook* 60.1 (2006): 5–29.

Ichikawa, Mariko. "'What Story Is That Painted Vpon the Cloth?': Some Descriptions of Hangings and Their Use on the Early Modern Stage." *Theatre Notebook* 70.1 (2016): 2–31.

Jauss, Hans Robert. *Toward an Aesthetic of Reception*. Translated by Timothy Bahti. Minneapolis: University of Minnesota Press, 1982.

Jonson, Ben. *The Alchemist*. Edited by Peter Holland and William Sherman. Vol. 3 of *The Cambridge Edition of the Works of Ben Jonson*, 541–710. Cambridge: Cambridge University Press, 2012.

Jonson, Ben. *Cynthia's Revels*. Edited by Eric Rasmussen and Matthew Steggle. Vol. 1 of *The Cambridge Edition of the Works of Ben Jonson*, 429–548. Cambridge: Cambridge University Press, 2012.

Jonson, Ben. "An Execration upon Vulcan." Edited by Colin Burrow. Vol. 7 of *The Cambridge Edition of the Works of Ben Jonson*, 165–179. Cambridge: Cambridge University Press, 2012.

Jonson, Ben. *Every Man Out of His Humour*. Edited by Randall Martin. Vol. 1 of *The Cambridge Edition of the Works of Ben Jonson*, 233–428. Cambridge: Cambridge University Press, 2012.

Jonson, Ben. *The Magnetic Lady, or Humours Reconciled*. Edited by Helen Ostovich. Vol. 6 of *The Cambridge Edition of the Works of Ben Jonson*, 391–540. Cambridge: Cambridge University Press, 2012.

Jones, Ann Rosalind and Peter Stallybrass. *Renaissance Clothing and the Materials of Memory*. Cambridge: Cambridge University Press, 2000.

Jordan, Thomas. "To his friend the Author." Vol. 2 of *The Plays and Poems of Philip Massinger*, edited by Philip Edwards and Colin Gibson. Oxford: Oxford University Press, 1976.

Kahn, Coppélia. *Man's Estate: Masculine Identity in Shakespeare*. Berkeley: University of California Press, 1981.

Kantorowicz, Ernst. *The King's Two Bodies: A Study in Medieval Political Theology*. Princeton: Princeton University Press, 1957.

Karim-Cooper, Farah. *Cosmetics in Shakespearean and Renaissance Drama*. Edinburgh: Edinburgh University Press, 2006.

Kastan, David Scott. *Shakespeare and the Shapes of Time*. Hanover, NH: University Press of New England, 1982.

Kastan, David Scott. "What's the Matter?" In *Formal Matters: Reading the Materials of English Renaissance Literature*, edited by Allison Deutermann and András Kiséry, 249–253. Manchester: Manchester University Press, 2013.

Keats, John. *Selected Letters of John Keats*. Edited by Grant F. Scott. Cambridge, MA: Harvard University Press, 2002.

Keegan, Daniel L. "Performing Prophecy: More Life on the Shakespearean Stage." *Shakespeare Quarterly* 62.3 (2011): 420–43.

Kerrigan, John. *Revenge Tragedy: Aeschylus to Armageddon*. Oxford: Oxford University Press, 1996.

Kiefer, Frederick. "Curtains on the Shakespearean Stage." In *Medieval and Renaissance Drama in England* 20 (2007): 151–86.

Kinney, Arthur F. *Lies like Truth: Shakespeare, Macbeth, and the Cultural Moment*. Detroit: Wayne State University Press, 2001.

Kiséry, András. *Hamlet's Moment: Drama and Political Knowledge in Early Modern England*. Oxford: Oxford University Press, 2016.

Kornbluh, Anna. *The Order of Forms: Realism, Formalism, and Social Space*. Chicago: University of Chicago Press, 2019.

Knoll, Gillian. "Binding the Void: The Erotics of Place in *Antony and Cleopatra*." *Criticism* 58.2 (2016): 281–304.

Knutson, Roslyn Lander. "The History Play, *Richard II*, and Repertorial Commerce." In *"Richard II": New Critical Essays*, 74–94. London: Routledge, 2012.

Knutson, Roslyn Lander. *The Repertory of Shakespeare's Company, 1594–1613*. Fayetteville: University of Arkansas Press, 1991.

Knutson, Roslyn Lander. *Playing Companies and Commerce in Shakespeare's Time*. Cambridge: Cambridge University Press, 2001.

Kuhn, Thomas. *The Structure of Scientific Revolutions*. 4th ed. Chicago: University of Chicago Press, 2012.

Kuzner, James. *Shakespeare as a Way of Life: Skeptical Practice and the Politics of Weakness*. New York: Fordham University Press, 2016.

Kyd, Thomas. *The Spanish Tragedy*. Edited by Clara Calvo and Jesús Tronch. London: Bloomsbury Arden Shakespeare, 2017.

The Lamentable Tragedie of Locrine. London: Thomas Creede, 1595.

Lancashire, Anne. "Dekker's Accession Pageant for James I." *Early Theatre* 12.1 (2009): 39–50.

Langbein, John H. "Historical Foundations of the Law of Evidence: A View from the Ryder Sources." *Columbia Law Review* 96.5 (1996): 1168–1202.

Langhans, Edward A. "The Theatre." In *The Cambridge Companion to English Restoration Theatre*, 1–18. Cambridge: Cambridge University Press, 2000.

Lennam, T. N. S. "Sir Edward Dering's Collection of Playbooks, 1619–1624." *Shakespeare Quarterly* 16.2 (1965): 145–53.

Leslie, John. *A Treatise Concerning the Defence of the Honour of the Right High, Mightie and Noble Princesse, Marie Queene of Scotland, and Douager of France with a Declaration, as Wel of her Right, Title, and Interest, to the Succession of the Croune of England.* Leodii [and Louvain]: Gualterum Morberium [and J. Fowler], 1571.

Lesser, Zachary. *Renaissance Drama and the Politics of Publication: Readings in the English Book Trade.* Cambridge: Cambridge University Press, 2004.

Lessius, Leonardus. *A Consultation What Faith and Religion Is Best to Be Imbraced.* Translated by William Wright. Saint-Omer, 1618.

Levine, Laura. *Men in Women's Clothing: Anti-theatricality and Effeminization, 1579–1642.* Cambridge: Cambridge University Press, 1994.

Lewis, Cynthia. "'With Simular Proof Enough': Modes of Misperception in *Cymbeline.*" *Studies in English Literature* 31.2 (1991): 343–364.

Lewis, Rhodri. *Hamlet and the Vision of Darkness.* Princeton: Princeton University Press, 2017.

Lewis, Rhodri. "Polychronic *Macbeth.*" *Modern Philology* 117.3 (2020): 323–46.

Lin, Erika T. "'Lord of thy presence': Bodies, Performance, and Audience Interpretation in Shakespeare's *King John.*" In *Imagining the Audience in Early Modern Drama, 1558–1642*, 113–133. New York: Palgrave Macmillan, 2011.

Lin, Erika T. *Shakespeare and the Materiality of Performance.* New York: Palgrave Macmillan, 2012.

Lin, Erika T. "Recreating the Eye of the Beholder: Dancing and Spectacular Display in Early Modern English Theatre." *Dance Research Journal* 43.1 (2011): 10–19.

Loewenstein, Joseph. "Marston's Gorge and the Question of Formalism." In *Renaissance Literature and Its Formal Engagements*, edited by Mark David Rasmussen, 89–114. New York: Palgrave, 2002.

Loomba, Ania. *Gender, Race, Renaissance Drama.* Manchester: Manchester University Press, 1989.

Look About You. Edited by Paul Menzer. In *The Routledge Anthology of Early Modern Drama*, 267–349. New York: Routledge, 2020.

Lopez, Jeremy. *Theatrical Convention and Audience Response in Early Modern Drama.* Cambridge: Cambridge University Press, 2003.

Lopez, Jeremy, ed. "*Richard II: New Critical Essays.*" London: Routledge, 2012.

Lopez, Jeremy. *The Routledge Anthology of Early Modern Drama.* New York: Routledge, 2020.

Low, Jennifer A. and Nova Myhill, eds. *Imagining the Audience in Early Modern Drama, 1558–1642.* New York: Palgrave Macmillan, 2011.

Lupton, Julia Reinhard. *Shakespeare Dwelling: Designs for the Theater of Life.* Chicago: University of Chicago Press, 2018.

Luttfring, Sara D. *Bodies, Speech, and Reproductive Knowledge in Early Modern England*. New York: Routledge, 2016.

MacDonald, Michael. *Mystical Bedlam: Madness, Anxiety, and Healing in Seventeenth-Century England*. Cambridge: Cambridge University Press, 1981.

MacDonald, William L. *The Architecture of the Roman Empire*. 2 vols. New Haven: Yale University Press, 1986.

MacIntyre, Jean. "Production Resources at the Whitefriars Playhouse, 1609–1612." *Early Modern Literary Studies* 2.3 (1996): 2.1–35.

MacKay, Ellen. *Persecution, Plague, and Fire: Fugitive Histories of the Stage in Early Modern England*. Chicago: University of Chicago Press, 2011.

MacLean, Sally-Beth and Scott McMillin. *The Queen's Men and Their Plays*. Cambridge: Cambridge University Press, 1998.

Maltby, Judith. *Prayer Book and People in Elizabethan and Early Stuart England*. Cambridge: Cambridge University Press, 1998.

Manley, Lawrence and Sally-Beth MacLean, *Lord Strange's Men and Their Plays*. New Haven, CT: Yale University Press, 2014.

Marchitello, Howard. "Science Studies and English Renaissance Literature." *Literature Compass* 3.3 (2006): 341–365.

Markell, Patchen. "The Recognition of Politics: A Comment on Emcke and Tully." *Constellations* 7.4 (2000): 496–506.

Marlowe, Christopher. *Edward II*. Edited by Martin Wiggins and Robert Lindsey. London: Methuen Drama, 2005.

Marlowe, Christopher. *The Jew of Malta*. In *The Complete Plays*, edited by Frank Romany and Robert Lindsey, 241–340. London: Penguin Books, 2003.

Marlowe, Christopher. *The Troublesome Raigne and Lamentable Death of Edward the Second, King of England with the Tragicall Fall of Proud Mortimer: and Also the Life and Death of Peirs Gaueston, the Great Earle of Cornewall, and Mighty Fauorite of King Edward the Second*. London: William Jones, 1598.

Marshall, Peter. *Beliefs and the Dead in Reformation England*. Oxford: Oxford University Press, 2002.

Marston, John. *Antonio's Revenge*. In *"The Malcontent" and Other Plays*, edited by Keith Sturgess, 57–116. Oxford: Oxford University Press, 1997.

Marston, John. *What You Will*. Vol. 2 of *The Works of John Marston*, edited by A. H. Bullen. London: J. C. Nimmo, 1887.

Massinger, Philip. *The Picture*. Edited by Lucy Munro. In *The Routledge Anthology of Early Modern Drama*, 382–468. New York: Routledge, 2020.

Massinger, Philip. *The Roman Actor*. Edited by Martin White. Manchester: Manchester University Press, 2007.

Masten, Jeffrey. *Queer Philologies: Sex, Language, and Affect in Shakespeare's Time*. Philadelphia: University of Pennsylvania Press, 2016.

Maus, Katharine Eisaman. "Horns of Dilemma: Jealousy, Gender, and Spectatorship in English Renaissance Drama." *English Literary History* 54.3 (1987): 561–83.

Maus, Katharine Eisaman. *Inwardness and Theater in the English Renaissance*. Chicago: University of Chicago Press, 1995.

Maxwell, Baldwin. *Studies in Beaumont, Fletcher, and Massinger*. Chapel Hill: University of North Carolina Press, 1939.

McMullan, Gordon. "'The Neutral Term?': Shakespearean Tragicomedy and the Idea of the 'Late Play'." In *Early Modern Tragicomedy*, edited by Subha Mukherji and Raphael Lyne, 115–32. Rochester, NY: D. S. Brewer, 2007.

Menzer, Paul. "Crowd Control." In *Imagining the Audience in Early Modern Drama, 1558–1642*, 19–36. New York: Palgrave Macmillan, 2009.

Merleau-Ponty, Maurice. *The Merleau-Ponty Reader*. Edited by Ted Toadvine and Leonard Lawlor. Evanston, IL: Northwestern University Press, 2007.

Merleau-Ponty, Maurice. *The Visible and the Invisible*. Translated by Alphonso Lingis. Evanston, IL: Northwestern University Press, 1968.

Middleton, Thomas. *No Wit/Help Like a Woman's*. Edited by John Jowett. In *Thomas Middleton: The Collected Works*, 779–832. Oxford: Oxford University Press, 2007.

Middleton, Thomas. *The Second Maiden's Tragedy*. Edited by Anne Lancashire. Manchester: Manchester University Press, 1978.

Middleton, Thomas. *The Revenger's Tragedy*. Edited by MacDonald P. Jackson. In *Thomas Middleton: The Collected Works*, 543–593. Oxford: Oxford University Press, 2007.

Middleton, Thomas. *Women, Beware Women*. Edited by John Jowett. In *Thomas Middleton: The Collected Works*, 1488–1541. Oxford: Oxford University Press, 2007.

Middleton, Thomas and Thomas Dekker. *The Roaring Girl*. Edited by Coppélia Kahn. In *Thomas Middleton: The Collected Works*, 721–778. Oxford: Oxford University Press, 2007.

Milton, John. *Paradise Lost*. Edited by Stephen Orgel and Jonathan Goldberg. Oxford: Oxford University Press, 2004.

Mollin, Alfred. "On Hamlet's Mousetrap." *Interpretation: A Journal of Political Philosophy* 21.3 (1994): 353–72.

Montaigne, Michel de. *The Essayes of Morall, Politike and Militarie Discourses of Lo: Michaell de Montaigne*. Translated by John Florio. London: Edward Blount, 1603.

Muggins, William. *Londons Mourning Garment*. London: Ralph Blower, 1603.

Mullaney, Steven. *The Reformation of Emotions in the Age of Shakespeare*. Chicago: University of Chicago Press, 2015.

Mukherji, Subha. *Law and Representation in Early Modern Drama*. Cambridge: Cambridge University Press, 2006.

Munro, Ian. *The Figure of the Crowd in Early Modern London: The City and Its Double*. New York: Palgrave MacMillan, 2005.

Munro, Lucy. *Children of the Queen's Revels: A Jacobean Theatre Repertory*. Cambridge: Cambridge University Press, 2005.

Munro, Lucy. "Comedy, Clowning and the Caroline King's Men: Manuscript Plays and Performance." In *Early British Drama in Manuscript*, edited by Tamara Atkin and Laura Estill, 213–228. Turnhout: Brepols Publishers, 2019.

Munro, Lucy. "The Whitefriars Theatre and the Children's Companies." In *Ben Jonson in Context*, edited by Julie Sanders, 116–123. Cambridge: Cambridge University Press, 2010.

Murphy, Jessica C. *Virtuous Necessity: Conduct Literature and the Making of the Virtuous Woman in Early Modern England*. Ann Arbor, MI: University of Michigan Press, 2015.

Murray, Molly. *The Poetics of Conversion in Early Modern English Literature: Verse and Change from Donne to Dryden*. Cambridge: Cambridge University Press, 2009.

Museum of London Archaeology. "Initial Findings from Excavation at Shakespeare's Curtain Revealed." May 17, 2016. www.mola.org.uk/blog/initial-findings-excavation-shakespeare%E2%80%99s-curtain-theatre-revealed.

Nashe, Thomas. *Pierce Penilesse his Supplication to the Diuell*. London: John Busby, 1592.

Nashe, Thomas. "Somewhat to reade for them that list." In *Astrophel and Stella*, by Phillip Sidney, A3r–A4v. London: Thomas Newman, 1591.

Nashe, Thomas. *The Terrors of the Night, or a Discourse of Apparitions*. London: William Jones, 1594.

Neill, Michael. "'Anticke Pageantrie': The Mannerist Art of *Perkin Warbeck*." *Renaissance Drama* 7 (1976): 117–50.

Neill, Michael. *Issues of Death: Mortality and Identity in English Renaissance Tragedy*. Oxford: Oxford University Press, 1997.

Neill, Michael, ed. *Antony and Cleopatra*. Oxford: Oxford University Press, 2000.

Neill, Michael. "Unproper Beds: Race, Adultery, and the Hideous in *Othello*." *Shakespeare Quarterly* 40.4 (1989): 383–412.

Neill, Michael. "'Wits most accomplished Senate': The Audience of the Caroline Private Theaters." *Studies in English Literature* 18.2 (1978): 341–60.

Nevo, Ruth. *Comic Transformations in Shakespeare*. London: Methuen, 1980.

Newman, Karen. *Shakespeare's Rhetoric of Comic Character: Dramatic Convention in Classical and Renaissance Comedy*. New York: Routledge, 1985, 63–64.

Ngai, Sianne. *Ugly Feelings*. Cambridge, MA: Harvard University Press, 2005.

Nicoll, Allardyce. *A History of Restoration Drama 1660–1700*. Cambridge: Cambridge University Press, 1923.

Nicosia, Marissa. "'To Plant Me in Mine Own Inheritance': Prolepsis and Pretenders in John Ford's *Perkin Warbeck*." *Studies in Philology* 115.3 (2018): 580–597.

Nowell, Alexander. "Mr. Noel's Sermon at the Parliament Before the Queen's Majestie." In *A Catechism Written in Latin by Alexander Nowell*, edited by G. E. Corrie, 223–229. Cambridge: Cambridge University Press, 1853.

Nunn, Hillary M. *Staging Anatomies: Dissection and Spectacle in Early Stuart Tragedy*. Burlington, VT: Ashgate, 2005.

Obermueller, Erin V. "'On Cheating Pictures': Gender and Portrait Miniatures in Philip Massinger's *The Picture*." *Early Theatre* 10.2 (2007): 87–107.

O'Callaghan, Michelle. *The English Wits: Literature and Sociability in Early Modern England*. Cambridge: Cambridge University Press, 2006.

Olivier, Jacques. *A Discourse of Women, Shewing Their Imperfections Alphabetically.* London: Henry Brome, 1662.

Orgel, Stephen. *Impersonations: The Performance of Gender in Shakespeare's England.* Cambridge: Cambridge University Press, 1996.

Orgel, Stephen. "The Play of Conscience." In *Performativity and Performance,* edited by Andrew Parker and Eve Kosofsky Sedgwick, 133–51. New York: Routledge, 1995.

Orgel, Stephen. "Shakespeare Imagines a Theater." *Poetics Today* 5.3 (1984): 549–61.

Orlin, Lena Cowen. *Locating Privacy in Tudor London.* Oxford: Oxford University Press, 2007.

Orrell, John. "Beyond the Rose: Design Problems for the Globe Reconstruction." In *New Issues in the Reconstruction of Shakespeare's Theatre: Proceedings of the Conference Held at the University of Georgia, February 16–18, 1990,* edited by Franklin J. Hildy, 96–118. New York: Peter Lang, 1990.

Orrell, John. *The Quest for Shakespeare's Globe.* Cambridge: Cambridge University Press, 1983.

Overbury, Thomas. *New and Choise Characters.* London: Laurence Lisle, 1615.

Painter, William. "The Lady of Boeme." In *Italian Tales from The Age of Shakespeare,* edited by Pamela Benson, 149–74. London: Everyman, 1996.

Pangallo, Matteo, *Playwriting Playgoers in Shakespeare's Theater.* Philadelphia: University of Pennsylvania Press, 2017.

Park, Katharine. *Secrets of Women: Gender, Generation, and the Origins of Human Dissection.* New York: Zone Books, 2006.

Parker, Patricia. *Shakespeare from the Margins: Language, Culture, Context.* Chicago: University of Chicago Press, 1996.

Paster, Gail Kern. *The Body Embarrassed: Drama and the Disciplines of Shame in Early Modern England.* Ithaca, NY: Cornell University Press, 1993.

Patterson, Annabel. *Censorship and Interpretation: The Conditions of Writing and Reading in Early Modern England.* Madison: University of Wisconsin Press, 1984.

Pavis, Patrice. *Analyzing Performance: Theater, Dance, and Film.* Ann Arbor: University of Michigan Press, 2003.

Peacham, Henry. *Minerua Britanna.* London: Wa: Dight, 1612.

Peacock, John. *The Stage Designs of Inigo Jones: The European Context.* Cambridge: Cambridge University Press, 1995.

Pedersen, Tara E. *Mermaids and the Production of Knowledge in Early Modern England.* Burlington, VT: Ashgate, 2015.

Pepys, Samuel. *The Diary of Samuel Pepys.* Edited by Robert Latham and William Matthews. 9 vols. London: Harper Collins, 1995.

Pérez Díez, José A. "Editing on Stage: Theatrical Research for a Critical Edition of John Fletcher and Philip Massinger's *Love's Cure, or The Martial Maid.*" *Shakespeare Bulletin* 34.1 (2016): 69–88.

Peters, Julie Stone. *Theatre of the Book 1480–1880: Print, Text, and Performance in Europe.* Oxford: Oxford University Press, 2000.

Peterson, Kaara L. *Popular Medicine, Hysterical Disease, and Social Controversy in Shakespeare's England*. London: Routledge, 2010.

Phelan, Peggy. *Unmarked: The Politics of Performance*. New York: Routledge, 1993.

Pickering, Danby. *The Statutes at Large*. London: Charles Bathurst, 1763.

Platt, Peter G. *Shakespeare and the Culture of Paradox*. Burlington, VT: Ashgate, 2009.

Platter, Thomas. *Thomas Platter's Travels in England*, 1599. Translated by Clare Williams. London: Jonathan Cape, 1937.

Plautus. *The Brothers Menaechmus*. In *Four Comedies*. Translated by Erich Segal. Oxford: Oxford University Press, 1996.

A Pleasant Comedie, Called the Tvvo Merry Milke-maids. London: Lawrence Chapman, 1620.

Plutarch. *The Lives of the Noble Grecians and Romanes*. Translated by Thomas North. London: Thomas Vautroullier and John Wight, 1579.

Pollard, Tanya. *Drugs and Theater in Early Modern England*. Oxford: Oxford University Press, 2005.

Pollard, Tanya. "Tragicomedy." Vol. 2 of *The Oxford History of Classical Reception in English Literature*, edited by Patrick Cheney and Philip Hardie, 419–32. Oxford: Oxford University Press, 2015.

Poole, Joshua. *The English Parnassus*. London: Thomas Johnson, 1657.

Popkin, Richard. *The History of Scepticism from Savonarola to Bayle*. Oxford: Oxford University Press, 2003.

Potter, Lois. *The Life of William Shakespeare: A Critical Biography*. Oxford: Wiley, 2012.

Preiss, Richard. *Clowning and Authorship in Early Modern Theatre*. Cambridge: Cambridge University Press, 2014.

Preiss, Richard. "Interiority." In *Early Modern Theatricality*, 47–70. Oxford: Oxford University Press, 2013.

Purkis, James. *Shakespeare and Manuscript Drama: Canon, Collaboration, and Text*. Cambridge: Cambridge University Press, 2016.

Prynne, William. *Histriomastix*. London: Michael Sparke, 1633.

Puttenham, George. *The Arte of English Poesie*. London: Richard Field, 1589.

Rabelais, François. *Gargantua* and *Pantagruel*. Translated by Burton Raffel. New York: W. W. Norton and Company, 1990.

Rackin, Phyllis. "The Role of the Audience in Shakespeare's *Richard II*." *Shakespeare Quarterly* 36.3 (1985): 262–81.

Rackin, Phyllis. "Shakespeare's Boy Cleopatra, the Decorum of Nature, and the Golden World of Poetry." *PMLA* 87.2 (1972): 201–212.

Rackin, Phyllis. *Stages of History: Shakespeare's English Chronicles*. Ithaca, NY: Cornell University Press, 1990.

Rackin, Phyllis. "Temporality, Anachronism, and Presence in Shakespeare's English Histories." *Renaissance Drama* 17 (1986): 101–23.

Rasmussen, Eric. "Shakespeare's Hand in *The Second Maiden's Tragedy*." *Shakespeare Quarterly* 40.1 (1989): 1–26.

Reinheimer, David A. "*The Roman Actor*, Censorship, and Dramatic Autonomy." *Studies in English Literature* 38.2 (1998): 317–32.

Ricoeur, Paul. *Memory, History, Forgetting*. Translated by Kathleen Blamey and David Pellauer. Chicago: The University of Chicago Press, 2004.

Ricoeur, Paul. "Narrative Time." *Critical Inquiry* 7.1 (1980): 169–90.

Roach, Joseph. *Cities of the Dead: Circum-Atlantic Performance*. New York: Columbia University Press, 1996.

Roberts, Sasha. "'Let me the curtains draw': The Dramatic and Symbolic Properties of the Bed in Shakespearean Tragedy." In *Staged Properties in Early Modern English Drama*, edited by Jonathan Gil Harris and Natasha Korda, 153–74. Cambridge: Cambridge University Press, 2002.

Robertson, Bartholomew. *The Crovvne of Life*. London: John Marriot, 1618.

Rochester, Joanne. *Staging Spectatorship in the Plays of Philip Massinger*. Burlington, VT: Ashgate, 2010.

Rodes, Francis. *Life after Death*. London: Thomas Dewe 1622.

Rodgers, Amy J. *A Monster with a Thousand Hands: The Discursive Spectator in Early Modern England*. Philadelphia: University of Pennsylvania Press, 2018.

Rosenfeld, Colleen Ruth. "The Queen's Conceit in Shakespeare's *Richard II*." *Studies in English Literature* 60.1 (2020): 25–46.

Rowlands, Samuel. *The Letting of Humours Blood in the Head-vaine*. London: W. F., 1600.

Rutkoski, Marie. "Breeching the Boy in Marlowe's *Edward II*." *Studies in English Literature* 46.2 (2006): 281–304.

Rutter, Carol Chillington. *Enter the Body: Women and Representation on Shakespeare's Stage*. New York: Routledge, 2001.

Rutter, Tom. *Shakespeare and the Admiral's Men: Reading Across Repertories on the London Stage, 1594–1600*. Cambridge: Cambridge University Press, 2017.

Salingar, Leo. "Jacobean Playwrights and 'Judicious' Spectators." *Renaissance Drama* 22 (1991): 209–34.

Saunders, Richard. *Physiognomie*. London: Nathaniel Brooke, 1653.

Schechner, Richard. *Between Theater and Anthropology*. Philadelphia: University of Pennsylvania Press, 1985.

Schmitt, Charles. "Philosophy and Science in Sixteenth-Century Universities: Some Preliminary Comments." In *The Cultural Context of Medieval Learning*, edited by J. Murdoch and E. Sylla, 485–537. Dordrecht: Reidel, 1975.

Schneider, Rebecca. *Performing Remains: Art and War in Times of Theatrical Reenactment*. New York: Routledge, 2011.

Schoone-Jongen, Terence G. *Shakespeare's Companies: William Shakespeare's Early Career and the Acting Companies, 1577–1594*. Burlington, VT: Ashgate, 2008.

Screech, M. A. *The Rabelaisian Marriage: Aspects of Rabelais's Religion, Ethics, and Comic Philosophy*. London: Edward Arnold, 1958.

Serlio, Sebastiano, *The First Booke of Architecture*. London: Robert Peake, 1611.

Sinfield, Alan. *Faultlines: Cultural Materialism and the Politics of Dissident Reading*. Berkeley; University of California Press, 1992.

Shakespeare, William. *Antony and Cleopatra*. Edited by John Wilders. London: Bloomsbury Arden Shakespeare, 1995.

Shakespeare, William. *As You Like It*. Edited by Juliet Dusinberre. London: Bloomsbury Arden Shakespeare, 2006.

Shakespeare, William. *The Comedy of Errors*. Edited by Kent Cartwright. London: Bloomsbury Arden Shakespeare, 2017.

Shakespeare, William. *Cymbeline*. Edited by J. M. Nosworthy. London: Arden Shakespeare, 2007.

Shakespeare, William. *Hamlet*. Edited by Ann Thompson and Neil Taylor. London: Bloomsbury Arden Shakespeare, 2006.

Shakespeare, William. *The History of Henrie the Fourth; with the Battell at Shrewsburie, betweene the King and Lord Henry Percy, Surnamed Henrie Hotspur of the North. With the Humorous Conceits of Sir Iohn Falstalffe*. London: Andrew Wise, 1598.

Shakespeare, William. *King Henry IV, Part 1*. Edited by David Scott Kastan. London: Arden Shakespeare, 2002.

Shakespeare, William. *King Henry IV, Part 2*. Edited by James C. Bulman. London: Bloomsbury Arden Shakespeare, 2016.

Shakespeare, William. *King Henry V*, Edited by T. W. Craik. London: Arden Shakespeare, 1995.

Shakespeare, William. *King Lear*. Edited by R. A. Foakes. London: Arden Shakespeare, 1997.

Shakespeare, William. *King Richard II*. Edited by Charles R. Forker. London: Arden Shakespeare, 2002.

Shakespeare, William. *Macbeth*. Edited by A. R. Braunmuller. Cambridge: Cambridge University Press, 2008.

Shakespeare, William. *Macbeth*. Edited by Sandra Clark and Pamela Mason. London: Arden Shakespeare, 2015.

Shakespeare, William. *The Merchant of Venice*. Edited by John Drakakis. London: Arden Shakespeare, 2010.

Shakespeare, William. *A Midsummer Night's Dream*. Edited by Sukanta Chaudhuri. London: Arden Shakespeare, 2017.

Shakespeare, William. *Much Ado About Nothing*. Edited by Claire McEachern. London: Bloomsbury Arden Shakespeare, 2016.

Shakespeare, William. *Othello*. Edited by E. A. J. Honigmann. London: Arden Shakespeare, 1997.

Shakespeare, William. *Romeo and Juliet*. Edited by René Weis. London: Bloomsbury Arden Shakespeare, 2012.

Shakespeare, William. *The Taming of the Shrew*. Edited by Barbara Hodgdon. London: Arden Shakespeare, 2010.

Shakespeare, William. *The Tempest*. Edited by Virginia Mason Vaughan and Alden T. Vaughan. London: Arden Shakespeare, 1999.

Shakespeare, William. *Twelfth Night*. Edited by Keir Elam. London: Arden Shakespeare, 2008.

Shakespeare, William. *The Winter's Tale*. Edited by John Pitcher. London: Arden Shakespeare, 2010.

Shakespeare, William. and John Fletcher. *King Henry VIII (All Is True)*. Edited by Gordon McMullan. London: The Arden Shakespeare, 2000.

Shannon, Laurie. *Sovereign Amity: Figures of Friendship in Shakespearean Contexts*. Chicago: University of Chicago Press, 2002.

Shapin, Steven. *The Scientific Revolution*. Chicago: University of Chicago Press, 1996.

Shapin, Steven and Simon Schaffer. *Leviathan and the Air-Pump: Hobbes, Boyle, and the Experimental Life*. Princeton: Princeton University Press, 1985.

Shapiro, Barbara. "Beyond Reasonable Doubt: The Evolution of a Concept." In *Fictions of Knowledge: Fact, Evidence, Doubt*, edited by Yota Batsaki, Subha Mukherji, and Jan-Melissa Schramm, 19–39. New York: Palgrave Macmillan, 2012.

Shapiro, Barbara. *A Culture of Fact: England, 1550–1720*. Ithaca, NY: Cornell University Press, 2003.

Shapiro, Barbara. *Probability and Certainty in Seventeenth-Century England: A Study of the Relationships between Natural Science, Religion, History, Law, and Literature*. Princeton: Princeton University Press, 1983.

Shapiro, James. "'Tragedies naturally performed': Kyd's Representation of Violence." In *Staging the Renaissance: Reinterpretations of Elizabethan and Jacobean Drama*, edited by David Scott Kastan and Peter Stallybrass, 99–113. New York: Routledge, 1991.

Sharpe, Kevin. *The Personal Rule of Charles I*. New Haven: Yale University Press, 1992.

Shepherd, Simon. *Amazons and Warrior Women: Varieties of Feminism in Seventeenth-Century Drama*. New York: Harvester Press, 1981.

Sherman, Anita Gilman. *Skepticism and Memory in Shakespeare and Donne*. New York: Palgrave Macmillan, 2007.

Sherman, Stuart. "Dryden and the Theatrical Imagination." In *The Cambridge Companion to John Dryden*, edited by Steven N. Zwicker, 15–36. Cambridge: Cambridge University Press, 2004.

Shore, Daniel *Cyberformalism: Histories of Linguistic Forms in the Digital Archive*. Baltimore: Johns Hopkins University Press, 2018.

Sidney, Philip. *The Defence of Poesie*. London: William Ponsonby, 1595.

Simonds, Peggy Muñoz. *Myth, Emblem, and Music in Shakespeare's "Cymbeline": An Iconographic Reconstruction*. Newark: University of Delaware Press, 1992.

Simpson-Younger, Nancy. "'The garments of Posthumus': Identifying the Non-Responsive Body in *Cymbeline*." In *Staging the Blazon in Early Modern English Theater*, edited by Deborah Uman and Sarah Morrison, 177–88. Burlington, VT: Ashgate, 2013.

Smith, Bruce. "Eyeing and Wording in Cymbeline." In *Knowing Shakespeare: Senses, Embodiment and Cognition*, edited by Lowell Gallagher and Shankar Raman, 50–64. New York: Palgrave Macmillan, 2010.

Smith, Bruce R. "Making a Difference: Male/Male 'Desire' in Tragedy, Comedy, and Tragi-comedy." In *Erotic Politics: Desire on the Renaissance Stage*, edited by Susan Zimmerman, 99–116. New York: Routledge, 1992.

Smith, Bruce R. *Phenomenal Shakespeare*. Malden, MA: Wiley-Blackwell, 2010.

Smith, Emma. "Author v. Character in Early Modern Dramatic Authorship: The Example of Thomas Kyd and *The Spanish Tragedy*." *Medieval and Renaissance Drama in England* 11 (1998): 129–42.

Smith, Emma. "Hieronimo's Afterlives." In *The Spanish Tragedie with the First Part of Jeronimo*, edited by Emma Smith, 133–59. London: Penguin, 1998.

Smith, Warren D. *Shakespeare's Playhouse Practice: A Handbook*. Hanover, NH: University Press of New England, 1975.

Sofer, Andrew. *Dark Matter: Invisibility in Drama, Theater, and Performance*. Ann Arbor: University of Michigan Press, 2013.

Sofer, Andrew. "Spectral Readings." *Theatre Journal* 64.3 (2012): 323–36.

Sofer, Andrew. "'Take up the Bodies': Shakespeare's Body Parts, Babies, and Corpses." *Theatre Symposium* 18 (2010): 135–48.

Sparke, Thomas. *A Sermon Preached at Whaddon*. Oxford: Joseph Barnes, 1593.

Spenser, Edmund. *The Faerie Queene*. Edited by Thomas P. Roche. London: Penguin, 1978.

Spiller, Elizabeth. *Science, Reading, and Renaissance Literature: The Art of Making Knowledge, 1580–1670*. Cambridge: Cambridge University Press, 2004.

Spolsky, Ellen. *Satisfying Skepticism: Embodied Knowledge in the Early Modern World*. Burlington, VT: Ashgate, 2001.

Sprague, Arthur Colby. *Shakespeare and the Actors: The Stage Business in His Plays (1660–1905)*. Cambridge, MA: Harvard University Press, 1944.

Squier, Charles. *John Fletcher*. Boston: Twayne Publishers, 1986.

Stage, Kelly J. "*The Roaring Girl*'s London Spaces," *Studies in English Literature* 49.2 (2009): 417–36.

States, Bert O. *Great Reckonings in Little Rooms: On the Phenomenology of Theater*. Berkeley: University of California Press, 1985.

States, Bert O. *The Shape of Paradox: An Essay on "Waiting for Godot."* Berkeley: University of California Press, 1978.

Steggle, Matthew. "Varieties of Fantasy in *What You Will*." In *The Drama of John Marston: Critical Re-visions*, edited by T. F. Wharton, 45–59. Cambridge: Cambridge University Press, 2000.

Stelzer, Emanuel. *Portraits in Early Modern English Drama: Visual Culture, Play-Texts, and Performances*. New York: Routledge, 2019.

Stephens, John. *Satyrical Essayes Characters and Others*. London: Roger Barnes, 1615.

Stern, Tiffany. *Documents of Performance in Early Modern England*. Cambridge: Cambridge University Press, 2009.

Stern, Tiffany. *Rehearsal from Shakespeare to Sheridan*. Oxford: Oxford University Press, 2000.

Stern, Tiffany. "Taking Part: Actors and Audience on the Stage at the Blackfriars." In *Inside Shakespeare: Essays on the Blackfriars Stage*. Edited by Paul Menzer, 35–53. Cranbury, NJ: Associated University Presses, 2006.

Stern, Tiffany. "Time for Shakespeare: Hourglasses, Sundials, Clocks, and Early Modern Theatre." In *British Academy Lectures 2014–15*, edited by Janet Carsten and Simon Frith, 1–34. Oxford: Oxford University Press, 2016.

Stewart, Alan. *Close Readers: Humanism and Sodomy in Early Modern England*. Princeton: Princeton University Press, 1997.

Stewart, Alan. *Shakespeare's Letters*. Oxford: Oxford University Press, 2008.

Stockton, Will. *Members of His Body: Shakespeare, Paul, and a Theology of Nonmonogamy*. New York: Fordham University Press, 2017.

Stubbes, Phillip. *The Anatomie of Abuses*. London: Richard Jones, 1583.

Suzman, Arthur. "Imagery and Symbolism in *Richard II*." *Shakespeare Quarterly* 7.4 (1956): 355–70.

Swander, Homer. "No Exit for a Dead Body: What to Do with a Scripted Corpse?" *Journal of Dramatic Theory and Criticism* 5.2 (1991): 139–52.

Syme, Holger. "The Theater of Shakespeare's Time." In *The Norton Shakespeare: Third Edition*, edited by Stephen Greenblatt et al., 93–118. New York: W. W. Norton and Company, 2016.

Tatham, John. *Knavery in All Trades, or, The Coffee-House a Comedy*. London: W. Gilbertson, and H. Marsh, 1664.

Taylor, Charles. "The Politics of Recognition." In *Multiculturalism: Examining the Politics of Recognition*, edited by Amy Gutmann, 25–73. Princeton: Princeton University Press, 1994.

Taylor, Diana. *The Archive and the Repertoire: Performing Cultural Memory in the Americas*. Durham: Duke University Press, 2003.

Taylor, Gary and John Lavagnino, eds. *Thomas Middleton: The Collected Works*. Oxford: Oxford University Press, 2007.

Tennenhouse, Leonard. *Power on Display: The Politics of Shakespeare's Major Genres*. London: Methuen, 1986.

Thomson, Leslie. *Discoveries on the Early Modern Stage: Contexts and Conversations*. Cambridge: Cambridge University Press, 2018.

Thomson, Leslie. "The Meaning of 'Thunder and Lightning': Stage Directions and Audience Expectations." *Early Theatre* 2 (1999): 11–24.

Thomson, Patricia. "World Stage and Stage in Massinger's *Roman Actor*," *Neophilologus* 54.4 (1970): 409–26.

Tilney, Edmund. *The Flower of Friendship: A Renaissance Dialogue Contesting Marriage*. Edited by Valerie Wayne. Ithaca, NY: Cornell University Press, 1992.

Todd, Janet and Elizabeth Spearing. *Counterfeit Ladies*. New York: New York University Press, 1994.

The True Chronicle History of King Leir, and His Three Daughters, Gonorill, Ragan, and Cordella. London: John Wright, 1605.

Tourneur, Cyril. *The Atheist's Tragedy*. In *Four Revenge Tragedies*, edited by Katharine Eisaman Maus, 249–330. Oxford: Oxford University Press, 1995.

Tribble, Evelyn. *Cognition in the Globe: Attention and Memory in Shakespeare's Theatre*. New York: Palgrave, 2011.

Tribble, Evelyn. *Early Modern Actors and Shakespeare's Theatre: Thinking with the Body*. London: The Arden Shakespeare, 2017.

Turner, Henry S. *The English Renaissance Stage: Geometry, Poetics, and the Practical Spatial Arts 1580–1630*. Oxford: Oxford University Press, 2006.

Turner, Henry S. "The Problem of the More-than-One: Friendship, Calculation, and Political Association in *The Merchant of Venice*." *Shakespeare Quarterly* 57.4 (2006): 413–42.

Turner, Henry S., ed. *Early Modern Theatricality*. Oxford: Oxford University Press, 2013.

Turner, Victor. *The Ritual Process: Structure and Anti-Structure*. New York: Routledge, 2017.

The Two Noble Ladies. Edited by Rebecca G. Rhoads. Oxford: Printed for the Malone Society by J. Johnson at the Oxford University Press, 1930.

Urkowitz, Steven. "Interrupted Exits in *King Lear*." *Educational Theatre Journal* 30.2 (1978): 203–210.

Veltruský, Jiří. "Dramatic Text as a Component of Theater." In *Semiotics of Art: Prague School Contributions*, edited by Ladislav Matejka and Irwin R. Titunik, 94–117. Cambridge: The MIT Press, 1976.

Vives, Juan Luis. *The Education of a Christian Woman: A Sixteenth-Century Manual*. Edited by Charles Fantazzi. Chicago: University of Chicago Press, 2000.

Walsh, Brian. "The Dramaturgy of Discomfort in *Richard II*." In *"Richard II": New Critical Essays*, 181–201. London: Routledge, 2012.

Walsh, Brian. *Shakespeare, the Queen's Men, and the Elizabethan Performance of History*. Cambridge: Cambridge University Press, 2009.

Warner, Michael. *Publics and Counterpublics*. New York: Zone Books, 2005.

Webster, John. *The White Devil*. Edited by Benedict S. Robinson. London: Bloomsbury Arden Shakespeare, 2019.

Weimann, Robert. "The Actor-Character in 'Secretly Open' Action: Doubly Encoded Personation on Shakespeare's Stage." In *Shakespeare and Character: Theory, History, Performance, and Theatrical Persons*, edited by Paul Yachnin and Jessica Slights, 177–98. New York: Palgrave Macmillan, 2009.

Weimann, Robert. *Author's Pen and Actor's Voice: Playing and Writing in Shakespeare's Theatre*. Cambridge: Cambridge University Press, 2000.

Weimann, Robert. "Bifold Authority in Shakespeare's Theatre." *Shakespeare Quarterly* 39.4 (1988): 401–417.

West, Michael. "Were There Playgoers During the 1580s?" *Shakespeare Studies* 45 (2017): 68–76.

West, William N. "'But this will be a mere confusion': Real and Represented Confusions on the Elizabethan Stage." *Theatre Journal*, 60.2 (2008): 217–33.

West, William N. *Common Understandings, Poetic Confusion: Playhouses and Playgoers in Elizabethan England*. Chicago: University of Chicago Press, 2021.

West, William N. "Intertheatricality." In *Early Modern Theatricality*, 151–172. Oxford: Oxford University Press, 2013.

West, William N. *Theatres and Encyclopedias in Early Modern Europe*. Cambridge: Cambridge University Press, 2002.

West, William N. "What's the Matter with Shakespeare? Physics, Identity, Playing." *South Central Review* 26.1 and 2 (2009): 103–26.

A Warning for Fair Women. Edited by Charles Dale Cannon. The Hague: Mouton, 1975.

Weber, Samuel. *Theatricality as Medium*. New York: Fordham University Press, 2004.

Wentworth, Thomas. Vol. 2 of *The Earle of Strafforde's Letters and Dispatches*, edited by William Knowler. London: William Bowyer, 1729.

West, Russell. *Spatial Representations on the Jacobean Stage: From Shakespeare to Webster*. New York: Palgrave, 2002.

White, Martin. "'When torchlight made an artificial noon': Light and Darkness in the Indoor Jacobean Theatre." In *Moving Shakespeare Indoors: Performance and Repertoire in the Jacobean Playhouse*, edited by Andrew Gurr and Farah Karim-Cooper, 115–36. Cambridge: Cambridge University Press, 2014.

Whitney, Charles. *Early Responses to Renaissance Drama*. Cambridge: Cambridge University Press, 2006.

Whittle, Jane and Mark Hailwood. "The Gender Division of Labour in Early Modern England." *Economic History Review* (2020): 3–32.

Wiggins, Martin. *British Drama 1533–1642: A Catalogue*. 9 vols. Oxford: Oxford University Press, 2012.

Wiggins, Martin. "The King's Men and After." In *Shakespeare: An Illustrated Stage History*, edited Jonathan Bate and Russell Jackson, 23–44. Oxford: Oxford University Press, 1996.

Williams, Raymond. *Keywords*. Oxford: Oxford University Press, 1983.

Wilson, Luke. *Theaters of Intention: Drama and the Law in Early Modern England*. Stanford: Stanford University Press, 2000.

Wilson, Thomas. *The State of England Anno Dom. 1600*. Vol. 16 of *The Camden Miscellany*, edited by F. J. Fisher. London: The Camden Society, 1936.

Womack, Peter. "The Comical Scene: Perspective and Civility on the Renaissance Stage." *Representations* 101.1 (2008): 32–56.

Womack, Peter. "Off-Stage." In *Early Modern Theatricality*, 71–92. Oxford: Oxford University Press, 2013.

Woodbridge, Linda. *English Revenge Drama: Money, Resistance, Equality*. Cambridge: Cambridge University Press, 2010.

Worthen, W. B. *Shakespeare, Technicity, Theatre*. Cambridge: Cambridge University Press, 2020.

Worthen, W. B. "The Weight of Antony: Staging 'Character' in *Antony and Cleopatra*." *Studies in English Literature* 26.2 (1986): 295–308.

Yachnin, Paul. "Performing Publicity." *Shakespeare Bulletin* 28.2 (2010): 201–29.

Yachnin, Paul and Myrna Wyatt Selkirk. "Metatheater and the Performance of Character." In *Shakespeare and Character: Theory, History, Performance, and Theatrical Persons*, edited by Paul Yachnin and Jessica Slights, 139–157. New York: Palgrave Macmillan, 2009.

Zaleski, Carol. *The Life of the World to Come: Near-Death Experience and Christian Hope*. Oxford: Oxford University Press, 1996.

Zerba, Michelle. *Doubt and Skepticism in Antiquity and the Renaissance*. Cambridge: Cambridge University Press, 2012.

Zimmerman, Susan. *The Early Modern Corpse and Shakespeare's Theatre*. Edinburgh: Edinburgh University Press, 2007.

Zucker, Adam. *The Places of Wit in Early Modern English Comedy*. Cambridge: Cambridge University Press, 2011.

Zucker, Adam. "Space and Place." In *A New Companion to Renaissance Drama*, edited by Arthur F. Kinney and Thomas Warren Hopper, 501–12. Hoboken, NJ: John Wiley and Sons Ltd, 2017.

Zucker, Adam and Alan B. Farmer, eds. *Localizing Caroline Drama: Politics and Economics of the Early Modern English Stage, 1625–1642*. New York: Palgrave Macmillan, 2006.

Zwicker, Steven N. "'On First Looking into Revisionism': The Literature of Civil War, Revolution, and Restoration." *Huntington Library Quarterly* 78.4 (2015): 789–807.

Index

Please note: page numbers in **_bold italic_** refer to footnotes

Printed in the USA
CPSIA information can be obtained
at www.ICGtesting.com
LVHW011854151123
763993LV00007B/320